Information and Organizations

California Series on Social Choice and Political Economy
Edited by Brian Barry, Robert H. Bates, and Samuel L. Popkin

Information and Organizations

ARTHUR L. STINCHCOMBE

University of California Press

BERKELEY   LOS ANGELES   OXFORD

University of California Press
Berkeley and Los Angeles, California

University of California Press, Ltd.
Oxford, England

© 1990 by
The Regents of the University of California

Library of Congress Cataloging-in-Publication Data
Stinchcombe, Arthur L.
    Information and organizations / Arthur L. Stinchcombe.
        p.   cm.—(California series on social choice and political econ-
    omy ; 19)
    Includes bibliographical references.
    ISBN 0-520-06780-0 (alk. paper).—ISBN 0-520-06781-9 (pbk.:
alk. paper)
    1. Industrial sociology.   2. Industrial organization.
3. Organizational behavior.   4. Management information systems.
5. Uncertainty.   I. Title.   II. Series.
HD6955.S84   1990
658.4'038—dc20   89-20289
                                                                  CIP

Printed in the United States of America
1   2   3   4   5   6   7   8   9

The paper used in this publication meets the minimum
requirements of American National Standard for Information
Sciences—Permanence of Paper for Printed Library Materials,
ANSI Z39.48-1984. ∞™

Contents

Acknowledgments

As I look back over my files, I find old syllabuses labeled "organizations as information," but in those days my desktop computer did not date my syllabuses for me. What that means is that many students for many years have put up with me thinking about the subject of this book. Some of the materials that went quite directly into the book were developed in lectures to undergraduate classes in "industrialization" and "organizations" at Northwestern University, and students' vague impression that I was reading an article from an encyclopedia in those classes may have been due to my writing on an encyclopedic effort at the time. I co-taught one of these courses with Arnold S. Feldman, which held me to enough higher of a standard as to make it believable that the lectures might someday be the basis for a book. My first debt, then, is to the students who put up with the ambiguous advantage of getting much of Chapters 2, 4, and 5 before they were ready for the rest of the world, and to Feldman for comments and stimulation.

Carol A. Heimer read the entire manuscript with an eye to the argument that should have been there rather than to the failures of the argument as written. She also thought that the book should be written in English, which agreed with my convictions better than with my behavior. Being married to a person who criticizes one's work has many advantages, but the most important to me was that she knew me well enough not to try to get me to change things that I would never change. Tempering the wind to the shorn lamb may not be the best thing for the reader, but it helped me to accept more improvements to the text than I would otherwise have done. Mayer Zald read the first eight chapters of the manuscript in an earlier version and was the primary cause of there being a conclusion. An anonymous reviewer for the University of Chicago

Press provided sufficient detail about why the manuscript was beyond redemption to help me repair some parts.

Others who have read and commented on parts of the manuscript include Alfred D. Chandler, Per Heum, Robert K. Merton, Charles Payne, Paula Rossow, James Sheridan, John Walsh, James Zetka, and Harriett Zuckerman. I suppose the general tone of these acknowledgments already demonstrates that I will often defend my faults rather than graciously accept correction, so these people will not be expected to take responsibility for the remaining imperfections.

I have tried to estimate the number of working hours for the manuscript that different sources have supported. Most of roughly 1,500 hours supported many years ago by the Stanford Graduate School of Business with Mellon Foundation funds went into Chapter 6. The Institute of Industrial Economics of Bergen, Norway, with funds partly from the Norwegian State Oil Company (Statoil), supported about 1,000 hours for the research reported in Chapter 3, and supported previously published work used throughout the book. I figure that the four-course teaching load at Northwestern University College of Arts and Sciences gives me about 200 hours per quarter for research; I have used five quarters, or 1,000 hours of research time, and in addition was provided with a course off one quarter, for a total of about 1,200 hours. This time was used especially for Chapter 9 and for general rewriting work. A couple of summers supported out of our household resources supplied about 1,000 hours. The Center for Urban Affairs and Policy Research at Northwestern University supported about 400 hours of work.

The total amounts to about two and a half years of full-time work, with office space, overhead, help in making research contacts, and the like thrown in. Since the salary and other expense involved are probably a good deal more than the gross sales the book will have, this level of support helps provide evidence for the basic argument of Chapter 9 about the rent of reputations. I am grateful to all these institutions, to their movers and shakers, and to the members of my household for support of my research. Aside from whatever value the research in this version may have for the scholarly community, it was great fun to do it.

Chapter 6 has been previously published by Norwegian University Press in my and Carol A. Heimer's *Organization Theory and Project Management*. I am grateful for permission to reprint it here. Chapter 3 is revised from a paper published in photocopy form by the Institute of Industrial Economics of Bergen, Norway.

1 Information, Uncertainty, Structure, and Function in Organizational Sociology

Rationality

Rationality necessarily involves an analysis of the future, because the consequences that give purpose to acts are necessarily in the future. Thus all rationality is based on predictions of one kind or another, not on knowledge. Assuming that actors are perfectly rational, of course, implies that they are certain what the future holds, that in all relevant respects our notions about the future constitute knowledge. The assumptions of neoclassical economics are that various financial quantities (e.g., the interest rate and the savings and investment rates if distinct) summarize all the relevant information about the future that one needs in order to make economic decisions, and that everyone else can have the same information that an individual actor uses to work out a strategy (the investor, for example, presumably compares a concrete opportunity [e.g., to invest] with the relevant financial quantities [e.g., the interest rate]; the assumption is that anyone else with resources has access to the same information about the future relevant to that investment as the investor does). The assumption of neo-Keynesian economics (and apparently of Keynes himself) was that the idea that investment can operate with only financial and universally available knowledge assumes a kind of knowledge about the future that human actors do not and cannot have (see Weintraub 1979).

Two main traditions of organizational sociology start from the Keynesian or neo-Keynesian assumption that the future is uncertain. The older one has as its stellar figures Herbert Simon and James G. March (e.g., March and Simon 1958). Its main thrust has been to try to describe what people acting in organizational contexts (and to some degree acting in organizational roles in the light of organizational purposes) actually do to deal with the imperfection of their knowledge or predictions of the future, what decision procedures they in fact use to fill in what neo-classical economists require them to know.

The other tradition, whose stellar figure is perhaps Oliver Williamson (e.g., Williamson 1985), looks at what organizational devices might be good for dealing with various sorts of uncertainty about the future (e.g., small numbers bargaining, which involves uncertainty about the future behavior of a partner who is not replaceable in the market—or is replaceable only at a higher cost). The organizational devices solve specific types of departure from perfect markets. The actual distribution of such organizational devices, then, is to be predicted from the distribution of the problems they are good for solving. The Williamson alternative is, in short, microeconomic functionalism. The approach to the microeconomic ideal of perfect efficiency in spite of uncertainty is the survival criterion for the practice in a functional argument.

To put it another way, the Simon-March tradition is concerned with the *causal explanation* of departures from rationality. The Williamson tradition is concerned with the *functional explanation* of organizational structures, such as hierarchies. The Simon-March objective is to explain why organizations use less than rational methods. The Williamson approach is to explain how organizations can come near rationality, if not quite there, by adopting organizational devices that deal with uncertainty. The clue to structures needing such explanation in the Williamson tradition is that they occur in the context of market behavior but depart in significant ways from the structure of decision making known to be optimum in a perfect market.

I propose in this book to follow a slightly different strategy from both of these, though the difference involves a minor shift from the received tradition. I propose that information about the uncertain future becomes progressively available *in distinct social locations*, depending on what sort of uncertainty it is. What resolves the uncertainty of particular actors, then, is the *earliest available information* that will show what direction the actor ought to be going because of the way the future of the world is, evidently, turning out. Structures that depart from idealized markets (none of the organizational structures we explain in this book work like ideal markets do) are then to be explained functionally, by the growth of the organization toward those locations where information for resolving uncertainty is chiefly located. That information then has to be processed quickly, both to adapt the previous tentative strategy and to work out the tentative strategy for the next period. The core of structure of organizations, then, is information processing, and the core information to be processed is the earliest information that indicates what sort of world (i.e., future) the decisions are being made for.

The explanation is, however, causal as well as functional. The organization controls neither where the uncertainties it is confronted with arise, nor exactly what sort of information is crucial. Those are determined by what the organization is trying to do and varies from one part of the organization to another, depending on what that part is trying to do. That is because different things one is trying to do have different bottlenecks, different main loci of uncertainty about the future, and consequently different information that will bring success.

It is, then, the factual distribution of information relevant to crucial uncertainties (crucial in particular, in economic organizations, for the net value of the object or service produced by the organization) that determines the actual structure of the problem confronting the functional structure. Structures of organizations, and of parts of organizations, vary according to the sorts of uncertainties they confront, and so according to what sources of information they depend on and to how that information is best got to the decision-making units. The board of directors is organized as a committee, the assembly line as a hierarchy, because the financial and trustworthiness uncertainties faced by the board are different from the labor cost uncertainties faced by the assembly line.

The crucial thing for an organization from this point of view is to be where the news breaks, whenever it breaks. Information is "news" for the organization when it is a first appearance of some sign of how the future is going to be, in a respect crucial for the organization. The argument then is that news about one sort of contingency facing an organization (e.g., fluctuations in the quality of raw materials) is likely to be found in a different place than news about another sort of contingency (e.g., the risks of a hostile takeover). One therefore needs a type of structure to gather and process information from raw materials sources to manufacturing different from that needed to gather and process information about suspicious movements of stock sales.

In both cases, however, the organization does not know what kind of world it is making decisions in, because it cannot predict the future very well—not well enough to stay afloat. It needs the news, and it needs to respond to the news as it breaks, not after the news gets to all the participants in the market in the form of price changes. It is in fact such reactions to news that inject information about what is happening to corporate futures into the price system.

Much of this book will apply the above approach to economic organizations, partly because the classical literature on economic organizations has been sensitive to risks and to information processing and partly because economic organizations is what I know most about. However, the language above may suggest more restriction of the problems of uncertainty and information processing to economic organizations than is appropriate. Certainly a university scientist, in order to establish that brief moment of monopoly reflected in his or her name as author on the first publication of a new finding, is highly uncertain beforehand about where new knowledge is to be found (see, for example, the discussion in Watson's *The Double Helix* [1968] 1981) of getting the x-ray diffraction results from Rosalind Franklin, which limited the possible structures of DNA) and how likely it is that someone else will get there first. Such a scientist (and therefore the university) must be very attentive to the news of scientific results related to his or her line of research. That uncertainty of research is compounded as deans and department heads bet on who is going to make the correct bets about where new knowledge is to be found, without themselves being able to make those bets as well as the people they are hiring (for example, see the evidence of wrong personnel bets by Watson and Crick's administrative head, Sir Lawrence Bragg, in Watson [1968] 1981, 37–40, 60–62).

Universities also tend to grow toward sources of news that tell them as soon as possible what the future of science and scholarship is going to look like, and to organize their "administration" so that decisions on research and hiring are taken primarily by people who have efficient channels to that news. We will treat a few problems in university administration in Chapter 9 to show that the approach taken here extends beyond economic organizations.

Uncertainty

The basic idea here, then, is that uncertainty is not an indelible characteristic of a particular decision. Instead it changes over the course of the decision. That is why people take decisions tentatively. They enter on the first branch that might lead to an investment (e.g., a "conceptual study" in engineering) in order to get part of the news that will reduce uncertainty (see Marschak, Blennan, and Summers 1967, 49–121, on the process of decision to follow or not follow a line of development in designing jet engines; see also Crecine 1969).

In general, the further a commitment to a line of action extends into the future, the larger the proportion of all the information entering into the final decision will be that is news coming in over the course of implementation of the decision. People do not decide to drill exploratory wells until after geological studies have shown a promising formation; they do not drill the first production wells until exploration shows that the find is "commercial" (i.e., that its rate of flow, costs of development, transportation costs, etc., combined with anticipated oil and gas prices over the course of the wells' lifetime, show "adequate" anticipated profitability); and they do not develop the whole field until the first production wells come in as anticipated (see Stinchcombe 1985e, 41–65, for a more detailed analysis of the uncertainties in oil field development). That is, they are not nearly as blind to the nature of the future at the time a major investment is made as they were when they first set out with sonic equipment to explore the shape of the rocks a couple of miles down from a given pasture.

But of course, at the very end OPEC may fall apart and the field turn out not to be commercial after all (Herskedal and Kristiansen 1987). At this point, after one has made tentative decisions to go a bit further, waiting for the final commitment until as much news as possible comes in, then one has to estimate the probability distribution of oil prices and of true rather than estimated construction costs, and "take risks." Uncertainty is reduced through news; then finally the residual uncertainty is transformed into risk, and people make their bets. Or perhaps better, people make small investments and build a small structure to collect relevant news; if the news is good, they make bigger investments and develop a larger structure to collect relevant news; and so on. Uncertainty is transformed piecewise into risk, with a large part of the risk at first being a guess concerning the value of the news that a news-collecting structure will bring in.

This orientation to news must partly explain the fact observed by Mintzberg (1973) that top business managers prefer their information "live," from conversation, telephone calls, inspections, problems brought in by subordinates. Top managers are primarily responsible for dealing with uncertainties, because they are nearest in the hierarchy to profit takers who ultimately take the financial risks. So the parts of the total communications structure they are likely to be most attentive to are the parts that follow the fast-breaking news, the news that reduces uncertainty. It will be important for them to use fast communications channels, voice and telephone, rather than waiting for a memo to be drafted, revised, and forwarded with appropriate signatures up the line.

Uncertainty About What?

The primary task of this book is not to follow the drama of taking risks in the light of the last possible reduction in uncertainty. Rather, it is to analyze the structure of organizations as determined by their growth toward sources of news, news about the uncertainties that most affect their outcomes. The basic notion is that those uncertainties are distinctive in different parts of the organization, depending on their distinctive tasks and environments. A way to conceive of this is as follows.

By analogy with the findings of linear programming methods for optimizing complex decisions, we can imagine that any particular process has from two to a few "constraints" on its success. At any particular instant, there are likely to be only one or two variable factors that will improve short-run success (such as persuading all the workers to come in Monday morning on time), but those may change from instant to instant over quite short time periods. Over longer periods there may be several constraints which may be overcome or removed, at greater or lesser expense. We can for convenience call these the "bottleneck" factors in a given type of work with a given set of historically derived assets. Many of the things that are essential for the process to go on are not constraints at a given time (ordinarily, for example, air for workers to breathe is not a constraint; at times in underwater construction, however, it is the crucial constraint).

The basic generalization is that only uncertainties about the constraints on success matter, and so only information about those constraints on success is crucial to the operation. Because the constraints are likely to change over time, the uncertainties that are relevant and the news that resolves those uncertainties are likely to change.

It may often be, however, that the changing information is structurally located in the same place, so that the same structures will carry it back to the organization. For example, the information relevant to figuring out the structure of DNA changed as the alternative hypotheses under consideration changed with the gusts and flurries of facts and ideas (Watson 1968). But most of the information relevant to *any* of the alternatives was located among physicists and physical chemists interested in biological problems, especially the "phage group" organized around Delbrück and Luria, the crystallographers working on proteins organized around Wilkins and Franklin, and the physical chemists organized around Linus Pauling. The informal network bringing in the news did not have to be rebuilt with each shift in hypotheses, because basically the same sources of news had the facts about each of the alternatives.

Similarly, as we will examine in more detail in Chapter 5, information about needed improvements in an innovation that will make it more marketable comes from those who are in contact with the innovation users. In the early days of computers, given the structure of maintenance agreements and software development at the time, these were likely to be the maintenance people or the "client representatives" of the vendor of a computer, the folks who would be in contact with the computer center of the vendor. So it was essential that information from the client contact people get back to the software and hardware developers in the vendor organizations, whether the design problem was with the software, the mainframe computer, or the peripherals, whether it was in the early days of the computer model or the last days before it was replaced by new models, and so on.

It is such repetitive use of information from a given source of news, as problems and constraints on success change and new uncertainties therefore affect decisions, that tends to cause dense and fast information collection and information processing in organizations to be oriented to particular sorts of uncertainty and particular sources of information. It therefore follows that different organizations, having different main constraints, hence uncertainties, and hence news sources, will need to grow different types of structures of information collection and processing. The basic functional postulate of the argument of this book is that such need produces a tendency to grow such specialized structures for processing information about the relevant uncertainties that differ in different organizations.

But the same logic applies to the uncertainties of different tasks in different parts of the organization. Different uncertainties matter for different products, for reaching different clients successfully, for arranging the flow of borrowing and repayment so as to give stockholders their optimum risks and rates of return (and so the maximum value of their stocks) in different states of the financial markets, for maximizing university prestige in molecular biology versus other parts of physics or other parts of biology, and so on. We will therefore expect that the structures for information collection about crucial uncertainties (and especially that part of information processing that involves rapid use of fast-breaking news) will in general tend to be different in different parts of the organization.

Information

Up to this point we have emphasized the temporal features of that sort of information that reduces uncertainty, that what is uncertain at one time becomes predictable (or becomes calculable risk) at another time because new information (news) comes in. But many other features of information besides its recency make it functional for reducing uncertainty. Consequently, many other features of an information-collection and -processing apparatus—besides being located where the news about the relevant uncertainties is breaking and getting that information fast to the relevant decision makers—determine the degree to which they "serve the function" of controlling uncertainty, turning it into calculable risk.

We will discuss these secondary features under the rubrics of: (1) units of analysis; (2) noise reduction; (3) level of temporal abstraction; (4a) trustworthiness and error estimation and (4b) agency problems in information trustworthiness; and (5) expertise of analyzers.

1. *Units of analysis.* The kinds of causal unities about which an organization needs coherent information are those that make several activities subject to the same constraints: then units made up of those activities have the same conditions of success. For example, in studying production delays in a steel mill in South America, I found that the hot rolling section of a tube mill collected and analyzed delay information but that the cold processing parts did not and their delays were not treated as part of the problem of the efficiency of the plant. The reason was that on hot rolling operations there is a high degree of technical interdependence of the different operations, and they have to be done in tight sequence because otherwise the steel will cool down so much that it cannot be worked. That meant that the success of any part of hot rolling depended on delays in every other part, so any constraints that caused delays in one suboperation were a constraint on all the others (Stinchcombe 1974; Stinchcombe and Harris 1969). It was very uncertain whether at any particular moment the line would run, because many interdependent difficult operations all had to run at once for the line to run.

Similar inputs (e.g., preventive maintenance for the whole hot line) would tend to remove all the constraints on operation, so information about maintenance problems of any part of the hot line would be useful in forming a remedial policy. Incentive systems that encouraged one shift not to leave steel hot, ready to be rolled, depressed productivity of the whole line on the following shift. In short, the technical unity of the line meant that it was subject to common constraints, that there were common remedies for those constraints, and consequently that common information would be valuable in increasing productivity of each of the parts.

For another example, we treat below in Chapter 4 the question of what Chandler means when he says that different lines of merchandise will require separate administrative divisions. One of the examples he gives is Pittsburgh Plate Glass. The firm added several lines of merchandise that tend to be used with plate glass, such as paints, brushes, putty, and the like, which have no technical unity with plate glass *in production;* they do not need to be heated and formed while hot or shipped in special ways because of their fragility. But the information about what is selling to finishing contractors in lumber yards and hardware stores around the country is located in the same place for glass as for putty, and for both of these as for paints and brushes. Consequently, the lack of technical unity in manufacturing did not require divisionalization of Pittsburgh Plate Glass.

When the firm started to sell some products to other manufacturers on a large scale, however, those products and their manufacturing and marketing staffs needed to be divisionalized because they had to respond to a completely different structure of uncertainties and information-processing requirements. The news about what was selling in lumber yards was not useful in forming an inventory policy about such industrial goods. The market constraints on plate glass and paint brushes, then, tended to be similar, and to be solvable with information from the same structure of contacts with lumber yards. The market constraints on industrial chemicals were not similar, and so they had to be placed in a different division.

For Sears, analyzed also in Chapter 4, the statistical system for inventory control in stores requires each distinct commodity to be treated separately, since all the thousands of commodities that Sears sells in its department stores are bought separately, reordered separately, inventoried according to the expected rate of sale and the reorder interval, and so have to be treated as separate units of analysis. The "unit control" system developed in Sears retail operations provided such a set of statistics on the sale and inventory of separate products.

There are two general points to be made about this. First, one can support a functional argument that an information system has its origin in a need to respond to a given sort of uncertainty, *if* it has the units subject to that sort of uncertainty as its units of data collection and analysis. Conversely, one can assume the functional argument and infer from the units of the information system what the uncertainties are. We infer from the units of a preventive maintenance system that the hot rolling section of a tube mill has as a principal constraint the maintenance of all its parts, while the cold processing operations are not subject to the same constraints and so do not need information about the same uncertainties.

2. *Noise Reduction.* The odds at the race track and the average price of a stock over a week or so are good estimates of the long-run relative merits of horses or of the expected earnings and risks of a corporation. But almost all the bets of particular people, given the odds, and almost all the minute-

to-minute or hour-to-hour fluctuations of stock prices are error noise around that good estimate. Race track touts and investment analysts cannot ordinarily beat, respectively, the odds or the market, so their advice about what horse to back or what stock to buy is random noise. What one wants in dealing with uncertainty is a system of fast analysis (as the track itself has for odds, for example) that will eliminate the noise and error and provide only the valid information about the constraint. IBM, in pricing a personal computer, does not want to know that a particular retailer always undercuts the official price by 3 percent unless it can learn how the retailer can afford to do that and then use that information to its own profit. But the company does need to know if all retailers are cutting the price by 3 percent rather than 10 percent, because 3 percent means it is meeting the competition in its pricing policy, 10 percent that it is not.

A central kind of noise is irrelevant detail in a report. A twenty-page output from the accounting department for department or project administrators has to be reduced, often by pencil calculations (usually by administrative assistants or the equivalent), to about three or four numbers that tell where they stand. In analyzing an information-processing system, then, one wants to know the four numbers that the best administrators of departments or projects have calculated for them, rather than what all is included in the twenty-page biweekly output that is stacked in a closet (after those four numbers are abstracted) until the auditors say it can be thrown away. Such detail is comparable to knowing how much each bettor has bet on each horse rather than knowing the summary (the track odds).

Another kind of noise is, of course, systematic error. Deans complain, for example, that all professors they talk to earn less than average for people of their rank and distinction. The fact about which they complain comes about because professors have reasons to select the set of people or institutions to average so as to make the average as high as possible without seeming absolutely ridiculous (see 4b below on agency). We will deal with the general problem of systematic error in the section below on trustworthiness, and reserve the term *noise reduction* for reduction of random error.

The basic device for reducing random error is to take a mean (or median or percentage); the larger the number of observations over which the mean is taken, the smaller the residual random noise. But a larger sample of fast-breaking news is always late. Consequently, the dilemma is to produce the most recent mean possible, compatible with its being sufficiently noise free to indicate what is happening to the crucial uncertainty, to indicate how the world is developing. If an information system shows signs of this tension between noise reduction and newsworthiness, for example by using a four-week projection of demand updated each week (as General Motors developed—see Chapter 4 below), this shows that it is oriented to getting noise-free information about that uncertainty that is recent enough to adapt to a changing and uncertain world.

The alternative strategy for dealing with noise occurs when each case has to be dealt with in the way it in fact turned out. In the textile industry, the mean strength of a thread being spun or woven does not tell when it will break; the weaver-loom system has to be set up, then, to deal with each break in the thread after it happens, and taking the mean time to failure only helps in buying thread, not in running looms (Blauner 1964, 59). The machine has to be stopped and the break tied up when it in fact happens; one cannot set up the work on the shop floor based only on the fact that an average stretch of thread in a spinning machine will not break.

Skills in the division of labor are primarily for dealing with variation in the situation: in the raw materials, in the design requirements, in the previous errors (for instance, previously built walls not being quite plumb), in the weather, and so on. The reason one needs the skill of a carpenter is that one gets the news that the wall is out of plumb when one is hanging the door, and so one needs to deal with it at that point. In Chapter 2, we deal with the skill composition of the labor force as a response to substantive noisiness of the work process, the amount of random variation that has to be dealt with rather than averaged out, drawing heavily on the work of Charles Sabel (1982).

3. *Level of Temporal Abstraction.* Different parts of an organization deal with uncertainties that develop over different time spans, and different organizations have crucial uncertainties that vary over different time spans. The abstractions built into the information-collection and information-processing structures have to be adapted to the time spans over which adaptation takes place.

For many manufacturers, much of their capital investment is in buildings that are reasonably easily turned to other purposes, with the old machines moved out and new machines moved in. But oil and chemicals firms build special-purpose capital equipment (often roughly 5 percent only is for the building, 95 percent being for the processing installations); such special equipment has to pay for its entire cost by a long time doing the single thing it is built for. Ordinarily in the oil and chemical industry, the total amount of labor that goes into building the equipment is of the same order of magnitude as the total amount of labor for running the equipment for twenty years. If the price of the product falls below the operating cost of the installation, that installation, and consequently that half of the total labor that built the installation, cannot be used for anything else. One reflection of this is that a large proportion of all the middle-class people employed in the oil and chemical industries are accountants, specialized in estimating financial outcomes into the far future under various long-term uncertainties about costs of raw materials, labor, and product prices.

Ordinarily the response to random variations in the raw materials, in the degree to which a particular wall is straight up and down, in what the latest client to walk in the door seems to have on his or her mind, in just what about quadratic equations a particular high school student seems to be having trouble with, is organized into an entirely oral information system—the informal world of skilled manual work, sales work, or classroom teaching. So the shortest temporal abstraction level is reflected in an information system within the individual, or at most in the interaction of a small group, and appears in our organizational analysis as human capital, as "skill."

As one goes up the hierarchy of most organizations, the time span of responsibility increases (Jaques [1956] 1972), which means in turn that the uncertainties one is responsible for responding to develop over longer periods. While the skilled worker or salesman responds from minute to minute to random variation, the manufacturing division responds to shifts in demand for automobiles that are updated each week, and the general office responds to quarterly or yearly profits, yearly shares of the market, and other indicators of where long-term investments should be made or where shifts should be made among executives who are not, evidently, responding effectively enough to weekly variations in demand. Research and development departments tend to be oriented to the very long run, though they are occasionally brought back to earth by a computation of profits on recent innovations by the central administration (Lawrence and Lorsch 1967; for critiques of this research, see Tosi, Aldag, and Storey 1973; Blau and Meyer [1956] 1987, 111–116).

The result is that information-processing systems have to aggregate information over different time spans, and when different parts of the organization respond over different time spans their information systems need to be segregated. We discuss in Chapter 5 how information systems for feeding market information back to engineering and manufacturing have to be faster and richer for innovations than for products from which the bugs have already been worked out. Consequently, the information systems for an innovation in general have to be segregated into an autonomous "divisional"–type structure.

Similarly, in Chapter 3 we discuss how the "well report" for past oil wells and the "well plan" for a well to be drilled in the same field bear an intimate relation over the very short run from the point of view of drilling operations. But all that absolutely critical detail disappears from long-term plans for connecting drilled production wells to the processing apparatus that prepares the oil and gas for shipment, for here the crucial question is whether the connections between the two have any leaks that could create a danger of explosion. From the point of view of commissioning the processing operation (starting production), the dates and mechanical details of the "completion" of the well are all the temporal detail one needs about drilling.

The level of temporal abstraction of any information system, then, serves as empirical support for an argument that the system is supposed to deal with an uncertainty developing at that time scale. Conversely, again we can assume the functional connection and use the level of temporal abstraction to find what sorts of constraints a given piece of the administrative apparatus is oriented toward—the constraints that operate at the time scale of the abstraction of the system. Such information flows with different levels of temporal abstraction are central to defining "decentralization" in Chandler's work, analyzed in Chapter 4.

4a. *Trustworthiness and Error Estimation.* Scientific papers are required to present the evidence on which the argument they make is based. Textbooks do not generally have to analyze the evidence, nor do they have to say what sorts of errors such evidence is subject to and what protections against error one has built into the experimental procedure. This difference is due to the difference in the degree of uncertainty about the arguments in question. In general, no competent chemist would disagree with any argument in a competent textbook in chemistry (for an exception, see Watson [1968] 1981, 110, 122). Scientists do not have to give their readers the basis on which to disagree with their reading of the evidence unless there is some uncertainty about how to read the evidence. It is assumed that if something is sufficiently uncertain to be worth publishing a paper about in a scientific journal, then it is sufficiently uncertain that one has to specify the evidence on the basis of which one makes a particular argument about it. Consequently, there are routinely descriptions of experimental procedure (in highly codified form, of course) in the scientific literature but not in the typical textbook.

A system of discourse that attaches qualifying information to assertions, so that the reader can go behind the assertions if necessary, according to the degree of uncertainty generally thought to attach to the conclusions, is a "trustworthy" system of information. Science, then, is a finely tuned trustworthy system because the relatively certain assertions of the textbook have little data that allow the reader to assess the uncertainty, exactly because there is not much uncertainty; the more problematic assertion of a new discovery has to have evidence presented and evaluated in the standard scientific way. Hence, the detail of the evidence is proportional to the uncertainty of the assertion. Such systems do not provide useless information about certainties, nor do they present uncertainties as revealed truth.

This does not mean that there are no errors in the information. If there was no chance that scientific papers were wrong, scientists could just publish the conclusions without the evidence. And of course, the textbooks of a generation ago have in them things that were consensual in the scientific community at the time but that are now "known" by consensus to have been disproved by research in the meantime. A trustworthy system of information, in short, is one that does not routinely deceive its users about the uncertainty of the conclusions reached on the basis of that information but at the same time does not burden them with information about stable features of the environment. One does not ordinarily watch the news from the scientific community to see whether a given paragraph in one's physical chemistry textbook is wrong; one does watch that news to see whether conclusions of experiments reported in the most recent scientific literature stand up to different procedures in different laboratories.

One is not surprised to have a Nobel Prize winner write a sentence like "The letter was not in the post for more than an hour before I knew that my claim was nonsense" or for him to be advised by a mentor, who had forwarded some problematic work for publication, that "in this way, I [Watson] would still be young when I committed the folly of publishing a silly idea" (Watson [1968] 1981, 110). Scientific research is not worth doing unless it is in an area where the right answer is uncertain, and consequently scientific work is required to give others the basis for assessing its own degree of uncertainty. It is exactly because Watson was working in an area where he was quite likely to be wrong that he was required to give the evidence and the details of the argument.

Similarly in the oil business, everyone knows that many "promising structures" on the basis of acoustic exploration have no oil or gas in them and that one knows for sure only when oil and gas comes into an exploratory well. Further, one has a reasonable estimate of the recoverable reserves only after several exploratory wells have "delimited" the reservoir. A report of acoustic exploration thus has attached to it a professionally well understood degree of uncertainty, the first exploratory well a different (smaller) degree of uncertainty, and an estimate of recoverable reserves based on several exploratory wells a still smaller degree. No one professionally concerned is likely to mistake one report for the other. The information system is "trustworthy," even if uncertain to different degrees after each estimate, because each estimate has attached a professionally understood assessment of its uncertainty.

If, however, an incentive system exists in which the executive in charge of estimating recoverable reserves is punished severely for producing an overestimate, while no serious consequences flow for him or her from an underestimate (presumably because one does not know one has lost money by not investing but always knows one has lost money by investing), that executive may not be rewarded for attaching the correct degree of uncertainty to the estimate. Then he or she may report lower reserves than the evidence justifies. The system becomes untrustworthy at that point, because there is a systematic bias in the estimate of the probable error. (It may be deliberately arranged to be biased downward if it is known that the decision based on the information will be taken by amateurs and so will not take account of the evidence on its degree of uncertainty; it would, however, be an unusual—and probably short-lived—oil company in which this was the case.)

4b. *Agency Problems in Information Trustworthiness.* One can tell that the travel voucher and entertainment expenses accounting system is oriented to contingencies of fraud and extravagance by the safeguards built into it. It is very hard to collect information on entertainment expenses that tells accurately how much entertainment expense it was rational to expend on the company's behalf, that provides a reasonable estimate of the marginal productivity of the last dollar of entertainment expense. In this case the low trustworthiness of the information is due to the fact that the person who has to report on the value of the entertainment to the company is also a person who benefits from a more expensive evening out.

Organizations write multiple rules about the external features of entertainment and travel expense (those governing travel by federal employees are a wonder to behold) that, one hopes, limit the degree of extravagance and fraud. Protections against error that an organization builds into its information system tell a lot about what the organization really wants to know.

Many of the sources of untrustworthiness of information are faults in the incentive system for providing accurate information and accurate estimates of how likely one is to be wrong. These are generally dealt with theoretically under the heading of "agency theory," which deals with the broad class of problems in which the agent has more information—later or better news—than the principal about the uncertainties involved in a decision that the principal has to take (or that the agent has to take on the principal's behalf).

Agency theory deals with such things as "moral hazard" in insurance, in which the policyholder has information about strategies for reducing loss that the insurance company does not, but is not motivated to use those strategies because the insurance company pays the losses; or "adverse selection," in which the buyers of insurance policies know that they are worse risks than the company has estimated, so the insurance is a very good bargain for them, while those who fail to buy policies know that they are very good risks and so can better self-insure.

In general, information sources are people, who have motives to distort information so that they look better or worse than they really are. Such motives make information untrustworthy. The multiple devices that insurance companies have developed to deal with these problems (see Heimer 1985a, 11–17 and passim) indicate that trustworthy information about expected losses requires special structures to shift the incentive system. These devices also indicate that getting accurate information on the risks being insured, against the possibility of moral hazard or adverse selection, is a crucial uncertainty for insurance companies.

As Shapiro (1987) has pointed out, devices to make information more trustworthy can be simulated to make fraud more effective (for case material and evidence on how hard it is to find fraud, see Shapiro 1984). For example, a scientist's conclusions look more certain than they are if he or she reports faked data than if he or she merely reports an "expert opinion." Simulating the devices that we use to make scientific reports trustworthy makes false results look more trustworthy. Every device for making information trustworthy provides an additional reassuring cover for a con game when the device can be simulated; financial insurance companies with slim reserves may have the initials FDIC, for example.

A baroque structure of reviews, signatures required, committee consideration, and auditing usually indicates that the information system is endangered by agency problems, problems of motivated distortion of the content of an information flow; the tenure process in a leading university is a good model for what an information-processing and decision-making system with severe problems of agency looks like. But those same structures, by the functional argument, are indicators that agency-induced errors in the information will tend to lead to important errors in the decisions.

5. *Expertise of Analyzers.* The maintenance of the quality of the flow of information is in general achieved by constant minding by people who

know what uncertainty is to be analyzed, where the news about it is to be got, what causal unities determine which units are subject to that uncertainty, how to make the tradeoff between currency of information and noise reduction, what temporal span the decisions cover, what degree of uncertainty different sorts of information are subject to and how to indicate the level of uncertainty correctly, who is motivated to distort the system, what auditing or control procedures will work, and who are the other experts to consult on all these questions. Data on the expertise of those who mind the information flow supports a functional argument about what sort of uncertainty, and which constraints on success, the information flow was developed to control. Conversely, assuming the functional argument, one can tell that if high-priced accountants are minding the information flow, the long-term financial outcomes are the crucial things being estimated; if engineers in charge of maintenance are minding it, the constraints are likely to be reliable performance of machines; and if auditors whose chief qualification is suspiciousness go over the accounts frequently, the validity of claims and the likelihood of fraud is a crucial constraint on success.

Structure and Function

Many functions never get fulfilled: getting accurate information on the quality of a used car when the place where the news is located is the used car salesman is not a social structural possibility. Conversely, many functions that are carefully fulfilled solve problems that were never there in the first place: certifying that high school teachers understand curriculum theory or audiovisual methods of instruction has a clear manifest function, though it seems to do no good (the movie projector in the school gives both teachers who have and those who do not have audiovisual training a few minutes peace and classroom order, a true and important function).

Functional arguments are always suspicious because they attempt to explain things by their consequences, and this obviously requires a reverse, consequence-governed, chain of causation, a causal loop so that a consequence can explain its cause. Such arguments are particularly suspicious when one is explaining the structure of information flows in a situation in which rewards depend on what information is given. Teachers and teacher professional organizations, through their certificates, create an information system that looks as if expert judgment is used to select instructional movies. Of course, the one way to select good instructional movies is actually to look at a lot of movies in the subjects one teaches and pick out the best ones. But no school board (that I know of) is willing to pay teachers a skilled worker's wage to watch movies all summer.

The function of the certificate is to monopolize positions as teachers for those who have gone to education schools (where they teach audio-visual methods) and completed liberal arts programs, and to provide something to justify having people around that education school who produce or market instructional films. Since the manifest function of selecting good instructional movies would be very expensive and no one believes in such selection enough to pay that much for it, and since the latent function of this certificate is important enough to some people to keep the system going, an information system is created with very little information in it (certification systems for skill are treated as information systems in Chapter 6; the origins of skill requirements are treated in Chapter 2).

In this case we can perhaps identify the causal links back from the latent function to the structure and content of the information system, having to do with the fluctuating power of education schools (which have more luck requiring such certificates when teacher training is popular and many teachers are required by the system). Consequently, we do not have to depend on the manifest function for an explanation.

But the first evidence we used to suggest that all was not as it seemed was to check whether the information system had the characteristics that would be required for its manifest function: is the information in the system about the principal source of uncertainty on instructional films—namely, whether the film is appropriate to the students and to the instructional purpose of a particular teacher? Since the judgment of whether a film fits is clearly best made by a teacher seeing the film, the characteristics of the required information system are clear. One can very often disprove functional hypotheses without examining the reverse causal chain, by examining internal evidence about what the structure would have to do for the functional hypothesis to be true.

The field we are mining in this book, however, is shot through with situations in which people's rewards depend on the information flowing in an organizational system. Because a sociologist's fundamental inclination is to look at the seamy side of life for explanations, the big socio-logical fact may seem to be that people are motivated to misinform. To convince the sociological community that explanation by manifest functions of getting the organizational job done is fruitful is therefore rhetorically difficult. Our main hope is to do so by showing that many details about the setup of organizations that are otherwise inexplicable are explained by the proposition that information systems tend to grow toward sources of news about the central uncertainties of that part of the organization, and that the structure of the information-processing system can often be predicted from the assumption that its design gets the job done. Thus, the alternative hypothesis that the information system is a sham, designed to give cushy jobs to its perpetrators, can sometimes be refuted by showing that that alternative does not explain the elegant fit between what an information system does and what is needed to get the job done.

A second problem with functional explanations is that they take such things as organizational constraints, and uncertainties bearing on those constraints, as real, as causal variables. These causes work not only by functional mechanisms, already suspicious, but at a supraindividual level of explanation as well. Since, of course, all the significant organizational acts that we will be explaining are done on purpose by conscious individuals, any explanation at the social level has ultimately to be shown to be adequate at the level of intentions of individuals. I address this problem in detail in Chapter 4, in connection with Alfred D. Chandler's (1962) analysis of the origin of the multidivisional structure in Du Pont. But we can sketch here the broad lines of attack that this book takes.

The first line of attack is that in fact, empirically, we often find that an organized structure of intentions of a lot of different organization members exists, and that that organized structure is such as to get the organizational job done. The interconnections of those intentions are of such a character as to cause organizational information systems to grow toward the sources of crucial uncertainties for organizational success, and the substantive content of the structure of the information processing system as created by those intentions is in fact such as to collect information on the right units—to reduce noise, to abstract in the right temporal frame and to segregate different temporal features of uncertainties, to assess the degree of uncertainty accurately and to control agency problems of information quality, and to put the right sorts of experts in charge. If in fact individuals make up functional structures, this is surely an important dependent phenomenon that people who specialize in explaining individual behavior ought to address. This individual-level explanation is God's work, but not my own particular vocation.

The second line of attack is to assume that people as individuals confront the problems posed to them in their individual work, and that a long series of solutions to such problems of how to do one's individual assignment are such as to make the organizations "climb the gradient" and grow a structure that responds to the crucial uncertainties that govern organizational success. We assume organizations climb that gradient faster if the people in charge of creating and maintaining information are truly experts, if the general organizational tradition is one that discourages corruption, fraud, and manufacturing evidence and the like. This leaves the intellectual challenge of specifying how organizational problems become problems assigned to individuals who have the "obligations, rights, incentives, and resources" (Heimer 1986b) to solve them.

A third line of attack is an evolutionary one, particularly relevant to Chapter 5 where we specify some features that administration of innovations needs to have. A careful reading of that chapter should suggest that many organizations are not well set up to introduce innovations, and may fail even if they are because introducing innovations is organizationally difficult. The uncertainties that confront an innovation are severe in all sorts of areas. But the high rate of failure of innovations means that the features we find in those organizations that innovate successfully are likely to be functional for innovation.

If in the long run business firms can be profitable above the interest rate only if they introduce innovations (as Schumpeter 1942 argued), and if organizations last longer if they are profitable, then organizations whose innovating arms have grown faster and more accurate information systems that reduce the uncertainties connected to the innovations are more likely to be around for sociologists to study (cf. Nelson and Winter 1982). Similar evolutionary arguments may be used to suggest that administrative structures in General Motors, Du Pont, or Sears may be more functional than those of Kaiser-Fraser, Lydia Pinkham, or Montgomery Ward.

The Plan of the Book

The overall organization of the book is to ascend the levels at which information and decision systems are organized, starting with individuals' skills and ending up with class relations in whole societies. We pass from individual skills to technical departments in manufacturing, then to divisional organization, to innovations that cause reorganization of these first three, to networks of contracts among organizations, to segmentation of labor markets in the economy as a whole, and to the formation of workers' information on their class and political interests. We then hop sideways from these materials (largely focused on economic organizations and their offshoots) to illustrate the application of the theory to university research administration.

In Chapter 2 we start with variations in the basic information-processing mechanism of modern social organizations: the employee. The main social structure to be explained in this chapter is the division of labor, the main information-processing mechanism is skill of individuals, and the main social effect is the stratification of employees by level of skill. This definition of the problem is implicit in Charles Sable's *Work and Politics: The Division of Labor in Industry* (1982), so we base our analysis on that book. Our main problem is to specify precisely enough what skill consists of so that we can build a theory of when it will be necessary.

We argue that all work is characterized by an inherent dilemma: that productivity is highest when all the activities necessary to production or delivery of a service are highly routinized but specialized human work is most valuable (and hence the incomes of organizations highest) when there is uncertainty about what to do. Routinized work is more productive partly because people work faster when they are doing something that is routine for them, but mainly it is because, once routinized, the work can be mechanized or computerized or otherwise improved, and the improvement will stay in the productive system as part of the routine rather than as a sporadic flash of genius.

But routines are in general effective only if used under the appropriate circumstances: only if the parts to be assembled are standardized, only if the clients in a restaurant come in with standardized wants and select from a limited menu, only if the pilot can depend on his (or her, if airline piloting were different) counterpart workers in the control tower to behave in a routinized fashion so that the information they give him has an absolutely clear meaning. This means in turn that uncertainty in the environment of work—unstandardized parts, unstandardized clients, or unstandardized fellow workers—undermines productivity by undermining routinization.

We will analyze skill as *the capacity to routinize most of the activity that comes to a given work role in an uncertain environment.* We will argue that skill is a repertoire of routines which the workers can do accurately and fast, as well as a set of selection principles among routines, such that the complex of routines and selections among them deals with most things that uncertainty brings to the worker. Thus, we will expect to find skill when a great many different things must be done to produce the product or service but when each of those things has to be done in several different ways depending on the situation. For example, more complex products are likely to require higher skill levels in the work force that produces them, but the highest skill levels should be found in industries with complex products that have to be customized for particular clients and constructed in varying environments, as in the building construction industry. Much of the chapter, then, consists in the analysis of variability and uncertainty in exactly what work has to be done at a particular time, uncertainty about which of the routines in workers' repertoires have to be pulled out.

Chapter 3 turns to the variation in structures of administration in different sorts of activities within manufacturing, by showing that the system for extracting, treating, and shipping crude oil has many different types of information problems, and so many different structures for processing the information. The data for this chapter come from a study of building such a manufacturing administration in the Norwegian State Oil Company (Statoil), the first such organization built by a Norwegian oil firm (other than the Norwegian branches of multinational oil firms, which of course are legally Norwegian oil firms). The different things one has to do, say, to build an information system adequate to buy a stock of spare parts rather than to develop accounting software or to drill a production well a couple of miles deep without killing anybody are especially clear. (Much of the material for Chapter 3 has been previously published in photocopy form by the Institute of Industrial Economics in Bergen, Norway [Stinchcombe, 1986d], which sponsored the research.)

Chapter 4 reanalyzes Alfred D. Chandler's classic *Strategy and Structure: Chapters in the History of the American Industrial Enterprise* (1962). The central concern of that book, we argue, is how information coming from different sources, especially different markets, is combined to make different sorts of decisions. Chandler argues that when the information needed to make money off a company's products or services comes from several sources and has to be related to several distinct systems of decisions, one has to form more or less autonomous divisions to integrate the information from a given market and then arrange for the division so created to pass on to the central office only abstract and general information relevant to financial and investment decisions. Chandler's argument then becomes a functional one: that *in fact* organizations that need divisional decentralized structures because they are in multiple markets tend to get them.

First we undertake to define more exactly, in terms of information-processing and decision-making structures, what Chandler means by his dependent variable, decentralization into divisions. We then examine in detail how Chandler builds this functional argument for a case where he has the most historical detail, the origin of the divisional structure of Du Pont. Chandler has a good deal of information on how individual actions inside Du Pont added up over the course of several years to a shift to a divisional structure. This gives a hint of how the methodological objection to the organization-level functional analysis (that is the basic strategy of this book) can be disaggregated into individual human action that is understandable.

The core of the analysis of Chapter 4, however, is the explication of Chandler's implicit definition of when a firm is in multiple markets. Our argument is that, for Chandler, a market is a matter of where the information about the central uncertainties about a flow of products or services lies, and how this information can be got to decision points and integrated in a sensible way, rather than primarily about who the firm's competitors are. Chandler uses the economic competition definition of what a market is only occasionally and tangentially; his main, implicit definition is that a market is a number of phenomena outside the organization that produce a common administrative problem—problem of relating information to decisions—within the firm.

In one sense, then, the subject of Chapter 4 is the origin of the overall variation among firms between divisional and centralized organizations. But the core explanatory principle is that *within* the firm the problems of different product lines are different enough to need different information-processing structures. One needs to separate into different divisions administrative dealings that involve different sorts of uncertainty, because different product lines have to attend to different sorts of news, collected in different ways, evaluated according to the particular situation of that line of goods, and integrated with engineering and manufacturing in a distinct way. One needs one information-processing system and set of routines for making decisions to sell explosives to a few mines or the War Department, and another for making decisions to sell paint to thousands of householders or housepainting firms. The central administrative mistake, according to Chandler's argument, is to administer news about one sort of uncertainty with a structure built to handle another kind. Thus, Chandler's argument is exactly in tune with the main thrust of this book.

Chapter 5 deals with the special kinds of uncertainties that are ordinarily associated with innovations and with the sorts of information-processing and decision-making problems that they pose. The analysis can be seen as an elaboration of Joseph A. Schumpeter's examination of the relation between economic innovation and routine administration (e.g., Schumpeter 1942). Schumpeter identified routinized administration with large bureaucratic organizations. But in order to have the economic effects Schumpeter urged, innovations must be produced by efficient—which means routinized—production processes and must reach the market in routinized channels. The temporary monopoly over a valuable product or service that in Schumpeter's analysis creates the profits from innovation does not in fact produce profits unless the innovation can be produced on a large scale and marketed to collect the extra margin created by the monopoly.

Our argument will be that the introduction of an innovation involves a higher level of uncertainty than do the production and marketing of goods that have been on the market for a long time. The news needed to improve the innovation, to find its market, to introduce elaborating innovations, and to penetrate new niches is likely to be found in a different place than those which the information system of an existing organization reaches. And it has to be dealt with simultaneously and rapidly by engineering, manufacturing, and marketing in much the way that Chandler argues for distinct product lines.

Thus, Schumpeter is right in stating that it should ordinarily be hard to introduce innovations by using an existing bureaucratic structure. Yet a structure with many of the characteristics of a bureaucracy is needed to get the profits out of the monopoly created by innovation. An innovation poses an administration with a problem similar in form to the dilemma that we argue in Chapter 2 produces a demand for skill. It also poses a problem of differentiated information collecting and decision making similar to that which Chandler argues produces divisional decentralized administrative structures, as we argue in Chapter 4.

The sociological answer to Schumpeter's argument about the unfitness of bureaucracy for innovation (aside from the empirical observation that most important innovations are produced and marketed by large bureaucracies) and the consequent necessity for an individual heroic entrepreneur is that the administrative problems posed by innovation are of the same sort that skill and decentralization ordinarily solve, though perhaps more extreme. Thus, the first functional argument here is that innovations should tend to create pressures for divisional decentralized administration, such that the innovation has a separate but integrated news-collecting, information-processing, and decision-making structure. The second functional argument is that, because the level of uncertainty of the work involved to introduce an innovation will ordinarily be higher than that of other production, such a division is likely to have a higher skill mix than a division with an equally complex product or service that is no longer an innovation.

A good portion of Chapter 6 has been published previously as "Contracts as Hierarchical Documents" (Stinchcombe 1985b). The argument is that many contracts between organizations are actually formal organizations themselves, with news collection, information processing, and decision making built into a joint social structure consisting of the two (or more) corporate parties to the contract. Thus, the contract creates a social structure to deal with uncertainty, just as the labor contract does. The chapter then challenges Williamson's argument (1975, 1979) that dealing with uncertainties produces hierarchy. (Williamson's later work [1985] is compatible with the argument presented here.) The argument is that anything one can do with social structures constructed by labor contracts, one can do with social structures constructed by contracts between firms.

Williamson's argument is of the same functional form as ours, namely, that when information and decision problems create certain kinds of uncertainties, then a social structure that tends to resolve those uncertainties (that is, a hierarchy) tends to grow to manage them. The only problem with his argument, we will allege, is that the functional requirements of hierarchy itself involve continuity of production, such that the heavy investments in building a hierarchy and training the people to do their roles in it will be productive long enough to pay for themselves. Consequently, when one is only going to be, for example, in the business of building oneself a factory or an office for a couple or three years, one does not want to erect a hierarchy able to build factories and offices on into the twenty-first century. Rather, one wants to hire organizations that know how to build factories and offices, and that have skill structures and incentive systems appropriate to the uncertainties of that business, to put together a temporary social structure to build the building. Then, if it turns out that the site is sand rather than rock, one wants to change some of the specifications for the building in the middle and still use the same system of contracts and subcontracts to build the new design.

We will show that when, for one reason or another, it is hard to build a hierarchy to do the job but when the problems that (Williamson argues) tend to produce hierarchies occur, the structures of hierarchy will tend to be built into the contract itself. Thus, we are supporting Williamson's functional argument by breaking down the variable of "hierarchy" into its components, so as to avoid identifying it with the legal unity of a firm or another organization. In short, when functional pressures toward hierarchy exist but there is difficulty building an ordinary hierarchy made up of employment relations, we find instead contractual means for creating hierarchies among corporate actors.

Chapter 7 returns to the problem of skill of Chapter 2 from a different point of view. If the division of labor in a set of activities produces a set of skills to deal with the uncertainties, as outlined in Chapter 2, then the personnel system of the organization has to create a status system to motivate the acquisition and utilization of those skills, as well as a recruitment system to fill the jobs with people who will turn out to have the appropriate skills.

One of the most complex uncertainties that organizations deal with is uncertainty about whether people will be willing and able to do the work. The information system inside the individual is just as complex as the information system of the organization. Measuring what that system is capable of, then, involves analyzing the relationship between the particular complexities and uncertainties of the work to be done and the complexities and skills of the mind and body of the worker or recruit.

It turns out to be very difficult even to measure how well people are doing their jobs because, in general, line management does not fully know the complexity of the workers' jobs, and personnel management knows even less. Unless one knows a job very well, it is very hard to differentiate explanations of low productivity that blame true variations in the world from those that involve lack of competence or will on the part of the worker. But even when one can measure performance accurately because one knows the uncertainties involved in the work well, it is very hard to predict what quality of skill and what discretion in the internal decision-making system a worker will develop over the course of his or her years of experience with the organization and, hence, what kind of productivity, in the environment to be confronted over those years, the organization will get. Further, it is exactly this sort of information about employees' performance that is hard to collect from the people who know most about it—namely, the workers themselves—because they have an interest in getting the rewards that come from giving good news about the uncertainty about their competence and avoiding the punishments that come from giving bad.

We deal with four main structures for dealing with the fundamental information uncertainty of the labor market: continuity in the job (seniority in a job as a basis for holding that same job), internal promotion systems ("internal labor markets" in the strong sense), certificates from schools, and certification by a body of peers. We argue that reliance on such imperfect information systems provides the structural basis for segmentation of the labor market, because the fundamental privilege in the labor market is the capacity to give reliable certification that one can do a job. We do not, however, show why it is that some groups (e.g., white males) are more able to give such certifications than others (e.g., blacks or females).

Chapter 8 uses the materials from Chapters 2–7 on how organizational structures originate to examine the problem of class consciousness.

It is very clear that working-class consciousness is a consequence of the formation, with industrialization, of new kinds of organizations in the economy. Much of the argument in Chapters 2–7 can be conceived as an analysis of how capitalist (and socialist) economic organizations differ from peasantries, agricultural villages under feudalism, and other preindustrial forms of organization. In particular, we argue that such reorganization of the economy tends to produce reorganization of the labor contract, such that the *same* labor contract is imposed on whole categories of people. Labor contracts in preindustrial social structures tended to be more individualized.

From this point of view, class consciousness is a product of collective contracts. At first, collective contracts are unilaterally imposed on the workers by urban industrial and craft employers, creating categories of workers subject to the same working conditions, the same measurement of performance, and the same wages. Worker class consciousness is simply organizing those categories to negotiate their side of the collective contracts already imposed on them. This is a caricature of the argument in David Lockwood's *The Blackcoated Worker: A Study in Class Consciousness* (1958); a more nuanced development is given in Chapter 8.

But class consciousness, in the way it is ordinarily used, is the projection of one's position in an employing organization onto the society at large, so that one's place in that society, one's interests in the economy and polity, are seen "as through a class darkly," in Kenneth Burke's phrase. We therefore reformulate E. P. Thompson's great book, *The Making of the English Working Class* (1963), to specify under what conditions a position in an employing organization will be projected onto the larger canvas of labor market organization and political movements as a definition of interests there.

We then apply this combined Lockwood-and-Thompson theory to the decline of class hostility in the more class-conscious (industrial and transportation blue-collar) part of the economy and the low level of class consciousness in many parts of the service sector of that economy. Chapter 8, then can be thought of as an extension of an analysis in Chapters 2–7 that is oriented dominantly toward economic employing organizations, to the explanation of some features of unions in the labor market and of left political organizations. It does so by showing how the structure of organizations may provide information to workers about their interests, information that is then interpreted by the culture of the larger system.

Chapter 9 carries out another sort of extension, into a field involving employing organizations whose purposes are education and research. We give a couple of case studies of administrative structures in universities, namely those that administer space and those that set teaching loads of professors.

A prestige university confronts the uncertainty about where new knowledge is to be found and who will find it. Clearly, unless a piece of knowledge has been highly uncertain beforehand, it is not much of a research accomplishment to discover it. Thus, as in professional athletics, research tends to be completely uninteresting if the outcome is certain and most interesting in cases where nobody knows for sure how a given line of investigation will come out. From an administrative point of view, the main implication of this situation is that the people who know both what work is to be done and who can do it are concentrated at the lowest hierarchical level of the organization—the professors—though they may be paid more than people with many subordinates. What these subordinates hopefully know how to do is to have good bets about where new knowledge is to be found, better than those of fellow scientists at the lowest levels of *their* organizations who provide the baseline of uncertainty.

Scientific results, and to a certain extent results in other scholarly disciplines, change the degree of uncertainty generally held in the scientific community. Those findings or theories that are most fruitful, in the sense that they most change other scientists' bets about where new knowledge is to be found, are the most valuable. That is why citations turn out to be such good measures of the subjective estimates of scientists of who has done the most important work.

But this deep uncertainty—in which other competent people cannot bet as well as the future Nobel Laureates one wants to hire, retain, and promote—makes management in the ordinary sense extremely difficult. Even the knowledge of what sort of work the organization will be doing in chemistry or physical anthropology is concentrated toward the bottom of the organization, and people in chemistry and physical anthropology at other universities can probably usually bet better than the dean what will occupy the space in the labs and the research time of the dean's subordinates next year and the year after.

But this means in turn that the information the dean needs in order to make organizational tradeoffs between departments, for example to decide on allocations of laboratory space or teaching loads of various faculty members, have to be wrested from subordinates who have no interest in providing the basis on which space might be wrested from them or in having students and courses added to their teaching load. Thus, the commitment of a university to research distinction is in essence a commitment by the university administration not to know how to manage the organization, not to know whom to hire, retain, and promote, and not to know how to organize the flows of the most crucial information; their subordinates, the professors, and professors in other universities, are the ones who know.

In the administration of the allocation of space we analyze why this inherent situation of university authorities tends to lead to departmental sovereignty over space, with only occasional invasions from above. In the administration of teaching loads we study the pressure for university administrators to ignore measurements of individual research productivity in setting teaching loads, even though the dominant reason for having few courses in the (more or less uniform) teaching loads of universities is to give time for research. The question to be answered, then, is why universities so seldom try to allocate more time for research to those who do it best and why instead they depend on the National Science Foundation or the National Institutes of Health to make the judgments about whose teaching responsibilities should be lower, whose higher, by judging whose time those institutions are willing to buy from the university (at cost plus 50 percent or so—the percentage of overhead is higher at some leading universities).

The objective of this brief exploration into the organizational aspects of the sociology of science to show that uncertainty and the information needed to reduce uncertainty shape the structure of administration of universities as much as they do that of economic organizations.

The objective of the book as a whole is to illustrate in a variety of contexts how the social structure of organizations can be explained by the structure of the information problem they are confronted with. The idea is that organizational principles differ radically from one situation to another because what is functional for an organization differs similarly. What individuals have to learn; what distinct types of information structures must be built into manufacturing management; which departments processing which information should group together into divisions; how the administration needed for managing innovations and that needed for managing more routine products differ; how management tells whom to hire, retain, and promote; what the content of contracts among organizations will be; what features of organizational position will be taken by an organization's members to define their fundamental economic and political interests; and why scientists go their own way regardless of their administrators—all are to be explained by the nature of organizational uncertainty and the form of information processing needed to reduce it.

Broadly speaking, we are trying to explain why the formal structure of organizations varies depending on what those organizations have to do. All the elements of this theory exist in the organizational literature. For example, the centrality of routines in organizations, emphasized in Chapter 2, is central to both Cyert and March (1963) and Nelson and Winter (1982). The dependence of skill levels on nonroutineness and the location of skills in those parts of manufacturing with much market uncertainty are analyzed by Charles F. Sabel (1982). But those pieces have not been put together into a systematic theory of the skill levels of organizations.

In particular, it has not been done in such a way that the same theory can be used to explain why innovations not only create such administrative difficulty but also require such high skill levels, as we do in Chapter 5. To make the transition, we have to use the complex theory implicit in Chandler's interpretations of various concrete business facts in *Strategy and Structure* (1962). But that theory is not systematic enough to use for our purpose. For example, Chandler writes as if the explanation for divisionalization of firms is the same as that for general office structure. But divisions respond to different uncertainties than does a general office, and so are differently explained. This distinction helps to untangle what Chandler's theory is and so to show why his analysis of Sears is not convincing.

Because Schumpeter had not read Chandler and had not studied Du Pont, he could not imagine making bureaucracies flexible enough to be innovators. He therefore placed all the burden of economic advance on heroic entrepreneurs. But Chandler's theory shows more exactly what kinds of bureaucracies can innovate, can turn an invention into a going concern making monopoly profits.

Thus, the work of this book is to make an overall theory of uncertainty and information sufficiently strong and exact to show where our geniuses in organization science went wrong. It does so by a systematic attempt to explain variations in the formal structure of organizations. These variations are often between parts of the organization. For example, to explain the structure of Du Pont, with product line divisions and a general office, we need to explain why decentralization to divisions involved first centralizing those divisions. But we also need to explain what uncertainties the general office responds to and therefore why it needed more abstract communication flows to it and a nonhierarchical committee structure of communication within it. The structure of the general office in Du Pont was a committee structure much like one that had been tried and rejected for internal administration of the divisions.

In some sense, then, the theory of this book is old hat. But by explaining variations in organizational structure by variations in the type of uncertainty dealt with, we can show the relations among the classics of organization theory. In the process, we make the classical theory empirically richer and make it stretch from the micro level inside individuals as they develop skills to the macro level of class relations in whole societies, from the General Motors assembly line to the university laboratory for research in biophysics. We hope, in sum, to make the theory we have used both more concrete and more general, so as to explain why the forms of organizations are at once so wonderfully various and yet so obvious once we see the uncertainties that they have to deal with.

2 Individuals' Skills as Information Processing

Charles F. Sabel and the
Division of Labor

Introduction

The basic argument of this chapter is that when we say a person is "skilled," "semiskilled," or "professional," we are describing what sort of an information-processing system he or she is. If organizations have to deal with uncertainties, then someplace in the organization there have to be people who bring information to bear on those uncertainties. The flow of unpredictable events to a worker's or professional's area of responsibility sets problems for that worker or professional. The capacity to use the news about what uncertainty has come in, to decide what to do and then to do it or arrange to have it done in a fast and effective way, is what a skill consists of.

Thus, to describe a skill is to specify what sort of information-processing mechanism a given worker is. We will argue that the best way to describe the individual as an information-processing structure is by the *routines* he or she can use, and then by the *principles* he or she uses to decide which routine to invoke as chance brings in now this, now that task to be accomplished.

If we then develop a theory of the conditions under which more complex information processing by individual workers is required, then we will have a theory of the skill distribution of different sorts of organizations, and of different parts of organizations. To develop such a theory we first develop the notion of routines, of routinization as part of what skill is, and the relation of the *number* of routines in the repertoire of a worker and the complexity of that worker as an information-processing system. We also discuss the routinization of the *relations among* workers' routines in "fordist" production. Fordist production allows the use of semiskilled workers in the production of complex products.

The theory of routinization and skill will then give us a theory of the conditions under which complex production requires complex information processing by individual workers. This provides the basis for describing what technical, raw materials and market conditions are necessary for fordist production, and conversely what conditions will require a high skill mix in the labor force of organizations.

Thus, the central dependent variable, the thing to be explained, is the skill mix of an organization or of parts of an organization, such as why maintenance departments cannot be deskilled the way mass production departments can. The ultimate independent or causal variables are technical, raw materials and market uncertainty, concretely enough described so that we can tell where that uncertainty is higher and where it is lower. The core mechanism that connects causes to effects is the place of routines, discretion, and information about how to respond to uncertainty that have to be trained into the worker; these determine his or her skill level. So it is to the theory of routines in skilled and semi-skilled work that we turn first.

Relations Between Routines and Skills

The key thing to get out of the next few subheads is a picture of *routinization within the individual*, that is, a skilled person becoming really expert and fast at doing some number of distinct tasks, which enter in different combinations into different jobs. The basic argument is that skilled workers' skill consists of a *set of routines*, a set of smaller skills for particular tasks that they do very well, and many *principles of decision* which tell workers when to use one routine, when to use another.

In preindustrial society, the skill that artisans had was by and large the ability to do *all the things necessary* to carry on a given business, such as baking or shoemaking or goldsmithing. What distinguished artisans, such as blacksmiths or wheelwrights, from outworkers, rural people doing one task in one routine like weaving, was that they had many skills, all that were required to produce some complex object or set of objects, and could switch among these task skills in an intelligent way.

First we need to specify more exactly what we mean by a routine, and what we mean by a complex set of routines tied together by worker discretion. We will do that by making an analogy between work and computer programs. The part of the total task in use of a computer that is programmed into the computer is a part that is *completely routinized*— all decisions are prespecified. The parts of an individual's skill that are completely routinized are those that he or she does not have to think about—once a routine is switched on in the worker's mind, it goes to its end without further consultation of the higher faculties.

Furthermore, a whole factory's work is like the work of a skilled person, a combination of decision-making parts, requiring human discretion, and more or less completely routinized parts, parts that can go forward without consultation of *either* the higher faculties within the individual workers *or* higher authorities for decisions. These completely routinized parts of a social organization consist not only of routines within the individual workers that do not require decisions (meaning that the worker can be either semiskilled, as an assembly line worker is, or highly skilled, as a symphony musician is) but also of relations among workers that do not involve decisions. The model of such a social structure is the early Ford assembly line, and Sabel (1982) has used the term *fordism* to refer to such socially organized routinization.

We treat briefly the variation across organizations of the total amount of routinization. For example, in universities we find highly routinized work in the registrar's office; in hospitals we find fairly routinized work in pathology laboratories. Overall, however, both types of organizations have many highly skilled workers using discretion in their work. At the opposite extreme, an automobile assembly plant has a high ratio of semiskilled production workers hooked together by completely routinized connections among their tasks. But there are still unroutinized parts of such assembly plants, in management and in maintenance departments or tool and die shops. We will analyze why some parts can be more completely routinized than others, and consequently why only a small part of a university is like an assembly line, only a small part of an assembly plant is like the professional staff of a university, but why small parts of each have an atmosphere much like the main part of the other.

Routinization within the individual without individual decision making (i.e., semiskilled work on complex products) is thus the outcome of a social process, the routinization of production. Historically, this has involved two causal determinants, which are analyzed separately later in the chapter: (1) the movement of work into factories and the winning by factory management of the right to specify the content and performance standards of jobs (the specification is often done by engineers, so we study in particular the establishment of authority of engineers) and (2) the finding of the kinds of markets in which firms using such fordist production systems are viable.

Two Relations Between Routines and Human Decisions

Let us start by deepening the analogy mentioned above between the structure of work and the basic structural features of computer programs.

A computer program is made up of two main parts, the part done by the machine and the part done by humans. The part done by machine has to be *completely routine.* That is, when the machine starts running, every single step that the machine is going to do before showing some output has to be completely specified and has to depend only on things that are already in the machine (by machine I mean the whole system, all the machines controlled by the computer). This part of the program is unforgiving; if the wrong directions are put in, the wrong results come out.

The human part can be arranged in two main ways. One is so-called batch processing, in which the humans try (and almost always fail) to put in everything necessary at the beginning to specify every part of the machine routine. There is only one set of human inputs, and one set of outputs that tells the programmer he or she was wrong or (more rarely) right. The other arrangement is called "interactive computing." The basic notion is that the program asks the person at the terminal to specify the first step or first few steps, then shows the results and asks him or her to specify the next step(s). Again, a person always makes mistakes but can go back to the previous step and correct each mistake as he or she goes along. So when people get to the end of a series of human inputs and computations on them, they are fairly likely to have corrected most of their mistakes already, and thus to have usable outputs. The contrast in structure between batch and interactive computation in outlined in Fig 1.

Similarly, the routines of an organization can be thoroughly pre-

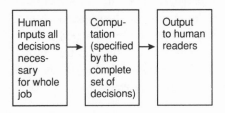

Batch Computer Routine

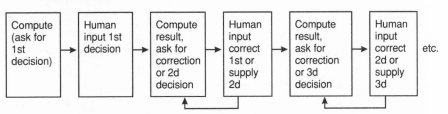

Interactive Computer Routine

Fig. 1.   Batch vs. Interactive Structures of Programs

specified, or they can have many stages at which human discretion can be applied. For an example of a system that is "interactive," consider the *whole* process involving the registrar's routines in a university. That system is built so as to have multiple points at which the human input of the professor (sometimes a committee of professors) is entered: in the title of the course, in the schedule of class meetings, in the flunk notices, in the grades; the input of the department and the school on what is required for graduation; and some more limited input of students at registration time and drop/add time on what courses they choose.

But *most* student input is fed not to the registrar but to professors, who translates pages of messy prose or check marks on a test sheet into the few alternatives allowed by the registrar's routines. So the sixty or so course grades that are most of the sixty or so professors' human input to the registrar about a given student are actually the result of the professors turning a mass of written and oral work into quarter grades, to be output as GPA's, and so on, which in turn qualify a student for this or that major or for remedial classes or get a student advised to take "poet's science." These multiple human inputs from multiple professors make this routine a more or less "interactive" one. This interactive structure is closely related to the use of *skilled professionals* in the "human" part of the routine.

The thing that the professors as "complex human translators" at intermediate points in the registrar's routines makes possible is an enormous variety of outputs—especially in the various "majors" or degrees that qualify people for different lines of work. That is, the process makes it possible to have simple routines or "programs" in the registrar's office, yet to produce a large variety of outputs that would ordinarily require great complexity in the registrar's routine. If it were the registrar, rather than the professor of biochemistry or biophysics, who had to decide what should go into a course on membranes, the registrar's routines would have to be much more complex.

But let us look now at the routines for producing biochemists (or sociology majors, or whatever). We do find some guidelines in the requirements in the catalog, but those are the result of pulling and hauling within the department faculty—occasionally with input from student complaints. It will turn out that if an important professor is working on membranes (and if, *mirabile dictu*, he or she likes to teach), then a course in membranes at least will be an option in the training of biochemists. (Some general difficulties of management of people who know more about the work to be done than their managers are treated in Chapter 9 on university administration.)

The content of the courses may "improve" to keep up with new scholarship, but the professor-hours per student graduated shows no general tendency to go down over time. Quite often the routine parts of the teaching—say, elementary calculus for engineers if taught in the mathematics department—tend to be slighted. People in mathematics may want to get rid of such courses because they cannot teach new and interesting things there. A university may get more and more efficient registration but no real "improvement" (i.e., rise) over time in the student/professor ratio, because the nonroutine parts do not "improve" much over time.

When an organization has routines that are "interactive," we usually find a very complex structure with many parts that do not seem very efficient. Hospitals, research laboratories, universities, law firms, and so forth tend to have most of their routines with such human inputs built into the middle; they therefore look inefficient and anarchic to a modern business school eye.

But let us go to the automobile assembly line, which more nearly resembles a "batch" computer program. A "batch" in this case may be a year's production of a few models of cars. The engineering of the car and the tooling up for model changes are supposed to be the *final* input for *all* this year's cars. Of course, there are more bugs in the production process at the beginning, so more cars do not pass the inspection at first and line speed is slower. And maybe the manager will not be able to be as flexible about producing several models in short runs on the same line at first because, for example, the supply and inventory system for parts for running several models interspersed is not fully developed. Still, the basic structure of an assembly line is the "batch" program. The parts of the program are fixed, and the management have enough control so that even if they have a carburetor attacher who is widely respected among his colleagues, they do not increase the amount of carburetors to be installed the way a university increases training in membranes.

In particular, the manager on an assembly line can really work on making each component part of the routine efficient. Taylorism—improving the pieces of the routine—will not work in a university (or it *mostly* will not), because a university does not want to teach the same courses efficiently year after year and end up producing 1950 model biochemists forever. Deans and college presidents cannot "engineer" the product and the production process in detail.

Similarly, when in a study of a hospital—a relatively unroutinized organization—someone finds that it takes, say, ninety minutes on average to get a neurosurgeon to an emergency room to operate on an accident victim, a time-study engineer specialized in improving routines would have difficulty knowing what to do about it. One does not know that a neurosurgeon is needed until someone makes a diagnosis of severe head or spine damage; a hospital is not trying to produce as many brain operations per day as possible, but only as many as are necessary (and the exact ones that are necessary) given the automobile accident experience and stroke or tumor damage on that day. On an unroutinized job, timing the elements of a routine may not answer the crucial questions. (One thing hospitals may do is to start trauma centers that can afford to have a neurosurgeon there on duty all the time; what can be routinized is the presence of a neurosurgeon, not how to move him or her from place to place or get operations performed faster [Schwartz 1975; 1978a,b]).

Notice that quite often in an unroutinized organization like a hospital there *will* be a big enough flow for *some* routines to warrant "assembly line" structures. In a modern hospital the pathologist (usually a man) is more an engineer for an assembly line of tests (usually carried out by women) than he is a person who does diagnoses. Pathologists do keep a monopoly over writing out the "interpretation," especially of things like biopsies. Similarly, in a university multiple choice test grading can be routinized, and an industrial engineer would be a lot of use in designing procedures for that. But an industrial engineer usually would not help much in turning a heterogeneous group of term papers into grades acceptable to the registrar.

That is, there are bit of work even in a hospital in which the physician specifies a lot of decisions for a laboratory worker's routine (check marks on a lab form), the routine runs, and the output comes back the next day to the physician. The "compute" boxes on the interactive diagram that would represent the production process in a nonroutinized organization, then, can be fairly complex batchlike processes, much like assembly lines. For example, the compute process in an American university for turning a transcript into a certification by the registrar that a given student has satisfied all the requirements for graduation is a pretty complex routine, but it does not require the discretion of a leading biochemist even when the person being certified is a student graduating in biochemistry.

So the first big distinction we want to make among routines is, Are there large elements of human discretion in the course of the routine (interactive) or are all the decisions preformed (batch programs)? Keep in mind here the model of the registrar's relation to the information coming from a student's term paper versus the assembly line. This first variable essentially asks, is there complexity *outside the routine* that is input (in simplified form) into the routine?

Complexity of the Routine

A second variable has to do with *complexity in the routine*. Compare the old Ford assembly lines that made black Model Ts or black Model As and nothing else to the modern assembly line that makes the same model in different colors and makes several variants of a given model. Now one may have several different bodies that are mounted on the same chassis, a couple of alternative engines on the chassis, and an automatic or stick shift variant of each of these, or maybe even a couple of different lengths of chassis. In order to make the modern complex assembly line run, one has to supply the appropriate sequence of parts so the line does not produce a two-door body with front seats that do not fold down.

Obviously each one of these model options on the modern complex assembly line itself has the structure of batch program. All the decisions are made in advance, so that everybody knows folding seats go into two-doors. One wants to build the routine of the assembly line so that as word comes back from the dealers that there are many station wagon liberals out there this year, one increases the frequency with which one "calls" the subroutine for station wagons, and one hopes all the links in that routine work as efficiently as all the other routines.

In such a complex assembly line, one has a bunch of subroutines, all very similar, and an overall routine that selects out or "calls" the subroutines according to results in the market. When that control routine says, "twenty station wagons, one hundred two-doors, and two hundred four-doors," this entails a whole set of twenty decisions about the special placement of the station wagon spare tire, one hundred decisions about two-door folding front seats, and maybe twenty decisions about a longer chassis. But once the quantities are selected, each production run of those quantities is a batch process and entirely routinized. That is, the hundred decisions about whether to put in folding front seats are part of a hundred-unit-long batch program for producing two-doors and within that routine are completely automatic, at least if the routine is working properly.

Obviously, this is a much more complex program or routine than that of the Model T assembly line and requires more flexible systems for inventorying and buying parts, for organizing the storerooms to put out the parts in the right sequence, and so on. The routine itself is more complex. This in turn means that it will be harder to make all its parts work smoothly. There are more things to go wrong with three kinds of seats than with one kind, and more color of paints to run out of when there are six colors, not just one.

Adding complexity to a computer program is one of the main activities of programmers, and it takes a lot of person-hours to write a modification, and even more to get it really running. The same thing is true of increasing the complexity of the routines of an organization so that they routinely yield a wider variety of options, in order to respond to a wider variety of states of the world. Batch programs with human parts need debugging, and the more complicated they are the more bugs they will have.

Artisans at the Beginning of the Industrial Revolution

It is useful in specifying the relationship among the organization of work, the division of labor, and the skill of individuals to examine artisan production in the early nineteenth century in England, as presented in E. P. Thompson's great *Making of the English Working Class* (1963). Somewhere around a fourth of the labor force of London was made up of artisans in the time Thompson was writing about, including masters who ran small businesses in a given trade, journeymen who had all the skills to do so but not the property or managerial responsibility of a master, and apprentices who were learning the skills. This ratio was probably somewhat less than a quarter in most other urban areas, except for a few places that specialized in metal goods (Sheffield, Birmingham).

The main thing that made up the skill of such an artisan, and that makes up the skill of a modern craftsman such as Sabel talks about (1982), is *flexibility*. The reason it took several years to become a craftsman was that a person had to be able to do many different things well in order to make the product. The reason craftsmen were so hard to replace by part-time agricultural laborers, who might also work as outworkers in a cottage industry like weaving, was that there was no one thing craftsmen did (craft workers were almost always men in those days, and still are *usually*) that one could teach a rural laborer to do in a short period of time. Running a loom to make one kind of cloth is one routine, making shoes of all different sizes and styles is more craftsmanlike, and making pieces for machines with the technology of metalworking of 1790 to 1830 required the worker to master many different routines. The first job, then, is not protected from the competition of unskilled rural laborers, while the last is subject to the competition only of very skilled artisans.

For instance, the way one ran a lathe in the days Thompson wrote about was to get the piece of work spinning, then to hold the tool up against it on a long, heavy lever that the machinist supported on his shoulder and, with practiced judgment, to adjust the cut by varying the pressure and angle of the tool with slight movements of the shoulder (see Wallace 1972, 148). Nowadays the machine holds the tool in place, in those days a person did, and it required strength and coordination. Since machinists had to make many different pieces to make, say, a spinning jenny, they had to know how to do many different things with this primitive lathe technology, and to do them fast and correctly.

This variety in the work, with a consequent variety in the routines that an individual had to master, gave craftsmen protection from some of the rigors of competition and made technical advance in their trades into *something they incorporated into their skills*, rather than something that drove them down to subsistence wages as they tried to compete—as technical advance did to the handloom weavers, for instance (see Smelser 1959, 245–264). A power-driven loom by about 1830 seems to have been about 25 percent more efficient than a hand loom (Smelser 1959, 205–209), so a cottage industry could compete if the folks were willing to be about 25 percent more miserable than urban workers were. But if one introduced, say, a new sewing machine into the shoemaking trade (until the development of automatic shoemaking machinery in the late nineteenth century), it became incorporated into the skill of the shoemaker and *increased* the difference between such an artisan and the untrained agricultural worker. The artisan knew how to operate a sewing machine as well as having other skills that the unskilled workers could not match. This contrast in the position of artisans versus the more single-routine trades gave the former a collective capacity to resist disruption of their system of work social relations by capitalism and technical change.

A modern carpenter does relatively few of the detailed jobs that an eighteenth-century carpenter did. Technical change has almost completely changed the *content* of the craft. But he (98.8 percent of carpenters were men in 1985; *Statistical Abstract of the United States, 1987*, 386) still occupies about the same place in the general labor market, union or nonunion, because as one after another element changed it got incorporated into the skill of a personally flexible craftsman. So it still takes about three years to learn to be a carpenter, though now an apprentice, rather than learning how to smooth logs into beams with an adze, learns to form a frame of a house with nails, glue, and plywood. The structure of the program that represents the carpenter's skill is still interactive, with many subskills that are almost entirely habitual. Carpenters are intelligent human decision makers who allocate their time among those subskills. The subskills have been almost entirely replaced, or at least very substantially modified, since the time Thompson wrote about.

To give a more concrete picture of what artisanal skill consists of, consider the example of a housepainter (because I have been a housepainter). The skill consists essentially of three elements: (1) speed and accuracy of *doing pieces* of routines (or subroutines); (2) efficient and accurate *switching among* routines; and (3) *creation* of routines for new purposes. (Roughly speaking, in computer systems the people responsible for these aspects of running the machine are, respectively, the *machine operators*, the *users*, and the *programmers or systems architects*.) For a housepainter, skill consists first of all in being able to paint windows so that the paint does not get all over the glass, to enamel or varnish a door so that the paint does not "sag" or "run," to slop paint evenly on flat surfaces at a high speed, to do small plaster-patching jobs so they are imperceptible when painted, and so on. Speed and accuracy in doing the subroutines, the parts of the job, are the first things an apprentice learns.

A second part of the skill is to adjust the trade-off between speed and accuracy, between cost and quality, in a way appropriate to the job. For example, if upper-middle-class people are going to be living with a window a few inches away, sitting in a soft chair and contemplating it, one wants the paint to go just enough onto the glass to make a clean smooth line, but the overlap onto the glass should be very narrow, very straight, and very neat at the corners. In a restaurant they want a considerably faster job, because extra accuracy will not pay off in restaurant profits except in *very* tony places. People do *not* contemplate windows in commercial establishments. In a factory they want to let the light through the glass—at least through the middle—and to make sure the metal sash is covered so it does not rust. They want to do it as cheaply as possible just so it looks good from the road. College students' dormitories or apartments were very likely painted at a "commercial" standard, while the homes they came from were likely painted to a "residential" standard. So painters really need three different routines—residential, commercial, and industrial—for painting windows, at three different speeds (industrial fastest), three different qualities (residential highest), and three different prices (residential highest).

In the construction industry, nonunion firms in general use less skilled labor than union firms. By hiring nonunion painters one is likely to get a commercial standard in a residence, because the painter cannot do residential-quality painting. A union painting company can pay about 30 percent more per hour and still compete with nonunion painters. For a given quality of work, people seem to increase in speed for about three to five years; thus nonunion contractors by and large employ these workers for the first three to five years, the union contractor after that.

This discussion of painters brings out the contrast between the first two components of skill: speed and accuracy within the routines and ability to switch among routines depending on the situation. Being able to paint windows at the three different speeds, qualities, and prices is the first kind of skill; knowing when each is appropriate is the second kind. These two components of skill correspond to the distinctions among computer programs that we talked about, between batch and interactive programs; the more elements of painter discretion built into a painting role, and the more routines painters are required to switch among, the more the role has the structure of an interactive program with decisions between one routine part and the next.

Skills embedded in the role of an individual painter depend on the overall routines of the painting contractor. In a big city one can find industrial painting contractors that never do commercial or residential jobs, and so their painters do not have to switch levels of speed and accuracy. And there will be commercial painters and residential painters (sometimes even outside versus inside residential). So the structure of the overall routines of the contractor, the degree of specialization, will determine what kinds of skills he or she needs in a painter. Linoleum laying and wallpapering are also (or at least were thirty years ago) in the painters' union jurisdiction. The larger the city, the more likely it is that there will be specialized linoleum and wallpapering firms. The more specialized the contracting firms, the more narrow the specialization of painters will be, on average—the less variety there will be in each individual painter's skill, the faster and better each will be with those subroutines or task skills he or she actually uses, and the less switching there will have to be between those task skills. But in the big city painters are still "artisans," in that they know all the skills and the switching routines that are necessary to produce their firm's product. The division of labor among occupations in construction is still basically the division of labor among firms, but the firms are more specialized in the big city.

The discussion above may seem to imply that only skilled jobs have multiple routines and involve worker discretion in choosing among them. Yet operators of simple machines and bank tellers, jobs that take less than two months to learn to do "adequately," have to use much technical knowledge and discretion too (Kusterer 1978, 45–62, 75–94).

The Division of Skill Between Workers and Professionals

We will now discuss three ideal types of ways people can learn to make the decisions involved in a skill. I will call them craft, young professional, and senior professional. I will discuss each of these in terms of three topics: (1) what kind of basic training each type of worker needs for the exercise of his or her decision-making skill; (2) what sort of knowledge this leaves him or her with; (3) how the "jurisdiction" of the occupation, the set of activities and decisions over which it normally has control, could best be described.

After analyzing these three ways of socially organizing to divide decisions about work routines within roles and to learn how to do those roles, we will turn to a big historical change in the social structure of decision making about manufacturing work, which Reinhard Bendix has studied in his *Work and Authority in Industry* (1956, 274–287), namely the introduction of time and motion study, or "industrial engineering," especially in the steel industry, between about 1890 and 1920.

Industrial engineering was central to the establishment in American industry of the right of management to enter into the jobs of the workers and to reorganize the work itself, to redefine its skill level, to break it up into more specialized occupations. This assumption of authority over the organization of each person's work was involved in the transition to a whole new way of organizing the definition of "skilled worker." The new skilled worker in the steel industry—or later, say, in the automobile industry—was not a person who knew how to do everything in the business of making steel (or automobiles). Instead, after the transition to a modern factory organization of production the highly skilled worker was either an engineer or manager on the one hand or a craftsman on the other, a person who was master of various routines or tasks that have to be done occasionally, adapting to the situation. The skilled craftsman in an industrial plant nowadays can almost be defined as a specialist in everything that has not yet been routinized by industrial engineers.

The point here, then, is that defining the skill of a skilled worker is no longer like the process that defined artisan skill in prefactory manufacturing (which still is found in construction). For an artisan enterprise, every skill needed to produce the product of the firm was part of the repertoire of the most skilled workers. Modern factory management got authority to define routines, to assign them to different workers, and to assign to factory-trained skilled workers tasks still requiring many routines used occasionally at worker discretion. After engineering authority was established in factories, skilled workers had skills created by managerial authority rather than by market processes. Further, routines or tasks now down by factory skilled workers could be reorganized, at any time it became economical, so that they could be done by semiskilled workers in mass production.

Three Organizations for Learning
Routines and Decision Skills

Table 1 gives a brief outline of the main ways different skilled workers learn their roles, what their knowledge consists of, and how the jurisdiction of the craft or profession is typically defined.

CRAFTSMEN

Craftsmen, in ideal circumstances, learn their job by *supervised experience*, the supervision often being one-on-one. First they learn the bunch of skills that hang together practically in a certain job, whether these involve the same principles or not. For instance, the thing that connects painting and paperhanging into the same trade union jurisdiction is that they come at the same stage of the finishing of the building and have the same purpose—looking good. They have to be coordinated with each other, so that the ceiling is not painted after the wallpaper is on, putting splashes on the paper. The knowledge of an all-around painter thirty years ago would have included both being able to paint (and to paint various things at different speeds) and being able to hang wallpaper; wallpaper has pretty much gone out of fashion since then.

So the training of craftsmen is in the first instance to learn these skills one after another from someone who knows how to do them, in the course of doing the work the journeyman or master assigns to them according to their developing skill. When they have worked enough so

Table 1. Ideal-Typical Ways Craftsmen's, Young Professionals', and Senior Professionals' Roles Are Defined and Learned

	Craftsman	*Young Professional*	*Senior Professional*
Basic Training	Supervised experience	Taught principles	Own experience analyzed in the light of principles
Knowledge	List of routines and "indications" for use of routines	Principles without routines	Analyzed routines
Jurisdictions	Bodies of routines connected "practically" to each other	Areas to which principles apply (e.g., mechanical vs. electrical engineering)	Creation of new routines and "higher management"

that they will have learned almost all the routines involved in the job, the apprenticeship will be over. There is nothing "intellectual" that connects the job of wallpapering to the job of painting, the physics of making the paper adhere, the skill of making the pattern of one strip of paper match another, and so on are very different from the physics of making a paint film cure into a viable wall covering or the skill of "cutting in" an edge where the woodwork meets the glass so that it looks good.

It is possible to train for the intellectual professions by an apprenticeship method. For instance, the Inns of Court in Great Britain have traditionally trained barristers (lawyers who appear in court and who are likely to become judges) by apprenticeship (Flood 1982; Abbott 1988). What lawyers end up knowing through such training is the law connected to a large number of practical situations that appear in the courts, and what painters end up knowing is how to cut in window sash, how to align wallpaper so the patterns match and so they still match when they get around the room and attach the last strip of wallpaper to the first one, how to get paint evenly on the ceiling in a hurry but without lap marks, and so on. That is, in both cases what people learn is a list of routines.

The basic training of craftsmen, then, is supervised experience in practical work. What they end up learning is a list of routines and knowledge of "indications" of when *this* routine applies, when *that* one; and the set of routines they learn are those that connect practically to get a given kind of job done, not a set connected by intellectual principles.

YOUNG PROFESSIONALS

Young engineers just out of engineering school are perhaps the ideal type of school-taught young professionals of a modern system. They are taught a series of principles in a set of courses. Courses in engineering schools are not so much a list of things engineers ought to know how to do as a set of principles that engineers will likely find useful in doing the various things (which we cannot very well anticipate now) that they will end up being assigned to do. So if the knowledge of craftsmen is a set of routines unbound by intellectual principles, the knowledge of young professionals is a set of principles they can apply. Young professionals go to work without much practice in the routines in which these principles are in fact applied practically, and certainly without practice in routines enough to cover all the sorts of things they have to do to get an engineering job done. So the job of young engineers is defined in some sense by what the school has taught them—by whether they have been taught as electrical engineers to solve problems with electricity or as civil engineers to solve problems with strength of materials for supporting heavy weights.

SENIOR PROFESSIONALS

Senior professionals have, of course, had the abstract training of young professionals and the hands-on experience of many years so they command the routines of working in a given field. In some sense senior professionals have the three years of actual coursework of the young engineer, as well as three or four year of apprenticeship of the electrician or plumber, and the advantages of both. But the crucial thing that a senior professional has, which craftsmen usually do not, is the experience of many years in *applying abstract principles to various routine situations, and so improving the routines.* In the civil service they sometimes say that a person "hasn't got twenty years of experience—he's got one year of experience repeated twenty times." A crucial thing about a senior professional is that one year of experience repeated twenty times is unlikely: each added year of experience of engineers add (on average) to their value, because they can do routines that have been developed *and improved* in their own experience—improved by the application of a deep abstract understanding of the objectives and the causal processes involved in the profession. So professionals' wages keep going up for a long time with experience, while the craftsman's wages level out after three or four years.

Earnings Curves for Craftsmen, Professionals, and Managers

In general, brand new professionals just out of professional school are not as valuable as craftsmen, simply because they have not really mastered any routines. But experienced professionals are a lot more valuable than craftsmen, and are eligible for positions in higher management. The two (or really three, with the upper management branch for professionals) wage curves look something like those in Fig. 2. (These curves are not based on systematic research, but on happenstance data seen in the course of paying attention to the problem for many years.)

The general picture is that craftsmen become more valuable at their craft for the first three to six years of experience but (except perhaps for promotion to foreman) do not increase in value after that time. They generally cannot do a lot more different kinds of tasks at fifty than they could at twenty-four, nor can they do them any faster. Engineers, in contrast, cannot really do anything until after graduation and are rarely hired at a skilled worker wage rate even after they have had as much training as craftsmen have. Young professionals may get their first job at

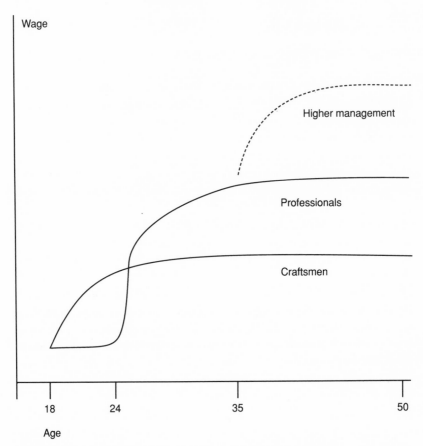

Fig. 2. Wage-Age Profiles (Idealized) of Craftsmen, Professionals, and Professionals Who Go into Management

below the wage rate of craftsmen (for example, an assistant professor of sociology often makes less than a fully qualified plumber).

But engineers do not (as they say in the trade) "burn out" until about thirty-five years of age. They keep increasing in competence because the routines they learn by experience are placed in an abstract framework of engineering knowledge and are improved by further applications of engineering principles to the engineer's experience. At around thirty-five one starts to perceive which engineers are "on the fast track," headed for managerial responsibilities. If they move into management, their incomes tend to increase substantially up to about age fifty. The flat places on these curves are not really flat, because people keep getting increases to keep up with inflation and with the general growth of real incomes (the curves in Fig. 2 represent wages relative to the median of a given year). In general, the jurisdictions of professionals increase in size up to about age thirty-five as they "get more professional experience," and of course managers have more general responsibilities than specialized professionals, increasing further after age thirty-five. So one feature of senior professionals is that their jurisdictions, the areas of competence within which they operate, may have been substantially modified since their education (Faulkner 1983).

It is important to keep in mind that these differences, say between young professionals and senior ones, are analytical rather than concrete. For instance, in graduate school in chemistry the work of a graduate student is more like the work of a beginning chemist than it is like the work of a student in a first-year undergraduate chemistry class. Graduate students do take classes; but to a considerable extent they are practicing the routines used in chemistry so that they can do them right every time, analyzing those routines in relation to their own scientific problems, finding new techniques, and improving a technique for their particular application of it. Already they are in the process of becoming "experienced professionals," and they are paid in graduate school at a rate that is in general already about equal to that of a craftsman (of a low level) rather than of an unskilled worker. When chemists with newly minted Ph.D.s go on the market for the first time, they will already be part way along the curve of "experienced professional."

A rather similar thing happens in medical education, with its division into the basic science years, the clinical years, and the residency years: by the time specialists get their board certification, they are quite experienced professionals.

Jurisdictions of Occupations

The jurisdiction of the craft union is not just a matter of union cantankerousness or self-interest, though it is certainly that also. It really is essential that it be defined which craftsmen should learn a given skill, so that at least somebody will know how to do the work. For example, is the list of routines for finishing plasterboard joints to be with the finishing trades (painters or plasterers) or with the ones who put up the plasterboard (carpenters), and if it is a finishing trade, should it be with plasterers or painters? The final decision is arbitrary. It went one way (carpenters) west of the Mississippi, the other way (painters) east of the Mississippi. The main point is that the bundle of things that fall in a craft's purview is determined by *practical* connections, not theoretical ones. No abstract principle says whether plastering and sanding the joints of wallboard should be considered plastering (because one uses a plasterer's trowel first), sanding (because one uses sandpaper, a traditional painter's tool, next), or carpentry (because it is part of installing things put up mainly with hammer and nails).

Similarly, both plumbers and electricians install pipe, one to put wires in (it is then called "conduit") and one to run water through (it is then called pipe or tubing). But pipe *and wires* are connected to the jurisdiction of electricians in one case, pipe *and waste lines* to the jurisdiction of plumbers in another, because of installation connections (one puts in conduit at the same time and in the same place as wires and connects them to switch boxes; the other puts in tubing at the same time and in the same place as sinks and connects these to waste lines). It is important to put the skills of pipe installation in *both* places because otherwise technically interdependent things (wire and conduit, tubing and waste lines) would not be done by the same people. Construction management would have a mess trying to coordinate plumbers with electricians (neither of whom ever come when they say they will).

Of course, there are also political resolutions of jurisdictional questions, as when the compromise was worked out saying that the painters would finish plasterboard in the East, the carpenters in the West. Once one has decided where the jurisdiction goes, then a whole series of social arrangements follows: painting contractors will bid on the job of finishing and painting plasterboard in the East, general contractors employing the carpenters will bid on it in the West, so the competence of the businesses follows the lines of the jurisdictions of the workers. The apprentices of painters (or workers for nonunion painting contractors) will learn to finish the joints of plasterboard in the East, the apprentices of carpenters in the West. When a big job involving plasterboard comes up in the East, the placement of finishing workers will take place through the painters' union; when in the West, through the carpenters' union. The jurisdiction of a craft is a central principle in the social organization of firms, of apprenticeship programs, and of the placement of workers.

The jurisdiction of an applied science tends to be some compromise between the reach of a given *cognitive* discipline and the practical unities of a job. For example, while from about 1900 to 1940 the best definition of the applied-science aspect of medicine was applied bacteriology (medicine did whatever one could do by killing germs, by preventing infections, and by quarantining sick people), there was also a sort of patient-educational task as well. A doctor had to learn the "normal course" of a lot of diseases in order to tell people what was happening and when they would get over it—not because we then knew scientifically the immunological response to bacteria or to viruses, but simply because the patients wanted to know. So the patients to whom physicians were applying what we knew then about the applied science of bacteriology happened to come to the doctor with a series of questions about the disease: Do people usually die from it? When will the fever go down? When will I be able to go back to work? When does the rash go away? How sure are you that this is really chicken pox? Doctors thus had to learn the course of various diseases, even though that was not particularly a part of bacteriology that made medicine into an applied science.

Now, in fact, the normal course of infections is a part of medical science. Physicians specializing in particular diseases write in *Scientific American* about the mechanisms that produce the fever, the mechanisms that produce the continuing tiredness after the fever goes away, the end of the contagious period when the free viruses (that can infect other people) will be killed inside the body and the only remaining function of the immune system will be killing the cells of the patient's own body that are infected (the fever is connected with the first phase). This is because now medicine, as an applied science, has a lot of knowledge of how the immune system works, and the immune system determines the course of most diseases.

Nevertheless, a lot of medical learning takes the form of learning a bit about a lot of diseases and about a lot of parts of the body—a sort of jurisdiction defined the same general practical way as craftsmen's jurisdiction. So medicine is (and even more *was*, between 1900 and 1940) a combination of an applied science and a "craft" of healing. Young professionals tend to be bad at the "accidentally" attached tasks of their profession, for these are not in the applied science taught in classes.

The jurisdiction of senior professionals tends to be much more vaguely and individually defined. Within the broad range of, say, surgery, one surgeon specializes in the thyroid. He (or she) can accumulate a wide variety of experience in the alternative ways that that organ can lie or can malfunction, guess the likely meaning of oddities on the X-ray of that organ, relate alternative treatments to the symptoms various patients show after surgery, and so on. A physician can only specialize solely in thyroid surgery if he or she has sufficient reputation, and the only way to learn enough to get that reputation is by analyzing a lot of experience, so it is somewhat a matter of chance who gets to be a world expert on surgery of the thyroid.

To some degree, the jurisdiction of senior professional is self-defined. But a general tendency is that experienced professionals' jurisdiction is in those parts of the professional practice that have the most uncertainty. Senior professionals in engineering are more on the preproject roughing out of the plan, less on the detailed work, then more again on the management of the actual building or starting up of the assembly line, where technical knowledge has to be combined with managerial experience. Similarly, senior surgeons are more likely to be referred difficult and esoteric cases, while junior surgeons do more routine surgery.

The Determinants of the Division of Labor Between Engineers and Skilled Workers

So far we have not said anything to indicate that one rather than the other of these methods of creating skill would be better for a particular economic operation, except for some obvious disadvantages of a newly minted degree; if average new engineers can get 70 to 80 percent of the questions right (which might be the percentage for a passing grade in an engineering class), then 100 percent of the bridges they design will fall down.

The big difficulty is that senior professionals are too expensive for operations involving a rapidly changing mix of quite routinized suboperations. For machining a die, senior engineers are too expensive, young engineers do not know enough about metal working, so it goes to craftsmen, to machinists. Frederick Taylor himself, the main originator of "industrial engineering" and an engineer with a lot of experience supervising workers in a steel plant, could figure out how to do skilled operations faster than skilled craftsmen—eventually. But someone with a new degree could not.

Often no one can tell early on which way of organizing a given kind of work is better. An example is the recent history of numerical control (Sabel 1982, 63–70; Noble 1984, 79–192). In numerical control a built-in computer controls the machine. That computer has to be programmed for each different piece to be produced. The question was, should it be programmed by "record and playback" or by an engineer programming a big computer? In the United States, the air force decided to have engineers do the programming before a skilled worker ever saw the operation. In Germany and Japan, in contrast, users of numerical control and machine designers mimicked the activity of a skilled worker by having their most skilled workers operate the machine, recording all the behavior of the machine during that person's operation, and then making that recording tell the machine to repeat those motions. Such tools provided for workers to correct certain bits of the recorded program (to go to the correct point, to rerecord a section, then to go to the end of the section and go on from there) as they learned to do that part of the operation more efficiently.

In the United States many managers and engineering departments put obstacles in the way of "machinist-programmed" numerical control. This was partly because they wanted the work for themselves, partly because they did not want to give the unionized skilled workers the power advantage of being the only ones able to run the machines, and partly because they really believed that programming by engineers would be the best in the long run ("technological utopianism" I call it in Chapter 5). Part of the air force's reason for choosing the engineer-programmed version of numerical control was that no machinists knew how to produce the complex shapes of aerodynamical surfaces that they wanted, so machinist-programmed numerical control simply would not have worked for what they wanted to do.

The result is that nowadays most of the machines are being programmed by less expensive skilled workers rather than by senior engineers who, much more expensively, know both the abstract language of numerical-control programming and the concrete routines of metalworking. This means that now the Japanese and Germans control the international sales of most machine tools, whereas thirty or so years ago the United States was the dominant force in that market. Obviously, someone in the United States made a big mistake in what kind of skill system to build numerical control into, and we are all paying for it in our negative balance of trade.

Part of the problem here is a general danger of trusting engineers too much. If managers go with what an engineer thinks is "state of the art," then generally no one can make it run all the time. And at any rate, they need engineers to run it. For instance, fighter pilots are trained to a considerable extent as aeronautical engineers, as well as in the routines of piloting. That makes a fighter pilot a very expensive product indeed. But even having engineers with years of experience flying our fighter airplanes does not work. Twenty-three percent of navy pilots, for instance, in an average career of twenty years, are killed in flying accidents (Perrow 1984, 126; citing Wolfe 1979, 17). Even senior engineers cannot always manage a "state-of-the-art" airplane landing on a "state-of-the-art" aircraft carrier.

Manufacturing Artisans in the Early Industrial Revolution

In this section I want to discuss how authority is organized in a typical artisan trade (above we treated the organization of *skill* in such a trade) and what this means for the structure not only of work but also of class consciousness. Then I want look at how the factory changed that organization, by discussing the erection of the authority of senior professionals and managers over the content of jobs. Authority over job content was the central thing that remained pretty much in the hands of the worker in a preindustrial "artisan" mode of manufacturing.

Because early industrial artisans (I will call such workers "he" in what follows, for the reasons discussed briefly above—women in manufacturing in the early nineteenth century mostly worked in unskilled work in the textile and apparel trades) had all the skills necessary to complete the manufacture of a product, artisans could, if they did not like the authority system or the wages where they worked, go elsewhere or organize their own firms. In many respects the artisan was invulnerable to employer sanctions.

This meant that there were tough social structures that could carry working-class culture, structures that did not get disrupted, that young apprentices were exposed to for years in a one-on-one supervisory relation in which they learned the trade. The government could not suppress the carriers of this working-class culture without suppressing the craft. Many of the traditions carried by these artisans in 1790, when E. P. Thompson (1963) took up his story (a very similar story is told for France in Sewell 1980, 1986), were sort of "trade union" traditions, about wages and working conditions. But there were also technical traditions, including in particular notions of what good work really ought to look like, tricks of the trade, an idea of how fast a good workman reasonably ought to be expected to work, and the like.

There were also political and philosophical traditions. For instance, the radical "Enlightenment" values of scientific belief (which in those days was more often antireligious than is true nowadays), republicanism, freedom of speech, and the whole complex of notions that Thompson connects with the writings of Tom Paine were part of the culture of machinists in England, France, and the United States at least from about 1800 to 1850 or so (on the United States, see Wallace 1972, chap. 5, esp. 211–219; on France, see Sewell 1980, 64–72, and chap. 9, 194–218).

A key fact in the stability of these deviant systems of working-class culture was that capitalists, the "masters," were themselves virtually always craftsmen as well. They really had to be, because otherwise they could not glance at the hundred different things their workers were doing and see whether they were being done right and at a reasonable speed. Another key fact was that in general the number of people in a given artisan trade even in the big cities was reasonably small, and that people moved around from shop to shop or from one construction job to another. There was therefore a dense social network in a given trade. The network crossed class lines (it included masters) but did not include the nonmanufacturing upper classes, which had a different culture from the artisan workers. Cross-class contact was still within craft culture.

Informal culture supported craft or artisan guild and union organizations when there were any and kept the traditions of organization alive during times of repression (Thompson 1963). Thus Sheffield, a metal-working center north of Birmingham, could come out of the period of wartime authoritarianism (ca. 1800–1815) with a lot of its radical tradition intact. When he was doing politics from about 1807 to the mid 1830s, Francis Place, the London working-class reformer, could still talk the language of the people he had helped organize in the 1790s (Thompson 1963, passim). Sewell (1980) shows for France that artisan corporate culture from the old regime still existed, in modified form, in the revolutions of 1830 and 1848, after periods of Napoleonic and restorationist repression.

Economic and Technical Threats to Artisan Organization

An artisan trade is threatened by one of two things: such big growth in the market that it pays capitalists to break the elements of a craftsman's skill into separate jobs and train a large number of semiskilled workers to do those jobs—the mass production threat; or radical technical change in the product or, more rarely, in the process of production. When E. P. Thompson talks about how the son of the boss wheelwright had to learn from the workers what was good work on a wheel (1963, 235–236), we as modern readers hardly know what a wheelwright is. The reason for our ignorance is that today the job of making wheels is broken down in an auto factory into its component parts, and these parts are done by semi-skilled workers who would never tell their boss what the customary way to do things was because workers no longer have authority over the content of the job.

This threat due to growth of the market is perhaps most dramatically manifested in what happened in the U.S. steel industry in the 1890s and the first decade of this century (Stone 1975). Through bitter strikes and reorganization of management, a well-organized craft method of production was reshaped into a system of mass production using semiskilled workers. The steel industry still has a high proportion of workers classified as skilled in the census, so not all the complexity of work was extracted from the work force and concentrated in management. In the 1890s, control of the definition of jobs was wrested from workers and relocated in the management of the biggest steel companies. From the point of view of the argument here, a crucial fact is that these were the companies making rails for the railroad boom (cf., e.g., Chandler 1962, 53; 1977, 258–269), companies with a large market for uniform goods.

In both wheels and steel, a huge growth of the market for uniform goods made the flexible wheelwright or the flexible steelmaker replaceable by a division of labor organized along rigid bureaucratic lines. We will return to this point later when analyzing the market conditions for the success of "fordism" (Sabel 1982).

The other main threat to artisan trades is a radical technical change that makes the whole product archaic. The craft of sailmakers was destroyed in the period between the decline of sailing merchant ships and warships around 1900 and the rise of the middle-class leisure sailor after World War II. Technical change made sails archaic for freight and passenger traffic, and they did not become modern again until a mass of middle-class people could afford leisure sailboats. More recent examples of technically archaic crafts (since World War II) are the plasterer and the marble-setter crafts, which both disappeared with the growth of new wall materials such as gypsum board and ceramic tile.

From the point of view of working-class culture, it is important not only that craftsmen or artisans can carry a deviant (working-class, trade union, or radical) culture and that they were relatively invulnerable to capitalist and governmental oppression. They were also respected in the working class. They could do things that other workers could not do. They had often traveled to far places because their skill was transportable (Tom Paine, for example, was a craftsman—a corset maker—when he left England, and eventually he became a printer, also an artisan trade).

Authority Reorganization and Artisan Skill

Let us go back to the problem of the disappearance of wheelwrights. Everybody started buying wheeled vehicles, the market expanded, and the wheelwright shop with artisans each of whom could make dozens of kinds of wheels was replaced by a factory with separate divisions of labor for each kind (cf., e.g., Buick Motors creating a wheel factory in Flint, in Chandler 1962, 117–118). Within that factory, management broke up the dozens of things a wheelwright did into specialized jobs for semi-skilled workers. So the skill of the wheelwright became the skill of the factory as a social unit.

The individuals within the factory may have a socially defined skill anywhere from unskilled worker to engineer (engineers have a college education about equivalent to the apprenticeship of a wheelwright—three years of actual experience in classes—but, as we have discussed, they keep gaining valuable experience up to about age thirty-five). But the crucial thing to notice is that the deskilling of, say, the person who makes the hole in the wheel fit the axle (once a wheelwright, now a semi-skilled machine tender) is an active *managerial* process. Deskilling is *creating* a semiskilled job out of a piece of a wheelwright job by management effort, authority, and thought. The job of the semiskilled workers is *designed* by someone (or a group) of higher skill. For instance, an engineer may specify what has to be done by the lathe (and by the foundry before that), and a tool and die maker may shape the tool to put into the lathe to do it. The engineers, die makers, and machine tenders are tied together by a social structure, a "management," which defines their jobs, their skill levels, the standards to which they are supposed to work, performance measurement to see whether they are working fast enough and well enough, the incentive or pay system, and so on.

This proliferation of *managerial* functions and relationships is the crucial development that turns a craft shop into a mass production factory. And the *authority* of management is absolutely crucial to making the whole thing work.

Reinhard Bendix (1956) is interested in the development of the ideology that justified managerial authority. That authority has to take from workers the right to define their own job, their own skill level, their own standards of quality, and put these rights into the hands of an engineer or manager. I am speaking historically here—of course the particular worker who is now a semiskilled lathe operator was not in general the *same* worker who was once an all-around wheelwright, so the process Bendix is talking about took the authority from a *social group* and transferred it to another social group, not actually (usually) degrading the work of someone actually on the job. An engineer's skill is, so to speak, half managerial, half technical. Engineers are not going to be making precise holes in wheels; rather, they will be designing the jobs and skill levels of folks that do. Engineers often move out of engineering into pure management (see, e.g., Chandler 1962, 317–319).

The Ideology of Mass Production Management

The idea of *efficiency* was the basic thrust of the early-twentieth-century campaign (Bendix wrote about the period from about 1900 to 1940) to establish the authority of management over jobs that used to be artisan jobs. A fine quotation from the *Review* of the National Metal Trades Association (comprising steelmaker and machinist managers) shows this clearly: "The employer is willing to pay for results, and in fact results are the only thing on which the value of labor can be based" (Bendix 1956, 271). The right to measure and determine results, and to specify what results are satisfactory and what they are worth, is the central component of managerial authority based on the idea of efficiency. This ideology of efficiency reserved to management not only the right to determine the *value* of labor, and hence what it *should* be paid, but also various other elements that went into the definition of a job.

The most developed paradigm of this conception of efficiency justifying the complete control over job definition by engineers and managers is the "Scientific Management" movement led by Frederick W. Taylor. Taylor, an engineer who worked as a manager in the steel industry, helped build up the bureaucratic version of steel management after the breaking of the craft system in the 1890s. The modern version of the same ideology is represented in the field of "industrial engineering."

The movement was based on time-and-motion study. This involved breaking down the job of the worker into its components and describing the motions that went into those components. Then, after redesigning the machine, the material, the work flow, or the worker motions to make the motions most efficient, the time-and-motion study engineer (or manager) tried to estimate what the *efficient* minimum time is for each of these motions, and hence for each task, and hence for the unit of output. This is the "result" referred to above by the National Metal Trades Association writer. Time-and-motion study gave management a *measure of result* on which to base their authority.

The first thing to notice about this process is that it theoretically reduces worker skill from a matter of the worker selecting from a repertoire of skills to do a certain job to a matter of making the motions he or she is instructed to make. Anyone who has tried to learn to do the motions required to play a Bach piano piece or do the butterfly stroke in a way acceptable to a swimming judge knows that doing the motions fast and accurately can still be quite a learning task. But the cognitive part of the skill, the *creation* of the routines, is moved to Bach or the swimming coach, and the performer or athlete only does the motions. The same is true for the lathe operator after an industrial engineer is through with him.

But for Taylor this efficiency picture of the worker's job entailed still more. He thought that this picture—*not* collective bargaining or craft traditions or a fair day's work for a fair day's pay—should determine the compensation scheme. First, the efficiency conception would determine what an efficient day's work *should* produce, allowing output quantity measures to be substituted for a craftsman's pacing of his or her own work. Second, the same conception allowed one to measure extra effort above the norm accurately, where the norm was described for all jobs because the engineer had supposedly described exactly the efficient time and motions for each job—what went into given worker outputs—in minutes required. The manager could translate the number of widgets produced and the number of wing nuts screwed on them into the same metric, the same system of measurement: "the number of minutes an ideal efficient worker" would take to do them.

This picture enabled management to base the compensation scheme of the whole factory on a set of efficiency models for each and every job. They could then compensate people who produced over the norm *above* the "competitive labor market wage" because they supposedly knew what was the absolute standard an efficient worker, hired off the labor market, could work to. In this ideology the skill and effort of the worker, and the definition of the job of the worker, come to be a "scientific" or "engineering" matter rather than a matter of competing interests, of class conflict over the division of the surplus, or of defense of skilled workers' stake in their investments in their skill. Further, it is the industrial engineer, the scientific specialist in management, who knows how to define all these things.

Scientific Management Authority in Practice

What happened in fact when time-and-motion study people went out to set up this "time needed by the ideal efficient worker" for a given job? They timed a worker, got an average for all the motions, redesigned the job by trying to improve the time-consuming motions, and timed it again. But what they now had was a measure of how long it took, on the average, for John Johnson to pick up a wheel blank, put it into a lathe, tighten the clamps, align it, cut the hole, remove it from the machine, and lay it on the conveyor. This was a detailed picture of John Johnson, not of the pristine idea of the efficient worker. If they were going to let John Johnson define the job, they would not have needed scientific management.

So the time study engineer supplied an estimate of *how far John Johnson was from perfectly efficient.* If he was working at a normal speed for workers, he might be marked down as 65 percent efficient. If this was a new operation (e.g., on a new design of the wheel), he would be marked down at 45 percent. Now the industrial engineer found the efficient ideal by dividing John Johnson's performance by the efficiency estimate, for instance:

$$\frac{20 \text{ pieces/hour (observed: 3 min. ea.)}}{.65 \text{ (estimate of J. J.'s efficiency)}} = 30 \text{ pieces/hour (efficient standard)}$$

Of course, this is exactly as "scientific" as the time-and-motion study people's estimate of what percentage of an "efficient" worker's speed John Johnson is working. And this is obviously a subjective managerial judgment, about as good as our wheelwright master's son's judgment as reported by Thompson.

If the industrial engineer is young, just out of industrial engineering school, and socially naive, an old hand in the factory will sweat and strain and move super fast and get nothing done—or, in the post office, a mail carrier will go to the crosswalk and wait for the WALK light to cross the street, which he or she would never do if the time-and-motion study person were not there—and still be marked 98 percent efficient. Then again, if the new industrial engineer is bucking to get promoted by setting high standards, he or she will not be "taken in" even by a worker who is *really* busting ass and will set a "scientific" standard no one can achieve.

The point is that if management conceals managerial standard-setting as a "scientific" estimate of a number, it may take a fairly clever union bargaining agent to find out exactly where they have built the speedup into their science.

The converse is also true. If "science" does not impress workers into working $1\frac{1}{2}$ times as fast for the same wage ($\frac{1}{.65} \approx 1\frac{1}{2}$), then managers have to shove it down their throats—which, especially if workers have a smart trade union specialist in time-and-motion study backing them up, may be difficult. Many managers felt that, since they had to assert their authority in the long run anyway, why do it with all these trappings? Management could just assert that it was management's job to get efficiency, ride roughshod over worker objections, and fire them if they continued to work at 65 percent of what management thought they might get out of them. Arbitrary authority of the "efficiency hero," not the science of efficiency, was the Henry Ford tack on the problem of speedup on the early assembly lines.

In the Ford plant, engineers had authority to redesign and set time standards for the jobs because otherwise the assembly line would not run—one could not tie hundreds of jobs to an assembly line without controlling all the workers in considerable detail. So the Ford management controlled them, science or not, and made a lot of cars—and *that*, not scientific management, justified their authority.

Conflict over the New Authority System

For all the reasons specified by Thompson (1963), a lot of craft workers were not very enthusiastic about this destruction of the social definition of their skill within the factory. The trade union organizations in the United States (Taylor worked in the United States) were quite generally, up until about 1937, powerful only in the crafts. When the steel industry was reorganized from a craft to a mass production industry in the 1890s, it became in many ways a model for the mass production factory of the twentieth century (and the place where Taylor began to develop the ideology that defended such a reorganization of the authority to say what a job was). The big steel companies explicitly beat a strike in order to get the right to define jobs and skill levels managerially, and then to set up hierarchies of jobs and training for those jobs by the factory rather than by other skilled craftsmen. This reorganization eventually resulted in about a 30 percent increase in productivity (Stone 1975). This is the opposite of what usually happens. Union plants are almost always more efficient (Freeman and Medoff 1984). In fact, in the construction industry union workers usually do about 30 percent more work per day. The increase in productivity by breaking the union must have been due to going over to a system of job description and control more compatible with mass production industry: managers do not need flexible workers when they are producing one ton after another of identical rails for a railroad boom.

Many further innovations in management, such as those described by Alfred Chandler (1962, and esp. 1977), depend on the system for defining work by management described above. Many of these techniques were first introduced into American managerial practice in the first large-scale industry, railroads. For example, Andrew Carnegie moved into making steel rails from the railroad industry (Chandler 1962, 406; Chandler 1977, 258–269; Beniger 1986, 240), bringing with him cost accounting (Chandler 1977, 267–269) and an orientation to precise specification of what time it should take to get a given bit of work done. This was part of his attitude in being willing to take on an expensive and violent strike in order to reorganize production management in the steel industry. Pierre du Pont learned the cost statistics approach to financial measurement of work in the steel industry before bringing it to Du Pont and General Motors. Cost accounting depends on managerial standardization of costs, and a very important part of costs is labor cost. So management definition of adequate work standards is intimately bound up with modern cost accounting and quantitative management technique.

But the engineering ideology of what a manager and a worker were like did not resolve all industrial conflicts. Not every worker believed his work was captured in full by a cost-per-piece figure in the cost accountant's statistics, or in the motions and times associated with specific tasks by a time-and-motion study expert. In fact, like E. P. Thompson's workers, steel workers often thought that depriving them of their status, self-control, and traditional levels of remuneration so that the corporation could make more money was a heartless way to proceed. And they eventually said so again with unions in the 1930s, with the "soldiering" on the job that Taylor complained about, and with cutting no corners when the time-and-motion expert measured their work. People were hard to manage heartlessly.

"Fordism"

A principal purpose of the conceptual development above is to have the concepts to define precisely "mass production," or "fordism" in Sabel's more evocative terminology (1982). "Fordism" we will define to be a productive system characterized to a high degree by five characteristics:

> 1. *Batch programming mode.* The main productive activity, the one that employs the most people, is one that has the structure of a "batch," rather than an "interactive," computer program. That is, for a great many activities in the firm, all the relevant decisions—and so virtually all characteristics of a given activity—are prespecified. The batch program may have a number of subroutines that are called with different frequency, depending on what the market wants; thus an assembly line, for example, may produce more four-doors, fewer two-doors, more black, fewer red, and so on, and still be running in batch mode. The key is that the discretion is only in the orders for the whole line, and once the numbers of red and black two-doors and four-doors are specified, the actions of almost all the workers are specified. Very little discretionary human input informs the decisions of what activity a given worker should carry out at a given time.
> 2. *Semiskilled production workers.* The skills of many

or most workers, then, include only a few routines, which they develop to a high degree so that they can do them fast and make very few mistakes. But their task skills do not form a large repertoire. This is what we usually call a "semiskilled" worker. After only a short time in the plant the workers can produce as fast as they are ever going to, and they know all the routines they are ever going to use, at least until the new batch program (the "model changeover") is brought in. Such workers are inflexible and know few routines, and are in that sense far from craftsmen.

3. *Management with authority to create jobs.* Management has the authority to create jobs, to specify the routines of jobs, and (quite often by way of collective bargaining) to specify the system of incentives and pay for the job and the measurement of performance (e.g., the speed, or the proportion of rejects, that will be satisfactory).

4. *Engineering staff as designers of work.* This authority to specify jobs that is "taken from" worker social structures like craft unions and put into the hands of management is used by professionals, especially engineers, to make the routines as efficient as possible, to rewrite the "program" of worker actions for a model changeover, and the like. The cognitive functions of designing a job are to a large extent located in a group of professionals rather than, for example, in supervisors who are flexible workmen promoted from the ranks because of their exceptional skill. The higher management tends to be recruited from senior professionals, and they design systems for creating routines for the workers, for enforcing them, and for measuring, rewarding, and punishing workers on their performance.

5. *Skilled maintenance and related workers.* The work of correcting difficulties, introducing changes in the productive process, and so on is not routinizable. This work includes maintenance, making the tools for stamping out metal parts, programming numerical control machines, "setup" of machines for producing different products, and mechanical drafting for the new products. Because many routines are involved, because the routines are not highly repetitive, and because the use of the routines has to be decided on according to the situation (they amount to "interactive" programming struc-

tures), they will tend to be done by skilled workers or semiprofessionals.

To put it another way, the remaining sources of uncertainty in the production process will tend to be "buffered" or "controlled" (J. Thompson 1967) by skilled workers or semiprofessionals as well as by professionals and higher management, because uncertainty is too great. Dealing with the uncertainty so that routine production can go on involves learning a lot of routines. There will generally be a separate set of skilled manual work departments (maintenance, tool and die making, and special departments that vary with the technology, such as the crew who lay firebrick inside steel furnaces) and skilled staff workers at the managerial levels (engineering, quality control and inspection, scheduling and inventory), besides the whole routinized structure of the production line and the "line" supervisory structure that keeps it running.

So this is what a "fordist" factory's social structure looks like: a large number of semiskilled workers doing many different jobs, each worker using a few routines and having little discretion; a smaller group of skilled workers in maintenance and related work; engineers designing the product and the production process, improving the routines in that process, and hoping to be promoted to management; and management, mostly former engineers, organized in a strong hierarchy ("line" management) to drive the people on the production line to work as fast as they can. Management also coordinates the engineering and maintenance process with the requirements of production.

It is characteristic of such production processes that, except for maintenance and related workers at the lower levels who have a great deal of discretion, the higher people are in the hierarchy the more discretion they have, the more time they spend planning how to do things in the more distant future, and the less hierarchical relations—the more "committee meetings"—they have in their own work situation. Authority and discretion are arranged very hierarchically toward the bottom, more democratically toward the top. The way such a system looks from the bottom is described in Walker and Guest's (1952) account of a General Motors assembly line; the way it looks from the top is described by Chandler (1962, 114–162).

The Impact of Certainty and Uncertainty on Fordism

For such a massive investment in developing and integrating routines to produce a fordist system to make sense, the production process must be

protected from uncertainty. If we contrast such a process as that described by Walker and Guest (1952) with, say, building construction, in
the latter the workers, as much as management, deal with the variability
in what the firm does one day as opposed to the next. It is construction
foremen who adjust the amount of labor the firm hires to the amount of
work there is to do. It is construction workers as well as foremen or managers who coordinate the work of different crafts. There is no particular
"buffering" of the work of the skilled workers in their routines to take
out the uncertainty; after all, the firm hired skilled construction workers
in the first place because it was in an uncertain work environment.

There are basically two ways of getting low uncertainty so that the
technology will not be disrupted and routinization can be made to pay.
The first is to select that part of the market that has demands with low
uncertainty (we will come back to exactly what that means), and the second is to "buffer" the routinized part from the fluctuations of the environment (Thompson 1967). The registrar does not need to know that
Sociology C-15 at Northwestern University is a fairly different course
when I teach it than when Arnold S. Feldman teaches it, so the registrar
can treat the grade that a student receives from me exactly like the grade
a student receives from him. This means that the registrar can completely routinize the processing of C-15 credits and grades. As long as we
keep the course basically the same so that students would not be permitted to take it twice, it will create no trouble. The registrar's routines are
completely "buffered" by the professors giving the same simplified
output, even though scholarship and the tastes of the different professors change the content of the course, the types of assignments that are
graded, and so forth.

That is, the professors "buffer" the uncertainty deriving from new
scholarship, from differences in approach to a problem within the discipline, from differences in teaching philosophy, and the like, and provide
the registrar with a standardized or "leveled" input, regardless of variations in the environment. The routinization of pathology work in a hospital relies on similar buffering by physicians of the variety of patients
that come in, changing their various conditions into a few checks on lab
test requisition forms.

One can get the same buffering from outside the work organization
itself. For instance, the outworkers in weaving that E. P. Thompson
(1963, 269–313) talks about were given their work by merchants, who
turned the variety of demands in the market, the difficulties of getting a
supply of raw cotton or wool, and the troubles of getting the wool or
cotton spun into yarn into parcels of routinizable tasks that could be given

to part-time rural weavers in small towns who had a loom at home. The "absorption of uncertainty" was done by merchants who did not run the weaving operation themselves.

Sources of Uncertainty in the Market

But the big determinant of routinization of the whole productive process of an organization is the lack of uncertainty in the flow of demands on the organization; only with low uncertainty of demand is routinization possible. We therefore need to analyze where uncertainty in the demands on an organization comes from. I will argue that there are four main sources of uncertainty which tend to prevent the development of fordism, or to undermine it later: (1) unstable markets; (2) unstable specifications of the product (short production runs or "made-to-order" goods); (3) unstable technology; and (4) variable raw materials, parts, or environments.

The basic argument takes the form that we will find fordism in one form or another more often when there is (1) stable demand (2) for a standardized product (3) whose technology of production is not changing rapidly and (4) which uses raw materials or parts that are easily available in standardized form and a technology that can be used in a stable environment (e.g., inside a building). It is in such conditions that firms can best use batch-program-like production processes, where there may be many decisions that have to be made once (such as for a complex product like automobiles) but once they are made the firm needs relatively low levels of discretion—there are few *new* decisions per unit produced.

Conversely, we will expect to find organizations with a lot of skilled workers or senior professionals when (1) the market has wide fluctuations, or (2) each product produced is more or less unique or is produced in small batches, or (3) there is rapid technical change, so that either the firm has to produce a new product because there are new possibilities that someone else will exploit if they do not or the firm has to change their production processes a lot to keep costs competitive, or (4) the work has to go on in very unstable environments or use very variable parts or raw materials.

1. There are very stable markets in industries like electricity production, gasoline, beer, food products (especially those such as dairy products that are not seasonal), some kinds of textile goods such as sheets or towels; there are very unstable markets in contract construction or in producing capital goods such as machine tools or airplanes, and so to a

slightly lesser extent in industries that market to those industries, such as building materials or steel. One finds markets of intermediate stability in "consumer durables" such as appliances, automobiles, furniture, or rugs.

In electricity and gasoline production, a lot of the decisions that need to be made for each kilowatt or gallon are actually built into the machines, so there are not very many semiskilled workers in those fields. Automation has gone furthest where production is most routinized. The main place where manufacturing firms still need flexible humans (and also where robots are most rapidly replacing humans) is in "quite routinizable" markets of intermediate stability. In such markets many decisions have to be made to produce each unit of the product, so routinization pays off even if one can only routinize for a year or so, and even if after a year one has to lay off half of the semiskilled workers, each of whom has been trained in a single routine.

It is also important that there be a *big* stable market for the product. When the oil industry was mainly producing kerosene for lamps and each consumer did not use much kerosene, oil refining was much more of a small-batch process, with workers moving the stuff from one stage to the next.

When routinization goes far enough so that the firm can completely automate the routine decisions, then they do not have so many semi-skilled workers. But to do that the firm has to build the electricity plants or the oil refineries to be useful for twenty years or so of a steady market for gasoline or electricity. Where there is a stable market but the product itself is reasonably simple (that is, fewer decisions, routine or not, need to be made because there are so few parts), as in some parts of the textile industry that produce standard white goods, then one often finds a lot of automation *and* semiskilled workers buffering the uncertainty (e.g., getting the loom running again when the thread breaks; see Blauner 1964, 59, 62–65).

2. Industries with unstable specifications for the final product include contract construction; the movie industry; some building of very big machines such as oil platforms (Alvarez 1986a,b; Stinchcombe 1985c); ships and airplanes (Newhouse 1982), where it pays to adjust the machine specifically to the environment or the size of the market of the firm buying it; art products or the artsy end of craft products (jewelry, for example); academic publishing (Powell 1978); and the fashion end of the apparel industry (Vernon 1960). In all these cases each customer, or each small batch of customers, wants something somewhat different, and so one has to adjust the work process to produce exactly that. In contract construction (Stinchcombe 1959), the building has to be fitted to the site and to

local building codes and has to be the right size for the market of the firm it is being built for (or the size that the family buying it can afford). To some degree there is a new design for every building, and the contract for each building will have a unique combination of tasks for the building work process to accomplish.

Similarly, one does not want to produce the same movie, even a smash hit like *Beverly Hills Cop*, over and over again until one can produce it in a month instead of a year and produce it with semiskilled actors (Faulkner 1983). Fashion goods need to be produced mostly after "the market" finds out what is going to sell in fancy shops this season, what will sell in the intermediate-level "women's department store" market, and what will sell in the mass ready-made market (Vernon 1960). So the specifications for what will be produced have to be adjusted to the latest market information.

In contrast, men's clothes, especially work clothes, or white textile goods, or work shoes, have a much slower changing set of specifications. Automobile specifications are set more by the factories than by the consumers, and at any rate mainly change once a year, and models of refrigerators or stoves often stay on the market for years. Quite a few basic industrial goods have very stable specifications (e.g., various grades of plate steel, steel I-beams, cement, bulk aspirin, or fertilizer).

We would expect more skilled workers (for a given complexity of product) in ladies garments than in other apparel, in contract construction than in the construction of mobile homes, in rugs than in other textiles, in the construction of big machines than in the production of standard machine tools or hand tools, and so on. Conversely, we would expect more fordism in appliances that sell in the same model for a year or more, in textiles other than rugs, in industrial chemicals or other industrial raw materials than in the finished goods made of them, and so on.

3. Unstable technologies produce unstable specifications when the developing technology makes new products possible. We would expect that at present computer manufacturers, as compared with builders of other machines of the same complexity, would have more skilled workers and professionals not only because their production processes are always changing, but also because their product this year is twice as powerful as it was last year (Fishman 1981; Kidder 1981). Changing technology in general produces changing specifications. Especially when there are powerful reasons for the consumer to be up with the "state of the art," as in weapons of a high-tech sort, rapidly changing technology will tend to produce rapidly changing specifications of the product and consequently

short production runs. By the time a company routinizes the production process for a fighter airplane, the order is canceled (Coulam 1977).

But a changing technology also produces changes in the production process, even aside from those involved in the changing specifications of the product. Computer chips are produced by a different technology this year than last year, while the locks on a car door are produced using pretty much the same technology this year as last. So one needs more skilled workers on the new production line of computer chips than on the old production line of car locks.

One expects, then, to find a high proportion of skilled workers and professionals in the high-tech industries: weapons, computers and computer software, telecommunications, pharmaceuticals, medical hardware, or scientific instruments manufacturing. Conversely, in industries with relatively low rates of technical change, such as canning, beer production, steelmaking, and most appliance manufacturing, one would expect to find more fordism.

4. Finally, variability of the inputs into the production process produces a need for a lot of decisions that are very hard to routinize. For example, fishing on the North Atlantic, at least in the old days, was done in boats small enough that the weather was a big determinant of whether one could stay afloat. Fishing is still one of the most dangerous industries in most counties where there is any substantial fishery, because a firm needs a small and economical boat to be economically viable, since in any given area of the ocean one can find only a relatively small quantity of fish. Fishermen do not want to sail an enormous boat around to be safe when they are only going to catch a few tons of fish before they have to take them back to shore. So the weather is a variable input into the fishermen's production process because the main way to control it nowadays, building bigger and more capital-intensive boats, is not economically feasible.

Similarly, underground mining, especially of soft rocks such as tend to be found in coal areas, is done in an environment that is very unstable, with variations in the width of the seam, the physical stability of the roof rock, or the underground water conditions. So although coal is, of course, a very simple product in both underground mines and strip mines, underground mines need more professionals and skilled workers.

In addition to such natural variability, inputs can vary greatly too. For instance, one reason factories are so much bigger in the Soviet Union than in the United States is that Soviet manufacturers cannot manage to motivate parts suppliers to supply highly standardized parts (Granick 1967, 144–147). Consequently, instead of depending on other firms for parts, a factory builds an annex and makes the parts itself so it can institute quality controls. The more routinized they want to make the assembly process, the more they have to be able to depend on standardized parts. One can go into an assembly plant in some underdeveloped countries and see people sitting and filing off the imperfections in the parts before assembly (I happened to see this in mainland China in 1975, but it occurs elsewhere). In these circumstances, a factory has to have workers with files making decisions about when a part is ready to be assembled, because it cannot trust the supplier to supply standardized parts. Finishing parts in a highly standardized way to eliminate workers with files may therefore require larger factories.

In particular, when the parts that an organization has to work with are individual people, it is in general quite hard to standardize them. And the more complex the thing the organization wants to do with them, the more difficult it becomes. Hospitals, psychiatric institutions, schools and universities, and other institutions that perform complex tasks on people have to take account of more variability in the qualities the individuals input to the process than do supermarkets, prisons, census takers, and the like. One can routinize the treatment of people more in the latter cases, less in the former (Leidner 1988). And the more one wants to influence individual decisions by clients, the more one needs to adapt to the clients' varying vulnerability to influence; thus it is harder to routinize the selling of expensive goods, especially goods that people buy only occasionally, like automobiles and houses, than of cheap repeat purchases like groceries or dimestore goods.

Conclusion

Let us now look back at what we have been trying to do. We start off with the fact that some things that people want to produce in the economy are inherently more complex, in the sense that somewhere along the way someone had to make a lot of decisions for it to turn out right. But fordism consists in making such complex products cheaper by routinizing not only all the decisions but also the production process to a high degree. The key here is that the more a fordist factory can routinize the whole process, the fewer decisions have to be made *anew* for each unit produced. So the real dependent variable here, the thing we are trying to explain, is, How many *new* decisions, nonroutinized decisions made by human intelligence and discretion, are there per decision that has to be made to make the product? Thus a formal measure of fordism would take the following form:

$$\frac{\text{routinized decisions}}{\text{total decisions}} = \text{fordism (routinization of production)}$$

This is the level of routinization or degree of fordism of production. The more complex the product, in the sense of the more total decisions required to produce it, the more time and expense will be saved by routinizing. Mass production in the fordist sense saves more on a complex product like an automobile or refrigerator than it does on a simpler one like a sheet or towel.

We have specified four variables that produce uncertainty in a production process, and have argued that the more uncertainty there is, the less the production can be routinized and so the less one can turn skilled work into semiskilled work by many different workers with different tasks (a "collective skilled worker with semiskilled parts"). We have also argued that the most opportunity for routinization will exist when there is *less* uncertainty from (1) unstable markets, (2) unstable specifications, (3) unstable technologies, and (4) unstable natural conditions or unstandardized parts that affect the process of production.

The ratio of skilled workers and professionals to semiskilled in any given industry should be raised by all these kinds of uncertainty, because there will be more decisions (out of the total necessary) that cannot be routinized, and therefore have to be built into the skill of the worker:

$$\frac{\text{skilled workers and professionals}}{\text{semiskilled workers}} = f(\text{level of fordism, complexity of product}),$$

where f is a decreasing function of fordism and an increasing function of complexity. The basic argument of Sabel (1982) is that there are many more industrial situations than we have imagined that are very uncertain, where both firms and individual workers have to adapt to a changing situation and yet do the tasks they do very efficiently to remain competitive. Further, the ratio of work settings that can be highly routinized to the numbers with irreducible amounts of uncertainty has *not* been going steadily upward, in the fashion argued by, say, Braverman (1974) and Noble (1984), because there are still just about as many fluctuations of the market, just as many people who want unique goods, just as rapid change of technology, and just about as much variability in the inputs to productive processes as there always was.

There is, then, no steady tendency to turn all jobs into semiskilled assembly line jobs. If anything, Sabel would argue the reverse. The total skill level of the work force is not going down. In industries with large stable markets for standardized goods, with stable technologies, and with stable qualities of raw materials and working environment, we will expect an approach to an equilibrium with a minimum of skilled workers and engineers, relative to the inherent complexity of the product, and a large number of semiskilled workers doing a few things each, with the routines of one intimately connected with those of another. Or in the extreme, we will expect that completely routinizable decisions will be built into automatic machinery.

The first variable determining the information-processing structure of an organization is how complex the information processed by each worker needs to be. This determines how skilled the individual worker needs to be: how many different routines he or she will have in his or her menu of things that he or she can do fast and well, and how complex his or her reading of the environment needs to be to select the right routine. Stability of markets, of product specifications, of technology, and of raw materials produces an opportunity to routinize. Routinization, or "fordism," lowers the skill level by simplifying the information that needs to be processed by the average worker to make decisions; it does this by decreasing the number of decisions that have to be made *anew* for each unit of product.

3 Manufacturing Information Systems

Sources of Technical Uncertainty and the Information for Technical Decisions

Introduction

The main argument of this chapter is that middle managers in manufacturing set up specialized information systems and keep them running. If most of the decisions in most organizations are "programmed," in March and Simon's language (March and Simon 1958), someone has to program them. In particular, they have to program them in the light of the uncertainties that affect the departmental part of the operations.

In this chapter we deal with lower level, "departmental," information and decision systems in manufacturing. We will find that there are different kinds of information systems in place in the different departments of a manufacturing firm. In particular, we look at the Norwegian State Oil Company (Statoil), which extracts oil and gas from under the North Sea and prepares it for shipment. We will be concerned with where different sorts of technical uncertainty come from, what sort of information is news about those uncertainties, and consequently what sort of information has to be fed in to make the routine decisions correctly.

"Correctness," as we will see, changes over time, as technical development (e.g., in software design), organizational experience (e.g., such as shows that the inventory of a spare part does not get depleted as fast as was at first estimated), or new knowledge about the environment (e.g., where there are soft rock formations that may collapse into the well being drilled) change the criteria of correctness. Thus, information systems have to be built to be adaptable to uncertainties about which baseline information changes over time.

The departmental routines of information and decision are, then, very analogous to skills. They do common things, that have to be done fast and well, because they are routines. They do the right thing because the choice of which routine to use, and when to build a new, better one, is a matter of managerial discretion.

The departmental information systems of this chapter together constitute the managerial system of the "manufacturing" part of a modern organization. It is such a system of differentiated complex parts that has to be coordinated with marketing and with production and process development engineering, integrating the information systems to create divisions, that we take up in Chapter 4. Without understanding how intricate the system for "routine" manufacturing is, it is hard to understand why special structures have to be built to coordinate it with marketing or with product design. Systems of comparable complexity, but quite different structure, exist in engineering and marketing.

People Driving versus Information Systems in Management

The first idea we have to get *out* of our minds is the "people-driving" view of what modern management is about, the Taylorist view. The data on what bureaucrats in manufacturing organizations do with their time are not really compatible with this picture (see, for example, the tables in chaps. 3 and 4 of Stinchcombe 1974). First, much of managers' time is spent reading, writing, calculating, drawing, and otherwise relating to documents. Second, they spend a good deal of time on innovations, rather than on routine operations; this is more true the higher their status but the fewer their subordinates. Third, the mean of their own estimates of how often they report to or are inspected by their superiors is in the general region of once a day, which is a small part of their total communicative activity, this low amount of "hierarchical" communication is not compatible with the higher part of the hierarchy having a supervisor-worker relation.

The general problem here is that organization theorists have very little idea of what there is to talk about (or write or calculate about), where such information has to flow and why. We therefore have very little idea of what relation the hierarchy that appears on the organization chart bears to the total flow of communication, because we cannot easily imagine what the communications are other than supervision.

One consequence is that we do not know what sorts of information there are in a manufacturing administration to be connected to engineering or marketing information. The answer that is implicit in the general hypotheses of this book, as outlined in Chapter 1, is that there are likely to be a lot of different types of information in the manufacturing system, for dealing with various sorts of uncertainty and consequently for making various sorts of decisions. For example, there are likely to be millions of pieces of information on the spare parts needed for maintenance work on any complex system of manufacturing machinery. The uncertainties that this information system is about are the uncertainties of how likely it is that we will need that particular part, what specifications it must have, and where one can get competitive bids on it. That information has to be connected periodically to the inventory of that part and, when the inventory is down, to the purchasing department to buy a new supply.

It will be very unusual that such information will have to flow anywhere in a hierarchy, except in very aggregated form as a budget estimate. But it has to buzz around at low levels all over the manufacturing system, and all over the construction project that builds the installation, so that the relevant millions of bits of information can be put together in orderly form and kept up to date. One of the many things that spareparts middle-level and lower-level technical managers in a manufacturing department do is set up this system, keep it running, update it, see to it that the routines are buying the parts when necessary and forwarding them to skilled maintenance workers when the time comes. But since there is almost no pyramid to this flow of communications, the fact that the managers are lower or middle level actually has very little to do with what communications they enter into. Their communications are determined by what it takes to keep a million pieces of information in order, not by the hierarchical pyramid.

The functional requirements of this system will be determined by where the information about reducing the uncertainty of how many parts one needs to have in stock, what parts will be satisfactory, and where one can get them cheapest are to be found. Thus we will expect that the structure of this system will look quite different from, say, the system of information in the software in the computer center. What has to be done to ensure that people can solve their problems with the software in the system is quite different from what has to be done to ensure that spare parts will be of sufficient quality, will be ordered on time, and will be bought from the cheapest supplier of that quality with the required short delivery delay. The social and organizational features of these two systems will therefore be quite different.

Some Data on Manufacturing Information Systems

I had a chance to study the buildup of the operations administration of the Norwegian State Oil Company (Statoil). The following descriptions of information systems reflect systems being built in preparation to operate a platform that was about to be delivered to them (by the construction part of Statoil's own organization). The platform was delivered while we, Carol Heimer and myself, were interviewing for the study. Our objective was to describe strategic aspects of getting ready for operations (the reports on this work are Heimer 1986a; and Stinchcombe 1986d).

In order to design the information systems, Statoil middle managers had to know what general kinds of information had to go into them. Then they could describe the problems of determining the systems' structure, of putting starting values on the pieces of information they needed for making the first decisions, and of making sure that one was ready to update the systems as new information came in. This descriptive material on what is actually in a manufacturing administrative system's various information files turns out not to be in the organization sociology literature (cf. Cooper and Gaskell 1976).

In what follows, the data on information systems' general characteristics come from only one organization, and that organization was not yet manufacturing anything. This is not the ideal sampling scheme for describing manufacturing information systems, but a sample of one is of course a great deal larger than any now in the literature, and the fact that the administrative system was being constructed meant that the people had recently thought a good deal about the structure of their part of the system. They were therefore probably better informants than people who merely operate a system handed on to them by their predecessors.

Operating Characteristics of Information Systems

The general purpose of this and the following section is to describe types of information used in manufacturing operations so that they are distinguished by the *operating characteristics* of the bodies of information—how information is generated by and incorporated into activities. An example will make this clearer.

A *preventive maintenance program* has the purpose of repairing all potential faults in machinery before the machines fail, by replacing or reconditioning them beforehand. These programs are especially crucial for machines whose failure might be fatal, such as airplanes or oil installations. Part of the information embedded in such a program comes from thousands of bits of experience: experience of the mean time to failure of thousands of parts, experience about how good a predictor this mean is for failure of particular individual parts (experience of the variance of time to failure), and experience of the costs of having that part fail unexpectedly before it is replaced or repaired. There is no useful general engineering theory from which such pieces of information can be derived ("reliability theory" in engineering [e.g., Green and Bourne 1972] is instead about combining that information for different parts of an interdependent system to get the temporal distribution of failures for the system; it does not generate the basic numbers about failure times for the parts). Variations in operating conditions mean that generalizing from, say, the general behavior of the parts of pumps to the behavior of a particular pump and its parts is not very useful. In addition, the incentives of the group planning a preventive maintenance scheme are strongly affected by their not usually being responsible for the budget for person-hours to be used in opening up a perfectly good pump just to make sure it is all right.

An operating characteristic of this information, then, is that it tends to be quite bad at the beginning of operations of a system and to improve rapidly with experience. So preventive maintenance plans are hard to create before operations begin and are not at first very good approximations to the plan that is in fact best for operation because the information in them is poor. Plans created before operations start, then, have a certain fictional or utopian quality and need to be adjusted drastically to reality in the first months of operation.

This *dependence on experience* makes the information contained in a preventive maintenance plan distinct from, say, the accounting information from the project that gives the capital value of the installation. The dollars paid for welding convey the same economic information as the dollars paid for compressors, as far as the tax authorities or insurance companies or financial auditors are concerned, and it is they who have to be satisfied with the numbers in the capital accounts. The capital value estimate for an installation does not improve with experience, and in fact perhaps gets worse, since depreciation is not usually calculated in a way that uses experience to reestimate an asset's economic value. The current economic value of an installation might be equal to the investment required now to create an equally efficient productive facility with the same capacity, and would not be estimated by the experience of the installation at all, nor by depreciating the cost of an old installation by any of the common accounting schemes. British Gas attempts to estimate the "current cost" of their capital equipment to assess their profitability and to set the appropriate rates for gas service, probably generally rational in the oil industry, where capital equipment is so long-lived. But tax authorities and credit institutions, who have learned to use historic cost figures, resist such innovations.

The main dimension that differentiates the information embodied in a preventive maintenance plan from that in a capital account is the degree to which operating experience improves the information. Operating experience gives information on—to give one example—the mean time to failure of a general class of pumps in the operating conditions of an oil installation. If a pump is left until it stops, the time to failure of that particular pump at that particular time is known with certainty, rather than from an estimate of a mean. The way we keep our financial accounts, the cost of a capital installation is not any better estimated after operating experience has been gathered, though of course the stock market will react to the profit outcomes of operating experience regardless of the book value in the accounts.

Such a dimension for differentiating bodies of information tells us something about how we would expect the respective information systems to be reorganized and updated as the transition from the project or building phase to the production or operating phase of a manufacturing establishment takes place. It also tells us to look at other systems of information to see whether change of organization of such systems as one moves into operations is affected by their degree of improvement by operating experience.

The following examples of types of information systems in manufacturing organizations and other similar organizations identify dimensions of differentiation that will be useful in analyzing the problems of creating information systems adequate to the manufacturing operating phase.

Types of Operating Information Systems

WELL REPORTS

The report of experience on a given well provides a great deal of detail about the geology in a particular field, and about the technical solutions that have worked to solve the problems that geology poses. That means that the well plan for the next well in the same field will be based, in great detail, on the reports for surrounding wells: where shallow gas with its danger of blowout is likely to be found; where the rock is solid enough to anchor the casings with cement; where the formation is weak enough that the weight of a mile or two of heavy drilling mud is likely to break out of the hole into the formation instead of returning to the top to carry the drilling chips and be reprocessed; and so on. I may of course have the technical details of what needs to be learned about the geology and what it implies wrong (an amateur's introduction to drilling can be found in Alvarez 1986a, 58–60), but my list gives the flavor of the information a well report contains that can be used in subsequent well plans.

This information is to a high degree environmental information about a particular field, is unique to that field, and is obtained within the drilling operation rather than from any outside source. Further, it is this unique internal information on which almost all crucial technical decisions depend, so that almost everything important that a driller or a drilling engineer has to learn to make his (or her, if drilling were other than what it is) operation succeed is internally generated. To exaggerate, everything a drilling engineer needs to know to plan a new well is generated within the drilling department from experience of previous wells. Drillers talk only to each other because other drillers (especially drillers in the same field) are the only ones who know anything of much importance. The respects in which this is an exaggeration are crucial for analyzing how drillers relate to the company's construction and operations organizations and information systems. For from one point of view, the drilling of wells is only the first stage of operations of a manufacturing installation (an oil well) that will produce oil, gas, or both in a condition ready for shipment. A closed circle of drillers' communication does not serve the larger organization well.

In the special case of the typical North Sea platform (until 1986, at least), in which the drilling equipment and the oil processing equipment are installed together on the same platform, the platform as delivered by the construction project is at first an extremely expensive drilling rig. The main operations that go on on the platform are drilling operations, until the wells are ready to produce gas and oil. So the first "operators" on the platform are primarily drillers, and drillers have to coordinate their schedule with the schedule of completion of construction and installation of equipment. They have to make sure the drilling equipment designed into the platform will in fact drill production wells efficiently and safely (or else they have to modify them so they will). In general, they have to collect information sufficient for their operations from the design and construction organization, to produce operations manuals for the drilling part of the platform, to prepare themselves to maintain the equipment, and so on, just as any other operations group has to do. From this point of view it is really the drilling division that "takes delivery" of the platform from the project organization that built it.

From another point of view, drilling is the last "investment" activity that prepares the platform for producing oil. Of the total investment preparatory for operations in the North Sea, roughly 60 percent is for the platform and the production equipment and 40 percent for the drilling and well completion. Drilling goes on for a relatively short period (roughly a quarter of the life of a platform), and after a well is drilled all that the production organization has to do is let the well flow. (If anything else has to be done, the drilling department comes back in to "open the well" and to "do a workover," producing a well with new characteristics.)

The completion of a well (that is, turning it from a hole in which drilling is going on to a hole from which oil and gas can be produced and delivered to processing equipment) has to be coordinated with the readiness of the production organization to handle the gas, oil, and water produced. The well has to be technically connected to the production system so that it has no leaks and can be controlled and shut down in emergencies. The product of a drilling operation is not simply a hole, but a production hole, a hole that can be operated to produce gas and oil profitably; thus it bears the same general relationship to operations as does the construction project that builds the installation.

The specifications for the output of the drilling operation ultimately come from production, and the hole that drillers drill has to be technically coordinated with the production system. The "specifications" for the characteristics of the production well need to be those that the operating or producing organization can work with, so the relations of production with drilling are much like their relations with the project that builds the installations above the seabed.

The withdrawal of drillers into communication only with each other is framed on each end by organizations with which they have to coordinate schedules, technical criteria, and economic criteria: the project or manufacturer that builds the drilling equipment, and the production operation that uses the hole drilled as a capital asset in its work. Drillers in Norway celebrated having made it through another week alive with coffee and whiskey on Friday; they had a rubber stamp to mark "Bullshit!" on the documents from other parts of the organization that distract them from the important matters of dealing with an open hole into which shallow gas may come at any time. These are informal reflections of drillers' dependence on the information generated by drilling operations, for they strongly mark the boundaries within which it is valuable to pay attention to what others say: the rest of the world does not know what is really going on. The delicate negotiations to get drillers to specify what spare parts they will need somewhat in advance so they can be ordered and inventoried with other spares by the production organization, or to get them to coordinate the design of the well completion with the project's design of the apparatus the completed well has to connect with, reflect the fact that drillers' withdrawal can be only a temporary phase of the total development of the oil field.

The dimensions that differentiate well reports (and well plans) from most other information systems, then, are that the information that is crucial to drilling operations is fairly unique to a single operating organization and that it is generated from experience in operating a particular installation in a particular environment. No one else needs to know exactly where the shallow gas or the weak formation that will let the drilling mud out of the hole are, but drillers cannot do their work without that information, and that information is generated within drilling.

This is an extreme case of a common feature of technical operations information systems, that much useful information is to be obtained only from operations and is of interest only to the people operating particular machines. It is called "plant-specific skill" by Charles Sabel (1982, 58–62). Operators and their supervisors all learn and use information about the peculiarities of the particular machines they use, or have useful classifications of the detailed variations in the raw materials they use, or notice variations in the environment useful to their work that are not noticeable to others. (The many words for snow in Eskimo languages is the standard anthropological example of such "local knowledge"; the many words in Norwegian for types of rain and rain mixed with snow or ice would serve as well.)

When a large share of the information used in a given activity is such "local knowledge," a subculture grows that is more or less isolated from the rest of the organization. That subculture is organized in large measure around an information system that is of little use or interest to anyone else and so is adapted to particular concrete features of the environment, uses an arcane language or system of notation, and resists invasions by standards from larger and more uniform information systems. Other extreme examples in the oil business are the culture of deep-sea diving, helicopter piloting (for both, see Alvarez 1986a,b), and the "systems" part of computer programming (see Stinchcombe and Heimer 1987). Work based on such specialized and bounded information systems is quite often subcontracted for rather than built into the hierarchical plan of the main manufacturing company organization, and may often be found in a section of an organization chart or a project plan under some such title as "specialized contracts."

SOFTWARE SYSTEMS

The distinctive feature of applications software systems in a large organization is that *after* they are put into operation they usually grow by about 10 percent a year (in lines of code or in the number of different reports they put out, two highly correlated measures; the revised program may not be integrated into a single file, and some of the additions may "stand alone"—these are included in the 10 percent [Lientz and Swanson 1980, 34]). The information embedded in a software system then grows rapidly as it is operated; programmers constantly write code to apply the power of the computer to produce new forms of information from the same data base or to increase the complexity of the data base.

The new subroutines' output is used in operations, in decision making, in reporting on activities to outside authorities, and so on. In the computer business as a whole, about the same rate of growth characterizes "systems" programming, such as operating systems or programming languages, with the main growth being in the number of "options" in the system.

We can guess that two sorts of processes go on here. The first is related to the fact that computer programs are still innovations. For all innovations, the first developments are directed at the main purpose of the innovation, or to functions where the innovation is highly productive. As the innovation persists, more and more "elaborating" innovations are added to it, fitting the innovation to occupy niches in the productive system that are more peripheral to its central contribution—where the market is smaller, the innovation less productive, or the value produced smaller (Grilliches 1957).

One writes a program for the main financial reports, for payrolls, for accounts receivable and accounts payable before one writes subprograms for cost analysis, which are in turn written before subprograms to take care of the special features of travel vouchers. One writes a programming language to translate algebraic expressions into computations before writing programming languages for matrix algebra (or before adding matrix options to the algebraic language), which are in turn written before packages convenient for solving systems of nonlinear equations.

Thus we expect that all innovations when they are new become more complex as they add progressively less productive complexities to the original major innovation. Since the hard part of making these supplementary innovations in software is apparently describing their specifications (which is often done by research about what the users really need) rather than inventing a way of satisfying those specifications, innovations in a particular software system tend to be produced at a more or less steady rate. Software is one of the few fields in which we have regular undergraduate educational programs for training "inventors" of new devices, so the movement to progressively less productive innovations in a given software system is more routine, regular, and predictable than in most invention.

A second possible explanation for the growth of software systems during operations is that user understanding of what they would really like to have is at first shaped by what they could have when they had to do it all by hand. As the cost of producing new types of differentiated reports decreases, people discover what they would really like to have because for the first time they can think about it realistically: what report format would be easier to read, or what further calculations in the report would involve less work with a pencil to get at the number that really tells them where they stand. People do not bother to think about what they might want until it becomes possible; the existence of an operating software system with most of their data already in it makes many more things easily possible, and so encourages the development of new specifications. Probably many of the new specifications of reports or other information products of the software system do not actually increase the productivity of the operating organization by much, but their marginal cost, once a basic information system and data base are computerized, is small (and the estimate by the software department of the cost to develop the elaborating innovation is often even smaller).

The situation with software systems is in some ways similar to that with the cost reduction use of cost statistics described below. The beginning of operations for both systems starts a systematic serial change of the goals for which the information system is being used. Just as one goes from the most obvious and productive cost-saving projects to the less productive ones after a detailed cost analysis system is introduced, so one goes from the most standard and useful reports from a data base to those that will be useful only for small audiences or will only slightly improve decision making. Similarly, just as one finds out by experience with a production line what cost-saving innovations need to be analyzed, so one finds out by experience what reports other than the standard ones are that one might want to get out of the data base by improving the software system.

This constant shifting in the goals of an information system requires detail, complexity, and flexibility—increasing "options"—to be built into the information system itself. Flexibility, detail, complexity, shifting purposes, and shifting applications characterize software systems, and the shifts of purposes and applications come more rapidly as the software system begins operation.

The dimension that differentiates software systems, at least in degree, from other information systems is that after a decade of operations about half the information structure in the system has been added since operations began. The continuous innovation that characterizes software systems makes the development phase of the system blend into the operating phase, because both involve a steady stream of capital investment in the capabilities of the system by a steady stream of technical innovative work.

The primary value of a system of cost statistics for an operating organization is to suggest where it is strategic to look for cost improvements. This is quite different from the main value of cost statistics for project or "building" organizations (see Stinchcombe 1985e), which use costs of component activities of the building process to construct estimates of the total cost of building proposed installations, depending on the amounts of the activities that will be involved in construction. Cost statistics are very little used in project organizations to minimize costs (except in choosing between installation designs involving differing amounts of different building activities and different materials).

The use of cost statistics for operations can be broken into two main parts: (a) comparing activities or products produced by a given organization with standards derived from productivities elsewhere or market prices elsewhere and (b) causal analysis of particular activities to seek modifications that will most reduce costs. I will call the first use "Cost Comparisons," the second "Cost Reduction." Then there is the traditional use of accounts for tax and financial purposes: (c) ledgers and financial accounts.

Cost Comparisons. Costs at a more gross or aggregate level can be used for comparison of lines of activity within a company with comparable lines of activity elsewhere, or with market price. These can be used to suggest lines of business a company might emphasize because of its comparative advantage or might go out of because of comparative disadvantage. In a rather similar way, they can suggest which components of a productive process it would be strategic to subcontract or buy (wherever the market price is lower than the costs of internal production) and which to internalize.

There are sometimes technical or economic reasons to keep activities within the firm, for example where there are strong technical or scheduling interdependencies with other activities (e.g., where prompt maintenance is required to keep production lines running—more generally, see "The Decoupling Principle in Project Administration," pp. 68–71 in Stinchcombe 1985e), where contracting would give the contractor access to sensitive information (this is common in defense industries and in software development), or where a contractor or supplier would be placed in a partial monopoly position (e.g., in running pipelines to a gas or oil field). In these cases cost comparisons can suggest low-performing activities among those which, for strategic reasons, have to be within the company—places in the organization where administrative energy and information about industry practice need to be injected into the operating system. High costs of a line of activity in the firm compared with industry standards show that such information and energy will be productive.

The principal operating characteristic of such a use of cost statistics is that the categories of costs have to be comparable to generally available cost standards. Costs may be aggregated into units that can be bought in the market, to allow comparison with available market alternatives; or they may be aggregated into units in common use in cost accounting systems elsewhere so that accounting consultants with wide industry experience will be able to locate costs that are above standard. Thus they depend on what Carol A. Heimer has called a "negotiated information order" (Heimer 1985b), in which a local information system must use the categories and standards accepted in a larger system of organizations rather than those that might be convenient for their own decisions. In particular, cost comparisons in an enterprise in which a firm goes into a new industry requires using the categories commonly used in the same business, which may not be the same as those used in the firm's original business.

Cost Reduction. To use statistics for cost reduction, one needs statistics that are broken down by *significant causal components* of costs (see the analysis in Stinchcombe 1974, 3–31). That is, one wants to know what costs can be manipulated, and costs subject to distinct methods of reduction need to be distinguished in the statistics. If an investment is required to change a production process, either formally, as with investment by buying a new piece of equipment, or informally, as with investment of managerial attention or retraining time for workers, the payoff can be evaluated if the cost contribution of the improved process to total costs is known. In general, as the opportunities for cost reductions with one piece of cost statistics analysis are used up, new analyses are appropriate, so it is important to build flexibility into the system so that different detailed categories can be used for analyses at different times.

The operating characteristics of cost statistics used for cost reductions, then, are somewhat in conflict with those used for cost comparisons. Rather than industry-standard categories at a quite aggregated level rigidly enforced throughout the cost system, one needs a detailed *dis*aggregated system of statistics, with easily changeable levels of detail so that one can analyze exactly the costs one is hoping to reduce with a new program. As one moves into the operations phase of a manufacturing enterprise being newly started, one wants to adopt more detailed and more flexible cost categories and to have an increasing part of the system of analysis not be standard reports but instead specialized studies dealing with changing cost reduction strategies.

An operating system is subject to a "learning curve" of cost reduction. That curve consists in reality of incorporating a long series of cost-reducing projects, involving improved equipment, improved procedures, improved skills, and the like, into the routine functioning of the production lines. It is information support to a series of such cost reduction projects that constitutes the cost reduction aspect of a system of cost statistics. Cost reduction uses of cost statistics are therefore distinguished from the cost comparison use by having the detail and flexibility that makes them useful for a shifting mix of cost improvement projects.

The dimension differentiating the two uses of cost statistics, then, is from rigidly enforced agreement with industry-standard aggregated cost statistics to shifting and flexible categories corresponding to the causal system that has to be manipulated to reduce costs. (An account of a similar problem in Norwegian oil insurance loss experience analysis—loss experience data are of course cost accounts for insurers—is Heimer 1985c, 216–221.)

Ledgers and Financial Accounts. Much the same dimension as distinguishes cost accounts for cost comparisons from those for cost reduction also differentiates all cost statistics from accounting for tax reporting and reports to owners—"ledgers" or "financial" accounts. Financial accounts have to provide statistics that cannot be fudged: legally enforceable numbers for taxation and auditable numbers of financial condition for use in the capital markets and for the assessment of management. There is an industrywide or economywide information order, though it might better be called "enforced" than "negotiated" (Heimer 1985b). Accounts are carried at a very aggregated level, so that capitalized values to be depreciated by the rules of the taxation system are comparable across all firms and profit and loss statements mean approximately the same things about the financial condition of different companies to banks, stockbrokers, and investors (Meyer and Rowan 1977).

But in addition to the dimension of rigid comparability across the economy rather than flexibility for internal use, all the data that go into financial accounts have to be auditable. There has to be a system for legitimating each figure of costs (e.g., an invoice that appears in some other company's accounts under accounts payable) and of profits or capital accumulation, which an outside auditor can check to see whether the figures have been produced by legitimate means. Financial accounts have to ensure financial discipline and honesty, as well as provide comparability between enterprises. (Of course, financial discipline and honesty are essential to the comparison process as well.)

PROJECT DESIGN

The drawings, specifications, quality control procedures, and the like that make up the description for a complex manufacturing installation are supposed to be a description that the fabrication and construction contractors who build the facility can bid on and use as a guide in their activities. Of course, the specifications have to be oriented to the way the equipment will be operated, since the purpose of the design is to produce commodities during operations. But the primary problem to which this information system is dedicated is the construction and delivery of the installation on time and within budget, according to the functional specifications and the broad strategy of design and construction specified (ultimately, at least) by the buying organization. We will call the information and decision system that guides fabrication of the capital installation "the project" (see Stinchcombe and Heimer 1985 for more descriptive material), and the one that operates the completed installation "operations."

But after the installation is constructed, some parts of the operations depend not only on broad functional specifications (such as "closing the fire alarm manual controls should shut down the processing train and close off the supply of oil and gas from the wells safely") but also on details (such as "for maintenance the screen in this instrument should be replaced with 90% fine platinum screen of the same size"). Broadly speaking, the maintenance activities, which in the case of highly automated production like that of oil and gas or chemicals may constitute up to 70 percent of the work to be done during "operations," depend on many of the details of the design, while operating activities depend largely on functional specifications. For example, the spare parts system needs to have categories of electric motors with feet versus those with flanges to distinguish those that can be mounted in different kinds of structures, so that the maintenance craftsman can mount the replacement motor where he has taken out the motor installed by the project. The operator, however, need know only that shutting a given switch turns on the motor that runs a given pump; he does not care whether it has flanges or feet.

Even in the case of maintenance programs (and corresponding spare parts buying programs), much of the information in the design for fabrication and construction will be useless, and some new information will be needed (e.g., mean time to failure of an electric motor in occasional use, alternative sources to buy particular spare parts). And particular pieces of information "needed" in the design may have much less importance for fabrication or construction than they have for maintenance. Which of several models of motors with flanges produced by a given supplier is used in a particular place is of very small importance in construction; it may be of great importance in sending out a supply of parts when the motor will be overhauled in preventive maintenance.

A particularly important difference in information usefulness for the project versus for the operations organization in that toward the last stage of building, what the construction or fabrication people need to know about a change is only what activities they need to do to change it; what the operators and especially maintenance people need to know is how it looks at the end—the "as-built" drawings and technical data sheets and parts lists.

Thus, while much of the technical information in the design is needed in operations, different parts of operations depend on different amounts and kinds of detail in that information, and need different amounts and kinds of supplementation to that information. The design information has to be reorganized in several ways to provide the technical information needed for operations. Some of that reorganization is ordinarily done formally by the construction and fabrication project, such as the production of "as-built" drawings and documentation. However, since the adequacy of this documentation is crucial for operations, but for the project it is merely one last bit of paperwork, there is a problem in getting the project to produce the quality needed. Similarly, some of the reorganization, such as finding competitive bidders for supplies of spare parts for maintenance, is ordinarily done by the operating organization, who need detailed supplementary information, partly not needed for the construction process but most easily obtained from vendors and contractors with whom the construction project has most contact. Since construction and fabrication do not depend (or at least not much) on knowing competitive bidders for parts, it is hard to get the project interested in supplying that information to the operating organization. In short, while most of the information that went into the design of the project will be buried in archives, never to be retrieved, much of it has to be massively reorganized to be useful to operations. Yet the project that has the information often has neither strong motives nor a strong sense of responsibility to provide quality information.

The dimension that differentiates design information from the other information systems we have considered is that in design the information guides one kind of activities, fabrication and construction, and is therefore organized subject to project imperatives—to have the information ready for use only once in the construction process but that once to have it ready on time. It has to be reorganized and supplemented to guide quite different activities (especially maintenance, but also operations) such that these can be repetitively performed and can be improved over time. So it has to be obtained for reorganization from project people who are geared by the incentive system to have information ready only once, and then on time; a core problem of such information systems is the organization of project responsibility and motivation for doing a good job on someone else's behalf (a question addressed in Heimer 1986a).

This problem, however, occurs in other information systems as well, as a leading software designer makes clear in the illuminating statement, "It takes only about a third of the total work on a system to get it to the point where *we* can make it run" (Allman and Stonebreaker 1982, 31). Unless software designers are strongly motivated by user-friendliness, one gets awkward solutions and indecipherable software manuals.

INFORMATION ABOUT AUTHORIZATIONS

Several information systems are distinctive because the information in them has been approved, so it can be used as a basis for action. Perhaps the most important systems producing approved information in oil operations, for example, are the budgeting process, the design approval process, and the complex of certifications and approvals involved in safety.

The design approval process for an installation in Statoil consists of two main parts: the approvals leading up to the "design freeze," perhaps embedded in the project manual with supplementary design documents; and the approvals that result in a "design change proposal," for a change slated to take place after the design freeze.

The budgeting process, resulting in the set of information that approves of expenditures in the production organization often stretches out over much of the year (though most people involved do not do budgeting full time for very long).

The safety systems in oil operations or chemical operations are comparable to those in airline operations, though they are generally more complex than in other manufacturing. In oil operations, the safety approvals system involves such things as the classification of areas according to the possibilities of the presence of explosive hydrocarbon and air mixtures. The classifications then vary over time—for the construction phase before drilling, from the start of drilling but before the startup of gas and oil processing, and for the normal operations phase of actual production. Other safety authorizations include special approvals for doing "hot" work (that presenting ignition risks, such as welding) or for performing lifting operations on platforms at sea while divers are under the water.

For all these systems there is a radical difference in the implications of a piece of information depending on whether it has been approved or not. The process of transforming information from proposed to approved is central to the whole formal part of the organization (Barnard 1946). The transformation from information for decision making to approved plan is much of what the authority system is for, what meetings among authoritative and high-ranking people are mainly about, and what causes much of the bureaucratic delay characteristic of decision making (Stinchcombe 1985c). It often takes quite a while from the time the information becomes adequate to show what the decision will have to be until that decision can be acted on, because the information about what we will (in fact) do has to be transformed into an approved decision, with an approved design, an approved budget, and a safety clearance, all attested by the correct number of signatures and meetings, all auditable by a quality assurance team, and perhaps by ordinary financial auditors as well. At any given time one could say that the formal organization consists of the body of information whose approval has made it a valid guide for action. (Occasionally people will in fact describe their responsibilities as seeing to it that people follow the approved procedures.)

The operating characteristics of approvals systems depend a great deal on the particular structure. One description of such a system (at a lower level) was "as a yo-yo": "I make a draft, it goes up to my supervisor, he returns it to me with comments, I revise, the revision goes to my supervisor, who sends it to his supervisor, who returns it with comments, I revise. . . ." Another description of an approvals system at a very high level in the oil industry is for design change proposals: after informal circulation in both the production and project organization for comments, leading to an informal approval to send the suggested change to be sent on for formal approval, the proposal may go through a premeeting and then a meeting of a cooperation committee made up of production and project people, then perhaps (for high-cost proposals) to a meeting of the general management committee for the whole organization. It is of course much easier to change a decision taken in a process of draft-comment-redraft-comment at a low level of the organization than it is to change one that has already required hours of higher management meeting time.

Such systems of approved information (or of "records of decisions and decision-premises") are "auditable," by ordinary financial auditors, by internal or external quality assurance auditors, by an "internal investigations department," by superiors, and so on. It is convenient to explain what goes on in modern quality assurance programs, for example, by making analogies with police versus contract law enforcement, with quality assurance more similar to contract enforcement.

The main limitation of ordinary police enforcement is that police must act within given uniform rules, so that everyone stands in a position of "equality before the law." The great contrasting advantage of contract law is that in each area of commerce, people can set up rules convenient for their purposes and write them into their contracts. Then if the courts enforce the contracts, they will be enforcing arrangements set up to be convenient for a particular line of activity, and the obligations that they enforce will be different for, say, the typical insurance company than for the typical manufacturer.

Financial auditors are perhaps the first example of enforcement organizations for formal administrations that are set up more like courts enforcing contract law than like police departments. Auditors try to see that the accounts of a firm adequately represent the financial implications of *whatever* the firm does and that those accounts are honest—though they represent quite different sorts of activities and legal situations for, say, a local government than for a manufacturer, and still different ones for an insurance company. For instance, an auditor concerned with enforcing honesty in an insurance company's maintenance of reserves, on the one hand, and a manufacturer's inventory evaluation, on the other, faces two very different problems. What the auditor actually enforces varies with the situation, as reflected in the accounts kept in a firm or other organization.

Some of the responsibilities of higher management are of this "auditing" sort, seeing to it that the procedures that reflect efficient manufacturing are enforced in the manufacturing division, those that reflect effective marketing are enforced in the marketing department, and those that reflect effective R & D are enforced in the laboratories.

In recent years some highly complex and differentiated companies, such as IBM, have developed internal management audits, which try to ensure that procedures in different parts of the organization adequately reflect the true management problems of those parts and that the procedures are adequately implemented in reality. One does not want a police system to enforce uniform ways of getting quality performance regardless of the actual managerial and technical situation. Instead one wants enforcement of what the best management in a given area thinks is the best way to proceed. What is being audited in such cases is the system in a particular part of the company for changing "decision information" into "approved plans," and for changing "approved plans" into "implementation."

The main dimension that differentiates such systems of information from the others we have considered is that attached to the specialized information system of a given part of the company is a supplementary information system that tells which pieces of information have been turned into approved plans. These are the routines of decision making, with their corresponding records of approved decisions. They are supported by a system for seeing that such approved decisions are either carried into action or else challenged by approved routines for changing decisions. This dimension is, then, the degree to which there is an authority system (both decision-making and enforcement aspects) attached to the information system.

A second dimension of such systems is that these decision-making routines have to vary with the situation. To take a very simple example, some decisions will need a technical review to see whether the engineering will work, while others will not. Likewise, some will require formal bids by letting specifications out for tender, others will not; some will need clearance with outside bodies such as insurance companies (and classification societies), governmental authorities, the work inspectorate, the aliens office of the police, others will not; some standing routines will need constant revision in the light of experience, others will not; some will need to be checked for evidence that people have padded their expense accounts, others will not. And so on through the relevant variations in decisions in different parts of the operation.

The variety of problems in different parts of the organization requires different systems of authority, so that one needs not only one organizational plan for the whole company (a broad sketch of the main divisions of authorizing responsibilities), but also routines and procedures in each of the subparts that differentiate approved plans from information in an appropriate way for that part of the administration. It is only at a very high level of abstraction that a whole organization "has" a formal organizational structure, for in the relevant respects each significantly different kind of activity has its own formal organizational structure.

An example of an authority system to be used only once, adapted to its particular task, is the system for startup of the process train in an oil processing plant. After each of the parts of this system is "commissioned" (tested and inspected as far as possible as an independent entity), the system needs to be connected together and then tested and inspected as a whole (especially for leaks) before letting gas and oil into it. This testing will never be done again.

But the pressure test mainly involved here (in 1986) is still not a perfect simulation of operations. It is done with helium rather than gas and oil; connections to the completed well and control of that well are not used; heating and pressure control of the oil-gas mixture is not carried out so as to reduce the gas content of the oil to what will remain dissolved in the oil at atmospheric pressure and environmental temperatures; the resulting gas is not compressed, dried, and shipped out; and so on. A lot of things can still go wrong on the first startup of the whole process.

Thus, one needs to set up a series of stages, each with a special set of safety provisions, each with a measurement of results, each with a way to stop and go back if something is wrong so that faults can be repaired, each with an appropriate approval apparatus to decide to go ahead to the next step. That is, the formal organization needed for startup is different from the one needed for building and commissioning the separate parts beforehand, as well as from the one needed for operating the system after it has been started. There will be many more engineers and managers per operator for the startup, many more special tests of how things are going, many more safety clearances, much more bureaucracy before going on. (See Gouldner 1954, 67–72, for an account of intensified supervision with the startup of a new gypsum board–producing machine system.)

The information that goes into this special system is much the same as that which goes into production operations; consequently, much of it must be extracted and reorganized from the information in the project design, just as an operations manual must be. What is different is the special structure of approvals that governs this part of the operations. Running the routine production organization with this many delays for special tests and approvals would, of course, be an economic disaster. The structure is entirely inappropriate for either building or operating the installation, though many of the people and most of the information used in the two structures are the same. The approvals system for commissioning is exactly—and only—appropriate for startup.

Summary of Dimensions That Differentiate
Operating Information Systems

The following list summarizes the seven dimensions of operating characteristics of information systems we have described.

Dimension	*Examples*
1. Quality of information improves dramatically with operational experience *or* information remains of same value.	Preventive maintenance plans, operations manuals, versus capital values of installations.
2. Information generated in operations is only useful for further operations of the same kind *or* operating information enters other systems.	Well reports, operator experience with particular machines (helicopters, diving equipment, process equipment), versus project design, cost statistics on operations.
3. Supplementary innovations in the information system add to the system rapidly during operations *or* information systems are stable.	Software versus invoice processing for payment.
4. Flexible, detailed, shifting categories are needed for cost reduction projects *or* constraint is exercised by categories of systems outside organization.	Cost reduction use of cost statistics versus financial and cost comparison accounting statistics.
5. Each figure is auditable by a "trail of paper" *or* figures are useful for decision purposes only.	Financial accounts versus cost accounts.
6. Information is generated to guide one kind of activity crucial for guiding other activities, requiring reorganization, *or* information is in a "closed loop" within a department.	Project design for construction useful for spare parts buying, maintenance plans, operating manuals, versus well reports, helicopter pilot experience.
7. Approvals systems for decisions are adapted to differing information and problems *or* authority is applied uniformly across cases.	"Audits" versus "policing"; budgeting versus ledgers; procedures for various special situations (e.g., startup) versus organization manual for production organization.

Each concrete information-processing system will, of course, have a value on each of the seven dimensions. For example, a spare parts information system is distinctive in having to be created mainly from project design information, an information system that responds primarily to different uncertainties. But corruption in parts buying is a risk; fraud, while not as routine as it is in entertainment expenses, may involve more money when it happens. There is therefore a careful system of approvals in the purchasing sector of the spare parts system, nowhere near as elaborate as the tax regulations for financial accounting, but there nevertheless.

In the above description I have chosen the most distinctive aspects of manufacturing information systems, having often found them out because they create problems for other people in the organization. The turning inward of the drillers, the rigidity of financial accounts from a cost reduction point of view, the lack of enthusiasm of the construction project for producing adequate documentation for operations, were all frequently mentioned as practical problems. The fact that one has to prevent corruption in spare parts buying is a routine and unproblematic aspect of the system (that is, of Statoil in 1986—this is an idiographic fact, not a law of organizational life).

Conclusion

Cross-sectional studies of occupational composition of organizations always show that the number of clerical workers is very well predicted by the number of technical and of sales workers. The computer programs for routine processing of organizational data are generally under the control of middle and junior managers in charge of this or that technical or sales function. The reason large human and electronic information-processing systems are connected to technical and marketing functions is that both of these require a great many decisions, each one of which is minor, but in the aggregate they all have to go reasonably well for the business to go well.

The thousands of decisions that have to be made in a spare parts system under a technical department about buying and inventory, or in a marketing department about which goods will be shipped to which clients, by which transportation system, with what insurance coverage, with what tax liabilities accruing, with what discounts on the "normal" price, with what dates of payments due, all require routine information systems that can be adapted readily to meet changing technical and market conditions. The fact that they have to be adapted means that the routines are not, in fact, entirely routine.

A technical or a marketing manager is primarily responsible for seeing that the routines are set up to respond quickly enough to changing conditions, by entering new information in the system, by basing decisions on that information in different (but still, for some period of time, routine) ways, and the like. While the discounts, shipping routes, insurance levels, and so on all have to be authoritatively resolved, there is no particular difficulty in getting people to consent to that authority within the organization—though there may be difficulties in getting them all to know what to do under various contingencies (to control errors, respond to complaints, and the like). But these authoritative systems are not, in any strong sense, hierarchical. Not everybody can say what discounts are available, and not everybody can decide which discount should go to a particular buyer, but the great majority of the people who have to do something about a particular discount, once it is decided, have no inclination to rebel against the decision. The problem instead is to see that once the discount is decided on, everybody who needs to know about the decision to settle other things (such as the size of the invoice, of the insurance cover, etc.) in fact gets it right.

There has been a great proliferation of these intermediate-level information systems in recent years. Organizations employ engineering and business school graduates to set up such systems, to adjust them to changing circumstances, to see that people follow the procedures with appropriate levels of discretion, and the like. In sociology the basic notion of what managers do is derived from a vague memory of Taylor figuring out first how to embody the skill of manual workers in a routine and then how to deskill those workers. That is, we have been interested in managers primarily as "people drivers" (cf. Stinchcombe 1983, 114–115, for an analysis of where people drivers are actually found in manufacturing). But many modern managers are not concerned with improving the productivity of manual workers, except indirectly.

The productivity of many workers is determined mainly by whether the machine they run is working, and sometimes by whether neighboring machines are working. This is especially true in continuous process plants, but also in such manufacturing operations as rolling steel (Stinchcombe 1974, 11–31). The quality of the information in the maintenance system—which determines, for example, whether or not the repair part for a machine that has just broken down is in stock—is likely to be a more important determinant of productivity than how hard either the operators or the maintenance workers work.

The purpose of this chapter has been to give a portrait of what else managers in manufacturing operations do besides driving people. The reason there is so much to that portrait is that the central uncertainties in productivity in a modern factory often are not whether the workers will work hard enough, but whether they will have the appropriate spare parts, or whether the cost accounts are flexible enough to focus attention on those parts of the line that should be improved first because they are bottlenecks in production. These determinants of productivity cannot in general be manipulated by driving workers harder. Instead they have to be manipulated by creating an information system that will routinely produce the right administrative details at the right times so that spare parts can be bought, or so that a decision to buy a particular machine for a particular place in the line to reduce costs can be evaluated correctly. Of course, how hard workers work also sometimes affects productivity, so middle managers do some people driving as well. The system for collecting information on worker performance and attaching rewards and punishments to different levels of performance is the subject of Chapter 7.

Because these different systems respond to different sorts of uncertainty, their relations to information generated in operations varies. The information in a preventive maintenance system is largely fictional until corrected by operating experience; the information in the present version of a software program is at a temporary resting place in a continuous process of innovation, which produces a software system with ever increasing numbers of options in what reports one will get; the information in a well plan comes quite directly from well reports on the drilling experience in nearby wells. In each case the operating characteristics of the system, and consequently what a middle manager has to do to make the system run properly, depend intimately on what sorts of uncertainties it has to control and where the information about those uncertainties is available. But all the responsibilities of middle managers in maintaining these various kinds of information systems generate clerical labor, computer time, routings for paper flows, data files, files containing catalogs of files, and all the other features of modern manufacturing bureaucracies peopled by engineers, programmers, and business school graduates.

The theoretical point of these examples is that the social structure connected with different manufacturing information systems, the technical skills embedded in them, and the problems of keeping information separate from approvals are all determined ultimately by what sorts of technical or economic uncertainty they are designed to deal with. The tendency of drillers to form a separate subculture in the organization and to be somewhat contemptuous of the information requirements of the rest of the organization is a product of an information system that responds to the central technical uncertainties of drilling. The constant tension between the demands of the cost accountants working in particular operating departments to produce more, and shifting, detail in the system and the demands of the financial accounting people for auditable and entirely standard figures reflects the different uncertainties of a cost reduction use of financial statistics and a taxation or profit measurement use of those statistics.

The conflicts between and within departments that arise from differences in what information systems are for and what uncertainties they respond to produce a "politics" of information systems. Information systems in departments are not merely organizational reflections of what objective reality is like; instead they are the outcome of much pulling and hauling about what the information systems *should* contain. The pulling and hauling may, of course, arise in part because this is one of many ways to get the responsibilities of one's department regarded as more important to the organization. But it arises also because a driller really has to pay attention to those who have the information he needs to drill a hole efficiently and safely—other drillers who have drilled nearby and specialized subcontractors who service drillers because they in turn have an expert and internally oriented subculture about, say, drilling mud.

The general theoretical point is that different parts of the information system of manufacturing are oriented to different types of technical uncertainty, ranging from the concern of software writers about what the next innovation should be to the repetitive buying of spare parts that have to be here on time; from the once-only system for safety approvals before the next stage of commissioning can begin to the repetitively auditable financial accounts for tax authorities and owners. This means that large parts of the information system that are responsive to one set of uncertainties are unresponsive to uncertainties that concern others. This is most obvious when divergent needs are built into the same information system in the same department, as when cost comparison functions, cost reduction functions, and ledger and financial functions are all under the accounting department and have contradictory "needs," different requirements for flexibility versus comparability versus auditability.

To see why such a manufacturing information system, with all its ill-fitting parts, needs to be coordinated with systems outside manufacturing, let us suppose that a manufacturing enterprise with a system something like the one just described has to decrease production because of a downturn in the market. Adjustments will have to be made in the spare parts inventory system to take account of fewer hours of operation causing less wear and cut parts inventory costs to correspond to the new requirements, while different adjustments will have to be made in the cost comparison part of cost accounting to spread overhead costs (downsizing usually does not lower overhead costs as fast as production costs).

Thus, the authority to demand adjustments in all the different parts of manufacturing information processing has to be located in a place that is highly responsive to shifting market demand, to sensible predictions of how long the market slump will last, and the like. It is precisely because the manufacturing information system is a ramshackle affair doing different jobs with the same basic informational materials that authorities over manufacturing who are responsive to the market need the authority to intervene throughout the manufacturing system. The creation of such authority is the core problem that Chandler addresses in his classic *Strategy and Structure* (1962), which we take up in the next chapter.

4   Market Uncertainty and Divisionalization

Alfred D. Chandler's
Strategy and Structure

Introduction

A central theme in organizational sociology for the last couple of decades has been the growth and distribution of "decentralized" management. Broadly speaking this has divided into two branches: the "contracts" branch that says that decentralization is often achieved by autonomous firms tying themselves together for specific purposes, and the "decentralized administration" branch started by Alfred D. Chandler (1962) and Peter F. Drucker (1946). We will treat the contracts tradition more extensively in Chapter 6. In this chapter we treat Chandler's argument. Since the richest source of data on the development of the multidivisional structure is still Chandler's own, this chapter is in effect a close reading of the theoretical aspects of Chandler's great historical monograph and of the relation of the theory to the data Chandler himself presents.

Our first task is to describe as exactly as we can what the dependent variable, the thing to be explained, is. It turns out that according to Chandler the central trouble with a centralized administration was not that it was centralized, but that it made centralization impossible where it was needed. Chandler's argument, especially in the treatment of Du Pont, is that in order to centralize the response in each of several markets that required markedly different tactics, one had to decentralize the firm as a whole. The main difficulties he points to that kept people at organizational reform derive from the firms' *lack* of centralized response to particular markets in which they were losing money. The reason they did not respond in a centralized way to those markets was that the firm had centralized at the firm level, which implied that the various functions (e.g., manufacturing, marketing, and engineering) that needed to be coordinated to respond to a particular market were each centralized *above* the level at which response to a particular market had to be organized. A central manufacturing executive would coordinate all manufacturing together (explosives and dyes, for example), rather than explosives manufacturing with explosives marketing and dyes manufacturing with dyes marketing; similarly for a central marketing executive and a central engineering executive.

This part of the argument, and the historical analysis of Du Pont, is also the place where Chandler best shows the connection between the firm-level problem of inadequate response to the various markets the firm was in and the resulting solution of administrative reorganization. In particular he treats in considerable detail how individuals in the firm came to see that they had a problem of market response, how they came to see that reorganization of the administration was a solution, and how they stuck to administrative reform until they came up with the solution: centralized administration in each market, decentralized administration in the firm as a whole. Consequently, it is in this analysis that we can best see how functional problems in large firms come to be posed as problems in the work life of executives, the problem that has come to be called "methodological individualism."

Briefly, methodological individualism is the principle that explanations at the social level are not adequate unless the individual actions that are required for the social explanation to be true can themselves be explained adequately. This idea has been treated in the literature primarily as a question of the structure of theory. We will show in the first section below that Chandler solved the problem of methodological individualism for this part of his argument without having a theory of the general individual rationality kind that methodological individualists generally demand.

The argument for the functionality of the general office, detached from operating responsibilities and responsible for investment policy, is made most intensively in Chandler's chapter 3, in connection with Sloan's reorganization of General Motors. The basic idea is that only if the firm has better knowledge than the stock market does of the market projections and cost picture of each of its divisions can it do better than a completely decentralized, holding company structure. What is lacking in Chandler here, first, is a demonstration that such general offices do in fact do better than the stock market as a whole in predicting the future value of investments in their "subfirms." Are the profit rates of divisionalized firms with a general office in fact greater than those of holding companies with investments in various firms, each of which must respond separately to stockholder interests in profits?

Second, we need to be shown that this low predictability of the rates of return on investments in the subparts of firms without a general office was posed as a set of problems to the executives, who then set up the general office working with abstracted projections of demand, costs, and capital improvement proposals, and that those executives had the power to institute their proposals. In the second part of the chapter we will try to show that Chandler's analysis of General Motors *almost* satisfies those requirements. General Motors in fact expanded a great deal and remained the most profitable firm in the industry for many years after its reorganization into a multidivisional structure with a general office. The individual-level analysis required turns out to be, in large measure, a biography of Sloan himself, based largely on Sloan's own accounts. It is clear that Sloan had an adequate theory of his own behavior.

We will have shown in these first two analyses that the explanation of why a company will invent divisions is quite different from the explanation of why a company with divisions will invent a general office. The divisions are to facilitate different responses in different commodity markets; the general office is to provide information to satisfy bankers and other investors, to provide them with better guarantees of continued profitability than they would have from a holding company without such a general office. Thus Chandler himself has two different dependent variables here, which have two different explanations.

In the third section we treat Chandler's analysis of Sears. This is a particularly useful case to look at in connection with the problem posed for General Motors. Sears in fact competed with a structure of wholesalers and retailers who were organized as autonomous firms, with no centralized office and no centralized buying. We can pose the problem Sears had when it tried to use a mail order firm's buying structure to supply an appropriate inventory to a dispersed set of department stores in automobile-oriented shopping centers, then, as one of building a bureaucratic structure that could do what a market-organized structure of wholesalers and retailers was already doing very well. This is not a functional problem peculiar to Sears, because during the period Chandler analyzes here chain stores with multiple commodity lines were coming to prominence in the novelty trade (the "dime stores"), groceries ("supermarkets"), auto accessories, and eventually hardware and furniture, as well as in department store retailing.

Our analysis of Chandler's study of Sears, then, involves a systematic treatment of what functions the structure of wholesalers in various commodity lines nationwide in fact served and still serves, which parts of those functions were already served by the extremely decentralized structure of buyers in the nineteen or so commodity lines that characterized the Sears mail order regime before the reorganization Chandler discusses (described at that time as "a coalition of merchants"), and where in the new Sears structure the remaining, unfulfilled, functions were located.

Our argument here is that the decentralization into commodity lines, already present in the old regime, remained the central functional structure in the new regime as well. It was apparently the addition of detail to the inventory control system in commodity lines, rather than, as Chandler argues, decentralization into autonomous regional divisions, that made Sears (and other chain stores) able to do the jobs that specialized regional autonomous wholesalers were already doing.

We argue that Sears had to begin with an organization in many different commodity-line markets, that had already created "divisions"—the autonomous buyers for the mail order business—to respond to those markets. This divisionalized organization already had a general office, the one that decided to invest in department stores rather than expand the mail order business. In short, it started with the very structure to be explained, and had that structure for the reasons that the theory says it should have had such a structure. It entered very few new commodity lines. So what it needed was regional offices as branches of the general office to decide on investments in stores, and it also needed new modifications of its commodity-line information systems to feed store inventory and sales data into the offices of the commodity-line divisions run by buyers.

We argue, in short, Chandler in fact has little to explain—and mistakes what there is to explain—because he believes the regional divisions of Sears are "operating" divisions. He thus has not interpreted his theory of the first two cases correctly in analyzing Sears.

In the final part of the chapter we try to unpack the empirical content of Chandler's main independent variable, "being in several different markets." The overall functional argument in Chandler's book is that a multidivisional administrative structure is required if a firm is in several different markets. We provide a detailed definition of a distinct market as market uncertainty ramifying into the manufacturing and engineering of a commodity line in a way different for other commodity lines. In Chandler's chapter 7 he analyzes a large number of manufacturing industries in terms of his overall functional theory. If Chandler's book had been a sociological article, say in *Administrative Science Quarterly*, chapter 7 would be the article, and a page or two about the histories of Du Pont, General Motors, Jersey Standard, and Sears might have been in the original draft as motivation, to be cut by the editors as not science but anecdote. But I believe it is more useful to treat the chapter as a careful analysis of what the phenomenon, as perceived by the corporation, of "being in several diverse markets" looks like as an "objective" variable spanning a number of industries.

We will treat the variable of being in several markets as a matter of the social organization of uncertainty, of the organization of information necessary to adapt to that uncertainty, and of the amount of uncertainty. This will constitute the explication of the implicit analysis in Chandler's chapter 7 of the conditions under which market uncertainty ramifies into the manufacturing and engineering of a commodity line, so forcing marketing, manufacturing, and engineering together into a division. We will find that the most successful parts of the case studies, as well as the cross-sectional analysis of industries in chapter 7, are neatly summarized by five variables describing how uncertainty of demand is organized in different sets of commodity lines.

The Concepts of Centralization and Decentralization

The first big conceptual trouble in understanding Chandler's argument at the structural level is that "centralization" and "decentralization" as Chandler uses them are really two different kinds of centralization: (1) centralization for administering *one* product (or a small group of related products) for *one* market, with *market control* (losses and profits) over the central authority; and (2) centralization for administering *one* product for *one* market *in a division of the company*, with *both* market *and* administrative controls over that division (the administrative controls are by a central office that also controls over divisions).

To see what is going on, let us start with the Du Pont firm making explosives or U.S. Steel making rails or Ford Motor Company making Model T's. In each firm there was a marketing or sales department—Chandler tells about the development of the marketing department in Du Pont, with explosives experts advising clients (for example, mines or tunneling projects) on efficient and safe blasting. In each firm there was some sort of engineering or chemistry department (or both). And of course there was a manufacturing department.

For any one product, the firm needed the engineering force to design the product to fit the tastes of the market and to design the production line so it could make the product cheaply, yet so production could be adjusted to variations in demand; the engineering had to be adapted to both marketing and manufacturing. The firm needed to arrange for feedback from marketing to manufacturing so that manufacturing would not make too much and get committed to an enormous inventory, or would not have delays in the delivery that could kill the market, or so manufacturing could produce the right mix of sizes and colors. And obviously the firm needed engineering to design a line that manufacturing could in fact keep going, work on bottlenecks in the line, or redesign the product so as, say, to eliminate a weld by stamping the piece differently or otherwise contribute to cheap or flexible production.

A big problem of all industrial administration is to get each of these three functional departments to work together, to do what the others need instead of what they are inclined to do. Manufacturing can always save money by making long runs at a steady speed, with inventory taking up the fluctuations in demand. But if it turns out that a market fluctuation is not just a fluctuation, if clients are really stopping building railroads with the firm's steel or if folks are really poor in the depression and cannot buy a Model A, then the firm is stuck with the inventory. Then (as Ford did) the firm could force dealers to take the inventory and pay for it, and the dealers (the smart ones) would switch to General Motors so they would not go bankrupt—and Ford would have screwed up its marketing.

Marketing wants each order treated as a special case: stop production and make us this thing for this good customer. But when that happens, manufacturing gets disorganized, costs go out of sight, and the firm cannot sell (and it is "manufacturing's fault"). That is, there is a true dilemma between the requirements of cheap manufacturing and those of effective marketing, a dilemma someone has to solve in the interest of overall profits on that line of goods. Some things that sell cars better make manufacturing more expensive; some things that make manufacturing cheap really ruin the market.

Since engineering (e.g., design for ease of maintenance versus design for engineering efficiency) has to depend on what the market wants, on how much the dealers complain about the costs of warranty service, and so on, engineering has to be coordinated with marketing. Similarly, the tradeoff between "getting it out the door" and making it "state of the art" determines engineering delays, and those delays are reflected in manufacturing costs.

There were, then, in such centralized firms true conflicts among departments, because there were true technical and economic tradeoffs between what one department and another were supposed to maximize. And this meant that somebody (or some group—but in fact, Chandler says, a firm needs somebody) had to tell engineering to do what manufacturing said instead of what *they* wanted to do, to tell manufacturing not to treat each customer as a special case but to control their production by an inventory depletion time criterion, and so on.

Note that the right decision about which department ought to give way on what questions depended on the product. Eventually Du Pont would sell enough blasting powder to use up a shipload of nitrate, but they might not sell enough of that awful artificial leather Chandler talks about to use up a shipload of wood pulp. The decisions Du Pont needed to make for a standard manufacturing ingredient like blasting powder and an ingredient of novelty goods like artificial leather were very different. There was a different combination of the risk of being stuck with an inventory the company could not sell (low with blasting powder, high with artificial leather), manufacturing cheapness (very important for blasting powder, not so important—as long as it is cheaper than leather—for artificial leather), marketing flexibility (not important for blasting powder, of the essence for artificial leather), and so on. That is, the contradictions between marketing, manufacturing, and engineering had to be resolved in different ways to make money on different products.

The centralized firm, the structure with which Du Pont started after Pierre reorganized it to look like a steel plant, puts one man with a staff of accountants, marketing specialists, production line managers, and so forth in charge of all three departments. He (it is always a he in Chandler's book, so this "he" is a historical fact) needed expert engineering managers, sales managers, and manufacturing executives under him, because it was hard enough to do engineering, marketing, and manufacturing in the first place. But he also needed to be able to order them to give up their own professional standards in the interest of one of the others. And he had to do it in the light of whether his firm was selling blasting powder or artificial leather, Model A's or Cadillacs, steel rails or "special shapes."

Centralized administration is represented by diagram A in Fig. 3; decentralized by diagram B. The decentralized firm looked exactly like the centralized one, except the thing in the decentralized firm that looks like the centralized firm is the division—and there was, in addition to the market controls over the division, also administrative control by the general office. The reasons for the similar organization for administering a single product were the same. For a given product, the engineering and the manufacturing boss had to be forced to resolve their different priorities in the light of how one really made money *on that product*, and the same held for marketing and the other two. Forcing departments to resolve their conflicts in a way appropriate to the product requires autono-

Diagram A: Centralized

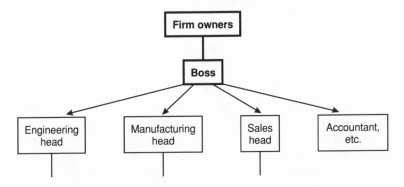

Diagram B: Decentralized

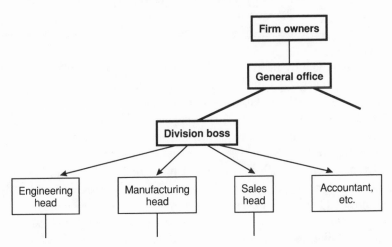

Fig. 3. Comparison of the Organizational Form of Centralized and Decentralized Firms in Chandler

mous operating divisions. Before we use Chandler's materials to develop our argument, it will be useful to consider a methodological issue: the role of individuals in organization-level functional arguments.

A Definition of Methodological Individualism

By "methodological individualism" we mean that every individual action that enters into some collective pattern must itself have an adequate explanation. The collective pattern may be, for example, that corporations that enter multiple markets with markedly different contracting patterns, spans of temporal adjustment, quality or service requirements, and so forth will tend to develop differentiated divisions to respond separately to those markets, and a higher-order integration mechanism (a "general office") to coordinate this divisional structure, because such a decentralized divisional structure is more efficient in responding to multiple markets. This is a functional connection at the level of the corporation: corporations in multiple markets "need" separate responses to the separate markets, and a decentralized divisional structure "fills that need." This is a way of stating the central argument of Chandler's *Strategy and Structure*.

The principle of methodological individualism, specified to this functional argument, says (1) that the actions of individuals in corporations that create the new structure should be adequately explained, in the sense that they should ultimately be shown to be a response to multiple markets; (2) that those actions should continue and aggregate in a way that ultimately creates the multidivisional structure; and (3) that such individual actions arise because the separate responsiveness to markets was "needed."

It has frequently been alleged that many functional explanations do not—and, in general, cannot—satisfy the requirements of methodological individualism (e.g., Homans and Schneider 1955; and Elster, e.g. 1983, 55–68). But obviously, if the explanations are true they must satisfy those requirements, since all social action is carried out by individual human beings.

Often the plea for methodological individualism is coupled with a preference for rational actor explanations: it is a concealed plea for utilitarianism. There is, however, no inherent reason why the model of individual action in a methodologically individualist account must be a rational one. For example, John Padgett has offered an account of how the Department of Housing and Urban Development (HUD) budget-making process "serves the function" of adjusting the departmental budget to the macroeconomic objective of the president's office, as transmitted through the Office of Management and Budget (OMB) (Padgett 1981, 85–92). The models of individuals in his treatment are specifically designed to take account of limitations on individual rationality, and have many random and nonoptimizing elements in them. The central point, though, is that the requirements set by the president's office enter as variables and constraints in the nonoptimal problem solving of the bureaucrats in HUD. Such models of a collective process satisfy the requirement of methodological individualism but are the opposite of any appeal to utilitarianism or to rational actor models.

Chandler's book is an especially interesting case in this regard, because he has followed some part of the strategy of deriving predictions from the collective-level theory and documenting them. His chapter 7 (1962, 324–382) tries to show empirically that in industries that function in single markets the multidivisional structure has not been adopted, while in those that function in multiple markets it has been. But Chandler thought it necessary for his purposes to write some three hundred–odd pages of history, mainly of four firms (Du Pont, General Motors, Jersey Standard, and Sears), to see how and why the multidivisional structure was invented and adopted.

As is typical for historians, many proper names of individuals appear in the accounts. Clearly Chandler does not believe the functional argument at the collective level is adequate with only collective-level evidence, for he includes additional evidence involving a large number of named individuals as well. If these people were optimizing, they took a long time about it and lost a lot of money in the meantime, and still disagreed about what was optimal when they adopted the new structure. That is, the Chandler book looks like a case of a functional argument with individual-level explanations, which is not the same as a simple rational actor model at the individual level. We will next examine Chandler's explanation of the origin of the multidivisional structure in Du Pont, with some side glances to his own theoretical statements and to the more formal models in Padgett for guidance on the logical and theoretical role that statements about named individuals in organizations can have (Chandler 1962, 52–113 on Du Pont; and Padgett 1980, 1981).

Individuals in Du Pont: Organizing Information Flows

In Chandler's discussion of the old-regime centralized administration at Du Pont, he emphasizes the systematic effort to create reliable flows of information, especially by Pierre du Pont. Pierre du Pont thought of the legal and financial changes that incorporated previously independent businesses into E. I. du Pont de Nemours Powder Co. as "only necessary preliminaries" to reorganizing the administration of all of them (44; all page numbers cited in the following with no further specification are to Chandler 1962). In that reorganization a central point was "to establish a system of costs in order that an economical manufacture could be installed throughout the business." Cost accounting introduced first and foremost in manufacturing (55, 58). Once sales were taken from jobbers and agents and done by salaried technical sales people, cost statistics were also created in sales, as were market share statistics (59–60). The treasurer's department, headed by Pierre du Pont, a member of the top management, came to develop a system of cost, performance, and sales statistics and projections (60, 66, 101–102). Since Pierre du Pont later became the power in the board of the company, the place of cost and performance statistics in defining the realities that confronted the company was secure.

At several points in Chandler's narrative, locating the difficulties facing the company depended exactly on the flow of differentiated cost, profit, and other performance measures (86, 92, 95, 100, 104). That is, a flow of differentiated statistics determined, in a general way, where people thought problems lay at various points throughout the administrative evolution. In one case, the fact that the statistics were inadequate to prevent problems of overstocking of supplies or of manufactured products (which were partly detected and diagnosed by statistics that came in later) was a crucial argument for reorganization (102).

Thus the environment in which administrative discussion went forward was shaped by information-collection technologies that could, for example, show that the problems after diversification were concentrated in lines where package goods were sold directly to the ultimate consumer, rather than in lines where tonnage goods were sold for further processing (92, 95, 100). In short, the problems people thought they had, and the fact that those problems persisted even after the company had reorganized to solve them (104), were features of an organizational intelligence system created largely by Pierre du Pont, and the results of that system were sufficiently persuasive that a negative decision on reorganization by the president, Pierre's brother Irénée, after Pierre had gone to General Motors, was overturned by the data (99–100 for the rejection in 1920; 110–113 for its acceptance in 1921), despite Irénée's continued skepticism.

The flow of detailed performance measurement information thus shaped the perception of the problem by individuals. In particular, it connected a systematic pattern of failure to individual perceptions in top management of that failure in a way that kept management looking for a solution even after rejecting the one they finally adopted (they obviously cannot have been optimizing in both 1920, when they rejected decentralization, and 1921, when they adopted it). The statistics to facilitate centralized administration thus ultimately helped cause decentralized administration. They also then became the basis of the general office's capacity to assess the work of the divisions they helped to create.

Individuals in Du Pont: Organizational Theory

In order for a problem, perceived through an organizational data collection system, to induce an organizational solution, it must also be analyzed by an organizational theory. The standard theory at the time of the innovations at Du Pont was one that ordinarily gave centralization and specialization as its answer (100 for Irénée's statement of these principles). But at least the theory's concrete manifestation at Du Pont was one that *could* diagnose a pattern in the data (e.g., the fact that other companies were making money in lines where Du Pont was losing money: 95) as requiring an organizational solution.

The most general guide to division of responsibility that could give rise to operational divisions specializing in a product line as stated by Harry Haskell (then vice president in charge of the high explosives department, but detached to head a subcommittee on organization): "The most efficient results are obtained at the least expense when we coordinate related effort and segregate unrelated effort" (69). He had already used that notion as an argument "to carry on the dye business as a separate entity. I think it would [be better] because it is a developing, unstandardized industry and should merit independent attention just as the Parlin chemical mixtures business was better by itself until standardized—when it was merged with the regular sales and operating departments" (68). The dye business needed "one individual in control of both production and sales, because the relation of the product and its qualities is so mixed up with the demands of the market for the product that to divorce them . . . would be detrimental to the business" (70).

This analysis meant that later evidence of interdependence of marketing, manufacturing, and raw materials purchasing (as shown, for example, in projections by manufacturing that were uncoordinated with marketing experience, resulting in inventory losses on raw materials or on manufactured goods in "merchandise goods" lines) was an argument for integration of those three functions. Further, it meant that the sales manager, Frederick W. Pickard, could explain the problems with the sale of package goods to the ultimate consumer by saying that he had products with "no logical sales connection with one another" (101). In analyzing these sales problems further, a subcommittee (which included Pickard) of the executive committee pointed out that (successful) competitors had one person in charge of both manufacturing and sales of each line and responsible for the profits of that line (96). Further interdependence provided a theoretical category that made the experience with "minidivisional" management of several new products (dyes, artificial silk) relevant to these problems of interdependence of sales and manufacturing on larger lines of products (96).

As is usual when evidence requiring a "paradigm shift" accumulates, the facts were at first explained away as a series of individual mistakes in a system of functional departments and centralized administration that had functioned brilliantly in producing munitions (96–100) and was still making much money on tonnage goods (104). In particular, "[we] have carried excessive stock . . . [have made] several unfortunate guesses on the purchase of raw materials . . . have been working against orders rather than setting up appropriate stocks. . . . Rearrangements, repairs, renewals, and replacements of plants have been high. . . . [There have been] miscellaneous shortcomings in factory operations such as poor routing, and inefficient piece-work, pay schedules, short-runs, etc." (98).

But the theoretical category of interdependence, and the proposed general solution in the theory that problems arising out of interdependence should be put under a single authority, maintained cognitive focus on the difficulty with the reigning centralized organizational paradigm. The category existed in the organizational theory of the old regime, and this made it possible to codify the experience to which it was relevant, so both the category and the experience would be available to diagnose the new problems in multiple markets.

Individuals in Du Pont: Responsibility for Inventing and Adopting a Remedy

The process outlined above provided the environment in which individuals could see functional need, which Chandler identifies at the collective level, as a problem whose answer was probably organizational. But individuals become aware of thousands of problems over the course of a couple of years (say, 1918–1920 in the Du Pont company). These problems have to become the *responsibility* of someone, of some committee, or of some routine process. Committees were central in Du Pont's higher management.

By the time Chandler began his detailed story, the Du Pont company had an overlapping set of problem-allocation mechanisms, by status and by committee jurisdictions. The status distinction was that each department had two chief executives, the higher of whom (a "vice president") was responsible for long-range policy matters, the lower (a "director") in charge of day-to-day or operational matters (57). There were both standing committees and task force committees (usually created as subcommittees of a standing committee). The committees had a shifting membership whose most active members were usually the vice presidents responsible for long-term planning. The main work of writing proposals for reorganization, writing critiques of those proposals, and passing or vetoing the final proposals was done by committees, though often one member of the committee was fairly clearly the author.

The mechanisms for creating committees, determining the charge to the committee (or the jurisdiction of standing committees), and specifying the membership are not clear in Chandler, probably because they were not clear to the people in Du Pont. There seems to have been more "constitutional" thought given to the composition and jurisdiction of standing committees with some decision-making authority, and much more ad hoc arrangements to give a charge and a range of authority to more specialized and temporary committees (58, 65, 93–96, 98–99, 103, 105, 113). Decision making was also apparently much influenced by rank; when Irénée du Pont, the company president, was being overruled on the issue of divisional organization, the executive committee was expanded to include the financial committee as well as Pierre du Pont and Raskob (who came back from General Motors to attend). In deference to the opinion of his colleagues, Irénée du Pont did finally vote for reorganization (110).

Two things are central to explaining how individuals got responsibility for devising solutions to the problems identified by the data flow and the existing organizational theory. The first is that the structure allowed for cutting the flow of "problems of subordinates" to the high executives, so that the latter could be detached from day-to-day problems to study, and restudy, problems of organization (303–304; see also Stinchcombe 1974, 24–25, 81–93). An executive directly in charge of a group of subordinates has to divert his attention to their problems when they need it, and so is not a deployable resource for analyzing long-run problems. The second factor is the existence of a flexible structure to tie together responsibility for solving problems and authority to implement the solution at the top levels of the organization. The top executives have to be not only free to study reorganization but also *authorized* to do so and *permitted to put the resulting proposals on the agenda of a decision-making committee.* The right to have one's proposals put on the agenda is the core of what we mean by "authorizing" a committee to study a problem, though of course the authorized committee also gets access to the intelligence apparatus of the top executives (58).

Although we do not get the details from Chandler of how this worked in Du Pont (the structure at the top seems to resemble that described by Cohen, March, and Olsen 1972), responsibility for the analysis clearly ended up being pinned on particular individuals (sometimes the individuals were drafting a committee consensus), and the proposals then usually went onto a decision-making committee agenda. (For a temporary hiatus in the second, see 99, where the first recommendation of a multidivisional structure was deleted from a subsubcommittee report by the subcommittee; this hiatus was only overcome in the face of a company financial crisis.) What we have, then, is not a description of the structure that authorized individuals to propose solutions to problems, but evidence that such a structure effectively existed in the top management at Du Pont—a sort of incomplete methodological individualism. It is incomplete because the collective-level solution is located in the behavior of specific individuals operating in a given structure, with their individual actions in fact linked in such a way as to create the collective-level pattern. We are not told how they came to be so linked, or why those individuals rather than others were authorized to act.

The submission by minorities to the decisions of the majority of the (expanded) executive committee is also not discussed in Chandler, though the lucky fact that one of the minority was the president, Irénée du Pont, gives us some evidence on the question. Aside from the uninformative phrase "in deference to the strong opinion of the majority of his colleagues," we are also told that he was appointed to the new executive committee, whose structure he had objected to. In addition, we are offered the speculation (in the final report to the board of directors of the corporation) that, after having experienced the operational running of market segment–oriented divisions by divisional councils (one member from sales, one from manufacturing, one from purchasing), managerial morale will improve by fixing responsibilities—which may be an explanation for minority acceptance. The failure to explain the submission of minorities is not unique to Chandler; the explanation of the acceptance of decisions made by authorized bodies is a weak part of social science generally.

Individuals in Du Pont and HUD: How Decentralization Works

What we mean by decentralization, presumably, is that the controls of a superior level of the organization over an inferior level are highly abstract. The performance measures that the general office gets about the inferior level in a decentralized organization carry few details that would enable them to penetrate the veil shielding the division manager from close inspection of his or her subordinates. If the general office knows too much about the performance of subordinates of the divisional manager, the knowledge that the general office is ultimately in command of their careers will lead those subordinates to try to make a good impression on the higher management rather than on the divisional manager. The goals that the general office specifies for the division must thus be somewhat abstract, so as to leave discretion with the division manager. Padgett describes the supervision of OMB by presidential-level bureaucratic politics as follows:

> Presidential decision making about fiscal policy and defense may be exceedingly complicated and convoluted. However, from the point of view of OMB, all that is produced from this within-level conflict is a single number—either of the form "your overall expenditure target is 500 billion" or of the form "cut 2 billion." The very top echelon of OMB may have some idea where this number came from, but whether they do or not is largely irrelevant to their task. Politics has been compressed into a single piece of information. (Padgett 1981, 80)

Similarly, Chandler points to the general office working mainly on "estimates and forecasts of anticipated conditions rather than on past or even current performance" (292). Clearly they cannot inspect many details of subordinate-unit behavior at any considerable distance into the future. They have to focus on one or a few numbers measuring performance (e.g., costs, market share, profits) and to supervise with a few numbers measuring constraints or goals (especially capital allocations and the description of which measures of performance will be used).

Thus the key feature of decentralization is the degree of abstractness of the information flow between the divisions and the general office. When that flow is, in Padgett's words, "compressed into a single piece of information," decentralization is maximal. It is the responsibility of the divisional manager to combine that one piece (or a few pieces) of information with the details about the world brought in by his or her subordinates and by the information-collection system of his or her division.

Padgett has shown that simple models of individual behavior in budget making at each hierarchical level are adequate to explain, on the one hand, the statistical dispersion of cuts across programs within HUD and, on the other, how the cuts come to add up to the totals specified by OMB, and therefore (more hypothetically) how OMB itself allocates cuts across cabinet departments so that they add up to presidential fiscal and macroeconomic objectives (Padgett 1980, 1981).

By analogy, we might construct a model of problem solving *within di-*

visions of Du Pont which could coordinate flows of information about purchasing, manufacturing, and sales of a particular product line from mines in Chile to the ultimate consumer. We could incorporate in this model investment and cost constraints imposed by the general office and specify the performance measures that office will use as objectives for the divisional manager to try to maximize. For our model to be workable, flows of information about what the problem is and flows of control communication about what the solution has to look like must be correctly segregated by degree of abstractness, so that each level has the right information to solve its level of problems. For example, in the abstraction process that turns divisional information into a flow to the general office, much information relevant to measuring subordinate performance within the division must be deleted, but information relevant to making market size, price, and cost projections must be retained.

The rather ordinary men at the general office deal with large time spans easily because information about daily and weekly time spans has been deleted from the information flow to them and because they allocate capital authorizations over large time spans rather than approving purchase orders. The rather ordinary division managers likewise have a manageable number of subordinates, given how often they have to confer with each or to force them to confer with each other, and the directions they get from the general office are simple enough that these can be integrated with the flow of communications with subordinates. A key indication of how well decentralization is working is the proportion of all communication of top executives that occurs in committee meetings (Stinchcombe 1974, 79–84); if they are talking to individual subordinates rather than to committees (often made up of the subordinates of the committee chair), they are probably not making long run policy with sufficient attention to data abstracted to reflect long-run trends.

To explain how abstraction and corresponding decentralization add up to the effective functioning in the U.S. federal government, Padgett uses the image of differentiated ecological control systems.

> Each level of organizational aggregation [of lower-level budget data] is embedded in a distinctive cultural context of "ecological control" premises which reflect, in highly compressed form, the historical residues of past political struggles—[at the lower level], program controllability [i.e., the degree to which future budgets are subject to executive discretion rather than fixed], whose roots lie in the legal structure; organizational priorities [of particular government departments], whose roots lie

in institutional roles and constituency relations; and
presidential fiscal targets, whose roots lie in macroeconomic and defense issues. Such ecological control premises change on different historical time frames. (1981,
121–122)

The point here is that through segregated levels of abstraction and the
time frame of responsiveness, different types of problems become problems to different hierarchical levels of the government. The same applies
in Chandler to Du Pont and General Motors. The solutions to the problems at each level go to the other levels in highly abstract form. For example, the presidential level sends out a target cut and gets back a proposal to cut certain programs by certain amounts; it need never know
how controllability and constituency relations were balanced in arriving
at these cuts.

Similarly, Du Pont's new general office need not know how much of
the capital and operating expenses of a division went into making manufacturing respond more quickly to market changes, how much into producing the product more cheaply; they need only know whether whatever the division did worked to preserve market share. But they need to
know this over the course of years, not weeks, as one does if one must
keep the inventory of unsold goods of many types within bounds. The
statistical techniques for abstracting performance records to the appropriate level to detect problems for the general office that require for their
remedy yearly shifts of investment are different from those for detecting
problems with too high production of one type of paint, too low of another. The hierarchical segregation of information is essential if individuals are to be able to respond to shifts in the environment by manip-
ulating resources under their control.

This sketch of Chandler's theory of what decentralized administration
does (considerably sharpened by a reading of Padgett) shows that his
main functional connection can also be disaggregated into individual behavior. Through decentralization from the central office *and recentralization at the divisional level*, authority to respond on different time scales is
coordinated with information adequate to detect problems on those time
scales, so each person's job is doable and yet the organization responds
correctly enough at all time scales. The sketch also shows that individual
rationality depends on appropriate decentralization. Only if a general
office executive gets information appropriately abstracted for making
projections, but *not* for promoting a division chief's subordinates, can he
or she respond strategically in making investment decisions.

Is It Still Sociology?

The historical chapters of Chandler's book are convincing partly because they disaggregate the functional connection to the individual level. But they are also convincing because they show that even if we do not always understand exactly why the individuals acted the way they did, they *in fact* acted in such a way as to create a multidivisional structure. So far his discussion could be either psychology or history, but nothing at the collective level, the level of the corporation, shows that the connections are social. Chandler's chapter 7 furnishes the evidence, in a form familiar to sociologists, that the histories are not merely unique paths leading from wherever it was to wherever the company happened to get to, as illuminated by what the individuals said they were trying to do.

Chapter 7 shows that there is a strong correlation between being in a single market and having a centralized structure and between being in multiple differentiated markets and having centralized divisions—but divisions decentralized from the central office. A sociologist would not ordinarily be satisfied with the four administrative histories in the first part of the book because there are more variables and contingencies than cases. Chapter 7 convinces that, almost invariably, firms that succeed after having entered many markets have a multidivisional structure, while those that stay in a single market have a centralized structure. This, then, is a functional connection that is decomposable into individual actions, yet it is clearly not the outcome of any simple aggregation of individual rationalities. If decentralization is an aggregation of individual rationalities to all, the majority of top Du Pont management who were against it for a year when they were losing a lot of money by not having it shows that it is a more complex rationality than we generally meet in microeconomics.

If a centralized firm, without changing structure, has one central executive coordinating engineering, manufacturing, and marketing of both explosive powder and artificial leather, the executive's job will be within his or her capacities only if he or she does the job by rule. If the executive is a powder person, he or she will say to engineering: make it cheap; to manufacturing: build up inventory, there will be rock to break up forever; to marketing: teach the customer how to do it right—get in there and help them run their blasting operation. But those rules will make the firm go broke in artificial leather for novelty goods.

The solution is to invent subordinate rule makers when the firm goes into many businesses: the bosses of divisions. The central management have to teach themselves not to meddle because they do not know artificial leather, only powder. Creating these subordinate dispute-resolving and rule-making authorities—the division heads—and getting the general office head of engineering, manufacturing, or marketing not to interfere are the first big achievements that Chandler talks about in Du Pont.

The Causes of Divisionalization

We have used our analysis of the details of Chandler's history of Du Pont to explicate his theory of the causes of divisionalization. The dependent variable in this story, then, is *the centralization of the management of product lines in distinct markets.* The first part of Chandler's explanatory problem is to explain why centralization at the divisional level, rather than at the firm level, is required for manufacturing in lines with distinguishable markets.

We have not explained why Du Pont wanted to maintain itself as a single firm, nor does Chandler (but see Chandler's later work [1977] for an explanation). Consequently we, and Chandler, have left aside the question of why there needed to be a general office at Du Pont. We have said only that if they had one, it needed to have abstract nonoperating information fed to it by the divisions.

Since Du Pont was already centralized, and since this fact did not change, we get no information from Chandler's history as to what brought about a general office, or what brought about firm unity when unity was not demanded by operational unity. To explain the multidivisional form, we need to explain the causes both of divisionalization *and* of a general office. But the second set of causes is better explored by looking at the creation of a general office than by looking at the creation of divisions. In Du Pont that process can be explained by what we now require the general office executives to do, now that we can no longer let them run operations.

To guess what general office executives would do after decentralization, one has to realize that they were the ones who controlled investments and had to answer for their profitability. But investment is a future-oriented activity, which means that an investment center like the general office has to form a picture of the future; this, then, will tell them returns from an investment made now in powder or in artificial leather. The general true answer they ought to be giving, of course, is, "Damned if I know what the future will be like!" But they cannot run a business on that truth, because they have to put their money somewhere or they will get no profit. So what the general office does is make projections—of market demand, of Japanese competition, of costs, of competitor efficiency. Then they calculate how these projections would influence profitability if, say, more money were to be put into artificial leather than into blasting powder, and vice versa. Then they decide where to expand, and how much.

The advertisements for Lotus 1-2-3 or Visicalc give an idea of what general office executives are doing. What the firm usually gets is an "exact" calculation (Lotus 1-2-3 does not give standard errors) of expected profit with a margin of error a mile wide; then it takes a decision. On average, the decision taken is the wrong one. Apparently the general office does not make its investment decisions any better than the stock market as a whole does, for the profits of multidivisional firms are not ordinarily any bigger than the average return in the stock market. Many firms with general offices that are very expert in highly abstract projections of future demands and costs go bankrupt. Chandler would argue that if the central management were not engaged in making such projections, they would be meddling in the business of the divisions and so would do worse than the stock market as a whole. But constructing an argument about what a general office is for, when, as in the case of Du Pont, it might well be a fossil left from the days when the company was a single centralized firm, is not a satisfactory way to proceed. Let us turn, then, to General Motors and its creation of a general office.

General Motors Creates a Multidivisional Structure by Centralizing

In Chandler's account of what happened to General Motors, the basic structure of William C. Durant's carriage business was just what Sabel (1982) says is the *alternative* mode to mass production, to "fordism," in organizing industrialism—what in Chapter 2 we called the "interactive" program structure. But Chandler does not describe how the skills of the workers in, say, the wheel maker's firm were taught and organized.

By subcontracting for the parts, Durant himself (or rather, Durant's company itself—Durant was off in New York talking to bankers) managed assembly, and especially marketing, directly. That way the carriage firm that preceded General Motors could respond rapidly to shifts in fashion. In particular, the whole structure could more or less turn around and make cars instead of buggies, using more or less the same marketing structure and the same set of subcontractors, but with different technical details, different volumes, and so on. The flexible structure in Flint, Michigan, was similar to that described by Sabel for flexible manufacturing in many classical industrial cities and was sufficiently adaptable to switch from routines for producing carriages to routines for producing automobiles.

If all these independent craft firms were doing fine, why did Durant buy out his suppliers to form General Motors? First, he didn't always. But when he did, the reason seems to have been risk management and capital flow problems; these led to vertical integration—to assemblers buying out suppliers or marketing firms. Small business owners could not afford to build to ten times their previous size, going deeply in debt, unless they knew they would have contracts. But the only game in Flint for these big contracts was (and still is) General Motors. Durant himself moved on the New York capital market, not in Flint. To borrow large amounts to finance a wheel plant's expansion, Durant could commit General Motors to buying from "GM's own" wheel plant (or from the Fisher Body plant after GM bought out Fisher Body). If Durant acquired a firm, he could afford to take the risk of making it ten times as big— which the owner could not—because he could guarantee the market for ten times as many wheels. Essentially, General Motors played "insurer" as its larger assets and secure market position guaranteed the loan or stock issue; in addition, it made the returns of the small business (say, the wheel maker or Fisher Body) insurable by providing a "guaranteed" market.

The firm becoming a subsidiary sold its human and organizational capital to General Motors, had that spread over a larger capital stock, and was given a secure access to the market (as secure as General Motors', that is). There was then no reason for Durant to intervene in the administration of the subsidiary unless it lost money, had too little capacity, or priced itself out of the market. The "private" wealth of the subsidiary's old owners was freed up (by having General Motors' purchase price in the bank), instead of further embedded in their parts firm. Especially, they did not have their wealth "leveraged" with a large debt that made the leverage very risky for them (which would have happened had they expanded with capital borrowed in their own name rather than letting Durant do the expansion) just because General Motors needed more wheels than they had capital to produce. General Motors needed the new, much larger capacity, so General Motors should take the risk, and not some little wheelwright who would have had to mortgage his house (or his race horses) to expand.

So what made this extreme decentralization work? In fact it is the thing that Sabel says makes fordism work, namely, a mass market for identical goods, organized into a bunch of reliable dealerships providing parts and service as well as selling cars and spread out around the country. This was what made Durant able to organize General Motors; he had made the carriage business work the same way. But what produced the money to invest in expanding the parts suppliers by, say, ten times was mass marketing. Durant's own innovations were not in fordism, but in mass marketing supported by craft skills; and that mass marketing provided backing for capital flows that eventually allowed parts of General Motors to fordize their production.

The basic generalization in Sabel (1962) is that mass marketing encourages the development of technical routines (see above, Chapter 2). But here we see that mass marketing first produced innovative technical firms tied together by subcontracts, with skilled, flexible workers producing whatever parts are needed this year. In short, it caused expanded craft production.

Perhaps the key is that at that time producing automobiles was technically new. A mass market in a technically new system may produce a flourishing "small-firm skilled worker" system. Only when the firm has mastered the technical problems at the operative level can the new knowledge of how to make, say, a million wheels a year *filter up* so that engineers can routinize the knowledge of how to make a million wheels. It is important to realize that a flexible system held together by flexible contracts and occasional vertical integration to redistribute the risks could compete successfully in the same market that the Ford Motor Company itself was producing in. Subcontracting can compete with fordism on fordism's own turf.

The Centralization Revolution at General Motors

To understand what the Sloan revolution at General Motors was, we have to note more specifically what functions it was that were created as new functions of the central administration (now the "general office"), what functions were not decentralized to the division, and what functions for the divisions and for the investors the general office had.

COORDINATING PROJECTED DEMAND

The crises that created the Sloan revolution at General Motors were centered in the marketing system. The basic problem seems to have been that the parts suppliers, being far back in the system from the dealers who have direct information from the clients, could not tell whether a slackening of demand was temporary or long term. (It is indicative that Sloan himself had experience in the parts production part of General Motors.) To keep their own production efficient, they needed to keep their trained technical workers on, to use their capital to the fullest, and generally to work up to capacity. So they had motives not to mistake a temporary downturn for a shift in demand. The main reason General Motors needed a general office, then, was to organize, and then universalize, an authoritative system for projecting demand, with projections revised often enough to control production and inventory policy far back into the parts and materials supply system.

CENTRALIZED DIFFERENTIATION OF GENERAL MOTORS' MARKETS

The second big thing Durant had developed was a class-differentiated marketing system, with the makes he had bought up into slots in a market organized from cheap to expensive. The cheapest line was Ford's, and it was a long time before Durant and Sloan could figure out how to produce a car to beat Ford in the low end of the market. Their short-run adaptation was to continue to produce and market the distinctive cars of the companies they had bought. Clearly, though, one should not encourage a successful Olds division, say, to expand to competitively damage the Buick division, when maybe no one else in the market was in a position to damage Buick.

As General Motors centralized, then, they did not want to go in a completely fordist direction, producing only one car. Diversified mass marketing was already a corporate strategy, an implicit result of acquisitions and letting the firms acquired continue to produce what they had been producing. In any case, decentralization as a way to deal with the administrative problems of producing several lines of cars was already institutionalized. What was new with Sloan and the general office was a deliberate plan to cover the spectrum of markets, to fill in (invest in) areas of the class system they did not cover, and to run down (disinvest or convert investments) in situations where subcorporations competed with each other for a class segment of the market. So the firm needed parallel feedback—parallel demand projections—to control production *in the several lines differentiated by class.*

COORDINATING THE SERVICE MARKET WITH THE CAR MARKET

The third general problem confronting Sloan, apparently solved in the operating divisions rather than by the general office, is that marketing cars ultimately depends on a reliable supply of repair parts. Producers of parts for, say, the Buick division had to cooperate as well with Buick dealers all over the country in supplying the repair parts needed to keep Buicks running. Having lots of Buicks in local junkyards for lack of parts ultimately depresses sales. The corporation thus had to have the marketing information collected from Buick dealers available for planning repair parts production.

Still, General Motors did not want Buick parts suppliers using monopoly power (e.g., being the only producer of Buick air filters) to jack up the price of repair parts. So while GM needed to supply information to the Buick air filter manufacturer, it needed also to keep that producer from exploiting his position as the only one who could supply the dealers. Sometimes such a problem was resolved by buying the parts supplier and putting it administratively into the Buick division, but such decisions would have been strategic ones made by the general office on recommendation of the Buick division.

CENTRALIZED FUNCTIONS NOT DELEGATED TO THE DIVISIONS UNDER SLOAN

It is important to note that some things were *not* left to divisional decision. The biggest example was purchasing. There are all sorts of reasons why people generally do not want purchasing to be under divisional (or any decentralized) control: corruption, price competition between divisions, integration of orders to get longer production runs for suppliers, relevance of purchasing information to the decision of whether or not to acquire a supplier, and so on. In any event, a crucial part of the administration of divisional supplier relations was not under divisional control. Similarly, standards of cost and profit accounting, calculation of investment returns, and the like were not decentralized. That is, mechanisms central to the integrity of general office control of the divisions (for the aspects that they mainly wanted to control) were not left in the division's hands.

THE GENERAL FUNCTION OF A GENERAL OFFICE

The main point of the specificity of our description of what was centralized is that when a firm already has a decentralized administration, imposing a new centralized structure on top of it threatens to centralize decisions that had better be left decentralized. Decentralization was the situation General Motors was left in by the acquisition strategy of Durant. When a firm like Du Pont has a centralized structure and then goes into various businesses that require different sorts of coordination among, say, production, engineering, and marketing, the firm is likely to end up running one of the businesses by a strategy inappropriate to that business, though it may work very well for another one—thereby losing money. Such a firm thus has to learn *not* to make so many decisions centrally. Chandler's point is that both firms—Du Pont and General Motors—ended up with pretty much the same structure, with coordination of the different specialties involved in a manufacturing operation going on at the divisional level and projections (and investment strategy based on those projections) being done at the general office level.

The functions outlined above for the general office are especially those in which information from one division, parts subsidiary, or marketing branch was useful for assessing the investment value of another division, parts subsidiary, or marketing branch. In such circumstances the general office has an interest in securing the following features in that information:

1. *Financial integrity.* The chains of information that link expenditures in a business to capital markets are more effective if they guarantee financial integrity. Centralized monitoring of purchasing, firmwide accounting standards, and coordinated projections all tend to make the standards for investment in each part of a decentralized firm as good as the standards for the whole firm. One function of the general office, needed to justify to an investment bank a loan of money to expand a wheel maker tenfold, is to guarantee the financial integrity of the information both on the wheel maker and on the buying division.

2. *Guarantees of markets.* If General Motors gives a long-term contract to its wheel-making subsidiary, this guarantees (within limits) a market for the wheels, which in turn guarantees (within limits) the profitability of the investment. Similarly, arranging that Olds shall not invade Buick markets, and vice versa, does not make either division secure from competition; but it does reduce the risks that completely autonomous divisions would autonomously invade each others' markets. A general office can make competitive destruction of the value of an investment less likely.

3. *Reliable external economies.* Reliable repair parts supplies and available retail installment credit are profitable businesses in their own right, but in addition, their reliability and availability are selling points for car marketing. Yet a completely autonomous firm supplying repair parts or installment credit might not find it profitable to supply exactly what a dealer needs. Being able to arrange reliable supplies of such externally generated selling points stabilizes the value of marketing investments, and hence of the manufacturing investments behind them. In turn, of course, stable marketing arrangements provide reliable opportunities to repair

parts suppliers and installment credit suppliers. Coordinated provision of complementary goods and services
makes a more profitable portfolio of investments.

Thus, the functions we see performed by the newly organized general
office in General Motors provide information crucial to capital markets
(cf. Zetka 1988). They also developed out of functions performed by
Durant as an individual, before Sloan created a committee version of
Durant. In this sense, Chandler's analysis of the causes of the general
office reduces to one cause, of supplying information of use to investors,
rather than of supplying coordination of response in commodity-line
markets. There is no general reason to believe that general offices will be
required wherever divisions are required.

The Theoretical Problem of Sears

This disjunction of the causes of divisionalization and the causes of general offices creates a problem for Chandler's analysis of Sears, for we cannot, I believe, understand the administrative reform of Sears without a
careful analysis of Sears's competition. That competition was a structure
of small and medium wholesalers in distinct commodity lines, with no
national commodity-line buyers and certainly no national general office.
Sears had to compete with this extremely decentralized system, and
could only do so if it could coordinate decentralized demands better than
that competition, through national "divisions" run by commodity-line
buyers. But I will argue that the central administrative innovation discussed by Chandler—Sears's regional divisions—could not do that work.

The problem Sears had was not to create commodity-line divisions, as
at Du Pont, because it already had them. Nor was it to create a general
office to govern investment, because it already had that too. Instead, it
was to build new structures of flows of information from retail stores to
autonomous buying divisions, inherited from the mail order business.
The regional divisions, I will argue, were not part of that flow.

The central argument, then, will be that neither the causes of divisionalization by commodity lines, nor the flows of information justifying
investments, changed. Hence the causes in Chandler's theory as developed above cannot explain what happened at Sears.

Regional Information in
Merchant Wholesaling and Sears

Let us take a problem of marketing administration from Chandler's analysis of Sears. We will try to illustrate again how Chandler argues, and in

particular how a *functional inadequacy of a structure* creates a *flow of problems for individuals* (or for small groups, more often) and how *structural change in a functional direction is caused by the solution of individual-level problems*. When we inspect Chandler's argument about Sears from this point of view, several inadequacies appear. We will look at the problem of adjusting the inventory displayed and on hand in a Sears store to the seasons and to the regions of the country. Obviously adjustments all the way back to the buyer (the person who arranges the contract between Sears and the factories that produce the goods) are needed if the overall "functional" problem of having summer goods gone and back-to-school goods on display by August, and of having different back-to-school clothes in Phoenix than in Seattle, is to be solved.

"The market" solves this problem by thousands of wholesalers stocking what local retailers are going to want to buy and sending travelers (traveling salesmen) around to the stores in their area with catalogs and samples, which results then in a large flow of small orders from wholesalers to manufacturers. If Sears was to have an advantage in this trade, it had to use the experience of, and the opportunity for, volume buying that it had developed in the mail order business.

But buyers for a mail order house need not time deliveries and displays for each store by the season and the region. They need to know how many raincoats and how many cowboy boots children whose parents order from Sears will want *this year* and to place both large orders rationally, thus allowing manufacturers to run their plants year-round and to process only one order for raincoats or one for cowboy boots. Sears did not need to build the buyers' information system to be attuned to seasonal and regional variations when it was a mail order business, and the buyer did not necessarily notice that the children's cowboy boot orders in August came from Phoenix and the children's raincoat orders from Seattle.

After going into the retail shopping center business, then, Sears had the "structural" problem that store-level problems were not the same problems their buyers were good at solving, namely minimizing manufacturing and wholesaling costs. This was because the functions of wholesalers—which cost so much—of adjusting inventories to seasonal and regional variations had no place to be solved in a structure created by "adding stores to a mail order house."

Chandler shows that when the aggregate performance statistics of the store division were not satisfactory, many people were set to work to find out what was wrong. They located many different kinds of problems—for example, a consultant with experience in cutting costs of government administration, found problems of cost minimization that Sears could work on. The structural strain of having a buyer information system that is not adequate to the new coordination problem does not necessarily mean the problem will be posed correctly. Many reforms may be instituted which do not solve the problem that Chandler (and we) locate by hindsight, that the organizational environment of Sears structures the buyers' problems in such a way that the buyers do not solve the stores' inventory adjustment problems as well as wholesalers in the open market solve competitive stores' problems.

If Chandler provides lots of evidence that Sears's people did not "rationally" solve their problem (instead, they "rationally" addressed a whole lot of problems in searching for what their problem really was), he still has to explain why "structure follows strategy," that is, why a functional result came about in the long run. His basic proposition is an "absorbing Markov chain" proposition: the organization will continue to throw up problems to individuals until they correctly identify the source of the functional inadequacy and build a structure that remedies it.

Commodity Line Rationality versus Store Inventory Rationality

Note that the buyer versus store problem will recur in many different lines. In Arizona, Sears should not stock as many gardening tools in the spring as in Illinois; above the glacier line, Sears probably should stock more fishing and hunting gear in the sports department; in the Southwest, the automobile lines should be adjusted for the large population of pickups. Buyers specialize in commodity lines because efficient buying requires a detailed knowledge of the characteristics and prices of competitive goods and competitive producers. Individual-level adjustments to problems of different store inventories in different parts of the country by particular buyers specializing in commodity lines is an inefficient strategy, because too many buyers in too many lines have to learn too much about regional variations. Individual-level rationality by buyers *in each merchandise line* is thus not a very viable "functional alternative" to reorganizing the connection between stores and buyers on a regional basis. Sears needed to divorce some of this flow of store problems to buyers (after being reanalyzed in regional inventory terms by a regional management) from the mail order flow to buyers, because the mail order flow has to solve a different structure of problems.

There are two kinds of connections from the functional outcome (adjustment of store inventories to season and region without losing all the advantages of massed buying) to the structural thing to be explained (operative divisions controlling wholesale buying and *some* kinds of regional administration of retail stores). The first is that individuals posed with problems of inadequate competitive performance in stores hunt for solutions. The second is that *until* they find a patterning of overall activity that solves the functional problem, people keep on being posed with individual problems that keep them looking for solutions.

So the basic problem Sears had, according to Chandler, was where to locate informational complexity in the organizational structure. The old regime, that of the mail order house, had something like nineteen decentralized divisions in the merchandise division (the number varied from time to time): nineteen lines in which the core executive—the buyer—had to keep track of what sorts of garden tractors were selling this year, of whether they could sell heavy goods like fertilizer competitively when they had to send it through the mail at a high transportation cost (they could not, when they were selling by mail order, buy carload lots locally, as a garden and lawn supply place in each town might do), of what manufacturer of lawn mowers could reliably produce a machine that Sears could guarantee customer satisfaction on without going broke, and so on.

The old Sears structure could be described as a "coalition of merchants" in these different lines, each functioning essentially as an autonomous buyer and "selling to" the mail order division, which in turn sold retail for the coalition. There was much decentralization of decisions to operative (i.e., merchandise-line) levels in which the big decisions about the sizes and contents of merchandise flows and inventories were made essentially by buyers in the different lines. This is *one* part of the essential information a wholesaler must have to be successful in the market; the other part is knowledge of local and regional peculiarities of the seasonal variations in how lines of goods move.

Sears's advantage was that they had a lot better buyers than commodity-line wholesalers for supplying a national market and for arranging for cheap production and response to changing fashions nationally in commodity lines. They had a big statistical base on which to estimate future demand and a developed routine for translating the necessary information from the buyer into a commodity-line section of the seasonal mail order catalogs.

The code word for this system in the mail order business is "quantity buying," by which, with that information and the big flow of goods through the mail order house, the buyer in a given commodity line could make it possible for the manufacturer to smooth out production of a good over the seasons and have long production runs, and so make it cheaper. The manufacturer could plan a smooth production schedule in much bigger batches before a changeover, reduce the amount of clerical work on a given quantity of goods because it was all for one buyer, and would ordinarily have *no* inventory risk because he or she would be producing to Sears's order rather than to what he hoped a lot of wholesalers in different parts of the country would decide to do.

Wholesalers both had and created for the manufacturer a much bigger burden of clerical work than the wholesale part of the Sears mail order business did, and they had and created a bigger inventory risk as well. This was because decentralized wholesalers' information was not as reliable and their expertise not as well organized to take advantage of big flows of goods. Wholesalers were more likely to have to write off or sell at cut prices if a line did not sell to retailers, for instance, because a competitor wholesaler had a slightly better model. Sears or Penney's might guess wrong about what would sell at the retail level, but at least as a wholesaler for their own retail outlets they did not have to mark down a lot of goods because of a few big retailer decisions to go with a competitor. The Sears buyer did not have to have salespeople out convincing each department head or buyer in each department store in many different metropolitan areas and small market towns to buy from her or him, as the small wholesaler did.

The clerical, inventory, and sales costs of wholesaling and manufacturing are cut down by chain stores generally, and it is these costs that are especially cut by a joint buying operation of a huge mail order house with a very big chain store. But what Sears had been sacrificing in order to make that saving (because the sacrifice was not important in the mail order business) was all the information about local peculiarities of demand that were built into the thousands of wholesalers adapting their buying and sales strategies to local markets throughout the country.

Now that Sears was going into the local department store business, they had to try to perform the functions that all those wholesaler clerical and sales people and all those autonomous buyers in each retail store did in the "free market" structure. The free market structure was very expensive, but it did that work of relating local demands to centralized "commodity-line" production by manufacturers who sold on national markets (Beniger 1986). Their competition, unlike General Motors', was already decentralized a lot more than Sears would ever be, because the competition was many autonomous firms scattered throughout the country. The average wholesaler in the United States even nowadays has about twelve employees (*Statistical Abstract of the United States, 1989,* 761). Sears had to compete against a structure that used a lot of clerks, a lot of salespeople, a lot of special ordering from factories, a lot of experienced small entrepreneurs in particular lines of wholesale trade in particular parts of the country, a lot of folks taking inventory risks because they knew their local market—a structure that was doing a very good job at something Sears had not had to do when they were only in the mail order business. But Sears had the advantage of knowing a lot better than that decentralized apparatus of wholesalers how to use the power and efficiency of buying on a large scale and of advertising nationally through catalogs.

The structure Sears had to compete with would never deliver swimming suits in midwinter in Maine or skis to a department store in New Orleans. What we see in Sears in the period Chandler studied is Sears trying to improve their accuracy and flexibility in wholesaling up to the level that their competition was already at, without losing their cost advantages from large orders placed well in advance.

Note that except for a very few comments on how to get good store managers and department heads in retailing, almost all of Chandler's talk about administrative reorganization is about the wholesaling end of things: how to relate the buying and supplying of mail order with that of stores (the long-run solution was to have separate inventory and quantity controls but to use the same buyers); how to adjust overall supplies to regional market variations; how to put controls on the buyers by forecasting demand so that Sears would not be caught (again) with excessive inventories; how to get the departments in the merchandise department (buying) down to a reasonable number; how to decide who was going to coordinate transport and select suppliers for different regions to minimize transport; how much Sears was going to intervene in giving technical specifications to manufacturers rather than just picking what was offered; and so on.

Sometimes (always, really) these decisions had retail implications. But these decisions were, in the competitive structure of small wholesalers spread around the country, all wholesaler decisions. Mass or chain store merchandising is mainly a reorganization of wholesaling by substituting bureaucratic or administrative control of wholesaling decisions for market control. Sears's decentralization had to cope with problems that the already decentralized wholesaling system had not had, and that Sears had not had when they had a terrifically decentralized system of buyers operating as more or less independent merchants but selling nationally through the catalog in a mail-order-only business. To see what was wrong with Sears's "buyer divisions" for coordinating inventories at many local departments stores, we need to analyze what Sears's competition, the system of tiny wholesaling firms, accomplished.

The General Problem of Wholesaling

Where does the problem that wholesalers have to deal with come from? The analysis has to start with a contradiction between what one needs at the retail store level and what the factories can produce. Each factory makes a restricted line of goods, goods related by a common technology. What a store like a Sears branch has to have is a flow of goods into the store inventory that is shaped by the consumption bundle that customers are looking for when they go to a "men's" department store, what a given kind of person or family buys on their monthly (or so) trip to a big store.

The job of wholesaling is to take the set of flows of homogeneous goods from a set of factories and to turn it into a set of flows of heterogeneous goods through a whole bunch of stores that is shaped to the current buying habits of each store's clientele. Price, style, quantity, performance criteria, and the like for the mixed flow at the store end has to come from folks who know what is moving, has to be adjusted for class and regional variations in consumption habits, and has to vary with the seasons and with what the seasons mean locally. That is where the ultimate information comes from, from the individual Sears big store responding to local peculiarities in consumption bundles that families buy on their once-a-month shopping trips.

But to turn all these dribbles of information on how many sofas we sell in the spring in each store into a large order for a factory, the information has to be aggregated into one decision about how many sofas to order of what styles and prices several months in advance—and it has to be aggregated separately for factories in different parts of the country, since shipping sofas is expensive. That aggregation is how a chain store gets its price break. It is what the economics of chain store wholesaling consists of. The chain store has to transmit that information to its wholesale buyer in a given commodity line in such a way that, when it looks as if things are maybe not moving as fast this year, the buyer can cut down the flow volume without completely disrupting the manufacturer and the traffic department in a way that will cost the chain a lot in the long run. The chain wants to make the adjustment before it has a cubic mile of extra unsold sofas.

It is because this problem can be solved by forecasting, by using expert buyers in each line of goods, by having regional executives manage wholesaling in distinct areas of the country, that we have chain stores that can sell at lower prices. It is because the competition of independent department stores and independent wholesalers spread out all over the landscape can do that adjustment, at a cost of more clerical and sales work and more inventory risk takers, that a chain store has to keep reorganizing until it gets a responsive system that solves the inventory problem of each local store and at the same time solves the manufacturer's problem of more expensive production if it cannot get larger orders far in advance.

Actually, the multiple-regional-divisional structure that Chandler focuses on was only a small part of the administrative innovation he describes. The main innovations had to be increased flows of market information from the various departments of the many stores to the wholesale buyers in specialized lines—information about what would move, how much of it would move, and at what price, style, and seasonal mix it would move. Regional top executives, even with larger staffs than they had, just could not do it. There was too much knowledge of too many lines of goods for them to administer it.

In fact, Chandler says as much, but he does not emphasize this point. He talks about the reforms undertaken by Barker, the vice president of retail administration and personnel, in the 1930s. As Huber says in his critique of Chandler's analysis of Sears, "Despite the centralized retail administration in place, Barker developed a policy of 'unit control' and other 'statistical procedures to ensure . . . that merchandise would be in stock in the right amounts at the right times' (p. 264 of Chandler). By 1934, according to Chandler, Barker had created a 'cohesive and capable retail organization,' even though it was to be more or less this same organization which would later be reorganized on territorial lines" (Huber 1985, 3). It may be that the regional divisional structure helped fine-tune this overall system for feeding buyers the adequate aggregated information that ultimately came from what was moving in the retail stores. But Chandler does not actually show the interconnection between the development of the information system that did the aggregating which functionally had to be done and the decentralization to regions *as well as* to buyers in each commodity line.

Another weakness of Chandler's evidence (Huber 1985, 3–4) is that Chandler does not actually show regional diversity. For example, the Pacific Coast territory must have stretched from Seattle to San Francisco, at least. But if one considers climatic variation, the wet mountainous market stretching out from Seattle and the desert market stretching behind San Francisco are probably no more alike than those of Seattle and Chicago. Instead, what may have been going on is that as Sears got a lot more stores in total, they needed to have lots of intermediate offices to handle the sheer quantity of decisions that are involved in running stores in San Francisco and Seattle, and then in Eureka, Portland, and Pullman. While Sears could run two stores on the West Coast with those stores' big decisions being made in Chicago, it was difficult to run twenty Pacific Coast stores that way simply because there would be ten times as many decisions to review and execute.

The same was particularly true of decisions involving investments in local stores. Manufacturing investments are in commodity lines; retail investments are in locations. The investment arm of the general office needed to know that stores in the Pacific region went in the right places. Once they were in the right places, the store-to-buyer information flow could adjust the store inventory. It therefore seems likely that regional offices were evaluating investments in stores in particular locations—a general office function—rather than aggregating inventory statistics— an operating division function. The more such localized investments had to be made far from Chicago, the more a regional division was required to advise on them.

Organizational Problems of the Service Sector

All of this illustrates why it is that the service industries tend to have a lot of the labor in the economy nowadays. The service sector as a whole has many clerks, salespeople, commodity specialists like the buyers and department heads in department stores, and the like. These people know about the prices, quantities to be sold, qualities, fashionableness, and so on of a line of detailed commodities for a local area or a particular store. In particular, they need to know what will be wanted in one department or boutique of this product from Janzen, this one from Dior, or of this product from AC Sparkplug, this one from Black and Decker.

Then all that information has to be translated into orders to a wholesaler for particular quantities at particular prices, shipping orders and bills of lading, addresses on the hundreds of pieces of mail that keep things in order so the mail carriers know where to deliver them, and so forth. A very large share of the work in the service sector, especially in wholesale and retail trade, transportation, and communications, is the processing of enormously detailed pieces of paper about how much of thousands of different commodities go to this or that store, when, and at what price. It is in this mass of clerical and routine sales work that the feminization of the service industry has progressed furthest; only about one out of five lawyers is a women (about one out of three new law school graduates is a woman), whereas something like nineteen out of twenty secretaries or clerks in retail and wholesale trade are women (*Statistical Abstract of the United States, 1987,* 386).

Sears's administrative problem emphasizes that what makes mass production possible is the processing and aggregating of this enormous mass of detailed information about commodity flows for thousands of commodities by all these women clerical and sales workers in the service sector. They are the ones who solve the problem of turning the particular demands of the clientele of a particular store into the factory's yearly plan of production, the plan that allows the factory to have efficient long runs of production of the same commodity.

The problem that Sears had to solve was this same one: how to make mass production possible when the information was concentrated originally in what was happening to this and that stock of lawn mowers in Seattle and in Phoenix, and in how much less demand for lawn mowers there was in Tucson than in Phoenix (because more folks in Tucson have desert plants on their "lawns," but people still have grass lawns in Phoenix). This is why Chandler's analysis of regional divisions is not adequate to explain all the changes made in information-processing structures using store data. Regional divisions did not usually have buyers to arrange for the production of goods with factories. What is problematic, what shapes the uncertainty, is the relation between store inventories and "quantity buying" by a decentralized "coalition of merchants," each in a single commodity line. For Sears to succeed, it had to coordinate its local store-inventory information so commodity-line quantity buyers could use it. Much of that information processing, as Chandler reports it, completely bypassed the regional divisions he thought were central.

But Sears did not gain its competitive advantage in wholesaling by regional organization. It gained it by using its mail order commodity-line buying divisions, by using information aggregated by commodity line from the stores. They used less sales and clerical labor, and created less trouble for factories, not because they had regional divisions, but because they had national commodity-line operating divisions. Thus, Chandler's main cause of divisionalization did not change. The divisions needed new information from commodity-line departments in stores, but their uncertainties were not substantially different from what they were in the mail order business.

Sears may have made its general office more competent to invest in retail stores by having regional divisions, but it already had a general office coordinating investment in commodity-line divisions. The causes for having a general office also did not change. Chandler's theory is more useful for explaining the structure Sears started with than for analyzing the administrative changes, including regional divisions, of the period he studied.

What Is Chandler's Independent Variable?

Chandler's analysis in *Strategy and Structure* is mainly about divisionalization; in *The Visible Hand* (1977) it is more directly about coordination and centralization. Consequently, his argument is clearest in *Strategy* when he argues about the causes for divisions becoming separated and internally centralized. We have only hinted above at these causes, as "being in several markets."

We have proceeded so far as if it were obvious whether a company was in several different markets. But since Chandler's argument as a whole depends on markets being a source of uncertainty that has to be adapted to (and since this book is about that part of his argument), we have to define markets such that they are *separable* sources of uncertainty. That uncertainty in turn has to ramify through the several functional departments (which make up the multifunction divisions whose origins Chandler is trying to analyze) in such a way that a coordinated response of the different functions to a market's particular uncertainties is necessary.

In this section we will be more specific about what "being in several markets" means. We will argue that in Chandler's argument being in more than one market had five elements: (1) that market uncertainties ramify into manufacturing and engineering; (2) that information on market uncertainties come from segregated social sources; (3) that those segregated social sources carry distinct information; (4) that the inventory risks that reflect the ramifying of market uncertainty are managed in similar ways within a market, perhaps in different ways in different markets; and (5) that total uncertainty is large. If all five conditions are met, then market uncertainty ramifies into the administration of manufacturing and engineering in such a way as to create divisions.

THE TRANSMISSION OF MARKET UNCERTAINTY TO MANUFACTURING

Consider, for example, Chandler's description of the steel industry (331–337), which ends with the statement, "If the market, apparently, has not been different enough [for different products] to bring about the growth of autonomous, integrated divisions, neither have strategic decisions been numerous or complex enough to demand the building of a general administrative office with general executives and staff specialists" (337). Yet this is in spite of the fact that "the big integrated steel works produce a vastly greater amount of a larger variety of products for more types of industries and businesses than do the copper smelters, refineries, and fabricating mills" (331). The key reason why vastly larger and more differentiated markets do not lead to differentiated multifunctional divisions (i.e., decentralization as defined above) is that

> the complex demands of scheduling and of coordinating departments require close centralized administrative supervision if the great integrated mills, the mines, ore boats, and distributing facilities are to be operated at a fairly even capacity and if loss and waste are to be avoided by piling up inventory in one department or another or through having temporarily idle facilities and other resources. The continuance and growth of the multidepartmental division may have been checked by the fact that the demands of a single market, whether it is in one industry or one region, is not enough to keep a single great mill operating at full capacity. Therefore such mills must draw on the larger national market. (336)

That is, for steel production in great mills, (1) there are great economies in producing all the stages up through molten steel (iron ore mining and transportation; mining and transportation of coal; coke production; reduction of the ore to iron; and burning off the carbon together with other alloying and chemical changes to make steel) for all the various products in one operation. There are also large economies of scale in combined iron and steel production (see, e.g., Scherer's and others' estimates in Scherer 1980, 96). (2) There are varying but substantial economies in producing many of the heavier steel products (plate, construction shapes, rails, large tubes) from semimolten steel at the same site. (3) The users of these products are willing to pay, in some delay between their orders and their delivery, for the cheaper products.

It has paid the great integrated steel mills to turn many markets in a given large region of the country into one market by administrative means. That is, they cut the connection between the order coming in and any special speedup or slowdown of the steel-making process. Instead they integrate all the orders for different products into a gross quantity of steel needed from the plant and govern the *first phases* of the process up through molten steel by that aggregated quantity. Then the flow of steel from the integrated part of the plant is sent to fabricating installations (especially rolling mills, but some to foundries), where it is differentiated to meet the needs of the different markets.

This means that the differentiation of the market does not result in differentiation of the main part of the manufacturing organization— mining, transportation, coke production, ore reduction, and steel production. The technology is not *dedicated* to serving a particular market, but instead is a general-purpose technology that produces a raw material for a wide variety of markets. But for a large share of steel products manufacturing in which that raw material is used, it pays to have the fabrication and marketing of that product near the furnaces. Fabrication near the furnaces in particular reduces transportation costs as well as energy costs for reheating.

When the market does get differentiated in what *kind* of steel it wants, so that smaller (usually electrical) furnaces must be dedicated to producing it (as in the steel minimills that have been expanding recently while the great integrated mills have been losing customers), then there are great advantages in producer autonomy and integration of molten steel manufacturing with the marketing of the products of that steel. So far, that autonomy has mostly been achieved by independent firms producing specialty steel products rather than by having autonomous divisions in the integrated mills.

The first requirement for there to be "differentiated markets" in Chandler's theory, then, is that the manufacturing apparatus serving the market be a *dedicated resource*, one of little use for servicing any other market with a different pattern and source of uncertainty. Otherwise the uncertainty from the market will not in general be transmitted to the manufacturing operation, except after being aggregated with the uncertainty that comes from other markets. Sears did not have regionally differentiated manufacturing, so its regional divisions did not amount to much. The differentiation of contact with manufacturing was already there in the nineteen commodity-line "divisions" of the mail order house.

When there are differentiated markets served by common, general-purpose manufacturing, then we will expect to find differentiation of the marketing structure and considerable autonomy of each marketing department. Of course, separate marketing departments may have to be hooked onto the administration of the last phase of fabrication (e.g., the rolling mill) in such a way that uncertainties from the market can give information on what exact products need to be produced in that last phase, how much inventory needs to be carried, what engineering improvements in the product might be required (for example, for fabricated steel products, the recent development of X-ray and acoustic inspection of the finished product has allowed the detection of many more flaws, resulting in much-changed quality control procedures in the last phases of production as an adaptation to customer demands; see Stinchcombe 1985b, 157). There will then be pressures in steel to have innovations that correspond structurally to the multifunctional division only for a late stage of the manufacturing process. But these pressures will not tend to penetrate to the management of the whole manufacturing operation—as happens when a given chemical plant produces only paint, another only explosives—and so will not actually result in multifunctional divisions.

The first point, then, in defining Chandler's independent variable—in defining when a firm is in several different markets—is this: whether the market of one *manufacturing operation* is different from that of another one depends on whether manufacturing operations are technically differentiated, so that the same general-purpose technical operation cannot serve now one market, now another. Even when there are reasons to administratively connect a general-purpose technical system—such as iron ore reduction and steel production furnaces—with technical operations serving different markets—such as rolling mills for producing plate (mostly sold to motor vehicle manufacturers), tubes (mostly sold to the petroleum industry), rails, and construction shapes (mostly sold through wholesalers and brokers to a dispersed clientele)—the differentiation of these markets tends not to be transmitted backward into the general-purpose technology that serves all of them.

More briefly, several markets with different sources and kinds of uncertainty may be transformed into one market by administrative means, if that seems wise and profitable. It is wise and profitable if a general-purpose technology can serve all the markets, especially when there are large economies of scale in that technology. (See 352–353 for Chandler's analysis of the same general pattern as is found in the steel industry for the early history of the petroleum industry, and 349 for similar considerations in the tobacco and meat-packing industries and for United Fruit and American Sugar.)

THE SEGREGATION OF PRODUCT INFORMATION

One of the ways manufacturing and engineering are connected to the market is that engineered and manufactured features like design, color or finishing treatment, chemical composition, quality control and reliability, maintainability and service cost, taste, and complementarity or compatibility with other products available in the market (e.g., software) largely determine a product's success in the market. Engineers and the manufacturing branch thus need to get market information in order to do their design, manufacturing, inspecting, or finishing work better. The question of whether some improvement in the product is worth its cost, then, is decided jointly by what the market will pay for it and what the engineering and manufacturing cost of the improvement is.

The social location of that joint market and manufacturing information for a particular product depends on the social organization of the selling process. The fact that information about what fertilizer sells in what sorts of packages to homeowners is concentrated in the same place as knowledge of what features sell garden tractors, while information on what fertilizer sells to farmers is concentrated in the same place as knowledge of what features sell gigantic field machines, is not determined by the technical interdependencies of fertilizer and tractor production. It may well be that the same machine manufacturers produce garden tractors and field machines, while one chemical plant produces both packaged fertilizers for the home gardener and carload lots for the farmer.

A commodity line that includes home fertilizers and garden tractors will therefore tend to develop information on the gardening market this year in a given Sears department in a given store, and that information has to be aggregated properly for the gardening buyer who deals with both the machine factory and the chemical factory. Similarly, outside Sears there will be a feed store commodity line with a farm implement department, which provides information on this year's demand for fertilizer in carload lots in a given part of the country and on the availability of credit for new field machines, and that information has to be aggregated by wholesalers and brokers for those same chemical plants and machine manufacturers.

The markets are different both because features that sell the products to homeowners and farmers are different *and* because the differentiated information is available in two different social structures. Of course, there is not much commonality in the concrete material features that sell a bag of fertilizer versus a garden tractor, and in that sense they address "different markets." But the gardening buyer in Sears (after appropriate reorganization of the Sears structure, as analyzed by Chandler) gets the information about the two products' features from the same flow of retail information, as aggregated by the appropriate inventory system and by informal transmission of sales know-how. The manufacturing commonality between field and garden tractors, or between a carload and a bag of fertilizer, does not mean they have common markets, because the information about what causes them to sell is not located in the same social place: the Sears buyer never learns what sells either carloads of fertilizer or great field machines, nor does the feed dealer learn what sells bags of fertilizer or garden tractors.

Chandler often talks as if selling more different products leads to differentiation into multifunctional divisions. For instance, in discussing why the chemical industry almost uniformly adopted the multidivisional structure, he starts with a quotation from Williams Haynes, *American Chemical Industry—A History:*

> Production of chemicals by the petroleum industry ap-
> peared to be economically and technically sound, but
> most petroleum executives could not see what appeared
> to them to be a tiny market for a multitude of chemicals
> produced by a complexity of operations and sold to a
> long and diversified list of customers, tasks for which
> they had neither the technical nor the sales staffs. (358)

Chandler's basic idea here is that the more products one sells, the more different markets one is in, and so the more pressure there will be for multidivisional organization.

Presumably this generalization is approximately true for the way diversity in chemical products is produced. In chemicals, diversity is due to the knowledge needed to produce one material being useful in producing a chemically related material whose uses may be very distinct. When the uses are very distinct, then the knowledge of product characteristics that help to sell the product is likely to be organized into different social structures.

This principle applies even to the same chemical product. The knowledge of what makes nylon bearings and runners sellable to the furniture industry, for instance, is not found in the same places as knowledge of what makes ladies' nylon hose sellable in supermarkets and department stores. Similarly, one could not learn in the department store that a bearing for a drawer ought to be white, whereas one could learn that nylon for hose ought to be "nude" and that nowadays "nude" is not the color of Rubens's nudes. When the information needed to perfect the manufacturing process or the product design is located in different social structures, the manufacturing process has to be organized to respond to information coming from those social structures separately.

This connection between segregation of information and divisionization is shown by what happened in cases where diversity of products was not generated by research or manufacturing commonality, but by the social organization of the market itself. In most such cases, multidivisional structures did not develop. For example, Firestone "took on automobile parts, rubber and plastic items, and other lines [other than tires] that used its marketing organization more than its production facilities" (352) but did not develop a multidivisional structure. Similarly, a General Foods memo is quoted:

> A single selling organization would be used in market-
> ing the several product lines, since "the demonstrated
> economics of selling a line of products through a single

sales organization would be increased by the number of items handled by each salesman" [footnote to the original source of this quotation omitted]. To administer the other activities involved in producing such a large line, the company promptly set up a centralized, functionally departmentalized structure. (347)

Earlier, Pittsburgh Plate Glass, "to make fuller use of its marketing resources . . . , turned after 1900 to developing a line of paints, brushes, and related items that could be sold through the same channels as window and plate glass" (342) without developing multifunctional divisional structures.

The example of many commodities using a single merchandising division is related to the steel one, except that in this case it is the marketing information resources that are general purpose and the engineering and manufacturing operations that are specialized and dedicated to a given product line. General-purpose marketing resources (rather than dedicated marketing resources) do not tend to produce multidivisional structures any more than general-purpose manufacturing resources do. Hence, it was not necessary for Pittsburgh Plate Glass to integrate its paint sales information and its paint production group separately from its integration of sales information about window and plate glass and its glass production group, since the sales organization could transmit product information about both from an integrated structure back to the differentiated manufacturing operations. Later, some of the separate production organizations at Pittsburgh Plate Glass developed industrial markets, and the sales organizations marketing to these customers were integrated with the manufacturing function in a divisional organization. Nevertheless, "merchandise division" sells the products of all these manufacturing divisions "to independent dealers, jobbers, distributors, and directly to small customers. Since the chemical unit sells only industrial goods, it has long been almost completely autonomous" (342).

Chandler restates his own hypothesis about the number of products as follows: "Those that sold a larger variety of *one major line* of products in much higher volume to a greater number of industries and businesses have consistently centralized the control of their activities through developing and rationalizing their functionally departmentalized structures; while only those making and selling quite *different lines* for increasingly differentiated groups of customers turned to the new multidivisional form" (343; Chandler's emphasis). Our point is to define more exactly just what makes a group of products into "one major line." In short, a group of products becomes one line when a single marketing social structure provides engineering and manufacturing with information on what characteristics help sell the products.

SOCIALLY ORGANIZED MARKET SEGMENTS CARRY DIFFERENT INFORMATION

The problem we pointed out above in our critique of Chandler's analysis of Sears's regional multifunctional divisions reappears in his chapter 7. In a number of cases regional divisions have disappeared, to be replaced sometimes by product line divisions, sometimes by centralized structures (334–335 for U.S. Steel; 341 for American Can; 348 for National Dairy Products; 354 for petroleum, ambiguously; 355–356 for Indiana Standard in particular, less ambiguously).

The basic fact here seems to be that although regional marketing systems are socially differentiated, serving different sets of customers through distinct staffs, the flows of information about product characteristics or product mix demanded are not distinct. Once one knows what the ratio of chocolate ice cream demand to vanilla ice cream demand is in one section of the country, one knows the ratio in other sections. Tin cans for tomatoes and applesauce have common characteristics, even if they are sold in different parts of the country, and milk cartons substitute for milk bottles at about the same rate in California as in New York. Only when distinct social structures carry distinct information do they have to be integrated separately with manufacturing and engineering. A difference that makes no difference is no difference. If my analysis above of whether Sears's regional divisions carry distinct information about product qualities is correct, we might expect to see the regional divisions wither away there as well.

CONSUMER PRODUCTS VERSUS INDUSTRIAL PRODUCTS

Du Pont started to differentiate its divisions when it for the first time entered the "package goods" market on a large scale, especially in paint (see above), while retaining its market for "tonnage goods," especially in explosives. Pittsburgh Plate Glass was already in the paint market, and it differentiated when various of its parts started to sell to industrial markets. The multifunctionality of Pittsburgh Plate Glass's divisions consisted in the fact that their industrial sales were administered together with their manufacturing, while their package good sales were still managed through the merchandise division. What is common to both histories is that selling to industrial markets and coordinating manufacturing with such selling is quite different from selling to consumer markets and coordinating manufacturing with that.

Part of the problem here is that the social structures that collect and aggregate information about desirable product characteristics are different for the two types of market (see above). Yet much of the problem is instead that the producing firm's job of projecting demand and the associated job of inventory control differ greatly for the two types of goods. With industrial goods, the customer typically predicts its own future demand, signs a contract for delivery in the future, and gives some warning if it is going to change that future demand. This procedure of course minimizes the inventory risk of the manufacturer. At the other extreme, the human capital resource of a regional wholesaler in a line of consumer goods is an informed projection of what will be sold in that wholesaler's area of the country; the wholesaler can then take the inventory risk involved in buying goods from the factory in hopes of a sale to local retailers. That is, the projection is not by the customer but by the seller, and the inventory risk associated with changes in demand is likewise typically borne by the seller.

There are, of course, intermediate forms. For example, building materials, though often sold to "industrial" consumers—construction firms—are not typically sold on long-term contracts signed far in advance, and so lumber yards and construction steel wholesalers carry large and risky inventories. And while Ford made the Ford dealers carry the inventory created in the depression by his continuing to produce at a higher rate than sales justified, other automobile companies took a good deal of the inventory loss themselves. Within a given industry, who does the projection, who carries the inventory risk, varies with administrative and contractual arrangements.

Nevertheless, the broad distinction is whether the buyer or the seller has to deal with the uncertainty of future demand, both in the sense of projecting that demand and in the sense of taking the risk. When selling consumer products, the manufacturer (or others on the seller's side of the market) has to do the projections and take the inventory risk itself. So manufacturers had better adjust their projection methods and their production response to fluctuations in the market—otherwise they, not the customer, will pay for projection and inventory mistakes.

The central rationalization of the information flow Chandler talks about in General Motors (146) is a set of running predictions of demand and of running corrections of those projections (projections for four months, updated and extended to a new month each month). The system of "unit control" introduced into Sears retail stores seems to have been similar, but with much-simplified projections based on recent sales (and resulting inventory changes). They had to be simplified because there were thousands of demands that had to be projected.

The pressure to form autonomous divisions tends to be higher where market knowledge derived from a large number of small flows of goods needs to be immediately translated into manufacturing and engineering decisions. This pressure is in general higher for goods in which the seller makes the projections of demand and takes the inventory risk. So in general, the integration of sales and manufacturing is higher in "package goods" than in "tonnage goods."

Where the demand is quite unpredictable at the level of the retailer or wholesaler, and so requires very rapid adjustment of product mixes and quantities (as in fashion goods in the apparel trade, novelties in dime stores, some building materials for buildings that are highly sensitive to the business cycle, and goods that are sold to secondary manufacturers in the fashion or other volatile trades, such as dyestuffs and artificial leather, information has to flow very rapidly back to the manufacturers (most of these examples come from Chandler's chapter 7; some are from Vernon 1960). No one can afford to take much inventory risk, but here, since sales are still basically from the retail inventory, the risk is on the sellers' side. The great firms whose administration Chandler studies generally stay away from these businesses, because such small flows are most efficiently managed only in entirely autonomous small and tiny firm structures, which rely a great deal on subcontracting.

Where there are large economies of scale in production, as in plate glass, or where specialized manufacturing knowledge is required, as in the manufacture of dyestuffs or artificial leather, the general rule excluding large firms sometimes breaks down. In such cases, however, sales of the specialized product has to be tightly integrated at least with manufacturing, and usually with some parts of engineering as well.

In commodity lines in which product differentiation is the basic form of competition, and consequently where small differences in the qualities of the product (real or merely advertised) can make large differences in market success, product design needs to be tightly integrated with market knowledge. In the sorts of enterprises Chandler mostly studied, product design (with attendant production-line design considerations) was in the hands of engineers. In such cases, engineers will also tend to be tightly integrated with sales (as well as with manufacturing, of course) giving rise to a typical integrated product division.

In the publishing trade, however, the relation of product design to the market is managed by authors and (especially) by acquisitions editors (Powell 1985), so it is acquisitions editors rather than engineers who tend to be tightly integrated with market information networks (often acquisitions editors are former book salespeople) and with manufacturing. There are no "engineers" designing books to integrate with marketing. Similarly, in the apparel trade the central design experts who respond to the market are artistic and style professionals, so it is they rather than engineers who are tightly integrated with market and manufacturing people in the same enterprise.

The general point, then, is that manufacturing units oriented toward retail markets and consumer goods, or other goods with a dispersed and variable market (e.g., industrial goods for agriculture or the building industry), are pushed to integrate market information into the administration of manufacturing and engineering. Hence, when incorporated into large diversified firms, they need autonomous divisions. This is more true when competition by product differentiation requires rapid shifts in design or product mixes to the latest marketing information, as for example in selling industrial goods to the apparel trades.

In particular, these sorts of retail product competition businesses cannot in general be run by an administration attuned to a market in which the customers themselves project their own demand and take the consequent inventory risks (and reduce them as best they can), as is typical in selling tonnage goods or other industrial products for concentrated manufacturing operations. If a company has manufacturing operations oriented to such industrial markets, it is very unlikely to go into consumer markets without organizing autonomous divisions to connect market information intimately with manufacturing and engineering (or the equivalent of engineering, such as acquisitions editors or dress designers).

SOURCES OF TOTAL AMOUNTS OF UNCERTAINTY IN MARKETS

The more total uncertainty there is in the markets to which a firm is oriented, the more total information has to flow to govern manufacturing quantities and product mix or to institute shifts in product characteristics. The more whatever market information there is has to be coordinated with uncertainties of other kinds in the environment of production or to meet technical changes in products or production processes, the more total information has to flow from manufacturing and engineering to the people who coordinate those two functions with market information. (If costs or technical characteristics of products are uncertain, that is in effect an uncertainty of markets: costs determine prices, and technical characteristics determine desirability.)

That is, the total uncertainty of a given market can be analyzed as in Chapter 2, when we were predicting routinization of production. We "specified four variables that produce uncertainty in a production process, and have argued that the more uncertainty there is, the less the production can be routinized, and so the less one can turn skilled work into semiskilled work by many different workers with different tasks (a 'collective skilled worker with semiskilled parts'). We have also argued that the most opportunity for routinization will exist when there is *less* uncertainty from (1) unstable markets, (2) unstable specifications, (3) unstable technologies, and (4) unstable natural conditions or unstandardized parts that affect the process of production." The same four variables should apply here to predict decentralization to divisions as are there applied to predict decentralization to skilled workers or professionals, *except* that they should be modified by the variables of linkage of manufacturing to markets, social structuring of markets, different information in different markets, and inventory risk by the sellers in the market.

In fact, we generally predicted in Chapter 2 that very high pressures for detailed response to vagaries of the market would produce so much decentralization that small firms of skilled workers would dominate a market, and there would be no decentralization of large bureaucracies to predict because there would be no large bureaucracies. Whenever large bureaucracies get into such uncertain markets, however, there would be pressure toward decentralization. Our question here is when that decentralization would tend to take the form of multidivisional organization.

The first four indicators of when firms are, according to Chandler, "in different markets" should tend to produce their effects more strongly, the more market or other uncertainty there is in a given commodity line. Chandler often talks about the degree of routinization in decision making as a determinant of how complex the coordination problem of operations is, or how complex the decisions about investment and long-run firm expansion are. Cases where he mentions routinization as a variable that depresses the tendency to form autonomous divisions include steel (337: "The selling of steel as well as the obtaining of ore and its production and fabrication still follows a fairly long-established routine pattern"); ambiguously petroleum, in its main markets (362, gasoline, fuel oil, and lubricants) and as a variable whose absence tends to increase divisionalization in the chemical industry (358–362, petrochemicals; 374–378, other chemicals); and the electrical and electronics industry (363–370).

There is also often an implicit argument in Chandler's analysis that corresponds to the argument in the Du Pont dyestuffs business, that more total uncertainty obtains in a new business (including a new business for the company), where closer coordination between marketing, manufacturing, and engineering is required than in more routine businesses. For instance, a proposal to incorporate the Stainless and Strip Steel multifunctional division into Jones & Laughlin's centralized admin-

istrative structure (333) seems to imply such a developmental routinization, after the innovation of building a stainless production and marketing operation in an autonomous division, leading to recentralization.

Multifunctional divisions responding to uncertainties of the environment rather than of the market probably include the extensive occurrence of divisions in the petroleum industry centered on regional crude
production. To produce crude, large risks have to be taken in exploration, and large investments have to be made in drilling, crude stabilizing
installations, and transportation to refineries. Both exploration and drilling involve great uncertainties about what is under the ground from
three hundred feet to as far as three to five miles down. Separate crude
production divisions are found in Jersey Standard (the Humble Oil Company, 173); in Standard Oil (Indiana) (the Stanolind group, 355); and in
Mobil (Magnolia and General Petroleum, 356).

Considerable autonomy is generally conceded to foreign raw materials–producing operations as well as to foreign marketing subsidiaries in
metals, petroleum, and some agricultural products companies. Sometimes it is not quite clear how far the presence of both marketing and
producing subparts in a foreign operations division is really an integrated
operation—sometimes, evidently, the foreign raw materials operations
also ship to the United States, and the foreign sales divisions also sell
goods produced in the United States. The uncertainty that ties separate
production and marketing organizations together administratively, then,
seems to come from the political foreignness of their common environment, rather than from the uncertainties of dedicated manufacturing
operations being tied to the uncertainties of the foreign markets they are
dedicated to.

Conclusion

The core variable to be explained in this chapter is the degree to which
the information-processing and decision-making systems in manufacturing, marketing, and engineering have to be authoritatively coordinated
by creating product-line divisions. The basic explanation has been that
when distinct market uncertainties ramify the manufacturing and engineering of distinct products, then divisionalization and decentralization
are necessary. But this statement is too vague to be of much use to a student of organizations. By reworking Chandler's data and argument, we
have tried to give a more concrete version of this explanation.

Let us start at the back end of the chapter, with the social organization
of information about market uncertainty. We argued that Chandler's im-

plicit definition of a firm as "in several distinct markets" was of distinct social structures bringing in information about market risks that affect manufacturing and engineering. Chandler's real independent variable might be conceived to be (1) the total uncertainty in a given market, including certain types of uncertainty of the environment of production and of technical change; modified by (2) a factor that describes how tied manufacturing uncertainties are to uncertainties in the market; modified by (3) the extent to which the information for adapting to the uncertainties is located in several different social organizations in the marketplace itself; modified by (4) the extent to which these different social structures actually carry different information, i.e., are not mere administrative conveniences such as regional arms responding to geographical distance; modified by (5) a factor that measures whether or not the projection of demand and the inventory risk are taken by the seller rather than the buyer in that market.

More formally,

MD = f[(total uncertainty) × (dedicated mfg. operations)
× (social segregation of markets) × (different information in
markets) × (sellers' demand projection and inventory risk)],

where MD stands for the degree of multidivisional organization, then each variable in parentheses describes a flow of commodities and is a matter of degree, varying between 0 and 1 for convenience.

This description gives concreteness to the explanatory side of the general argument. The argument now says that whenever all five of these conditions obtain to a high degree, then the information-processing task of an organization breaks into separable divisional parts. Consequently, these five conditions predict divisions with distinct authority and that such divisions will be units in the profit, investment, and performance measurement systems of the general office, in the case of multidivisional organizations, or of the stock market, in the case of divisions becoming separate firms.

Only if divisions do not become separate firms will we need to explain the existence of a general office and of "decentralization" to operating divisions. The theory of market uncertainty and market information segregation *does not* predict anything about the general office, except that if it exists it will tend to restrict itself to investment, profit assessment, and performance measurement functions, much as the stock market or investment bankers do.

In sum, the variable to be explained in Chandler's central argument, as we discussed at the beginning of this chapter, is really *centralization within product lines.* This only becomes an organizational problem when manufacturing, engineering, and marketing might not be coordinated within product lines—for example, when they are coordinated at a corporation level and the corporation is producing and marketing for several types of markets, as at Du Pont. When this is the case, internal processes may take place in the firm to produce decentralization. Information flows that focus attention, organizational theory that facilitates correct diagnosis, a structure of detachable high executives to study long-range organizational problems, a shifting committee structure allocating responsibility for solving these episodic structural problems—these are some of the conditions that facilitated such an internal evolution at Du Pont.

When the problem is instead how to manage investments centrally for a firm that is already very decentralized, as at General Motors, an evolution of more abstract information flows to a general office will tend to be instituted. We argued that the way Durant built General Motors showed that he (and General Motors as a corporation) functioned as an investment service for decentralized car parts suppliers, car assemblers, car sales finance companies, and car dealers. To continue to serve that function, Sloan (and the Du Pont financial crew who supported him) thought they had to build a system of more abstract projections to evaluate internal investments without destroying the operating efficiency of the autonomous divisions already in place.

Sears posed a still different problem for Chandler. This company was, in the mail order days, already decentralized (a "coalition of [nineteen or so] merchants") and already had a unified structure to coordinate the commodity-line "divisions." Sears's task, then, was not to build a Du Pont–General Motors–type of structure, because they already had one. Instead, it was to attach an information system that translated the behavior of store departmental (and specific commodity) inventories into information that the quantity-buyer divisional structure could use. Because Chandler misidentified the core of that structure (because in turn he was not looking very hard for the crucial links that ought to have existed, according to his own theory, between the regional divisions and the buyer divisions), he failed to interpret much of the administrative reform he reported at Sears.

His central trouble here was not applying a principle he often used in his chapter 7 analysis of manufacturing firms, having to do with whether the distinct regional markets really carried much distinct information to the manufacturing installations or buyers. Our argument here is that commodity line–supplier relations at Sears remained distinct with distinct buyers but that the regional markets by and large conveyed the same information to those buyers.

When Chandler's vague connection between ramifying market uncertainty and divisional organization is theoretically elaborated, it helps us to identify difficulties in his treatment. General Motors did not have the same reasons to develop investment expertise in the general office as Du Pont had to develop divisions. General Motors already had divisions. Sears's commodity-line divisions and general office were already in place; their regional divisions did not substantially change this structure, because they did not transmit much information that buyers needed.

What Chandler, modified, adds to our theory that formal structure is to be explained as information structures growing toward central sources of uncertainty, then, is a specification of the conditions under which operating information systems will tend to be integrated into divisions. He also gives a few hints about when investment decisions will be taken by a general office that is fed by very abstract information flows from the divisions. We have not had much success in developing a theory of why such decisions are sometimes taken by the stock market and investment bankers, sometimes by an internal corporate general office. That problem is left as an exercise for the reader.

In the next chapter we study in detail a particular kind of force that tends to produce divisionalization, namely the introduction of major product innovations. We treat this problem by analyzing how the findings of Chandler on making bureaucracies flexible fundamentally change the antibureaucratic premises on which Schumpeter (e.g., 1942) predicted that innovations would always tend to be introduced by autonomous entrepreneurs.

5 Turning Inventions into Innovations

Schumpeter's Organizational Sociology Modernized

Introduction

The general purpose of this chapter is to elaborate the fundamental distinction made by Joseph Schumpeter (1942) between invention and innovation. Since Schumpeter was interested in the transformation of the economy by the development of new technology, he was concerned only with innovations that could produce a continuous effect in the market, not with inventions that remained visions of isolated discoverers. He made the distinction between invention and innovation to distinguish those new ideas that revolutionized the economy from those that did not.

The particular lines that Schumpeter drew between inventions and innovations are not very useful in a modern economy. The basic problem is that Schumpeter thought that anything that could be done by large-scale bureaucratic organizations could be done routinely. Since (according to Schumpeter's argument) it was exactly the nonroutine character of innovations that produced the economic effects of monopoly, entrepreneurial profits, business cycles, and economic progress, this specification of the problem led him to predict the disappearance of many of the relevant economic effects as innovation became routinized (1942, 131–134). Even if innovation continues, he argued, its routinization destroys the entrepreneurial function; this destruction in turn undermines the argument in defense of capitalism that entrepreneurs are needed for economic progress (if innovation is only bureaucratic routine, then socialist governments can carry it out just as well). The routinization of innovation also means that innovations can spread rapidly in the market. This creates a lowered expectation of monopoly profits, which previously motivated excess investment in boom times and so decreases the amplitude of business cycles.

The argument below is that building a social system around an innovation is still not routine, even though it is (sometimes) done in large organizations. Not all organizations successfully innovate, but when they do monopoly profit positions and a heady flow of new investment are established, because not everybody can follow their lead. Turning inventions into innovations is difficult, because inventions need a particularly complex information and decision system connected to them to become innovations. For example, all organizations must create incentives so that workers will work hard to do what needs to be done; but creating incentives for the personnel who have to solve all the nonroutine problems of a division producing an innovation is a substantially different, and more complex, problem. Innovating workers and managers have to work into the night, go out and help the salesmen when the solder comes loose, help engineers understand marketing problems, and in general be motivated and authorized to take more responsibility than is needed or tolerable in a more routine production operation. This means that an incentive system that works fine for routinized production will not serve for producing an innovation, which in turn means that the information and decision problems for an incentive system in an innovating part of an organization will need special attention.

We have already argued that routine industrial administration is not so routine as all that (Chapter 3 above; and see Stinchcombe 1974, 3–39). Below we will argue that there are many structural impediments to be overcome in building the social organization that can carry an innovation—that can, in the phrase John R. Commons (1924) adapted from legal terminology, make the innovation into a "going concern."

In the first sections we will ask why it is that innovations create monopolies. That is, we develop variables that determine how long the monopoly created by an innovation is likely to last and, consequently, that determine the size of the economic impact. Schumpeter argued that the monopolies produced by innovation set in motion a disequilibrating cycle of profits, investment, and reestablishment of competition. Under some conditions innovations create larger and more durable monopolies than under other conditions. Longer duration and larger size of monopoly advantage both increase the incentive for introducing an innovation and increase the duration of the market's departure from competitive conditions, making the business cycle effects larger.

Many of the variables we identify have social components, or are technical and economic determinants that take social form. For example, it is quite clear that the learning curve of cost reduction after the introduction of an innovation creates a monopoly advantage for innovators, because at any given time they can expect to be further down the learning curve and so to have lower costs than potential competitors. But the actual process of cost reduction seems to be mainly one of introducing minor labor-saving and capital-saving innovations into the production process. Introducing such innovations requires not just thinking of them, but introducing them into an ongoing system of activity in which people's interests and skills are invested. Social arrangements determine whether such labor-saving innovations can be introduced easily. Consequently, the rate of "learning" of a production line has social determinants.

For another example, network relations between vendors and buyers that establish the advantages of the current vendor in some product markets have more stability if there are many reasons for the vendor to visit the buyer. In industries in which vendors visit for maintenance or to introduce innovations into the buyer's system, as frequently happens in computer systems, networks will be more stable. An innovator's market advantage partly consists of having stabilized networks that connect it to buyers. An innovator's monopoly advantage will thus tend to be longer lasting when the vendors typically provide maintenance or sell innovations on a system.

After this sociologizing of Schumpeter's basic economic observations on the relations between innovation and monopoly, we turn to sociologizing his view of entrepreneurship. The basic purpose of the middle sections of the chapter is to describe what has to be added to a technical idea in order to make it into a continuously producing going concern. To make an innovation viable, there has to be a market, as well as a social structure that can reach that market. Otherwise the innovation will not create a monopoly that will be worth anything. An investment group with control over the necessary resources has to be convinced that the innovation will work, which usually means in particular that it be convinced there is a market the innovation can reach. A manufacturing (or service producing) process has to be created that can produce the prototype of the innovation at a cost only slightly above what people will pay. This production process has to be started down the learning curve so that, to get the item's price, one need not add a profit to the cost at which the first prototype model was manufactured but instead can add a profit to a product the innovator has learned to make more cheaply. The benefits and profits have to be divided up in such a way that the people who as investors make the innovation viable feel they are sufficiently rewarded, that workers will tolerate the introduction of cost-saving improvements in manufacturing, and the like. And personnel adequate to all these purposes have to be added to the technical group from the R&D department to complete the social system for carrying the innovation.

This theory of what it takes to produce a social system that can carry the innovation, then, provides the basic outline for a theory of the social conditions of innovation in organizations. It is because that theory has so many variables, because there are so many things that can fail in the process of developing that social system, that introducing innovations is not in fact routinized even in large organizations.

In the final section of the chapter we turn to the question of administrative organization for innovation, using the theory extracted from Chandler in Chapter 4 above. The basic observation here is that innovations very often have market uncertainty that ramifies into manufacturing and engineering, and so need to have an autonomous "divisional" organization. Early in building the social system that will carry an innovation, many manufacturing adjustments have to be made in the light of market information, many engineering innovations are involved in solving the manufacturing problems of early production, and many customer service problems of the marketers require information from the engineering or manufacturing staff. Consequently, there is much interdependent uncertainty, requiring rapid information flow among the various parts of the innovation-carrying organization. This is the condition that Chandler argues requires an autonomous, fast-acting, product-oriented administration. That is, innovations must be administered with minidivisions.

But in large organizations it is difficult to create a special administration whose marketing is detached from other marketing, or whose manufacturing is not under the supervision of the vice president for manufacturing. The special reward system needed to get employees to work all night to get things going, to bet their careers on an innovation that may not pan out, is hard to justify to a personnel department trying to get uniform fair standards instituted throughout the corporation. In short, divisionalization on a large scale was not easy for the corporations Chandler studied, and it is not easy on a small scale for building up an organization to turn an invention into a going concern. As a consequence, routinization of innovation is not administratively easy, and large corporations very often fail at it.

Innovation, the Learning Curve of Cost Reduction, and Monopoly

Two main processes account for monopoly advantage: advantages in production, such as cost advantages; and advantages in the market, such as having networks in place through which firm products can be marketed. A central part of the advantages in production, as outlined first by

Schumpeter (1942, 81–106), is the temporary advantage a firm has when it has just introduced a successful innovation. An innovation monopoly advantage consists mainly of better production performance than the earliest imitators.

Let us start with the cost advantage of an innovating firm. The curves in Fig. 4 show the decline of costs with increasing numbers of units produced (the horizontal axis is the units produced by the innovator). The general pattern of decline of costs has been estimated for the production of airplanes and is known by the name "the learning curve." The basic shape is given by the fact that, for airplanes, the manufacturing cost of the second plane of a given model produced is roughly 75–80 percent of that of the first, the cost of the fourth plane is roughly 75–80 percent of that of the second, and so on, with the manufacturing cost of a unit being cut by between 20 and 25 percent each time the number of units produced is doubled. So the cost keeps going down with increasing production (or with time), but at a decreasing rate.

We have imagined that this cost curve describes the experience of the innovator and the first follower. That is, they both learn from experience in production at the same rate, so that, for example, the triangles B and C in Fig. 4 are the same shape. At the time the follower enters the market, the innovator has most of the production problems well in hand and is quite far down the learning curve. Obviously, the larger the distance A

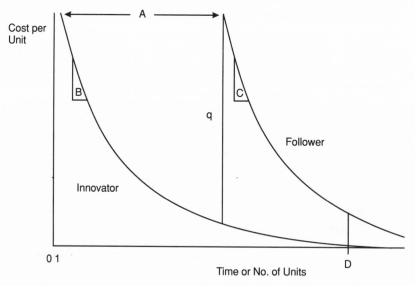

Fig. 4.   Cost Reduction Curves with Increasing Production ("Learning Curves") for an Innovator and a Follower

(the number of units the innovator has already produced before the follower gets into the market), the larger the innovator's cost advantage from learning at that time and at all succeeding times.

We might imagine that at point D, the cost advantage of the innovator over the follower is trivial, so that they are by that point truly competitive. The total size of the monopoly advantage of the innovator, then, is roughly the area bounded by the two curves and the double-headed arrow A, up to point D when the two are essentially even competitors. Between the time the innovator starts production and the time the first follower starts, any other follower may be assumed to be able to start where these two firms started, at some point on A. So up to the point of entry of the first follower, the innovator has an advantage for each unit produced, its size being measured by the distance between its own learning curve and the arrow A. When the first follower enters the market, the innovator's advantage starts to be reduced as the competitor learns to produce more cheaply than a new entrant would. The innovator's loss of advantage is progressive, because the innovator's learning goes slower after many units have been produced, allowing the follower to gain on the innovator. So the distance between the innovator curve and the arrow (before the follower enters) or the competitor curve (after follower entry) measures the cost advantage. The area between the two curves and the arrow is therefore the cost advantage multiplied by the number of units (giving total excess profit up to unit D) or by the time (giving total excess profit up to time D).

That is, if a follower were to enter the market at the same time the innovator produces its first unit, it could presumably make its own first unit at the same cost, and there would be no monopoly advantage. Both innovator and follower would go down the left-hand learning curve and would have equal costs of production. Since, however, the follower is presumed to enter later, after a period A, the innovator reaps all the advantage of learning. It can still sell in a market where a potential competitor's price would have to cover costs at the top of the curve, even though the innovator has learned to produce the product more cheaply. As the innovator comes down the left-hand curve with no follower, its cost advantage (over a fictional follower) increases from zero on the first unit to a quantity q when the follower starts. As it produces the first unit it has zero monopoly advantage; on the second it has, say, 20 percent, on the fourth 36 percent, over the fictional new entrant, and so on up to the advantage q for the $(A + 1)$ unit.

To get the total learning-curve monopoly advantage created by having no entrant up to time A, then, we need to sum up zero times the cost of the first unit, 20 percent of that cost for the second unit, 36 percent of the initial cost for the fourth, and so on, up to q for the unit produced at the time of the follower's first unit.

If we imagine a series of rectangles one unit wide, each with a length from the arrow A down to the left-hand learning curve, the advantage got from any one unit will be the area of that rectangle (the cost advantage times a width of one unit). Summing up all the rectangles for the total monopoly advantage due to the follower starting after time A will give the area between the left-hand cost curve and line q and below arrow A (which is at the level of the cost of the fictional early entrant).

Similarly, the $(A + 2)$ unit of the innovator (the first after line q), produced in competition with the *second* unit of the follower, has a markedly reduced cost advantage. The follower has cut 20 percent (say) off its costs, while the innovator is producing at a stage when it is harder to find production economies of the same size. This would be a cost advantage equal to a rectangle one unit wide and having a length equal to the distance between the two cost curves (extending just to the right of the line q). This cost advantage is fairly quickly reduced to the distance between the curves at D. By summing up the cost advantage of the innovator at each point, times the number of units to which that advantage applies, we get the area between the curves—between lines q and D—as the total monopoly advantage after the entry of the first competitor. (Complications of different rates of production at different points on the learning curve are ignored here, for the sake of simplicity. They would not change the conclusions.)

Clearly, when learning is fast, the monopoly advantage will be larger. This is shown in Fig. 5. Here we have added to Fig. 4 two learning curves with a flatter slope, one for the innovator and one for the follower. That is, if one compares triangles B and E, it takes more added units produced in triangle E to give the same amount of reduction of cost as in triangle B. Learning is slower. It might intuitively seem that the faster followers could learn, the quicker they would catch up with the innovator (one might, for example, guess that learning is very rapid in the computer industry, as competitors imitate each others' innovations quickly). But if we assume faster learning for the innovator as well as for the follower, the head start of the innovator is larger because it has been going down the learning curve faster. Another way to see this is to compare the total cost savings for the innovator up to the point F from faster learning (the area with vertical hatching) with the total cost savings for the follower to that same point (the area with horizontal hatching). If the learning curve is shallower, the total advantage of being farther along is not as great.

Obviously in either case, the longer the "lead time" between the inno-

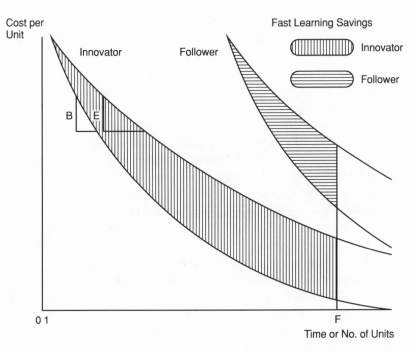

Fig. 5. Graph Showing That the Monopoly Advantage from Innovation Is Lower When the Learning Rate Is Lower

vator's introduction of the good into production and the beginning of production by the first innovator, the larger the cost advantage of the innovator at any given time and so the larger the total size of innovator advantage. Many of the proposed antitrust remedies against IBM's dominance of the mainframe market have involved demands that IBM give the technical details of an innovation in central computers to possible competitors as soon as these were released to its own peripherals and software divisions, so that at least in manufacturing peripherals and developing software the followers would have an equal start with IBM's own divisions. That is, the proposal was to reduce the distance *A* in Fig. 4 so as to reduce the monopoly advantage of IBM's software and peripherals divisions (Fishman 1981, 233–245).

Cases in Which the Follower and Innovator Have Learning Curves of Different Shape

So far we have noted that a pair of learning curves can be flatter or steeper, or closer together or farther apart on the x-axis (the axis indicating number of units produced or time spent in production). Both affect the size of the monopoly advantage, with steeper curves farther apart being advantageous to the innovator. A third difference in the relationship between the curves is that the imitator may learn faster (e.g., if imitation is not as hard as innovation, or if the imitator can hire experienced labor from the innovator, leading to a steeper learning curve). Even if the imitator approaches the learning curve of the innovator as an asymptote, never producing more cheaply than the innovator, faster learning for the follower reduces the distance between the curves and so reduces the total monopoly advantage of the innovator. Ordinarily, faster learning of the follower will eventually bring the follower to a lower overall cost of production than the innovator.

In Fig. 6, the right-hand curve is steeper than the left-hand one, so the follower curve approaches the innovator curve faster than in Figs. 4 and 5. This is shown by triangle *G*, with its shorter base, indicating that for the same amount of cut in costs (the vertical of the triangle), the follower needs to produce a smaller number of units (or a shorter amount of time has to pass). Because the follower curve approaches the innovator's curve faster, the point at which we judge the innovator advantage to be trivial comes at point *H* rather than, as before, at point *D*. Because the follower reaps cost advantages in less time, and because the follower more quickly reaches a point at which the innovator's advantage is trivial, the total area representing the excess profits of monopoly is smaller.

For example, IBM apparently learned something that was essential for success faster than Remington Rand (Univac) in the computer market, since Univac started with the innovation and IBM was a follower (Fishman 1981, 29–47). Relatively soon after IBM entered the market, however, it could compete at least equally with Univac. That is, point *H* occurred earlier than point *D* (the point of follower competitiveness with identical learning curves for follower and innovator) because of IBM's more rapid learning than Univac's.

Obviously, if some component of costs is lower for the follower—for example, a follower in Hong Kong may have cheaper labor, making its total curve lower from the beginning—the advantage of the innovator will be smaller after the competitor starts because the right-hand curve is in general shifted downward. Unless the firm with higher labor costs learns faster (it may be that innovation itself is a measure of the capacity "to learn," in the sense measured by the curves), the Hong Kong producer will eventually have lower costs than the innovator and should be able to drive the innovator from the market.

In Fig. 7, the right-hand curve starts lower than the innovator's curve did, because of the lower cost of some factor of production, though at

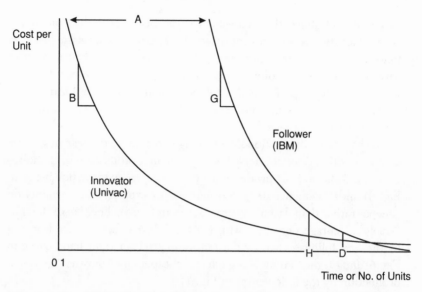

Fig. 6. The "IBM Effect": A Steeper Learning Curve by the First Follower Reduces the Monopoly Advantage of the Innovator

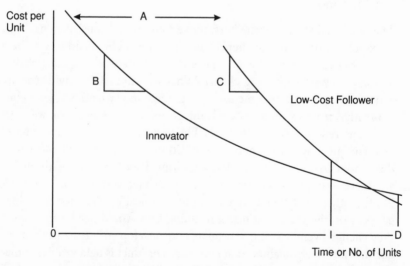

Fig. 7. The "Hong Kong Effect": A Follower with Cheaper Labor Reduces the Innovator's Monopoly Advantage, Eventually Driving the Innovator Out of the Market

first it is still above the innovator's curve because production in the cheaper location is not yet routinized. As experience moves the low-cost follower along the learning curve, it becomes essentially competitive with the innovator at point *I*, rather than at point *D* as before. Further, with increasing experience the follower in the low-cost location has lower costs than the innovator, eventually perhaps driving the innovator from the market it created.

So the size of the monopoly advantage created by the learning curve increases with: (1) longer delay between the first production of the innovation and the start of production by the first competitor (longer *A* in Fig. 4) and (2) steeper decline of costs with experience in production (steeper rather than flatter learning curves in Fig. 5). The size of the monopoly advantage decreases with (3) the "IBM effect," faster learning by the first follower than by the innovator (steeper right hand curve in Fig. 6) and (4) the "Hong Kong effect," cheaper labor or other factors of production by the follower (as in Fig. 7).

Innovation, the Marketing Network, and Monopoly

The *market* advantage of the "first mover" in general consists in having a more solid relation to the client than latecomers. One main way to be a first mover is, of course, by innovating, but there are others (e.g., getting the first contract with a big client). What we want to do now is specify what determines whether a contact in the marketplace is solid (and consequently creates a monopoly advantage for a first mover) or weak (is easily entered into by competitors). The network advantages that tend to maintain an innovator's monopoly position take three main forms: (1) the vendor in place may develop a multiplicity of contacts with clients and serve multiple functions for them, with each such contact reinforcing the others; (2) clients may become technically or economically dependent on the vendor in place, meaning they would pay heavy costs if they changed vendors; and (3) clients may develop such trust in the vendor that information about that company's product is believed while that about a competitor's product is received with suspicion.

The multiplicity of contacts between vendors and clients is increased when the client depends on the vendor for maintenance, for a flow of technical innovations adapted to the installed system, or when the client is involved in continuous buying (including when the equipment is leased from the vendor rather than bought). The responsibility of the vendor for maintenance builds the vendor into the technical system of production, so that day-to-day operations of the client require continuous interaction with the vendor. This provides many opportunities for the vendor to find out what the client needs and to give advice about how the vendor can satisfy that need, to exchange information informally about the economic relation and about sources of client dissatisfaction, and otherwise to support the capacity of the vendor to sell the next installation.

The "maintenance" relation established in the computer industry involves not only maintenance, but also access to a continuing supply of technical innovations. When one leases software from a vendor, one ordinarily gets the rights (without cost) to improvements in the system. Similarly, in the days when clients typically leased the machines, technical improvements in the hardware were often installed free of charge. But whether they are free of charge or not, innovations developed for software or hardware around which the client's operations are already built are more useful to the client than are random innovations. IBM's advantage over other mainframe computer manufacturers in selling peripherals was that any peripheral adapted to an IBM machine had a larger market than peripherals adapted to any other machine; their advantage over the plug-compatible manufacturers was that they could earlier and better adapt their improvements to their own systems, as well as make the systems harder for peripherals manufacturers to plug into.

When the client is buying a continuing stream of goods (as when an assembler buys from parts manufacturers) or a continuing stream of services (as when the client leases a building or a computer), continuity of supply is an important consideration. If the present supplier provides continuity, while changing suppliers would create an interruption, then the present supplier has an advantage. Further, the continuous flow of goods tends to be accompanied by a continuous flow of information, giving the vendor an information advantage in future sales. The vendor can in extreme cases make what Oliver Williamson calls "transaction specific investments," which are especially adapted to efficient and satisfactory delivery of what the client wants. A common case is remodeling by the landlord in a leased building, but transaction-specific investments may involve innovations made especially for a client, such as modifications on software for a specific client application.

The technical and economic dependence of clients on the vendor is increased when clients' operations are adapted to specific features of the product, such that they would have to reorganize many of their routines in order to go over to a competitor. For example, as long as the only people who use the computer are in the computer center, the costs of going over to a competitor system tend to be small. But when many people in the accounting department use a particular software program for invoicing, accounts payable, and so on, it can be very expensive to go over to a slightly superior or slightly cheaper competitive software system. Since software itself often depends on the hardware, it is often the case that building software into an organization's routines makes the organization technically dependent on the hardware as well.

One of the most common forms of technical and economic dependence is moving costs in real estate relations. Because it would cost us a good deal in time and effort, and often a good deal of money as well, we do not easily choose to move to gain small advantages in the real estate market. The costs of moving are even more substantial for a business, for it must move a social system with recalcitrant parts. (Moving a clientele is often extremely difficult; cf., on moving a labor force, Mann 1973.) There are often similar costs in changing equipment. For example, IBM for a number of years simultaneously rented two functionally equivalent memory systems, the "Mallard" and an older one, with the latter costing more per unit of performance. Although clients renting the older, more expensive system were free to change and save money, many kept it simply because finding out about the new one or moving the old one out would have been too much of a disruption (Fishman 1981, 235). If such moving costs are required when switching vendors, the first vendor in the market has a monopoly advantage in the amount of the moving costs, whether it got its first mover advantages from innovation or not.

Economic dependence can take the form of special credit arrangements with the current vendor. Because the current vendor may enjoy an information advantage, it may be willing to give credit when other vendors would not. Or the vendor may have got inadvertently into an exposed credit position with a client which another vendor would not rationally get into. Nevertheless, the client now depends on the vendor.

An obvious source of stability in vendor-client relations is mutual buying. IBM, of course, buys a great many telephone services, and arranges for its clients to buy many more. Bell was IBM's largest customer for computers when it was a single system, though this relation has been somewhat undermined by Bell's breakup. If either company is being difficult in its buying behavior (e.g., threatening to go over to competitors), it may face the sanction of the other being difficult in *its*.

In continuing client-vendor relations, trust grows out of a history of trustworthy behavior. In many cases the trustworthy behavior is making the system in which the product functions run, which may mean getting the bugs out of that system (e.g., out of the interfaces between the vendor's machine and the rest of the production line). Clearly, the vendor already on the scene has an advantage in having got the bugs out and is more likely to be able to deliver adequate system performance than another vendor. The long-run delivery of such adequate bug-free performance (or minor-bugs-rapidly-fixed performance) creates an atmosphere of trust.

In addition, the vendor's representatives can deliver information useful to the client on the vendor's own probable future behavior (e.g., products coming out, early warning of delays in release of those products), on its financial situation, on who to call to get action in the maintenance department, and the like, which may not improve the vendor's behavior but at least renders it more predictable by the client. Insofar as trust is based on predictability, it will tend to grow in an information-rich relationship with the current vendor rather than in a new relationship.

Further, because the vendor on the scene is in a continuing relationship itself, its own behavior will in general be more trustworthy. One is less likely to imagine that a continuing relationship can be maintained by lying to one's clients than one is to imagine that one can sell for the first time by misrepresentation. The client may be able to use continuing small sanctions on the vendor to improve its performance, and so to make the vendor in fact more trustworthy (Rogers and Larson 1984).

The sum of these advantages in creating trust results, for example, in managers of a company or university computer center using as a clinching argument a phrase like "I feel comfortable with IBM."

It is important to remember that one can destroy one's own advantages. Apparently Univac sent out engineers to maintain its machines—engineers perhaps too honest about Univac's problems. IBM sent maintenance people supervised by marketing specialists, who, whatever their other disadvantages as maintenance supervisors, were not excessively honest about technical details they did not know (Fishman 1981, 38, 44).

Thus one would predict that the more the vendor-client relationships in a market involve a multiplicity of contacts, technical or economic dependence of the client on the vendor, and developed trust between the client and the vendor, the greater the innovator's monopoly advantage in that market would be. The argument to this point has been that the monopoly advantage of an innovator is also a social system advantage. To gain and preserve a monopoly advantage by being farther down the learning curve, an innovator must first build, then constantly improve, a production social system. To gain a monopoly advantage in marketing, an innovator must build and solidify ties with clients as the first vendor in the market. The next section specifies what kinds of information-processing and decision-making structures it takes to create social systems that can exploit an invention by building and maintaining such monopoly advantages.

The Theory or Doctrine of an Innovation

In this section we hope to describe what sort of a social system an "innovation" is. Schumpeter (1942) is very clear that an "innovation" with a potential economic impact is quite different from an "invention" that might be patented. In the first place, a number of things that cannot be patented are innovations, such as the marketing in the big Eastern cities of lettuce from irrigated desert farms by packing it in ice and getting through service on the trains. In the second place, an innovation is what John R. Commons (1924, 143–213) has analyzed as a "going concern"; that is, it is a social system that can in fact regularly produce and market the innovation.

An innovation, then, is the unit of analysis, and we are talking about things like introducing word processors into an office, bringing out a new computer (Kidder 1981), designing and building a wide-body passenger airplane (Newhouse 1982), developing hybrid seed-corn (Grilliches 1957), and introducing multidivisional administrative structures (Chandler 1962). I have written elsewhere about some of the variables describing administrative innovations, whose essence is social, which determine how much opposition they are likely to meet (Stinchcombe 1986b), such as whether they involve the redistribution of status symbols. These variables described innovations by variations in the impact those innovations had on the interests embedded in the old regime, and consequently predicted whether or not they would be adopted at all. But here we want to describe what kind of social system it takes to make innovations that have already got past this adoption barrier into going concerns.

Obviously, the social systems created to administer an innovation differ a lot in size and complexity. When IBM embeds a number of improvements in a new board to slip into an old machine, they are very careful to design that board so that it interfaces with the rest of the machine and with the software having the same structure, so that the maintenance workers can just haul out the old one and put in the new one, and the users do not have to change a single line of code in their programs, appoint or fire anyone, change any human routines, or learn anything new. The innovation requires some modification of *IBM's* system, but nothing from the user. This is an innovation where the client's adaptation involves only lower costs and fewer mistakes, and it has already been paid for (in the old days, at least) in the maintenance contract that went with the lease. For the replacement board, the value of all the variables we describe below—what one has to do to make the social system attached to the innovation go—is very near to zero for the user; very little social system with this innovation needs to be made to go. So what we will try to describe with the variables below is a series of ways that innovations can depart socially from this ideal-type of an innovation with zero social system requirement, the replacement board.

I will organize the description of the social requirements of an innovation around six elements. Since a proposal to institute an innovation (or to implement a decision to introduce an innovation) must have a theory of the social requirements of the going concern, or be forced to develop one as it goes along, I will call each of these elements a *theory* of the social requirements in question. I have previously used many of these ideas to describe the theory one has to have to create an organization (Stinchcombe 1973). Here I use the same approach to describe the elements that must go into a theory of an innovation for that theory to be sufficient to build a going concern that can create and maintain a monopoly advantage. The complete theory of an innovation, then, requires the following elements:

> 1. A *core theory* of the innovation, of what is centrally involved technically in the design of the innovation, and a corresponding *theory group* (sometimes a "group" of one) that develops and defends this core theory
> 2. The theory of the *investment* in the innovation (and the risks and profits theory that justifies it), and the *investment group* responsible for collecting, safeguarding, and spending the money or other resources
> 3. The *technical-costs* part of the theory of the innovation, which is about what it will take to produce the innovation and what that will cost, and a corresponding *engineering* or other *technical-costs controlling group* that designs the technical productive system
> 4. The *market* or *benefits* part of the theory, about who wants the good or the effects produced by the technical-costs part, what price will they pay for the benefits, how the organization can reach those who want the benefits, and the concrete sales apparatus or clientele networks that the organization needs to build up for these
> 5. The *division-of-benefits* part of the theory, about what promises of future profits or interest payments can motivate the investor group, and about how benefits are to be distributed so as to provide careers for motivation of personnel
> 6. The *personnel* part of the theory, and in particular

answers to the problems of competence of personnel, trustworthiness of personnel, motivation of personnel, and the arrangements for the corresponding personnel flows.

A "Zero Resources Innovation" Described in Detail

Let us describe briefly how these elements enter into our "zero innovation" of the improved slip-in board, but now looking at it from the point of view of IBM, for which this is a "small" rather than a zero innovation. (The details of the following picture come mostly from Fishman 1981, 51–151, 379–411.)

1. The core theory involved in a replacement board is built up out of a series of maintenance problems brought in by service personnel, special fixes in the operating system to get around a limitation in the old board collected from folks who consult on software (some even from IBM's plug-compatible competitors), and perhaps some engineering innovations that came after the original design. There will be a small group of engineers and others who collect these, look them over, design modifications in the board, test them to make sure the "interfaces" are the same and that new bugs are not built in. That is, there is a flow of detailed information about problems with the old board flowing to a group dedicated to improvements of the design of the hardware, a "theory improvement" group.

2. The "investor group" is of course ultimately IBM stockholders, who allow IBM to retain earnings to invest at IBM's internal rate of return. More immediately, the group within IBM responsible for the system will have allocated such "upgrading investment" funds as part of their normal budget, probably financed out of returns from the particular machine being upgraded. IBM does this because they know that one main thing users buy is the reliable operation of the system, which is why IBM sells maintenance contracts. (When technical change is as fast as in the computer industry clients cannot provide reliable maintenance for themselves; see Stinchcombe and Heimer 1988.) A system executive committee of some sort will invest in the upgrading.

3. The technical-costs part of the theory is an engineering *cum* software theory about how the various glitches can be alleviated by rewiring the board.

4. The market theory of IBM has changed over time, especially in response to antitrust suits. The basic IBM market philosophy is that a cus-

tomer buys the service of a computer system, not the hardware. For a long time they would not even sell the client the hardware. Originally the client bought (i.e., rented) the system package, which included the maintenance agreement (which included the upgrading). Part of the system package was general access to all sorts of technical innovations—that is, the client bought a flow of improvements as well as the latest system. Much of IBM's advantage in the market consisted of the faith (assiduously maintained by the marketing person in charge of the account) that an IBM user would not be trapped with a big investment in an obsolete machine.

A second part of the market theory is that *if* IBM makes clients rewrite their software and reorganize their data-processing department when IBM introduces an innovation, *that* is the time they will go over to Control Data or DEC or some other company. So the interface stability criterion for the new board is part of the IBM market theory.

5. The central part of IBM's division-of-benefits theory is that 20–30 percent is a reasonable expected return on an investment. A second is that the company should not lay anybody off—the worker has a job at IBM regardless of business conditions. Market uncertainty is to a large degree put off onto the suppliers; when demand goes down, IBM is likely to start manufacturing parts that it once bought from suppliers, in order to keep its own workers busy (on this strategy in general, see Sabel 1982, 47–56). Related to the security of employment, however, is the practice of demotion. While employees are more or less guaranteed a job, they are not guaranteed the job they have now or one at the same rank (Goldner 1965).

A third part is market criteria dominance in IBM's reward system. At IBM, marketing dominates over engineering much more than at Data General (Kidder 1981). People get rewarded in IBM if their product does well in the market, not if it is only technically superior. The division of benefits is then made up of administration and profit criteria and career-structure rules that are traditional at IBM.

6. The personnel part of the theory at IBM is embedded in the company's general personnel system, by which people's careers organizationally depend on satisfying the users of the systems they sell. So the engineers in IBM will be part of a group dominated by the contact people who service the big users. The contact people, not the engineers, will be close to the managers for the system involved. In IBM the engineers are closely controlled so they give the users what they want, not merely a state-of-the-art product. These engineers, even more than other IBM engineers, are dominated by market people, whose big aim is

to hold customers. Bell, for example, in going competitive has imported a lot of IBM marketing people, modeled their new marketing departments on the IBM marketing structure (IBM has systems people responsive to marketing people, who are divided according to type of customer and type of system). Obviously, the personnel *also* have to understand electrical engineering, some computation theory, and so on.

Overall, then, this innovation process makes use of parts of IBM's general structure, which is set up to introduce client-serving innovations on a regular basis.

The Multidivisional Structure of Chandler as an Innovation

Let us now go through these elements with Chandler's innovation (1962), the multidivisional structure.

1. We note Chandler's comment about the innovations coming faster *if* people took time off from operational tasks to study organization, *if* they had a general tradition of organizational thinking, and *if* an engineering-rationalizing tradition dominated the organization. These are characteristics of a "theory group" that is likely to develop the sort of theory involved in an organizational innovation. But we also note that the problems could be misdiagnosed if a company had experts from outside without access to the details of the problems.

In general, though, adaptive response—or "muddling through"—was a main way of developing a theory of the new situation. For example, if Du Pont executives theorized too much about organization in the abstract, they tended to come up with the traditional theoretically optimal solution according to the organizational theory of the time, namely centralized, departmentally specialized administration. Chandler argues that a theory group with a decentralizing innovation was less likely to develop among older executives and more likely to form among younger executives (which means people about forty to fifty years old, apparently), and it was less likely to form when the organizational arrangements were strongly determined by family ties (though Pierre du Pont and Henry Ford II were leading advocates of the decentralized system).

2. "Investment" for administrative reform has to be the time and attention of authoritative people. Only a few managers are inclined to be reflective, to develop a theory. Sloan was very unusual in this respect. Top managers in general like to live in a bustle of activity, to be on the phone, to pay no more than five minutes' attention to a given subject (Mintzberg 1973). So it is not an easy thing to develop an "investment group" when the time of top administrators is the investment required.

3. The technical-costs theory has to break down the idea that minimizing administrative costs is the most efficient approach and also that part-time generalists (the "cabinet ministers" system) are good enough for strategic management. In Chandler's analysis, generalists who also had operating responsibility, especially responsibility for a functional department that was likely to develop goals of its own and a distinctive worldview, were not sufficiently attentive to general problems. Generalists with specialized responsibilities were less likely to depend only on market forecasts and an analysis of the distinctive competence of the organization and less likely to invest without fear or favor in different company activities; instead they tended to favor investments in more of their own specialty. Operative executives, too, were generally likely to invest more money in trying to solve their problems, rather than deciding that their area of operations was so full of problems that it ought to be scuttled.

Further on in the technical theory of the innovation the innovators had to decide what sort of abstraction techniques *could* be built into the information system so that the general office would not find the general contours of the strategic problems buried in a mass of operative detail. A crucial intellectual innovation in all this was to see that committees of generalists are good for making some kinds of ("strategic") decisions, while individuals (with advice from committees subordinate to them) are better for making operational ("routine") decisions. Different kinds of decisions required different administrative structures.

The technical-costs theory described by Chandler was embedded in many details about how particular decisions are to be made, what information about the basis and quality of decisions goes on to the general office, what controls the general office puts on those decisions, and so on. In short, as a theory, administrative decentralization was pretty helter-skelter, which is why Chandler had such a hard time explaining exactly what it was.

4. In Chandler's description, the benefits of the innovation were supposed to go ultimately to the stockholders. What the stockholders supposedly wanted was managerial control of investment in the activities of the corporation's subsidiaries by the criterion of long-run profits. Ultimately the innovators had to sell the active part of the board of directors—that is, the active top managers—that the benefits would show up in long-run profitability. The market for the innovation was, thus, internal to the company.

5. The benefits of innovation mostly went into the pot of general corporation profits. There may have been career benefits, such as becoming general officers or having full charge of a division, but Chandler does not

discuss this. Sloan has endowed many programs in business schools, so he must have got something out of his work of introducing the innovation at General Motors.

6. The main personnel part of the theory of administrative decentralization had to do with the full-time dedication of central office people to central office problems. The comparable thing in government is the relative role of the White House staff, especially the Office of Management and Budget (playing the role of the general office) versus the cabinet. If we imagine putting the White House staff *on top of* the cabinet, we have the personnel arrangement that Chandler saw as central to the innovation he was describing: a full-time top staff with general and abstract responsibilities supervising a group of heads of operative units. In general, the hierarchical superiority of the central office tends to lead to "problems of subordinates" gobbling up the superiors' time (see Stinchcombe 1974, 81–90). This had to be avoided by limiting communication between the general office and the divisions to general matters.

To put it another way, the innovation theory has to figure out how to make a hierarchical superior in the general office into a "staff" advisor on the implications of strategic policies on operative decisions, rather than a "line" executive. It involves having technical executives in the general office make reports to a committee, rather than making decisions. The crucial personnel question, then, was to create "general officers." The companies Chandler analyzed already had experience producing operative executives, so that was not a new personnel question.

Social Predictors of Success in Introducing Innovations

The basic point of the preceding sections is that if we want to describe an innovation in social terms, so as to bring sociological insights to bear on what happens to it, we can use this simple six-point outline (theory, investment, technical costs, marketing, division of benefits, and personnel) for descriptive purposes. We will next specify some variables that make it difficult to introduce an innovation. Obviously this bears directly on the question of monopoly, because the longer a successful innovator has the innovation while its competitors scramble to build the social system needed to carry it, the larger the monopoly advantage of the innovator will be. As preparation for this task, let us briefly reconceive the requirements of making an invention into a going concern as a set of information and decision requirements.

The first requirement is that the information system be set up so as to receive the information that needs to be processed in all six areas. The most common way this fails is to have engineers or inventors build a system that is equipped only to make technical decisions. That is, information leading to sensible investment, marketing, production management, division of benefits, and personnel decisions is not incorporated into the plan of the innovation, so these decisions get made by default. We will call the failure to satisfy this requirement "technological utopianism" below.

The social origin of this deformation of an information and decision system for producing an innovation is that one needs the invention first. The social requirements for producing an invention do not in general lead to a theory adequate to produce an innovation, because the theory built by inventors does not create a structure that allows social information to get through. If the inventing group were good at processing social information and making social decisions, they would likely be managers instead of inventors.

That is, the variable we will be describing as "technological utopianism" describes a specific common type of inadequacy of the information and decision system: confinement to technical matters and to administrative structures useful for getting the right technical answer. This deformation is particularly likely to happen in a part of an organization dedicated to introducing an innovation, precisely because innovations tend to start with inventions. It is a deformation because a theory adequate to describe an invention will not produce an information and decision system adequate to introduce an innovation.

In the following sections we will develop a theory of the information and decision difficulties that inventions get into, by discussing the information requirements of each part of the necessary social structure and the information problems they are likely to create by ignoring the requirements of the rest of the going concern being built.

Technological Utopianism

The basic argument of this section is that a common feature of *theories* of innovations is that they are seriously incomplete about what it will take to make the innovation a going concern. Let me illustrate this by giving a somewhat idiosyncratic reading of Engels's *Socialism, Utopian and Scientific* ([1882] 1935). The main thesis of that work, as I see it, is that the utopian socialists want to give a theory of how society might be organized better; Saint-Simon, for example, had scientists running everything. The utopians think of the process of introducing socialism as basically one of teaching people the advantages of socialism, whereupon, being convinced, they will institute it. But Engels says a "scientific" socialism has to specify the social forces that will bring this ideal state into being: specifically, the proletariat, subject to oppression in a capitalist market, and class conflict as a way to organize this group into a political force. That is, Engels's argument involves a theory of what the social system has to be to make it a likely carrier of an innovation like socialism. And that theory does not look like schoolteachers giving lectures from socialist texts.

The big first variable about theories involved in innovations, then, is "technological utopianism," by which we mean the degree to which the theory is merely describing the technical way to achieve some end, with no analysis of the social and economic forces needed to bring the innovation into being. A very good example is Apple's scheme a few years back to give one computer to each of one hundred thousand schools. It is not quite, but almost, fair to say that the scheme said nothing about how six hundred children in a school were going to practice using one computer, how teachers were going to plan their science or mathematics or writing curricula around it, how the teachers themselves would learn how to do it, who would pay the costs of their training, which children would be able to do their homework on a computer at home, what it means to have an academic training program that cannot have homework, and so on. There was, in short, no analysis of the investment and investor group, the benefits and who gets them, the training and motivation of the personnel, how the social system relates to who gets promoted in the schools, and so on. It was a very utopian theory, worthy of Saint-Simon or Fourier. Of course, if it was not intended to be a theory of an innovation, but merely a way of distributing samples to schools for advertising purposes, then the technological utopianism of the theory behind it was perhaps not a business disadvantage—merely a disadvantage for the adopting school.

A good many technologically utopian theories like this can be found in education, ones not based at all in the realities of thirty children in a room six hours a day for 180 days with one teacher (or five teachers one at a time) and no money for extras. People proposing innovations in education rarely say how many minutes their innovation should take, whether the time should come from the time now spent on arithmetic, reading, social science, or whatever. They are often utopian in the even narrower sense of not even having a technology for how to do it and when. When social scientists interview teachers about why they did not follow up on some jazzy program, the most common response is that after they got their enthusiasm up, nobody told them how to institute it concretely. So the educational theories tend to go skating over the surface of the schools, earning education professors lecture fees (small ones) and ending up being entertainment for teachers who get an hour off to go hear them.

The social significance of utopian theorizing is, first of all, that the computer sits in a closet or the reform movement disappears without a trace. The first consequence, then, is failure of the innovation to be truly introduced. It remains a technological utopia, without social flesh.

A second consequence is that *if* the technical solution is a real advantage but is nevertheless embedded in a technologically utopian scheme for bringing it to reality, there tends to be a long period of thrashing about until a viable social vehicle for it is found (a good description of such thrashing about, which has informed the discussion here, is Smelser 1959, 50–179; see also Hirschman 1963, 12–91). In such situations the innovation in a particular organization often depends on some enthusiast working eighty hours a week to put together the pieces to make the innovation go. For all innovations there is a long period of "social debugging" of the scheme for the innovation, with someone needed to carry the scheme through when unexpected difficulties (mostly market, personnel, division-of-benefits, and investment difficulties) arise and when the benefits of the technical innovation are delayed.

But there is more muddle in the muddling through for innovations introduced with utopian theories. If the plan has not specified the social forces needed to bring the going concern into being or described the market and who benefits from the innovation, how to divide the benefits that return to the organization, or who invests how much and why they do it, or the training and motivation of personnel, or the measures of success to be used, then the organization has only a "neural itch" of an innovation, not a theory.

One generalization in this field comes from Karl Mannheim, in a great book, *Ideology and Utopia* (1929, 117–122, 211–219, 229–239). The basic argument of that book is that theories of activities already embedded in ongoing practices tend to be disintegrated theories about how to solve particular problems, emphasizing the wisdom of institutions and the value of experience, with no overall scheme of how the whole thing works. Theories associated with movements for innovation ("utopias"), in contrast, tend to cover great areas of social life with one simple theory, one master mechanism to drive it all, involving a cataclysmic crisis or revolution that will quickly create a new society that runs on different principles, with no hard work of building that society up piece by piece involved.

To put it another way, the conservatives (he calls them "ideologists") typically believe that no reform can ever work because it would upset all the specific solutions we have worked out to deal with the various problems of coping with human nature, while the utopians or radical reformers typically believe there is no work to do after the revolution, that things will all fall into place. If one takes the advice of checking out the theory of the innovation implicit in the above analysis, and asks the reformer about who benefits, how much it all costs and who pays, who is going to run it and how we can arrange things so that we can trust them, one is likely to be ranged on the side of the conservatives, the "ideologists." Obviously Engels did not think he was a conservative, but the anarchists and other types of utopians did.

So our first big social variable about a prospective innovation is "utopian versus scientific," the degree to which the social structure necessary to bring the innovation into being is analyzed in the theory.

Investment Approval

In general, an "investment group" is a set of people who have to believe in the innovation enough to decide to put money and time into it. The first variable describing investment is the relation between authority to invest in an innovation and authority to keep running the routines. The core variable is how much harder it is to get authority to innovate than to get authority to keep going. To be sure, the ultimate source of money may not be the group that controls its investment, for instance the stockholders, who never hear of the innovation until it has either succeeded or failed. But the yearly report of the corporation and whatever appears in *Business Week* or the *Wall Street Journal* have to be convincing to the stockholders, even though the power to invest has been delegated to a set of managers.

An analysis more detailed than the one that may appear in the annual report has to be approved by a management committee high in the hierarchy, a strategic management group. Sometimes the plan for the innovation must go outside, as when the airline that is going to buy the new airplane has to approve the manufacturer's plans and to promise to buy a certain number before the manufacturer can borrow money to make them (Newhouse 1982).

Often even quite small innovations involving "capital expenditures" have to go much higher in the organization than does approval of how to spend already budgeted resources. For example, a manager who controls ten thousand dollars worth of labor *per day* (in 1989 that might be roughly one hundred factory workers) may have to go to a higher-management committee for all capital expenditures over, say, five thousand dollars. The higher management have already said they believe in the theory that explains how the ten thousand dollars per day is spent, but not the theory for new capital above five thousand. In the civil service or a university, the control is often much more minute, so a person with subordinates worth ten thousand dollars per day (somewhat fewer than one hundred because civil servants and professors are more expensive than factory workers) may have to ask for approval by line item of all capital expenditures whatever.

In a certain sense, then, investment groups are ideological groups. The reason nonprofits often have tighter investment controls is that almost everything they do is ideological, so nearly all expenditures are "investments." One has to believe in a university before one will invest money in it, even as a client, because one is not buying a well-specified good. New research projects (presumably all innovations) whose total budget will amount to less than a year's salary plus overhead of a leading professor may be reviewed by several levels within the university before going to be reviewed by a body of peers at the National Science Foundation (NSF), while decisions to renew the contract for that leading professor for another year are not ordinarily reviewed at all, or only reviewed if he or she gets an offer from another university. But when businesses are making investments, they conduct themselves much more like nonprofit organizations and universities, with endless committees and discussions among high-level executives about small expenditures.

The general point is that a clear functional distinction is made even at the lowest hierarchical levels between "operational" and "strategic" decisions, with the strategic decisions getting kicked upstairs, and innovations are almost always considered strategic if they involve any substantial capital investment at all. The approval of investments in innovations usually takes place in a committee-type decision-making structure. People ask whether they believe the theory involved in the innovation enough to put some freely disposable resources into it, resources not already committed to running the operations on which there is already consensus. The formation of beliefs in a theory quite generally goes on more in discussion groups ("congregations") than in an individual mind as a person reads a memo on the innovation.

A second variable in the investment process is the relation between the theory group and the investment group. Ordinarily, an investment group will require more in a theory than a technological utopia. Suppose we examine the difference between an NSF proposal (addressed to an "investment group") and a seminar paper delivered early on in a line of scientific work. The seminar paper is *supposed* to be a technical utopia, outlining the possibilities of a line of work in a way not much constrained by practical realities of money and time. The NSF proposal, in contrast, will have (1) a specific description of activities proposed (though the concreteness will be to some extent specious, and NSF specifically provides that within reasonable limits researchers do not have to pursue a line of activities that turns out not to be productive, but can invest the resources in another that appears more promising); (2) a budget; (3) a set of vitas of the people in charge; and (4) a statement of how this research will advance the science. The proposal is in a sense a routine extension of the technological utopia presented in the seminar paper into a theory of the social system that will accomplish this utopia, what its benefits will be, and so on. The additions are sometimes called "boilerplate" in the survey research business, are quite often already in standard files in the word processor, and are very often written or calculated primarily by administrative rather than technical personnel. In general there will be a conflict in points of view between a technical theory group and the business group that makes the investment decision, a technical-business conflict (Veblen 1919 makes this conflict central to modern capitalism) about adding to the technical theory enough social (especially financial and market) information so that the investors can judge the viability of the innovation *as a social system*. The technical group will often resist doing so much "irrelevant" work on the details of administration and finance.

A third general variable in the investment process is that investment groups have to trust each other with large quantities of money or other resources. There is a strong tendency for people to trust only those others whose behavior they understand well—people of the same culture, often the same people they see socially (Kanter 1977, 47–63). If one knows seven of a person's friends, one knows whether he or she plays the horses too much or likes women or men who are too expensive for his or her personal income.

One consequence is that people of different cultural backgrounds (for example, blacks, women, or foreigners) may have a harder time breaking into an investment group than into a technical theory group (see Stinchcombe 1986b, 255–264). There may be women executives at the middle levels (e.g., department heads and buyers in a department store) long before there are women at the top investment levels. There may be women selling houses long before there are women selling industrial real estate, because the industrial real estate broker is a central participant in an investment group. There may be minority groups in a country (for example, Chinese in Southeast Asia) who control most of the country's business because they trust each other enough to carry out the investments but do not trust members of the majority (for example, Malays). Social distance between the innovator group and the investor group reduces the likelihood that the innovation will be carried out, because it undermines the process of convincing the investment group of the theory of the innovation.

A big variable among investment groups is whether they are already a part of an organization (in the case of the IBM board, for example, the investment group is an integral part of the IBM organizational structure) or whether they have to be assembled from scratch to start a new company. The crucial people in the first case are decision-making executives, usually acting in a committee. The crucial people in the second case are *brokers*, who go around from one to another investor or approval body with a partially worked out investment coalition and persuade one after another to come in until the coalition is complete (cf. Banfield 1961). If a structure with money available for investment already approves of an innovation, it is ordinarily easier to bring the innovation into being. On the other hand, if the distance one has to go in the internal structure of the organization before reaching those with authority to invest is too long, then assembly of *new* enterprises, with short distances between investors and innovators, may work better.

Cost Reduction and Manufacturing Improvements

Let us now turn to the creation of a technical system to carry out the job of introducing an innovation—the process of coming down the learning curve. As we have already discussed, a crucial thing that creates a monopoly position from an innovation is being ahead of other firms on the learning curve. "Learning" here is the process of developing routines; of using cost statistics and other knowledge derived from experience to improve the efficiency of a productive system; of setting up incentives and social mechanisms so that workers who figure out a faster way of doing the work will let the company know about it (quality control circles as discussed by Cole and Siegel 1979, 134–155, 160–168, 202–211, 222–223; the idea that worker cooperation in technical improvements is more crucial for workers in pilot plants is suggested in Whyte 1961, 198–217); of making opportunistic improvements in capital equipment when it is down for repair (see Stinchcombe 1974, 3–41, for a series of managerial strategies used in a steel rolling mill to reduce down time). That is, learning as described in the learning curve is a set of innovations associated with the initial product innovation that improve the efficiency with which the innovation itself can be produced.

This translation of theories into technical action may show the technical-costs theories on which the innovation is based to be mistaken. The engineering theories that allow people to estimate the net benefits of an innovation by estimating its costs are very unreliable, especially when the innovation itself is more fundamental. The theories may, for example, be false or radically incomplete only in a specific environment, as I illustrated earlier in discussing Granick's book on the Soviet Union (Granick 1967, 161–164): a mass production theory of machine assembly lines depends on being in an environment that can standardize parts. If a company's parts suppliers do not have adequate quality control, the company cannot run an assembly plant, but instead needs assembly craftsmen or craftswomen with files and calipers to make the pieces of the machine fit together.

The bugs in engineering theories are often in the details, as when a machine tool that is supposed to work to the nearest thousandth in fact works to the nearest two thousandths, or when the clay that looks solid turns to jelly if it gets too wet (and so causes an earth dam to come sliding down the valley). Generally, though, the theory is likely not to work quite right at first not because crucial details were wrong, but because they were simply left out.

A big first variable that causes variation in turning technical theories into production systems is the *engineering adequacy* of the theory—its truth and completeness, how many bugs it has in it. Obviously, then, the speed with which the theory improves and the adequacy of feedback about mistakes are crucial as well.

This brings up a second feature of the whole startup process. The engineers and factory managers for an innovation need to be got down into the shop looking at the details. But this means that production workers who are used to running things for themselves have to get used to an engineer or manager always looking over their shoulders. If they have been used to starting work at 8:15, after fifteen minutes of joking and bullshitting, and the big boss comes down at 8:05 to a shop with no machine noise at all, the situation becomes strained. All sorts of illegitimate little arrangements (though they may be agreed to by lower management and tolerated through careful not-noticing by higher management) for making the work easier and more pleasant, the "indulgency pattern" (Gouldner 1954), tend to be undermined. Gouldner found this attentiveness of an innovating management to be a cause of wildcat strikes in a plasterboard factory he studied.

When the theory is known to be uncertain, the company quite often builds a pilot plant, say one-quarter of the projected efficient size. In general, the relations of workers to managers, the variety and excitement of work, the chances of promotion, the pressure for production, are better in the pilot plant. Hence, the creation of the actual production system involves making the pilot plant workers give up their close relations to engineers and higher bosses, making them do more boring work, cutting down their speed of promotion, and putting them under productivity standards that are more demanding. This transition from a sort of test laboratory for the theory on which the innovation is based to the production system that is actually going to produce the innovation thus creates strains that are the reverse of those documented by Gouldner when the innovation was introduced on the assembly line that he studied (Gouldner 1954; see Whyte 1961, 202–217).

Markets and Innovation Success

The market structure with which an innovation is faced determines how much profit the firm in which the innovation might take place may expect to make. This in turn depends on (a) whether the *competitive costs* are within or outside the organization—that is, whether the destruction of other economic opportunities, which Schumpeter (1942, 81–86) calls "creative destruction," also destroys economic opportunities and advantages *that the innovating organization has* (as in the case of the cheaper disk drives that IBM developed under the code name Mallard, mentioned above), or whether only economic advantages held by *other*, competitive, organizations are affected; (b) whether there is an *easy market niche* to pay for the period when costs are exceptionally high (cf. Grilliches 1957); and (c) whether the *profits of monopoly can be retained by continuous improvements*.

a. If the costs of competitive damage to unattractive alternatives by the greater attractiveness of the innovation are outside the innovating organization, the innovation is more likely to be introduced. Schumpeter (1942) argued that the central virtue of capitalism was that it could carry out "creative destruction" of technically and economically archaic social structures, primarily because the losses from an innovation occur in a different place than the gains, and in particular because there is no (in actual practice, very little) political communication from one to the other. People hurt by competition with an innovation cannot in general sue those who hurt them for damages, and they cannot stop those benefitting from the introduction of the innovation from introducing it (for a more formal analysis, see Commons 1924, 97–100).

We can immediately see some ways in which this virtue of capitalist social structure is limited in the United States, and we would expect lower rates of innovation because of these limitations. (i) Competition may be politically vulnerable. For example, innovations by the Japanese in the steel industry or by Hong Kong in the textile and apparel industry that damage their competitors in the United States are often limited through political constraints on free competition: tariffs, "voluntary" restraints, and the like. When AT&T was the common carrier for telephone traffic, they defended their monopoly on the manufacture of transmitting instruments by not allowing instruments made by competitors to be hooked up to the telephone lines. Political vulnerability of an innovator can transfer costs of competitive damages to the innovator by political means.

(ii) Benefits may be displaced automatically outside the organization that makes the innovation. For example, no one inside the garbage collection department would ordinarily get the benefit of a more rationalized work plan that saved labor—only taxpayers would be benefited. The "Scanlon Plan" of measuring base-rate efficiency and then giving the workers half the savings from labor-saving innovations introduced at their suggestion (or the rather similar arrangement of the West Coast Longshoremen's Union with the longshore employer's association [Finlay 1987]) retains some benefits for the workers, and so increases the rate of innovation insofar as worker resistance would significantly impede innovation. That is, the Scanlon Plan uses the benefits of innovations within public organizations to motivate innovation. When all costs of the innovation's introduction are costs within the innovating organization, then innovation is likely only if some of the benefits of the innovation can be transferred in, for example by special incentive plans.

(iii) Innovations discovered by one organization that would be in the jurisdiction of a competing organization tend not to be developed. For example, navy research rarely develops weapons that would fall under the jurisdiction of the air force, although their technical expertise in aircraft to be based on carriers might make that otherwise likely. If only a competitive organization can exploit an innovation, that innovation is not likely to be pushed.

b. One can classify market segments by how easily they can be penetrated by an innovation. Two sorts of market segments are often reached only by reducing the levels of profit from monopoly over the innovation. First, some segments of the market can be entered only at increasing cost, such as smaller ecological niches for hybrid corn or smaller users of computers requiring larger marketing costs than OEMs (OEMs are "original equipment manufacturers," a description of computer brokers invented in government bureaucracies—they sell large systems to large computer users by integrating other manufacturers' parts into a system). Second, some sections of the market do not gain particularly large benefits from the innovation, so they buy only when the innovation is cheap. An innovation, then, may depend for early success on being able to identify and reach those sections of the market that will give quick and lush returns.

(i) Government markets, especially the military, are often the first users of expensive innovations. Electronically read Hollerith punch cards (the starting innovation of IBM) were first sold to the Census Bureau; the first computers were sold to the government; the Navy Advanced Research Projects Administration is now a main client for the most advanced computers. Similarly, many transport planes for civilian freight were first developed either for military transport or for civilian passenger traffic, while the electronics for landing and taking off in bad weather was first developed for military use and only later applied to civilian air transport. The government payoff for having the innovation, especially the military payoff, may be very high, making it a lush market for innovations.

(ii) Raymond Vernon has argued (1960, 1966) that rich countries and rich cities are more likely to introduce innovations than poor ones. The argument has three parts. First, many innovations can be sold as luxury goods before they become cheap enough to be sold to a mass market. In a world where "rich" feudal landowners in poor South American countries often have about a fifth the income of North American steelworkers, the real luxury market tends to be concentrated in rich countries, and within those countries in the cities where the rich and powerful live, such as New York, Paris, or Tokyo. Innovators in those countries and cities, then, have the best chance of reaching the lush luxury markets that can sustain the costs of the high part of the learning curve. Second, advanced countries are advanced in part because they have developed ways of marketing innovations and of concentrating that marketing in great metropolitan centers; the rich of poor South American countries may often be more easily reached from New York than by an innovator in the South American country itself. The Marcoses and the Shah of Iran used to come to the United States or Europe to spend their billions. Third, the productivity of an innovation in capital equipment is likely to be proportional to the total volume of production to which it is applied, and that total volume is likely to be higher in countries with more production per capita.

(iii) Rank, prestige, and the network density of a consumer is associated in many fields with likelihood of adopting an innovation, even when someone else is paying for it (see Coleman, Katz, and Menzel 1957). If a firm or its members are close, in network terms, to the center of the network of consumers of the innovation, then the firm can reach the likely early adopters more easily. Thus we would expect innovations that are made at leading teaching hospitals to be diffused earlier among physicians, or those made at prestigious departments of a scientific discipline to become known earlier by people doing related work. Innovations connected to the centers of consumer networks should find the richest market niches more quickly.

(iv) In some lines of business, geographical similarity between the locus of the innovation and that of the adopting unit facilitates adoption of the innovation. Thus, in early modern times a pattern of crop rotation, artificial fertilization, and other innovations whose center was Flanders increased the yield-to-seed ratio (a rough measure of productivity in grain agriculture) from around 4:1 to around 12:1. This complex of innovations spread across the geographically similar rich plains of northern France at a more or less steady rate of about ten to fifteen miles per decade (Slicher Van Bath 1964, 330–333), but stopped at the borders of granite and sandy soils: the hills and mountains of Brittany, the *massif central*, the Ardennes, and the Alps. Just as many plants native to the isolated valleys of the Himalayas or Ethiopia only spread outside them into protected gardens and houseplant pots elsewhere (e.g., many roses, African violets), so innovations can have a limited radius because they are developed in an environment inhospitable to their spread. Such innovations may not find a niche rich enough to sustain them because they are not fitted for other geographical environments into which they would have to spread (Wallerstein 1974, 1980).

c. The monopoly advantage of innovators may be sustained by introducing new innovations that are tied to or elaborate on the first innovation. Boeing, for instance, often seems to come down the learning curve to manufacture a new airplane faster than its competitors by introducing production innovations more quickly. IBM manages to continue to sell its computers partly by making it easy for its customers to get new software and peripherals that will increase the productivity of their current installations. Hughes Tool in the oil business can sell innovations better than many of its competitors because it can service the tools anywhere in the world through an existing service apparatus (Boeing has the same advantage).

All these companies can market their secondary innovations relatively easily because the links they have with their customers have induced those customers to trust the vendor. Such trust is particularly crucial in selling an innovation, because the client cannot turn to alternative sources—such as competitors—to check out the vendor's sales information. Put another way, companies that have innovated successfully in the past are most likely to have access to that part of the market that will buy innovations.

The general point here is that features of the information-processing and decision-making structure attached to an innovation can determine the market success of that innovation. If that social structure does not have to take into much account the losses created by investments in the goods it replaces; if its competition is not protected by tariff or other barriers; if the benefits of the innovation do not automatically accrue to clients; if the innovating social structure's contacts are with the richest markets in government, in metropolitan cities, in innovative and educated groups, in the geographical area where the innovation applies; if the innovation has a stream of other innovations connected to the first one— then the innovation brings prosperity. If the innovating social structure's market contacts are poor, isolated, behind a prohibitive tariff or other barriers, and uninterested in buying improvements, the innovation fails.

The Division of Benefits

The market theory of an innovation says that there will be benefits to the innovating organization that must be divided up, but it does not say how. At least in economic organizations, the basic notion is that the total benefits that come back to the organization itself (the appropriable benefits) have to be divided up to motivate the activities that go into the innovation. I will analyze this under two headings: (d) whether rewards are closely tied to the *growth rate* of one's section or organization, and consequently generally whether the innovation is a new product (growth inducing, hence rewarding) or labor-capital saving (decline inducing, hence punishing); and (e) whether there are powerful *residual claimants* on the profits or benefits of the innovation—people whose interest is in reducing costs and taking the profits out rather than in motivating and rewarding everyone generously out of monopoly benefits.

d. Growth dependence of rewards is actually a complex variable. It takes a positive growth in the size of the innovating organization, *plus* some "firm-specific human capital" or "job rights" to tie the rewards to the people already employed in the enterprise, to produce from an innovation career advantages for presently employed people. It is because civil servants in the garbage department or West Coast longshoremen

(Finlay 1987) cannot be fired to allow the work to be hired out more cheaply that the Scanlon Plan or the sharing of the benefits of labor-saving changes by longshoremen motivates acceptance of innovations. If the workers expected that as soon as the innovations pushed their wage rate above the market rate they would be replaced by new workers at the market rate, they would not be inclined to support innovations; hence, job rights in the innovating organization are essential to turn growth into an incentive for workers. If a whole labor market area is involved in the innovations, as Houston was (once) for offshore drilling in the Gulf of Mexico, then engineers may participate in the boom even if their own firm goes under. In such cases the job rights are in the industry rather than the firm.

In some cases, labor-saving innovations may produce enough of a competitive advantage to maintain positive growth of the labor force, and so to maintain job rights—for instance, Japanese and Korean steel plants have at times expanded production when the world steel market as a whole was in glut.

Product innovations may not produce growth if they are nonpatentable and easily imitated. In general, then, the connection of innovation to growth of the firm is through monopoly, either monopoly of lower production costs through labor-saving innovations or monopoly of the market niche through product innovations and established market position. And the connection of growth of the firm to career rewards for workers is through worker control of their jobs, which in turn can come through indispensability, through labor union power, or through civil service regulation or other legal or customary tenure provisions. These interacting forces on career incentives for building an invention into an innovation are outlined in Table 2.

e. "Residual claimants" are those people who take up the excess of revenues over costs, and in particular those who can be expected to get most of the benefits of establishing a monopoly through introducing an innovation. These residual claimants can range in power from the anonymous and disorganized clients of a city's garbage system, who will pay one-tenth of a mill lower tax rate if garbage workers work more efficiently, to the family-owner majority of Du Pont's board of directors in the days Chandler was talking about. The basic and easy generalization is that the more powerful the residual claimants are, the more likely a profitable innovation will be introduced.

The probability of an innovation's succeeding may be drastically increased by changing the residual claimants—for example, when the developers of an innovation leave the firm in which they have developed

Table 2. The Impact of Innovation Type and Labor Market Control by Workers on Worker Career Motivation to Favor Innovations

	Innovation Type	
	Labor Saving[a]	Growth Inducing[b]
"Free" Labor Market	Mechanization producing unemployment (e.g., in farm labor)	Spreading career benefits in boom towns (e.g., Houston) or replacement by cheap labor.
"Internal" Labor Market	"Featherbedding" or "deals" in West Coast longshoring; effective union resistance to innovation	Career rewards for innovations (e.g., Data General)

[a]Without large compensating competitive impact.
[b]Product innovations and labor saving innovations with large competitive impact.

the competence to introduce an innovation, to exploit that competence in a firm of their own. Leaving is especially likely if the company where the developers were employed has already disapproved the innovation. Many large computer and software firms were started in this way (for example, the Data General firm analyzed by Kidder 1981; for software, see Stinchcombe and Heimer 1987). Passing out equity interests to leading technical innovators is one way computer firms have tried to stay at the leading edge of technology.

Merton has argued that the capacity to establish priority through publishing makes the person who publishes the residual claimant for innovations in science—that is, the one whose fame is increased by the innovation. His argument is that priority established by publication increases the motivation to carry out an innovation (Merton [1942] 1973b, 273–275). Joseph Ben-David (1968–1969) has extended Schumpeter's argument above by arguing that prestige competition among universities is crucial for the development of leading scientific nations, for then the costs of older discoverers whose fame is decreased are displaced outside the university introducing the innovation. He holds that nations with many regional universities, such as Germany and the United States, tend to be more scientifically productive, particularly in new fields, than countries with more centralized university systems, such as England and France.

Examples of Incentives for Innovation

We can specify which ends of these marketing and career reward variables predict easy introduction of an innovation by considering the account given by Tracy Kidder (1981) of the design and introduction of a new computer at Data General. (a) DEC VAX, the competitor to the machine with a soul, takes the losses if the Data General computer comes up to its promised level of performance. Contrast this situation with the introduction of a new computer at IBM, where most of the users who buy the new machine will be replacing an IBM machine. (b) The original equipment manufacturers (OEMs) provided an easy market for technically better products, which they in turn marketed as systems to the military and other large users; Data General could start making money on the innovation before any general marketing was required. (c) A series of "downward compatible" and "upward compatible" related models, improved software, and the like enable computer companies in general to maintain their monopolies created by providing an element crucial to the whole system, such as a main computer, so Data General expected to benefit from the innovation for a long time.

(d) Career rewards for computer folks are in general tied to their firm's growth rates. As we suggested above, innovations in the product itself tend to spur firm growth, whereas innovations on the production line tend to depress growth. The Data General innovation was a product innovation, and most of the people Kidder describes as being crucial in the innovation were employees rather than owners or stockholders; they could thus expect their rewards to depend on growth in the size of the labor force rather than, say, on increased profits from cost reductions. And (e) the powerful group in the company was the group who would collect what was left over of the benefits of the innovation after costs were deducted—the residual claimants. The chief executives at Data General were large equity holders and had killed the last innovation, one carried out by some of the people who implemented the innovation studied by Kidder. That is, the control over the introduction of this particular computer was not in the hands of those most committed to it and most motivated to see that innovation introduced—the engineers who worked on it. The top executives did not care whether this one or the one being developed in a competitive company group at another installation in North Carolina was ultimately put on the market. The technical group had to convince the money group. But once convinced the innovation would be profitable, they were strongly motivated to introduce it.

In contrast we can consider a labor-saving innovation in schools, such as teaching two hundred children at once by television. (a) Competitive costs are paid by teachers who are laid off. (b) There is no special market for easily automatable classes; students will not flock to required lecture-demonstration classes such as civics, American history, and English because they are automated and so cheaper. (c) Schools are already virtual monopolies, and there is no monopoly advantage of a more efficient school that could be maintained by spreading the innovation to related areas, because the school already has all the monopoly it will ever get by law. (d) Saving labor reduces the growth rate of the school labor force, and so reduces the number of supervisory or other lucrative and prestigious positions that will be created. And (e) there are no powerful claimants of the excess profits; any benefits go to the taxpayers. But since the constraining law on schools is that they should have *equal expenditures*, not equal effects, if they save money one way they will probably have to spend it another and there will probably not be any benefits for the taxpayers anyway.

It would be difficult to set up a social system less hospitable to labor-saving innovations than American elementary and secondary schools, and it would be difficult to set up a situation more encouraging to product innovations than that described by Kidder for Data General—except perhaps by making the engineers in the innovation group shareholders in the company.

Divisionalization and Innovation

Innovations not only require a complete social system with markets, division of benefits, personnel policies, and the like, just as any manufacturing enterprise does; but they require rapidly adjusting social systems as well. Because the market for an innovation is untested, new information about what will sell and at what price is always coming in, and manufacturing and engineering have to be adjusted to that rapid flow of new market information. Marketing people selling machines need, for example, machines that will actually work, and if the machines have been improperly soldered at the factory (because the soldering is also a procedure carried out under new conditions for this innovation), they need to be able to call on engineering and manufacturing people to come out and solder them correctly at the client's place of business (see Fishman 1981, 43). Since getting production costs down requires introducing innovations on the production line, and since innovations on the production line also have bugs, engineers have to come down and take a hand in manufacturing. That is, the introduction of a product innovation typically requires the sort of intimate relationship between manufacturing, engineering, and marketing that Chandler argued produced the requirements for divisional organization in Du Pont, General Motors, and other chemical, electrical, and automobile manufacturing organizations (1962, 52–162, 363–378).

Of course, Chandler was usually arguing that once a corporation began to market to distinct markets it would be under pressure to introduce a divisional organization. Here we are asking not whether an innovation that is successful will cause divisionalization of the corporation, but whether an innovation will be introduced successfully in the first place. What interests us, then, is not why the chemicals industry, which often introduces innovations requiring responses to new markets, is divisionalized, but rather what it is that makes the chemicals industry capable of introducing many innovations.

The functional argument of the last chapter can however be reversed to say that it will be easier to build a system that can introduce an innovation *if* it is easy in a given organization to organize a new division, largely autonomous from central manufacturing, marketing, and engineering, so as to allow rapid response as the news needed to make the new social system go comes in.

We noted in Chapter 4 that the Du Pont divisionalization was based partly on an analysis of Du Pont experience in introducing innovations. Let us quote again from Harry Haskell of Du Pont (in Chandler 1962, 68) on why a minidivisional arrangement was needed for the dyes business, which was at that time an innovating organization, before Du Pont became generally organized into product divisions:

> It may be that it would be better for a few years to carry on the dye business as a separate entity. I think it would because it is a developing, unstandardized industry and should merit independent attention just as the Parlin chemical mixtures business was better by itself until standardized—when it was merged with the regular sales and operating departments.

And then the conclusion of the committee based on this analysis (Chandler 1962, 70):

> [Dyes should have one] individual in control of both production and sales, because the relation of the product and its qualities is so mixed up with the demands of the market for the product that to divorce them and segregate the business into a clearly defined production

department and an independent sales department,
would be detrimental to the business. Later on when
the production of dyes becomes standardized it will no
doubt follow the evolution of other portions of the
business.

In the final analysis, then, the dyes business required what Chandler calls
(when it happens later) a divisional administrative structure because it is
carrying an innovation. But this means not only that Du Pont had the
category of division in its organizational analysis before it introduced divisionalization on a large scale; they were also used to introducing autonomous divisions to manage product innovations, and although this was
treated as an exception to normal good centralized management, it was a
"normal exception."

Presumably the causal relation between innovation and decentralized
minidivisions goes both ways. Innovating companies learn to create autonomous minidivisions easily; companies that create minidivisions easily
are more successful at innovation. Stated more generally: one can easily
create a new social system to fit a given niche only if allowed considerable
autonomy, and larger social orders that allow considerable autonomy to
new social units are therefore advantaged in introducing innovations.
This is one of Schumpeter's main arguments in favor of capitalism—that
it allows innovating entrepreneurs enough autonomy to produce economic progress. Thus Schumpeter's advice on how to organize an economy can be turned into advice to bureaucratic corporations: only routinize and subordinate an innovating minidivision of a large bureaucracy
when its adaptation to its niche and its viability as a going concern are
established.

Conclusion

Our first task in this chapter was to show that the monopoly advantage
from innovations, which Schumpeter saw as the driving force of capitalist progress and of business cycles, is increased and decreased by social
structural variables. The profitability of innovations depends on how fast
the innovator and potential competitors come down the learning curve,
and on how solid the network connections an innovator builds to its clients are.

Our second task was to show that turning an invention into an innovation—into a going concern that can regularly produce benefits for an innovating firm—is in fact creating a social system. A social system has to
meet its functional requirements in order to produce benefits over the

long run. This means it has to nurture technical ideas, to make investments in risky situations, to build a production system that can produce effectively and can come down the learning curve rapidly, to reach the market that can afford the innovation while it is still expensive, and to arrange the division of benefits so that both investors and personnel will be motivated to develop the competences needed to do all these things and then do them.

In short, because routinizing innovations is still a difficult and risky process, even in large bureaucratic organizations, it still produces excess profits when well done, creates investment booms as followers try to catch up, and induces creative destruction of archaic social forms during the recession that follows the investment boom. Furthermore, since there are special problems in administering viable innovative social systems within large bureaucracies, in that adaptation occurs on a shorter time scale than in more routine production and marketing, divisionalization serves in part as a social process for making innovation possible; it is the organizational creation of entrepreneurial social structures, taking the place of the heroic individual in Schumpeter's model.

In one sense, this chapter is merely a specialized application of the theory developed in previous chapters, especially Chapter 4. It says that in introducing innovations, market uncertainty ramifies into manufacturing and engineering and so tends to produce divisionalization. But turning an invention into an innovation also involves the special task of creating information-processing and decision-making routines. It therefore has distinctive pathologies. As an invention, for example, the normal state of the information-processing system is that of a "technological utopia." In general, the people who developed this technological utopia are not good at collecting and processing the information needed to satisfy an investment group, knowing little about "business plans." They may well not know where the lucrative markets are to be found (unless they developed the innovation for an engineer who is also a colonel in the Pentagon). They may be bad at estimating how fast the bugs can be got out of a production line for the product. And so on.

When we describe what is lacking in a technologically utopian plan for introducing an innovation, we are describing the information-processing requirements for a new product-line division. Each of those information criteria in turn requires skills in the people (as analyzed above in Chapter 2: innovation is a situation of low routinization and hence requires a high average skill level) and the building up of all sorts of departmental information systems (as analyzed in Chapter 3), responding to the distinctive technical uncertainties of the innovation. For example, the cost-accounting system needed to find the cost bottlenecks in a production line for an innovation would have to be much more flexible than would the cost system serving the overall firm in which the innovation is likely to be embedded.

In Chapter 6, we will analyze some of the distinctive problems of building a system to produce innovations through networks of contracts and subcontracts (see also Stinchcombe and Heimer 1988); and in Chapter 7 we will focus on the information system that has to be embedded in the incentive system for workers. As should be becoming clear, what this book is developing a theory of is the things that have to be added to a technologically utopian theory to turn it into an organized going concern.

6   Organizing Information Outside the Firm

Contracts as Hierarchical Documents

Introduction

Coase (1937), Dahl and Lindblom ([1953] 1976), Williamson (1975), Teece (1976), and Lindblom (1977, 27–29, 237–309) have all built and used a contrast between market transactions among firms and hierarchical administration within firms. The basic notion is that when many adjustments will have to be made during the course of contract performance, the transaction costs of negotiating and enforcing contract rise, and the great flexibility of a labor contract used to create a hierarchy saves transaction costs (see Williamson 1975, 64–72). Thus, whenever it is difficult to specify the required performance in advance (Marschak, Blennan, Jr., and Summers 1967, 64–72), when the costs, prices, or quantities to reign at the time of the performances are uncertain (Macaulay 1963), when team interdependences do not allow separate measurement of performances (Alchian and Demsetz 1972), hierarchy is preferable to market coordination through contracts.

The argument of this chapter is that contracts are often signed between a corporate client and a corporate contractor when this theoretical tradition predicts hierarchical integration. Although research and development in commercial life is ordinarily carried out by a subordinate R & D staff, as Mansfield et al. (1977) predict,[1] the government buys weapons R & D by contracts under the same conditions of uncertainty of performances.[2] Uncertainty about costs, prices, and quantities frequently leads to vertical integration, as Thompson predicts (J. Thompson 1967), but automobile franchises and weapons procurement often involve contracts for shifting quantities, uncertain costs, and prices to be determined (see Macaulay 1966; and Scherer 1964). Team performance of technically interdependent production often leads to hierarchical controls, as predicted by Alchian and Demsetz (1972), but airlines penetrate deeply into the technical work of airplane manufacturers.[3] And in rushed megaprojects in energy production, the intimate technical dependence of engineering and construction does not prevent their being split between contractors. Performances can be adjusted to changing situations by contractual means; administrations of performances can be set up by other kinds of contracts than labor contracts.

If the easy way to get flexible continuous performance over time is with a hierarchy isolated from direct market processes, we need to ask how people manage who are forced by their situation to do it the hard way. The literature that predicts why, for example, weapons development or building construction will be vertically integrated should predict what kinds of difficulties weapons and construction contracts will run into. Then we can look for attempts to solve such problems by writing administrative provisions into the contract. What we will be looking for is ways to construct social structures that work like hierarchies out of contracts between legally equal corporate bargaining agents in a market.

In the next section, we will analyze very briefly what kinds of social relations hierarchies consist of, and what functions they perform. This then provides an outline of what the functions are whose occurrence in contractual situations will lead to hierarchical elements in contracts. It may also suggest the nature of the structures that may intrude into the ideal type of market transaction, producing a variant of the ideal-type contract. The ideal-type contract is defined here to include all market transactions in which one firm or person makes an offer and another accepts. An offer and acceptance create legal obligations, whether or not a written contract is signed. In the ideal-type contract, the performances the offering party offers to perform are clearly specified, and the performances it will require in return are clearly described, though these may be implicit. Thus, a store's display of papayas with a sign, "Papayas, $2.39 each," is an offer, and carrying them to the cash register and paying the money is an acceptance, creating a contract. This contract is hardly ever written, except as a cash register receipt. The papayas are specified by being on display; the performance of the buyer has a meaning defined by laws of legal tender and sales tax laws and by the sign. Legal obligations created include the store's obligation to let the customer have the papaya and the customer's obligation to take it away, to suffer the consequences if it is dropped on the way home, and the like. A contract with hierarchical elements departs in many ways from such an ideal type; those bring it closer to the description of a hierarchy we offer in the next section.

Some conditions make it difficult, uneconomical, or impossible to specify the performances to be required at the time a contract is signed. Our argument in the third section is that difficulties in arranging market transactions in the way specified in the ideal-type papaya-buying contract tend to cause the addition of hierarchical elements to the contract. These may be divided broadly into (1) difficulties of prediction of specifications the client will want to make of a contractor's performances (e.g., one cannot describe what weapon one wants manufactured until one has done the development work, yet one wants to start tooling up for manufacturing early so as to reduce the time between development and operational availability; Marschak, Blennan, and Summers 1967, 49–139; see also Stockfisch 1973); (2) client or contractor uncertainty about the costs of carrying out the performances, resulting in a wish to make strategic readjustments either in the performances or in the compensation during contract performance; and (3) inability to measure clearly the performances to be demanded or the conditions determining compensation (e.g., the inseparability of engineering mistakes and construction inefficiency in cost overruns in major construction projects means that engineering and construction performances cannot be measured separately, even though they are often in separate contracts.

The "markets and hierarchies" literature assumes that the usual optimal way to arrange work is through a market. Hence, what has to be explained is "market failure." Since most work by individuals is not arranged directly through a market, there is a good deal to be explained. The explanations of market failure most often have to do with failures of information (uncertainty), monopolistic advantages of either the buyer or seller (small numbers in a given market), or difficulty in measuring outputs or commodities ("teamwork," etc.). Hence they predict that uncertainty, small numbers bargaining, and teamwork should produce nonmarket arrangements such as vertical integration or hierarchy. Our general argument takes the form of finding situations in which work is arranged through contracts (and hence through markets) that are characterized by uncertainty, small numbers bargaining, and teamwork. The received theory predicts hierarchy, but we observe contracts. We will show that hierarchy can be arranged through contracts, hence "through the market."

Section 3, then, sets a series of functional requirements that various contract devices will be called on to solve. The general argument of the literature is that hierarchy is a general-purpose structure for fulfilling these functions, for adjusting performances to an uncertain future flow of events. But since we will observe these functions being required in parts of the economy that are in fact arranged through contracts, there must be contractual functional substitutes for hierarchy, perhaps ordinarily of lower efficiency but called forth by the special circumstances of particular industries.

If hierarchies ordinarily do some things better than contracts, we can look for those contractual devices that simulate the operation of hierarchies to do those things. Section 4 below decomposes the functions served by hierarchies in adjusting to a changing world, in order to specify what contracts have to do to simulate hierarchies. We will argue first that contracts often specify authority systems, in the sense of specifying how one will recognize a communication requiring a change of performance as binding. In particular, if a client specifies a change in contractual conditions in midstream, it will ordinarily have also either to assume the risks this exposes the contractor to or to compensate the contractor for assuming the risk. In short, to specify the right to change the contract, one must ordinarily specify many aspects of the consequences of issuing an authoritative communication.

To back up this authority, contracts often specify an incentive system, in the sense this has within the firms: a method of tying rewards to performances that does not give all the revenue due to better performance to the employee. In order to achieve maximum flexibility, the client should reserve the right to change the incentive system as conditions change. Within a firm, for example, one may get a lower commission for selling popular goods, bonuses for moving things that turn out to be turkeys. Similarly, a contract may specify how the compensation scheme may be changed.

To control uncertainties in costs and prices, contracts often provide an administered pricing system. This may in some cases mean an authoritative way to determine the market price; the "administered" aspect in such a case is then only that the parties to the contract are in the future required to accept the market price so determined, whether they want to or not. But the devices may be much more complex than this, as for example in the English system of bidding on bills of quantities in construction projects. The quantity surveyor describes the project as a list of quantities of various kinds of work (such as cubic feet of concrete foundation to be poured). The contractor bids a price for each quantity in the list, which then specifies a unique pricing system for change orders for that particular contract: they are described in the same way by the quantity surveyor, as a list of quantities, and priced according to the prices originally bid by the contractor.

A hierarchy provides for resolution of conflicts within the firm, without routine appeals to a court. Similarly, contracts often provide a system for resolving disputes, sometimes with several layers. English construction contracts, for example, often provide that a named engineer (presumed to have nonpartisan professional standards) will resolve all disputes between the client and contractor for the interim so work can proceed, but that the engineer's decision can be appealed to a named structure of binding arbitration. These structures, internal to the contract, are subject to the usual appeals to the courts (as are decisions in hierarchies in firms), but they are intended to serve the functions of keeping disputes from hardening into expensive and disruptive legal battles.

Finally, hierarchies establish standard operating procedures for organizations—to secure efficiency and dispatch in processing organizational matters, to ensure that unobservable qualities in the output will be regularly achieved by quality control, to prepare for unusual dangerous events such as fires, and so on. Similarly, contracts for large projects often include a schedule (whose legal status is in general precarious), orders for components of nuclear plants often specify a series of quality control documents and X-ray films to be supplied for each weld, and marine insurance contracts implicitly specify standards of readiness for emergencies ("seaworthiness"; see Heimer 1985a).

A structure with legitimate authority; with a manipulable incentive system; with a method for adjusting costs, quantities, and prices; with a structure for dispute resolution; and with a set of standard operating procedures looks very much like a hierarchy, very little like a competitive market. Yet all these features of hierarchy are routinely obtained by contracts between firms in some sector of the economy.

Section 5 below asks what it means for the theory of the market that one common use of the market is to set up joint administrative structures between a client and a contractor, rather than to trade specified performances for specified compensation. That is, the model of the market in Coase, Williamson, Teece, and others is not a description of the construction contracting market, the market for weapons R & D, the market for the services of franchised automobile dealers (see Coase 1937; Dahl and Lindblom [1953] 1976; Williamson 1975; Teece 1976; and Lindblom 1977); instead it is an abstraction from the economics textbook, in which the administrative ingenuity embedded in the contents of contracts has disappeared. But when hierarchy is defined by contrast to this idealized version of the market, its features are indefinite. A common danger of the ideal-type method used in this literature is that one of the types, usually the most interesting one, is defined residually, by contrast with an empty ideal-type into which few empirical observations fall. This means not only that intermediate cases are misanalyzed, but that even the poles of contract and hierarchy are poorly defined.

An Extended Definition of Hierarchy

We will describe below how a series of functions that are not included in the simplified ideal-type market contract can be achieved through modified contracts. We need to show that they are in fact routinely achieved by those structures we usually call hierarchies. It will therefore be useful to show how hierarchies themselves, created in the usual way by chartering corporations and by decisions of boards of directors, carry out the functions that can be done by contracts. We will try to show how corporations create a structure with a working authority system, and an effective incentive system with observations of individuals' performances and rewards for differential performance, accepted operating procedures, legitimate dispute resolution structures, and internal pricing systems that contribute to organizational rationality.

First we will try to specify the elements out of which these functions are constructed within firms, the formal elements of hierarchies. Then we will try to describe briefly how the structure so constructed deals with uncertainties of specifications, uncertainties of costs, and unobservability of performances. Our main purpose here is to cast our traditional knowledge of organizations into a form that describes its relation to the contractual materials we will go through.

FORMAL ELEMENTS OF HIERARCHIES

We will argue that most of the hierarchical intra-firm structure we need to analyze is made up of five elements: (1) labor contracts yielding subjection to authority systems by employees; (2) fiduciary relations, especially involving boards of directors, entrusting them with wide discretion as representatives or trustees of the stockholders and others; (3) the legal personality aspect of organizations that defines them as origins of decisions, allowing them to set up performance measurements and wage, salary, pension, career development, or other incentive systems, to enter into contracts to motivate other firms by appropriate incentive systems, and to change these by organizational decisions; (4) the governance of the activities set up under these structures by production programs or standard operating procedures; and (5) meetings (with agenda controlled by the hierarchy or by standard operating procedures) for internal dispute resolution. A normal hierarchy, then, consists of labor contracts, fiduciary relations, the exercised right to measure and reward performances, standard operating procedures, and decision-making and dispute resolving meetings.

Labor Contracts. Simon (1957b), in a fundamental paper on the theory of the employment relation, showed how the central phenomena of authority can be generated in exchange relations.[4] Briefly, the argument is this. The central phenomena of authority are related to a "zone of indifference" of the subordinate (the term was invented by Chester I. Barnard). By a zone of indifference we mean a set of activities, all of which it would be rational for the worker to exchange at his or her wage rate. The higher the wage rate as compared to alternatives available to the worker, the more costs in terms of unpleasant or dangerous jobs the worker would be willing to do to retain the advantage of the wages. The higher the wage rate in a given job as compared to the competitive wage rate, the larger in general will be the zone of indifference of the worker. Conversely, as the competitive wage rate goes down, for example by unemployment during a recession, the size of the zone of indifference at a given wage rate goes up. Authority is strengthened by paying high wages and by bad times outside the firm. The zone of indifference is also increased if the tastes of the workers do not make a less desirable activity much more costly to them than another activity. The more equal different activities are in the minds of the workers, the more flexibility authorities have. One hires as traveling salespeople those who do not mind traveling, and one tries to so arrange work activities that one particular choice of activities does not result in the employment of the worker's lover at high wages.

Under what conditions will an employer prefer to buy a zone of indifference rather than particular activities (e.g., by subcontracting)? If the employer knew it wanted particular activities in advance, it could buy them on the labor market at the competitive wage rate or set up an incentive system in which the powerful motives of, say, employing sons and lovers at high wage rates could be mobilized. And clearly this is often done. Rather than run automobile sales bureaucratically, car manufacturers allow families or small corporations to own the job of selling cars through the franchise system. This allows car dealers to use their business power to reward their children and relatives, producing a small aristocracy with inheritable status in the core of the most modern bureaucracy. Presumably, car manufacturers do this for rational reasons, since they know perfectly well how to run bureaucracies of employed people, with nepotism rules, orderly careers, and all the rest.

The central question of rationality from the point of view of an employer is the distribution of uncertainty. An exchange partner is likely to want authority when it does not know which particular activity it is likely to want but is reasonably sure it will want some activity. Under these conditions it is rational to become an employer, to buy a zone of indifference rather than a set of particular activities.

Provided one is continuously in a given line of work, if one is faced with uncertainties of specifications, uncertainties of costs, or inability to divide up the work so that it forms decoupled packages, one will prefer to buy a zone of indifference rather than specific performances. But the situations in which we will find the uncertainties and the coupled activities above and yet also find contracting are those in which either one is not continuously in a given line of work (e.g., when one is a client for a building or an oil refinery, one is not continuously in the construction business) or when one is not competent to run such a business (as in weapons development or buying a software system). Under those conditions one wants a zone of indifference but also wants to contract for the work.

For our purposes, however, it is enough that authority systems can be constructed if one can buy zones of indifference, and the labor contract, combined with careful differentiation of family from work, will usually do the job. Organizations that have tasks requiring hierarchy will tend to have employees.

Fiduciary Relations. Historically, the law of corporations developed out of the law of trusts and the law of agency rather than out of that of master-servant relations. That is, from a legal standpoint, the central element of a corporation is not that it employs people but that others entrust it with their money. Boards of directors are also employees of the corporation, but they are mainly, legally, trustees. And operating executives of a corporation are also employees of the corporation, but mainly they are, legally, agents of the board. Stockholders, like minor children for whom a trust is created, cannot legally exercise their ownership of firm goods by disposing of them or using them. Only the board, like the trustee, has operating control (e.g., "possession") over the resources of the firm. Likewise, an officer of the corporation is legally bound to exercise his or her agency in good faith and not to exceed the authority granted, but his or her acts (if legal within the law of agency) commit the corporation and its resources.

What the stockholders buy in hiring a board, and what the board buys in hiring officers, is not so much a zone of indifference as a promise of responsibility, a promise to carry out a fiduciary role as a trustee or as an agent. The capital market is shot through with these fiduciary exchanges;

in fact, the ponderous conservatism of bankers and stockbrokers and corporation lawyers is more an ethical imperative of fiduciary exchanges than a character type of the very rich.

Inheritance law provided for trusts because the heir was often not trusted (either by the court or by the person who died) to administer the estate rationally. Children were always presumed incompetent. So the basic purpose of the trust was to provide wisdom in the management of an estate when wisdom was presumed lacking. The choice of a trustee generally required not only wisdom but either disinterestedness or identification with the interests of the heir.

The first of these aims of the laws of trust, wisdom, is reflected in the legal provision that trustees (and often agents) must act as "a reasonable man" would act in the circumstances. The norms do not specify what specific actions the trustee or agent should carry out. Nor is it any excuse in the law that the action taken is not forbidden in the document creating the trust or the agency; if that action was not one that a reasonable man would have taken under the circumstances, the trustee or agent can be held liable. It is a defense for the agent, but not for the trustee, that he or she was specifically instructed to carry out the unreasonable actions.

The second of these aims, disinterestedness, is reflected in "conflict of interest" norms, which try to ensure that the trust or agency is used in the interest of the beneficiary or principal rather than in the interest of the trustee or agent. Identification with the interests of the beneficiary or principal is often achieved by norms of election and dismissal, as in the case of boards of directors, or precarious or discretionary tenure, as in the case of cabinet officers, officers of corporations, or commercial agents.

The problem with both of these normative provisions is that they are easily corruptible, and the law is a very inefficient way to prevent corruption. Hence, the norms of wise and disinterested service are often supported by structural devices providing for continual review of their performance. The most common such devices are collegiality (a committee as trustee, e.g., a board of directors), publicity (e.g., annual reports with specified contents), and auditing. In their full development, then, the norms of trust or agency provide for six features (aside from the obvious one that the trustee should be well paid for the service): (1) reasonableness or wisdom as the performance standard, (2) disinterestedness, (3) election or precarious tenure, (4) collegiality or committee decision making, (5) publicity, and (6) audit. In general, large transfers of capital to new enterprises take place in the context of exchange relations with all these features. These formal provisions are ordinarily supported by extensive norms of gentlemanly business behavior and mutual relations among the people involved as trustees and central agents of the corporation that are well described by the Spanish phrase of the group, *hombres de confianza*—men of (that is, in whom we have) confidence.

Status Systems and Performance Incentives. If a central distinction between the times a client uses contracts and the times it builds a department to do the work is the continuousness of that line of work, we should expect that a chief feature of the hierarchical incentive system would be continuity of the exchanges between employee and employer. When an exchange relationship is continuous, such as bureaucratic employment, marriage, or the exchanges among subsidiaries of the same corporation, current exchange is modified by the expectation of future exchange. That is, in the future there will be a flow of valuable goods if the exchange relationship is not destroyed by the current exchange.

The rule of *caveat emptor* is not appropriate because the person who commits fraud or renders a poor performance gains only a small amount in the current exchange but sacrifices the whole (discounted) value of the flow of future exchanges (Becker and Stigler 1974). Norms about "fair" exchanges thus serve the interests of both parties, in that whatever disadvantage they may sustain from unfair norms of fairness, those norms protect them from the destruction of the relationship and hence protect the capitalized value of future exchanges. Further, a reputation for fairness may advantage one or more of the parties, so that, for example, an employer may keep on high seniority workers who no longer pull their load because firing them would undermine profitable exchanges with younger workers who hope someday to have seniority themselves (Becker and Stigler 1974; Caplow 1964).

The first requirement of such a system is that the future exchanges should in fact be secure, so that the future advantages for which one sacrifices his or her current interest will in fact be there. The basic phenomenon in an effective commitment is that each party be satisfied that at all relevant points in the future the value sacrificed by the partner by stopping the exchange will be greater than the advantage that partner can get by stopping unexpectedly. Giving hostages does this, for example, because the hostage is more valuable to the person giving the hostage than to the one receiving it; thus the latter can sacrifice the hostage if the relationship is broken. Evidence of giving the partner a monopoly position by leaving the market (e.g., by stopping flirting upon marriage) shows that one intends to sacrifice the whole value of the relationship in case of rupture, not just the difference between the value of this stable exchange and the value of well-explored alternatives. Passing control to the part-ner—for example, by a supplier selling out and becoming a subsidiary to its customer (see the analysis of Fisher Body and General Motors in Klein, Crawford, and Alchian 1978, 308–310)—guarantees the relation-ship by transferring control over the fulfillment of the selling partner's obligations to the parent.

An important concrete manifestation of commitment norms is norms of seniority. If the contract of commitment were established in a timeless instant, on model of a marriage that starts at the wedding and lasts "until death do us part," the risk arises that only one of the parties will turn out to be truly committed. A one-sided holding of hostages, a one-sided mo-nopoly, a one-sided transfer of control over one's resources, all lead to slavery. One general solution to the risk of one-sided commitment is to move the commitment by small stages, so that at each point (if all goes well) the partners will lose more by bugging out than is being risked by increased commitment. And in the employment relation and its ana-logues, the growth of seniority rules, of security of tenure in an agricul-tural tenancy, or of tenure in a university is sufficiently vital to the nature of the relationship that its absence is a sign of ruthless exploitation.

If a commitment is effective, it establishes an area of bilateral monop-oly for the two parties. The skilled autoworker has seniority only in Packard Motors, and the workers who know Packard's production pro-cess are the workers with seniority. Within the range between the price of labor at which Packard is willing to go out of business and that at which the workers will quit in spite of their seniority rights, any price is possible. A bilateral monopoly does not have a unique equilibrium rate of exchange, and the range of possible rates is set by the degree of commitment.

The reason all of this is important to the incentive system of continu-ous hierarchies is that many of the incentives used, especially at the lower managerial levels, are status system rewards. The value of a promotion is not mainly this month's increased paycheck, but the expectation that the rate of exchange in this particular exchange has permanently altered for the better. Thus, the reward for a worker improving his or her human capital is a commitment at a new rate of exchange. Unless the whole sys-tem is organized as a permanent status system, the investment (and the continuous disciplined pursuit of objectives specified by the superior) does not seem so worthwhile (Becker 1960).

Status systems with promotions as incentives are also more appropri-ate for executive and managerial jobs, in which one wants to reward discretion whose results are only observable over quite a long period (Jacques [1956] 1972, 22–42). It would be quite hard to devise a piece-rate system for jobs whose span of discretion was a month or six months.

Continuous exchange between the firm and its employees, then, makes it possible to construct a more effective career incentive system. Max Weber's specification of career incentives as a central defining feature of bureaucracy was shaped by his realization that such an incentive system produces the highest level of discipline for complex interdependent tasks. Thus we will expect hierarchies to have a permanently organized status system in which rights are attached to positions rather than to performances, with indirect attachment of rewards to performances coming from linking promotions to judgments of competence (but see Cole and Siegel 1979).

Standard Operating Procedures. Continuity of work in the same line makes standard operating procedures productive. Much of the transaction cost of contracting for specified work is actually the inefficiency of prototype production. If experienced airplane manufacturers can produce the second airplane of a given model for about 80 percent of the cost of the first, the fourth for about 64 percent of the cost of the first, and so on, then contracting one at a time with unique specifications rather than buying off the shelf can be extremely expensive. The virtue of standard operating procedures and of production programs is not that they are standard, but that they embody organizational learning (Newhouse 1982; see also Scherer 1964, 120–121).

One of the main things a hierarchy uses its control over a zone of indifference for is to make improvements between the prototype and the second, between the second and the fourth, between the fourth and the eighth, and so on. At the beginning of a production run there is not much one can do that is as inefficient as buying the same activities today that one bought yesterday. Even after the production process is running smoothly, we can project from experience in producing software that about 40 percent as much again as the investment to that point will still be spent on improvements of the sort that programmers call "maintenance."

In production processes these improvements range from simple jigs or patterns to the trained efficiency of an experienced machinist's movements (Burawoy 1979, 46–73; see above, Chapter 2). In cost accounting the categories of the system evolve so that they can be efficiently aggregated for all relevant cost analyses for deciding about products, or about executives, or about investments to improve a given process (see Chapter 3). Production-line maintenance programs are improved by better estimates of when parts should be preventively replaced, by development of better diagnostic tests of what ails a machine, and by replacing hard-to-repair motive systems with easy ones. In many ways, the central thing one sets up firms to do is to develop standard operating procedures, and then to improve them incrementally.

Meetings. Perhaps the central illusion of the novice organizational analyst is that the organization chart is a picture of the authority system. In the upper part of the corporate hierarchy the relations between ranks are more like that between courts of original jurisdiction and the appeals courts over them than like that between privates and sergeants. The higher ranks organize meetings in which problems and disputes of the lower ranks are ironed out. The organization chart serves as a constitution that specifies who will organize committee meetings, not who will make decisions.

Further, for the most important decisions there will be a sequence of meetings, or at least a sequence of reviews and initials culminating in a meeting. Standard operating procedures usually specify the route of the paper on which the decision contents are recorded, and this in turn specifies the sequence of meetings or reviews that make decisions; in practice, all important decisions appear as authoritative after a meeting on them has been held. Tyranny in such organizations is most often organized as it was in eighteenth-century France, where the king expressed dissatisfaction with a series of outcomes by inventing a new court, one more under his thumb, to treat matters of royal interest (mainly taxation matters; see Stinchcombe 1982, 90–92). Executives institute tyrannies by controlling meetings.

Using the hierarchy as a constituting mechanism for meetings creates an agile system for resolving disputes—though perhaps not one we would be happy to entrust the administration of justice to. The agility is particularly important in securing decision on things that have to be decided in a hurry. If disputes are appealed up the hierarchy, of course, the meeting of the board of directors has the final say. Hierarchies are seldom paralyzed by internal disputes, though as the late-eighteenth-century French royal administration shows, this can happen.

HIERARCHY AND UNCERTAINTY

The combination of labor market contracts involving a zone of indifference with career incentives in a more or less stable status system makes it possible to embark on a line of activity without knowing precisely what one is about. Within a wide range, the employees will obey, and a career executive who has done his best on a canceled model is happy to be promoted to assistant production manager for the successful model, if perhaps a bit piqued not to be production manager of his own model. Thus the progressive concretization of specifications, which we will find below is created by contractual contortions, is a normal hierarchical course of events. Dispute resolution machinery produces the legitimation of the decision on the model, and the disappointed executive was probably cowed in a meeting he attended.

Similarly, cost uncertainties do not require the payment of a risk premium to the department that may overrun its budget. The corporate funds that bear the cost uncertainties are the same ones that obtain the returns. The incentives to manage costs for the firm are as good as can be arranged, for the firm collects all the benefit of all the cost savings.

Finally, the capacity to reorganize information flows, authority, and measurement of outcomes so as to administer interdependent activities together reduces the problems of unobservable performances. The career incentive system can rely on the overall judgment of the superior on the quality of work, rather than observing separate performances.

In spite of the tendency of superiors to give all their subordinates equal ratings, and in spite of mutual recriminations between interdependent people about who caused the difficulties, one can keep an incentive system going and more or less correct its faults. One might still have to agree with Ecclesiastes, that "under the sun, ... the race is not to the swift, nor the battle to the strong, nor yet bread to the wise, but time and chance happeneth to them all." But time and chance can be adapted to in organizational performance measurement better than they can in the rigidities of normal contracts.

Prediction of Performance Requirements and Performance Measurement

The central reason for writing administrative provisions into contracts—provisions that contractual stipulations may be changed by specified methods—is that the future is uncertain. When that uncertainty involves so many contingencies that it is too expensive to give alterations of contract performances for all of them in advance, some mechanism for change or adaptation needs to be built into the contract. For convenience, we can treat these uncertainties under three broad categories: (1) uncertainties of the client about what it will want, or uncertainties of specifications; (2) cost uncertainties, due to contractor technical or cost uncertainties, to client ignorance, or to commercial or legal uncertainties in the client-contractor relationship; and (3) problems of observability of contractor defaults, so that without continuous intervention the client does not know whether the contract performances have been delivered.

If the client can anticipate that it might change its purposes, it will want to provide for changing the performances. If the actual costs of performances differ from the estimates made at the time of signing the contract, the rationality for the client of completing the contract may change if the client has to pay those costs; on the other hand, the contractor might not be willing to sign the contract without a prohibitive risk premium if it is to assume all cost risks. If the client anticipates being uncertain whether the contract has been fulfilled, it will want to be able to institute detective work or record keeping to reassure itself.

UNCERTAINTIES OF SPECIFICATIONS

Clients may anticipate that they will want to change their specifications of performances over the course of the contract for three main classes of reasons. First, the contract itself may involve exploration of the possibilities in the world; for example, in an R & D contract: one wants to buy research and development work on a particular airplane engine concept only if such an engine could be built, as judged after some preliminary workup is done (Marschak, Blennan, and Summers 1967, 63–90). Second, the client may anticipate changes in the state of the world to which it wants contractor performances to adapt; for example, a car manufacturer will want the dealers to push models that are selling slowly so no money will be lost on the production-line tooling for that model (Macaulay 1966, 12, 15, 18, 33, 46, 89, 167–168, 171). Finally, client preferences may change because of a change in the regime of the client organization or because of experience with the performances or products of the contractor during the contract. Sometimes such changes in preference can be anticipated; for example, the Department of Defense knows that operational experience will suggest modifications of the engineering specifications for weapons, but the exact modifications cannot be predicted (Stockfisch 1973; Bendor 1985).

The anticipation that one will know more about the possibilities as the contract runs its course is at the core of contracts for professional services. When people contract for a physician's advice, they find out what medical services they want. The special institutional protections of professional-client relations are designed in part to protect buyers who cannot know what they want until they find out what the world is like, what disease they have (Parsons 1939, 34–49).

When professional contracts are signed for large-scale projects, as when an oil company contracts for an engineering consultant firm to develop specifications for an oil platform, the exploration of what is possible is part of the contract. Such contracts are very generally negotiated on some sort of cost-plus basis—almost a sure sign of "hierarchy" penetrating market relationships.

In weapons development, the R & D part of the contract is very often written on a cost-plus basis, while production contracts after a weapon has been shown to be a real possibility are much more likely to be fixed-price incentive-fee or fixed-price contracts.[5] The cost plus basis shows that what performances the government will require in an R & D contract depends on what engineering possibilities turn out to be viable. Engineering theory is quite uncertain in predicting the performance characteristics of a high-technology system from an early paper plan. It is also very uncertain as a basis for predicting the costs of reaching a given technical possibility until that possibility has been specified in detail (Marschak, Blennan, and Summers 1967).

Even after a possibility has been developed and manifested in prototype production, the client cannot always explore its costs in the market without additional expense. A drawing that lacks many details of exactly how to produce the item can be clarified (within the same firm that did the development) by conversations between the engineers and a crew of skilled workers. To translate this conversation into detailed shop drawings for the production process for a complex weapons system or a computer so these can be produced elsewhere can cost millions of dollars.[6] That is, to draw up the client's specifications in specific enough form that the client can buy from several suppliers rather than from only one developer costs a lot of professional work, because it is the R & D contractor, not the client, that knows what the client wants.

Sometimes the uncertainty about the possibilities involves determining natural facts rather than exploring technical possibilities. In the development of the large Ekofisk oil field in the southern Norwegian North Sea, the first technical judgment was that the field probably was "not commercial" because the rock type was not permeable enough; each well would drain only a small area and would not pay for itself. In the "contract" between the Norwegian state and the oil companies exploring the field, there was a limitation on exploiting the field too fast—for example, not wasting the gas by burning it off but waiting until the gas pipelines were built. But the only way to get information about the permeability in a reasonable amount of time was to exploit a few wells "too fast," to estimate when the production started to fall off. Uncertainty about the state of the world a couple of miles down, then, required that the exploitation rate conditions of the contract be suspended for a time—until the production features of the rock were determined—and then reinstated. This suspension and then reassertion of the exploitation rate is a shift in specifications over time due to exploration of production possibilities (Moe et al. 1980, pt. 2, 7, 11). Hidden features of the world may be revealed by contractual activity and may require changing specifications as the hidden becomes manifest.

One very common form of client change in specifications in construction is due to failure of the imagination. The classic example is the light switch drawn behind the door—when the craftsman sees the location he can tell the switch would be better on the other side of the door. A typical, more subtle example occurred in the building of early concrete oil drilling platforms in Norway. In the tall concrete shafts of these rigs, a lot of plumbing and electrical work has to take place after the shaft is poured. If the shaft has supports for scaffolding poured into the inside wall, one can install and repair equipment by scaffolding supported by the walls, rather than having to build scaffolding from the bottom. But scaffolding does not appear on design drawings, so no one saw this possibility until a prototype existed. Contracts for the other rigs under construction were changed to specify such supports.

The general point is that in some kind of contracts it is contractual activity that discovers the production possibilities. As those possibilities are progressively revealed, one wants to change the specification of performances in the contract accordingly. To specify all possible states of the world would be expensive and otiose, since mechanisms to adapt performances as possibilities are revealed can be built into the contract.

The purposes of the client may change, not only because it finds out about the world, but also because that world changes. In many contractual situations the client can anticipate that some general kind of change in the world may change its purposes, without wanting or being able to specify all possibilities in advance. Perhaps the simplest of these is a change in the overall volume of the market for the line of goods a client produces. In contracts with franchise car dealers, for example, it may be reasonable to specify a market share for a dealer but not an absolute number of cars to be sold. In a recession, there is no reason to expect the proportion of Ford Motor Company cars among all those sold to decrease, but every reason to expect the absolute number to decrease. In developing informal standards of reasonableness to define the operational meaning of franchise contracts that allowed the manufacturer to require "satisfactory" sales, market share calculations of dealer performance requirements became standard. These market share standards replaced practices toward the beginning of the Great Depression in which Ford continued to force a constant stream of unsellable cars on the dealers (Macaulay 1966, 13).

In high-technology industries, technical developments outside the client-contractor relationship often make specifications of performances archaic. This is most obvious in military technology, when technical development is carried out by the potential enemy. Military supply contracts change as the Soviet Union develops defenses or offensive weapons. But in addition, for example, IBM has in the past followed the strategy for keeping its technical specifications secret for as long as possible so as to preserve its monopoly over sale of peripherals for longer, while Apple has followed the strategy of encouraging others to develop and sell add-ons and software. Both clearly expected technical developments elsewhere to change their relations with their clients. IBM thought that others would undermine contracts for peripherals; Apple thought that others could increase the value to the client of their computer, and so increase future sales (Toong and Gupta 1982). In both cases, the companies could be expected to modify their contracts with suppliers so that the monopoly or developments would be encouraged, leading in turn to different responses to technical developments among those suppliers.

When an accident happens to a given sort of ship, the classification societies that certify the ships for insurance companies often require changes in the ships before they will recertify them. Such societies routinely investigate accidents with a view to requiring preventive measures on other ships. Thus, the provision in marine insurance contracts that ships must be classed by a named classification society is an indirect requirement that the policyholder respond to changes in knowledge of the world, in particular knowledge of causes and accidents as represented in classification standards (Heimer 1985, 63–67). Changes in the standards of regulatory authorities, such as the CAB requirement for new inspections and new maintenance procedures for the engine supports of the DC-10 after the 1979 Chicago disaster (Newhouse 1982, 98), are also embedded in insurance contracts in provisions stating that the policy is not valid unless the planes satisfy government regulations.

Accidents that often happen during the course of construction, such as cave-ins, collapse of heavy structures before completion, and weather or fire damage to partly completed structures, will cause clients to want to change the activities required of contractors in order to achieve the performances specified in the contract. The reason construction has a much higher accident rate than the operations phase of the same buildings is that the construction process is not carefully designed for safety, and there are stages when the incomplete structure is weaker, more exposed, more unstable, than the complete structure will be.

Theoretically, this risk is assumed by the contractor or the contractor's bonding company, unless otherwise specifically provided in the contract. In actuality, however, the schedule, the degree of financial stability of the contractor and hence its financial capacity to carry out the performances, and sometimes even the technical possibility of construction plans are generally affected by severe accidents. In such a situation various standard contractual clauses are traditionally generously interpreted by the courts, creating a requirement that both parties adapt to the situation. The requirement for such adaptations are therefore generally implied in the contracts by the traditional legal interpretations.

Uncertainty of the law itself, especially uncertainty of substantive regulations such as environmental standards, create changes in client purposes. For example, nearly a year of work by an engineering crew was required to modify the design of the Statfjord B platform in the Norwegian North Sea to conform to new, stricter safety standards (Stinchcombe 1985e, 1985c). The extra engineering work thus entailed involved a change in the contract between the oil companies holding the concession in the field and the engineering contractor. Environmental and safety regulations virtually always change during the construction of a nuclear power plant in the United States, requiring changes in the performances demanded of both the engineering contractor and the fabrication and construction contractors (Cohen 1979, 76–77, 90–95).

In the case of software development, where it is very difficult to specify in advance what the client wants, adaptation of the software to client needs depends on placing the user-oriented members of the programming staff (the "architects") in authority on the project team, so that they guide the implementation programmers. When this authority structure in the contractor (the "system producer") fails, it takes more time to repair the software system to satisfy users than it would have taken to design it correctly in the first place (Brooks 1975, 47–50). The client's preference is not really changing; rather, what the client really wants departs over time from what the contractor is interpreting as the client's specifications—unless architects have authority.

Finally, we can recur to the contract for professional services in which client specifications—for weapons, for example—are developed by professionals. Professional "malpractice" or incompetence then produces specifications that do not in fact reflect client preferences. The avionics for the F111 fighter airplane (the F111 was also known as the TFX; avionics are the plane's navigational and aiming electronic systems) ended up being much more expensive and much less reliable than previous systems, though they did do more whenever they worked. The Department of Defense revised specifications in midproduction to get a cheaper and more reliable system. The bad performance was due to a mistaken set of engineering predictions about what was possible in a given "state of the art." Contractual activity can change specifications of performances by showing that some performances are not among the production possibilities, as well by finding some that are (Coulam 1977, 127–132).

The specifications changes we have discussed so far basically reflect changes in knowledge of the world or changes in the world. But client preferences can change in a more direct way. A simple example is a change in regime in the client organization. When Kennedy was elected and McNamara became secretary of defense, the military philosophy of the government changed. For example, the role of aircraft in support of ground troops increased in importance compared to the nuclear bombing mission, and the objective of common weapons for several services was introduced. An attempt was therefore made to modify the TFX airplane, whose range and speed (and therefore weight) were adapted to strategic retaliation, for carrier operations and support of ground troops. The management of the actual design was delegated to the air force. The fact that the modification was a failure enables us to observe the conflicts in objectives between the new top regime and the air force, for the air force preference for fast, long-range planes warred with the new preferences of the president and the secretary. In the long run, the air force won over McNamara, and the plane was not useful for the missions of the other services (Coulam 1977, 237–336).

A second source of direct preference change is client experience with the product. Operational testing of weapons almost invariably shows that the military did not want what they asked for in the engineering specifications, but instead wanted a modification of it (Stockfisch 1973). And in order to sell a satisfactory software system, one needs to adapt it in the design stage so that clients can modify it easily when they learn from experience what they really want to use it for (Brooks 1975, 117–118). Even those modifications of software that are called "maintenance," which are done by the supplier and are included in the contract of sale, are really changes in client specifications due to client experience. They come about because the test problems that software designers use to debug software do not adequately represent the problems the clients will use the system for. So client experience finds the *new* "bugs," that is, functions for the programs which the original program design does not allow for but which can reasonably be construed as a legitimate client expectation for system performance. For a heavily used software system, such postsale redesign or "maintenance" may easily amount to 40 percent of the total development cost (Brooks 1975, 121).

A third direct source of changes in client preferences derives from the fact that most clients are organizations. When a central authority in an organization delegates decision-making power (or revokes a previous delegation), it often changes the operating organizational preference function. The air force predilection for heavy, long-range, fast airplanes poorly adapted for ground support or carrier operation meant that the delegation to the air force in the TFX-F111 development resulted in a fighter adopted only by the air force (Coulam 1977, 237–336).

A common shift in preferences by delegation is due to professional perfectionism. Many professionals have a strong preference for technically elegant solutions, which often overrides cost-benefit considerations that are more important in the centers of ultimate power in the client organization. Organizations often go to great lengths to put "more reasonable" professionals in charge of design units (Kidder 1981; 119, 142), which shows they fear that internal delegation may change organizational preferences. For this reason, contracts normally administered by a professional department may provide for periodic review (with possible reorientation away from technical perfectionism) by higher authorities or operational arms of the client organization. R & D contracts and engineering contracts are especially likely to provide such review points.

Many client organizations determine their concrete preferences by a general preference for profits. Shifting profitabilities therefore change the client's preferences among concrete alternatives. For example, car manufacturers tool up each year for a large number of model changes. Some of those models sell well, but some move slowly. Since tooling for slow-moving models is a sunk cost and not useful for other purposes, the addition to profits made by selling a less popular model car is greater than that made by selling a hot-model car. But if franchise dealers control investments of selling efforts, car manufacturers would like to change performances demanded of franchise dealers to get them to move the slow models.

The purpose of this extended list of examples is to show that there are large parts of the economy in which the basic assumption of the labor contract—that the employer may change its mind about what it wants the worker to do (Simon 1957b)—holds between organizations.[7] Corporate and governmental clients change their minds about what they want from corporate suppliers and contractors. They know ahead of time that they may want to change their minds without destroying the contractual relationship, just as employers do not want to hire new workers on the open labor market for each change of task. Of course, the court will demand that the contract be written in such a way that the performances required at any particular time—or the options, such as contract cancellation, that can be used to reward or punish conformity with changed requirements—be definite.

Both the normal economic models of a market transaction and the legal model of a contract tend to obscure the degree to which large numbers of contracts are (realistically, though not legally) agreements to deliver an indefinite good or service for an indefinite price. A system for adapting to clients' shifting purposes as they discover production possibilities, determine how the world has changed, or change their preferences can render the performances required by the contract "piecewise definite," yielding an unfolding definiteness to be enforced by the court. And as clients will have been making those piecewise respecifications in the light of costs or of forgone alternatives as specified in part by pricing mechanisms built into the contracts, the contractors' compensation will likewise have been rendered piecewise definite.

The assumptions of our simplest models of market transactions, that clients know what they want and will continue to want the same thing throughout the transaction, do not therefore fit a large number of actual market transactions. Economists who analyze weapons research and development throw away the Economics 100 assumptions almost without noticing (Marschak, Blennan, and Summers 1967; also Scherer 1964). Similarly, practical seminars for contracts specialists in the construction industry discuss the techniques for writing the provisions dealing with "change orders" so that work can go forward on the change while compensation for it is in dispute, with hardly a glance at the legal theory of definite performances and considerations. Our purpose here has been to focus sustained attention on situations in which rational clients will want to provide contractually for being able to change their minds, without wanting to create a whole hierarchy of which they are the bosses.

COST UNCERTAINTIES

In many of the same industries in which we observe provisions for clients to change their minds we also observe contractor incapacity to project costs accurately. Scherer (1964) shows that when defense contracts are not renegotiated partway through, the standard deviation of the percentage cost overrun or underrun is about 10 percent. That is, aside from any bias induced in the mean cost estimate by strategic bargaining incentives (which bias in different ways with different types of contracts), sheer variation among contract outcomes causes a particular estimate to be within 10 percent of the mean percentage overrun or underrun for that type of contract only about two-thirds of the time; the other third of the time it is more than 10 percent from the mean (see Scherer 1964; 192, 195–196, and the graphs 196–199). Defense contractors simply do not know how much a weapon will cost. The standard deviation of costs as compared to estimates is large compared to the average percentage profit on the contracts.

Systematic data from other areas is rare, because cost data are not routinely public. A Swedish study of building construction suggested a range from 10 to 27 percent for working time spent in different projects on coffee breaks, walking to and from the locker rooms, and other nonwork activities (Kreiner 1976, 97). Clearly the contractors could not predict this variation very well, or they would have taken preventive measures. Since labor time is a large share of construction costs, cost uncertainty for construction contractors would seem to be in the same range as for weapons contractors.

Thus, even when performance specifications are definite, the appropriate compensation is very generally misestimated. Since often a single project is a large share of the total sales of a contractor, such cost uncertainty is a serious risk. This risk may be aggravated by penalties for not meeting a schedule. In one case of constructing missile silos with such penalty clauses, contractors apparently added about 50 percent risk premium to the cost the government had estimated for the work. The government shifted the risk to itself with a cost-plus-fee contract, and built the silos more cheaply.[8]

Because the client pays for the cost risk, it may be to everyone's benefit to plan to adapt to the risk, to agree to work together to minimize it, rather than merely shift it between parties. As background to the devices useful to such adaptation (devices short of hierarchy), we can specify some of the causes of cost uncertainties.

The first source of contractor cost uncertainty is uncertain technical information. An R & D contract would have no research element in it if the technical solution were obvious and all that had to be specified were the details, details that could be described (see Marschak, Blennan, and Summers 1967; on civilian R & D projects, see Scherer 1964, 178). The part of software development that can be accurately costed, for example— the writing of lines of code—accounts for only about a sixth of the development cost. The high remaining costs result because disaggregating a user's functional requirement into an implementation strategy ("system architecture") requires a good deal of expensive time, and then the implementation never works because it has bugs. The inaccuracy of the estimate of debugging time is so great, Brooks says, that a software project usually spends half its debugging time with debugging "90 percent complete" (Brooks 1975, 154–155). R & D and software development have in common that performance criteria for the product set by the client cannot be achieved in a technically routine way. Only routine technology can be accurately costed.

But any large unique project can meet technical surprises. The soil samples on the basis of which foundations for a building were costed may not have been a good enough sample, and much extra foundation work may have to be done (Kreiner 1976, 95–97). An oil platform base may sink improperly when being settled on the bottom and have to be discarded (itself not a trivial job) (Moe et al. 1980, pt. 2, 113–114). A new, lighter material for the huge fans that make bypass jet engines practical may break when a chicken corpse is thrown at a prototype fan at a high speed to simulate the engine swallowing a duck in flight; the titanium that replaces the new material may require new weight adjustments throughout the plane (Newhouse 1982).

In addition to technical cost uncertainties, estimators' manuals in construction warn the estimator to take account of the skilled labor market in the area (Page and Nation 1976).[9] If there are many more jobs than workers, the foreman's authority is undermined; if there are more workers than jobs, both the skill and the discipline of work crews can be increased. But how tight the labor market will be at the time a project is done cannot generally be predicted accurately when the project is estimated.

Tightness within the firm has the opposite effect in the defense industry. If a defense contractor has many employees but few positions on projects because of bad luck at the Pentagon, the projects it does have will have high official overheads inflated by salaries of people working on new bids, as well as high concealed overheads as projects are loaded up with extra workers. Scherer (1964, 183, 187) shows that lean efficient weapons projects are done by contractors with a lot of work, fat inefficient ones by contractors trying to retain valuable personnel for better times. Of course, this strategy is only possible because many defense contracts are cost-plus-fee contracts.

The cost of large, specialized machines such as airplanes, ships, heavy presses, or drilling rigs tends to decline rapidly with experience with a particular model. The rule of thumb among airplane manufacturers is that as one doubles the number of machines produced one cuts the cost of each additional one by 20–25 percent (Newhouse 1982, 19–21; Scherer 1964, 120–121; see also above, Chapter 5). This means that the average cost of production is as unpredictable as the size of the market. The size of the market for capital goods is very unpredictable, highly responsive to the business cycle, and strongly related to the prosperity of particular clients. Contractors cannot predict their costs for large capital machines because they do not know how far down the learning curve they will get. It is in part for this reason that airplane manufacturers will not design and produce airplanes unless they have a large advance order book for them.

Contractors very often depend on subcontractors who are themselves exposed to cost uncertainties. When a large number of large subcontracts are let on a fixed-price basis, at least one subcontractor on the project will likely get the job because it made the biggest estimating mistake. Since such a large subcontract may be a large share of the subcontractor's turnover, bankruptcy is not out of the question. Rolls Royce went bankrupt (to be saved by nationalization) because of overruns in developing the engines for Lockheed's wide-body airliner (Newhouse 1982, 62–72); if Rolls Royce had not been rescued, Lockheed would have gone bankrupt as well. Similarly, the computer development crew featured in Tracy Kidder's *The Soul of a New Machine* was substantially delayed because the chip manufacturer started to go bankrupt (Kidder 1981, 231–232, 268). (In this case, since the contracts for delivery of computers were not yet signed, the chip supplier was not technically a subcontractor.)

Contractors can misestimate their costs also because their historical cost data are bad. For many large contracts, the contractor's estimated cost is synthesized from estimates of what quantities of various elementary actions need to be carried out (e.g., how many yards of excavation), multiplied by a cost per unit derived in part from organizational historical cost data. But if the categories of elementary actions are not fine enough, the finished work may be costed with data that include rough work, the clearing of irregular terrain for a pipeline may be costed with data collected from work done on less broken terrain, or the job of locating survey respondents who are drug addicts may be costed with data on locating respondents who are physicians. The cost per unit may be misestimated from the historical data. Further, the multiplier may be out of date owing, for example, to inflation, technical change in the activity, or a decline in the quality control standards of a crucial semifinished goods supplier.

Such sources of inaccuracy plague all cost accounting, but they are more serious and harder to detect when production is not continuous. For one thing, since contractors often have to build up and tear down their organizations rapidly, a constant overhead cost such as a competent cost-accounting department is often an expensive luxury (Stinchcombe 1959).

Even when the contractor knows the costs (or even to the degree it knows them), the client may be excluded from that knowledge. The cost of bidding on a building construction job runs from 3 to 5 percent of the value of the job, even after the specifications are completely drawn up.

Contractors are therefore not willing to bid if there are many serious bidders, because bidding on many jobs they do not get increases their overhead and can make them noncompetitive in the long run. Ordinarily, then, a client gets a sample of three or so from a roughly normal distribution with a standard deviation of 10 percent (Scherer 1964, 192, 195–196, and the graphs 196–199).[10] Because the client often does not know what accounts for the differences among contractors (Kreiner 1976, 80–81), it may not be able to obtain good information from the market about costs even insofar as the contractors know them, nor can it legally penetrate the contractor for direct cost information.

The government sometimes tries to penetrate defense contractor costs. Even when they ask for separate pricing of components of a weapons development contract and devote government engineer and accountant hours to it, they cannot always get cost information to allow them to choose among alternative strategies (Scherer 1964, 204–207).

In addition, often contractors know of technical possibilities that they do not reveal because they do not effectively have a professional (fiduciary) contract with their clients.[11] I once knew an operations research consultant who had discovered that the main scheduling decision task a skilled executive did could be reproduced by a transformation of variables and a simple linear equation. By concealing that equation, he raised the price of his advice on the scheduling problem. A plastering contractor will rarely tell a potential client how much drywall would probably cost. Technical information that would allow clients to cut contractor profits is hard to come by.

The traditional theory in this field says that when clients are confronted with uncertainties that may impinge on delivery dates, on supplier solvency, on quality control problems as contractors desperately make up for costing mistakes, they will tend to incorporate the uncertainty within their organization, so they can control it as far as possible and predict when they cannot control it (J. Thompson 1967, 36, 40–42). But we have observed that in much of the economy they build whatever adaptations they do make into contractual relationships. They do this even when it puts contractors in a position of information advantage that may be (and often is) used to the clients' disadvantage—though the theory argues that the chance of exploitation by the contractor is a principal condition favoring vertical integration.[12]

OBSERVABILITY OF PERFORMANCE

When two activities depend on each other (are "closely coupled"), they should be administered together under the same responsibility, and only when activities are decoupled should they be divided between different firms or be done by different departments within a firm. The more two activities are interdependent, the more information has to flow between them, the more combined authority is necessary for making adjustments in both, and the more difficult it will be to allocate responsibility among activities for costs, delays, inferior quality, or other difficulties (Alchian and Demsetz 1972). This decoupling principle or team production principle means in particular that highly interdependent activities should not be separated by contracting parts of them, for that separates information flows, authority, and measurement of outcomes between two or more firms.

A derivation from this principle is that activities that have to be performed in series should only be separated among different firms if one is not in a hurry, so that delays (to give a breathing space), inspections, and inventories of partly finished work between stages can buffer interdependencies (J. Thompson 1967). Yet we observe that weapons development contracts are nearly always rushed to stay ahead of the Russians; that delays in construction administered by contracts are often the primary determinant of net present value of large capital projects, so such projects are rationally rushed (Moe et al. 1980, pt. 1, 111, 241); or that airline airframes stand waiting for the delivery of engines from a separate engine supplier at thousands of dollars a day lost per frame in interest alone (Newhouse 1982, 166).

Similarly, when the system being produced is highly technically interdependent, the quality control determining the reliability of components determines also the reliability of the system (Green and Bourne 1972). This means that the quality of work on a subcontracted component determines the effectiveness of another: faulty delivery of hot or cool air through a building's heating system leads to complaints about the fact that the windows do not open, and unreliable avionics causes a fighter-bomber to fly very fast in the wrong direction. To get the contractor to take responsibility for the performance of the whole system, a client often has to allow the contractor authority over the components (Scherer 1964, 110–112)—authority that is often administered and set up through contracts.[13]

The central difficulty for contractual arrangements that such technical interdependencies among components create is that the performances in two or more separate contracts are intermixed in such a way that the quality, timeliness, or cost of the separate performances are not separately measurable. This in turn means that it is difficult to establish which contractor was in default when the joint performance was inadequate. Several other common conditions have the same effect on performance observability. When performances are difficult to observe yet hierarchy is also difficult, special provisions may have to be made in the contract to render the performances controllable—which means to simulate a hierarchy by contractual means.

The most obvious problems of observability come when the performance is literally hidden, as in the length and composition of piles for a building, the second coat of paint on a three-coat paint job, the mean time to failure of a computer or copy machine just being bought, or, in international trade, the fiscal and monetary policy of the government that backs the currency in which the contract is to be paid.[14]

In the nature of the case a contract for professional services poses great difficulties in performance measurement. One cannot evaluate the quality of a service accurately if one could not have provided it oneself. One may know, for example, that the rate of ceasarean sections in the United States is much higher than it is in other countries where the maternal and fetal-neonate death rates are lower (e.g., the Netherlands or the Scandinavian countries), meaning that the procedure must be excessively prescribed. Yet an individual mother is not in a position to evaluate the professional advice she receives in her particular case. The extant economic theory predicts that the physician will prescribe the procedure that brings the highest fee; since such incentives could be corrected, one hopes it is this rather than incompetence that accounts for the over-prescription.[15] Except in very gross cases, defaults in performance of professional contracts are difficult to prove, and alternative control mechanisms are written into the norms of professional practice rather than into the contract.

In many contractual systems for large-scale projects, the client builds a large professional system within its own organization to supervise the administration of the contract. Scherer collected rank data from expert judges separately on the performance both of the government team supervising a set of defense contracts and of the contractor. The performances were highly correlated, indicating that client performance and contractor performance are too intermixed to be separately observed.[16]

In the Norwegian North Sea, the ratios of engineers in the client project organization to engineers in the engineering contractor's project organization have apparently ranged between 1:3 and 1:7. Under such conditions there is a large flow of information, consultation, approvals and disapprovals, and the like from the client's engineering crew to the engineer's crew; this means that at each step of the way the client's and the engineer's performance are deeply intermixed, and every step on the way to an engineering contractor's default has been approved or caused by a client directive. When things go wrong, when the project is delayed or becomes more expensive than planned, there is a flow of recriminations across the boundary that is nearly as large as the flow of information. In general, such deep intervention makes the contractor's responsibility for defaults very difficult to prove in court.

We see the same process in reverse when we observe that defense contractors on fixed-price contracts tend to refuse to introduce engineering changes, even though they will supposedly be reimbursed for the costs of such changes, because they cannot recoup the full cost of the disruption of production (Scherer 1964, 180, 237–238). When the client intervenes with a change order, it is not possible to discriminate exactly the costs attributable to client intervention from the costs normally due to activities for which the contractor is responsible.

The general point here is that when elements of hierarchy are built into the contract, by high Defense Department control of contractors, by supervision of the details of engineering work by a large client project crew, or even by an "isolated" engineering change in a fixed price contract, the separability of contractor performance is undermined. Thus, hierarchical elements built into the contract tend to undermine the legal obligation of the contractor for the performances specified and to require further reliance on hierarchical devices to adjust to the consequences of poor observability of performances.

Finally, we should note that when the contractor is in default, many contracts provide that the client (and sometimes also the surety bonding company) can resume authority over the performances and arrange to have them done by other contractors or by its own work force. The costs of such substitute performance are an element in determining the legal valuation of the contractor's default. That is, substantive hierarchical discretion and activity supervised by the client is involved in determining the damages of the default.

UNCERTAINTY AND THE REQUIREMENTS FOR HIERARCHY

Future contractual performances under certainty give no difficulty for either economic theory or the legal theory of contract. But the manufacture of large machines such as airliners or computer systems, the production of advanced weapons systems, and the building of large capital construction projects all frequently take place under conditions of *ex ante* shifting and uncertain client specifications—major cost uncertainties that it is rational to adapt to rather than to insure—and *ex post* uncertainty about whether the contractor has indeed done the performances. All of these uncertainties generate pressure to create structures connecting the client with the contractor (and the contractor with any sub-contractors) such that adjustive moves can be made authoritative. That is, such uncertainties create the requirement that hierarchical elements be built into the contractual system.

Elements of Hierarchy in Contract Contents

In the last section we showed that the functions for which hierarchies are set up are often necessary to accomplish the client's purposes in contractual relationships. We have also seen, in the preceding section, how hierarchies in fact fulfill those functions. The setting can provide some guidance in modifying our Economics 100 or Business Law 100 model of the papaya-buying contract to take account of the complexity we find in construction, weapons, airplane, or computer system contracts. We start by taking from our model of hierarchy the elements that we expect to be present when people have to solve hierarchical problems by contractual means.

"Hierarchical elements" in contracts can be described as consisting of five structures: (1) command structures and authority systems; (2) incentive systems, supporting authority systems and also guiding the use of a contractor's discretion by a structure of differential rewards partly isolated from the market; (3) standard operating procedures, that describe routines that involve actions by both contractors and clients; (4) dispute resolution procedures, partly isolated from the court system and from the market; and (5) pricing of variations in performances partly isolated from the market, including especially pricing based on contractor costs. Clearly a structure with relations of command, an incentive system partly isolated from the market, standard operating procedures, internal dispute resolution structures, and subunits whose "price" is determined mainly by costs is quite near to what we have described above as a typical "hierarchy."

COMMAND STRUCTURES AND AUTHORITY SYSTEMS

The naive notion of an authority system is one involving "command": a supervisor selecting an action for a subordinate to carry out. Above the level of foreman or secretary, authority systems rarely depend on command, though an authoritative description of an end to be achieved by an individual is perhaps not so uncommon. At middle management levels and above, revised minutes of committee meetings, a string of initials approving a proposed budget allocation, standard operating procedures adopted by the relevant authorities and written into the organizational regulations, or the question of a superior, "And what do you think you (or we) ought to do next?" with its implicit approval of whatever comes next, are more common ways of exercising authority.

Authority systems are systems by which flows of information are certified as legitimate or authoritative, so that the risk of being wrong is removed from the person who acts in accordance with the information and is laid instead on the legitimators of the communication (Barnard 1946). What we have to look for in contracts, then, are systems for certifying a given communication (other than the contract itself) as authoritative, and therefore as redistributing the risks of being wrong.

An elegant example occurred with the introduction of X-ray and sonic inspection of steel products. These inspections made possible a much more accurate determination of whether a given piece of steel actually satisfied the standards specified in the contract, not just on the surface but all the way through. Since almost all the increased accuracy was in detecting heretofore undetectable faults, the new devices enabled clients to raise the de facto standards for steel. The steel producers argued that the specifications for steel in the contracts extant at the time really incorporated the certifying procedures that were available when the contracts were signed; the clients argued that hidden defects violated the specifications as much as visible ones, and that inspection procedures not specifically described in the contract were implicitly left to the discretion of the client. (The decisions apparently went against the steel producers in most countries, and now inspection procedures are specified in new contracts.) The legal issue, however, was clearly, By what standards is the quality control certification to be taken as legitimate?

Such quality control systems are common features of contracts and constitute a clear example of an authority system in Barnard's sense of marking specific communications as authoritative. It is obvious that they distribute the risks of mistakes, since the steel producers were clearly claiming the right to their traditional proportion of mistakes, on the basis of which they had made their bids.

An approvals systems that is more clearly supervisory is that described above for defense contracts and large oil installations, in which a large staff of client engineers reviews and approves plans drawn up by R & D contractors or engineering consultants. The larger the client's engineering organization that reviews the contract's engineering work, the finer the net of approvals can be. This makes the sequence of steps that have to be approved more dense, which means that sketches, drafts, preliminary specifications and drawings, final specifications and drawings, tender documents, technical evaluations of the bidders' replies, technical changes proposed after contract start, and costs for all of these must all be approved by the client.

Aside from the extra work involved in creating a document for approval for each intermediate decision, such a fine net of approvals strains out any discretion or originality the contractor's engineers might have been afflicted with. Such a system makes the client engineer into a supervisor with restrictions on his or her oral and visual contact with the work, thus structuring the incompetence of the supervision and increasing its bureaucratic complexity (see the hearings on this problem in missile programs cited in Sherer 1964, 375–376).

A large number of inspection or "commissioning" provisions have the same general effect. In general, the inspection structure set up by the client is not specified in traditional construction contracts but is assumed according to industry practice. In large capital machinery construction, such as refineries or power generating stations, the contract often specifies a separate commissioning phase, during which authority is generally reconcentrated in the client's hands and the engineers or project managers from the contractor are put at the disposal of the client's supervisor of commissioning to aid in the testing of all equipment. In shipbuilding, some part of the inspection and testing is carried out by the classification societies that certify the ship to the marine insurance companies. Since clients do not want ships they cannot insure, and since producing an insurable ship is part of the contractual responsibility of the shipyard, this step serves also as an inspection on behalf of the client; indeed, it is paid for by the client rather than by the insurance company (Heimer 1985a).

More direct provision for command structures are often written into contracts. For instance, a standard form for subcontracts by a prime engineering contractor contains the language:

Physical Expediting

> When (company name) deems it advisable, this order
> shall be subject to physical expediting by (company
> name) representatives who shall be granted access to
> any and all parts of the seller's or sub-supplier's plant
> involved in the manufacture or processing of this order.

No actual capacity for the expediter to order people around is specifically provided, but authority is clearly being allocated.

The provisions about change orders in construction and large engineering project contracts quite often contain language to the effect that the contractor is to accept the orders of a specified person (in England this person, typically called "the Engineer," is employed by the client and is named early in the contract) on all change orders, even when the compensation for the change has not yet been agreed. The command authority of the Engineer over contractor personnel is thus established by designating the work to be a change order and not part of the original contract. The original contract, however, specifies this intermediate hierarchical phase, until the amendment of the original contract by the change order can be agreed on (or arbitrated).

Macaulay (1966) reports that in the bad old days, the automobile manufacturer's "regional representative" (the member of the manufacturer's marketing staff who dealt directly with the franchised car dealers) in effect had power to set quotas for sales, for car inventory, for parts orders, for sales and display space, and for other features of the dealer's business conduct not specified in the contract. These came to be points of dispute mainly when they increased costs and investments for the dealer and increased gross volume for the manufacturer but could decrease profit rates or increase risks for the dealers. The contract was written to provide that the manufacturer could cancel the franchise unless the dealer's performance was satisfactory to the manufacturer; but this meant that, lacking any other source of judgments of satisfactory performance, the regional representative could give orders with the sanction of the risk of cancellation. Again the authority structure is not specified in the contract, but the sanctions in the hands of the regional representatives were, and the practice of accepting their judgments created the command authority in practice.

INCENTIVE SYSTEMS

By an incentive system we mean a way of measuring or otherwise observing levels of performance of a contractor or of a contractor subunit and allocating differential compensation based on the level of performance, without further recourse directly to the market. An incentive system, then, is an enclave in the market within which special rules of reward and punishment apply. Of course, the broad levels of compensation tend to be set with an eye to the market, and a compensation system must produce a correspondence between output and costs that is viable in the market. But, for example, the piece rate systems in most American factories pay less for each additional piece (above the quota that merely earns the guaranteed daily minimum wage) than they do for each piece included in the minimum, which reverses the pattern to be expected on the basis of marginal revenue productivity. The older "Stakhanovite" Soviet incentive systems were closer to the neoclassical ideal.[17] Hence piece rates are incentives in a rule-governed enclave, rather than merely market reflections of differential machinist talent.

Actually, by this definition a normal fixed-price forward sale contract creates an incentive system. For the term of the contract, the contractor can sell the client a given quantity at the fixed price, even if it manages to reduce costs during the course of the contract. Thus the contractor collects the full value of all cost reductions, and none of that addition to contractor net revenue is dissipated by competitive reactions to these new cost possibilities. This superior incentive effect of fixed-price contracts is consciously used by the Department of Defense and some large corporate clients as the basis for a policy preferring such contracts. The average profit as a percentage of total sales on fixed-price defense contracts runs about three times as much as that on various types of cost-plus contracts (Scherer 1964, 159–60). Yet the Department of Defense believes it gets cheaper weapons from fixed-price contracts; their superiority as incentive (and competitive) systems thus apparently overrides the higher rewards to the contractors.

Once the basic device of building an incentive system into the contract is recognized, it can be extended to a wide variety of substantive measures of performance. In sharecropping and putting-out piecework systems, the incentive is based on the quantity of (acceptable) output. The difficulties of such an incentive system in a modern economy have been most fully studied for the Soviet Union (Granick 1976).

In the agency relations much analyzed in the modern economic literature, financial outputs provide the measures, which one would not want to do if the workers could eat part of the output before sale (Ross 1973; Becker and Stigler 1974). Many construction contracts provide for penalties (liquidated damages) for delays beyond an agreed-upon completion date, and often rewards for early completion as well. Franchise contracts for sales outlets generally in effect set up an incentive system to motivate sales efforts and sales-enhancing investments by the franchise holder without recourse to competitive bidding for the franchise.

The Department of Defense has experimented with making fees on R & D contracts depend on engineering performance criteria as measured on the resulting weapon. They have mostly discarded the system because contractors successfully argued that if the government had disapproved intermediate proposals that would have resulted, if followed, in a higher compensation, then the government owed the compensation; thus, the incentive system was incompatible with the degree of detailed authority over the development that the government wanted to retain (see Scherer 1964, 179, quoting U.S. Defense Department, "Incentive Contracting Guide," 43). More generally, the government's cost-plus-incentive-fee type of contract tries to create an incentive system partway between that of a fixed-price contract and a cost-plus-fixed-fee contract.

As one would expect, it appears that when the risk is higher, the contractors force the government to assume greater proportions of the cost overruns (and correspondingly, the contractors give up a larger part of the cost underruns, which would be profits under a fixed-price contract); that is, as one moves toward higher levels of inherent risks and cost uncertainty, one moves toward more hierarchical incentive systems (lower contractor shares in the cost risks) (Scherer 1964, 308).

STANDARD OPERATING PROCEDURES

The list of documents required by the operator of an oil field before it will pay a requisition (Stinchcombe 1985e) is a contractual practice that constrains everyone else to produce the appropriate documents; it provides an orderly way of proceeding in making purchases, a "standard operating procedure." But the companies operating in the standard way producing the standard documents are the consulting engineering firms, the manufacturers and assemblers of machinery, the construction contractors, and so on. It is the power implicit in the right to award contracts that enables the oil company to set up a standard operating procedure for a complex of firms involved in supplying goods and services to them.

The purpose of requiring all these documents is only rarely that the information is needed for some decision by the client. Instead it is to make sure, as far as one can with documents, that the contractor has followed routines specified by the client in making purchases, creating a trail of paper for auditing if necessary, providing documentation in case the regulatory authorities question a decision, and so forth. The information, then, is mostly not in the contents of the documents but in their existence, and what that existence communicates is that the contractor has in fact followed standard operating procedures specified by the client.

Tenders often require that the bidders on a large project provide PERT diagrams or other formal schedules with estimated elapsed time until various project "milestones" are reached. Generally associated reports on the achievement of the milestones are required as well, so that clients can estimate project completion delays as early as possible. This means in fact that clients will usually intervene to speed up projects that fall behind. The interventions often have the legal effect of transferring part of the risk for delays to the client, which is considered to have taken responsibility for meeting the schedule by taking it (partly) from the contractor's control. The legal disadvantage of intervening is often suffered for the sake of establishing a standard operating procedure to govern the schedule.

Sometimes the standard routines are established by traditional practice. For example, the marine insurance contract still contains a "sue and labor" clause, which was much more important before radio communications. It required the policyholder and its agents (in effect, the captain of the ship) to take whatever legal, physical, and commercial measures were necessary after a covered accident to minimize the total loss. Claims against the party liable for the damage had to be filed, repairs essential for the safety of the ship had to be made, perishable cargoes had to be sold, and so on. The costs were to be borne by the insurer. Such provisions provided routines for transferring the captain's agency relation to the new principal, which now would suffer the loss. The substantive contents of the obligations were defined by the situation (possible sources of loss), by the precedents in marine insurance adjudication, and by traditional requirements for good judgment on the part of captains (Heimer 1985a, 255–260).

DISPUTE RESOLUTION

The same "Engineer" in English construction contracts who is supposed to administer disputed change orders is also generally charged with authoritative (interim) interpretation of the contract in case of a dispute between the client and the contractor. The ideology here is that the Engineer is an independent professional who, though employed by the client, will give an objective interpretation of the contract. In England itself, this usually works to resolve the dispute; when the contract language is exported abroad, however, it tends to result in an interim client dictatorship through the Engineer's agency, because professional institutions protecting the Engineer's autonomy are not well developed elsewhere. Many such contracts also specify arbitration in case either the client or the contractor disagrees with the Engineer's decision. That is, a hierarchy of nominally independent appeals is specified within the contract, before the contract is appealed to the courts.

Under pressure from threatened legislation to protect franchised car dealers, car manufacturers developed a hierarchy of hearings and appeals, programs to help lagging dealers, and voluntary compensation for dealers who were canceled (usually by arranging for a new dealer to buy them out), before applying the market sanction of looking for an alternative dealer. Since the legislation was in fact ineffective in protecting dealers, these procedures were protections for the dealer from the manufacturer's market judgment that it could do better elsewhere, rather than an actual form of precourt dispute resolution (Macaulay 1966). If these devices applied to unionized workers, they would be called "grievance procedures" and they would be taken as a clear indication of the development of industrial justice with bureaucratization (Selznick, Nonet, and Vollmer 1969; see also Williamson 1975, 30, 73–80).

There are a great many informal equivalents of these formal hearings involving a contractor and a client. Many items on the agenda of a weekly or monthly meeting between client personnel and contractor personnel are disputes between the two organizations: technical disputes; disputes over what costs will be allowed; disputes over schedules, quality of workmanship, disruption of the client's business, where to put the fill dirt; or disputes over a client's employee who likes "to go over and rattle the contractor's cage a bit." Often the purpose of such meetings is described as "to clarify" the points of the agenda, which avoids naming them as disputes.

NONMARKET PRICING

Perhaps the surest indicator that a client intends to change a contract during its life is pricing based on contractor cost. This ordinarily involves complex procedures that supposedly ensure that costs are reasonable, such as the list of procurement documents mentioned above or the complex cost-accounting practices required of defense contractors. The general idea of such contracts is that the reward for the organization's competence—the fee or profit—should be separated from the costs incident on client change in specifications, client adaptation to cost uncertainties, or client control to secure faithful achievement of unobservables. Hospital services, engineering consultant services, R & D work, change orders in construction contracts, "sue and labor" work of a ship captain in marine insurance—all are usually priced on a cost basis. And cost pricing usually means hierarchy.

Cost pricing, though, in general means completely leaving the market, and so giving up competitive controls on pricing. When the technology of a line of work is not changing too rapidly, the institution of a "quantity surveyor" system, as used in construction in England, becomes possible. The quantity surveyor takes the architectural and engineering drawings of a project and translates them into quantities of technically distinct activities. Thus for example, welding pipes together fifty feet in the air is technically different from welding them on the ground and will have a different price. The contractor then bids on the bill of quantities, giving a price to a unit of welding fifty feet up, another price to a unit of welding on the ground, and so on. This pricing system yields the contractor's bid on the contract. For the contract itself, this practice has the advantage of stating precisely what is included in the contract (the bill of quantities is taken as final), of avoiding many contractor mistakes in reading drawings (meaning that the bids are serious), and of saving contractors estimating work so that more contractors are willing to bid.

But the contract usually specifies that a reasonable amount of work under change orders will be performed with the same pricing system. The quantity surveyor takes the quantities off the drawings for the change and determines the price. This is not cost pricing *post hoc*, but pricing of work outside the contract by a schedule of prices per unit built into the contract. But presumably the prices per unit reflect the contractor's estimate of its minimum costs plus a reasonable profit for the kind of work specified, under competitive pressure. Further, this process produces a fixed-price incentive system during the work on the change order, even with the contractual provision of hierarchical intervention by the client. It in effect uses market processes (and some very expensive and time-consuming work by a quantity surveyor) to get a market estimate of costs rather than a cost-accounting estimate of costs.

CONTRACT SIMULATIONS OF HIERARCHIES

The analysis of typical contract contents in several fields shows that when the extant theory predicts vertical integration but we do not *find* vertical integration, we find instead contractual provisions that may be expected to produce the effects of hierarchies. These provisions provide for clients to legitimate communications that will be taken as authoritative by employees of the contractor; they arrange incentive systems by rule partly outside the market; they establish standard operating procedures that involve regular flow of information between the contractor and the client and govern the procedures of the contractor as well as its objectives; they establish rule-governed systems for making fair decisions in case of disputes between the contractor and the client without recourse either to the courts or to client choice of another contractor; they price variations in performance by nonmarket rules, especially by costs or by quantity measurements of outputs.

These provisions often have a negative effect on the traditional obligations under the contracts. The difficulty when the Department of Defense sets up an incentive system to get the contractor to do what they later decide they do not want it to do, resulting in governmental liability for the incentive even though the contractor does not satisfy the performance requisites for it, is typical of the legal difficulties one gets into in writing contracts with hierarchical elements. The general point is that one cannot require the contractor to do something else than is specified in the contract without undermining requirements elsewhere in the contract or accruing liabilities that one would otherwise not have had. While much contractual ingenuity has gone into building hierarchical elements into contracts in these fields such that the legal obligations of both parties are clear, ingenuity does not always satisfy the judge.

Theoretical Conclusion

Our main descriptive conclusions are embedded in the preceding section. Briefly they are that five elements that make up hierarchies are often found in contractual language and that these elements achieve purposes of dealing with uncertainties that rational clients will often want to deal with. The fundamental conditions that call forth such contractual elements are those that ordinarily produce hierarchies in the ordinary sense of the term.

In a sense, the theoretical conclusion is that the law and the economy can arrange between firms in the market everything they can arrange in the labor market. When stated this way, the main proposition is unsurprising and a priori quite likely.

It does not follow that there is no use forming a concept of hierarchy with five elements (or some other number), an ideal-type concept whose contrasting concept is an ideal-typical market transaction. Such a strategy will be useful only if in fact the various elements cohere empirically. Since in our case they cohere (if at all) in a market subject to competitive evolutionary pressures (Nelson and Winter 1982), we have to argue that the various elements of hierarchy are functionally related.

We have occasionally noted above various empirical correlations in hierarchical features of contracts: for example, the usual nonmarket pricing of change orders in construction coheres with arrangements for the Engineer's hierarchical command of those changes. We could go through the other nine relationships between the five hierarchical elements we have found in contracts to show their empirical relationships as well.

To some degree our analysis of existent corporate hierarchies argues such an empirical correlation. When one is serious about setting up a hierarchy for the long run, one takes out a corporate charter, hires people, sets up an authority system and an incentive system, resolves disputes internally, and the like. The concretization of all five features in the normal corporate hierarchy therefore argues in favor of the empirical unity of the concept of hierarchy.

The functional unity of the features of hierarchy is implicitly argued above in the section entitled "Prediction of Performance Requirements and Performance Measurement." The argument takes the form that all five features of hierarchies (authority systems, incentive systems, standard operating procedures, dispute resolution procedures, and nonmarket internal pricing) are useful when a client may want to change specifications, when a contractor or a client cannot predict costs very well, or when performances are not easily separately measured. The end result of this argument, if it is accepted, is actually a continuous dimension between markets (or papaya-buying simple contracts) and hierarchies. For example, the work on a large capital construction project done hierarchically under change orders is normally about 20 percent. One could think of such a construction contract, then, as normally about 20 percent of the way between a pure market sales arrangement and an intrafirm hierarchical arrangement. Perhaps the normal R & D contract for weapons is 80 percent of the way toward making the contractor's engineering department into an arsenal development staff—a department of government (Stockfisch 1973; also see note 6). There is nothing wrong with describing such a dimension, along which decision systems range, by its two ends, contract and hierarchy. It simplifies theoretical discussion.

The continuous nature of the variable from "inside" to "outside" the firm does, however, make it hard to do empirical work with the dichotomy. When, for example, Teece gives statistics on what percentage of the distributors, pipelines, or oil wells are owned by the refiners and concludes that the oil industry is not very vertically integrated (Teece 1976, 36, 63–64, 96), one wants to tell him to come in out of the rain.

In the light of this discussion, the Williamson hypothesis (Williamson 1975) can be restated in continuous form.[18] Roughly it is that the greater the possibility of changing client specifications, the more the cost uncertainty, and the more difficult it is to measure performances, the higher the transaction costs of obtaining performances in the interfirm market rather than the labor market will be. Whenever these costs are not paid for by the compensating advantages of contracting (e.g., owing to being a construction client for only a short time, or to difficulties of R & D performance in government arsenals), we will expect to find hierarchical administration in the everyday sense of the term. We merely add to this some specification of what contracts will tend to look like when the compensating advantages of contracting are high.

Another way to look at these same theoretical conclusions is to ask, What else besides legally binding performance demands will we expect to find in contracts? Or, Why else are things put in contracts besides to establish the right to damages if specific performances are not carried out? The basic answer we have given is that the additions to contracts serve as the regulations of a formal organization. A corporation has a lot of authoritative "constitutional" writing that is not in the charter or other legal documents and that has the force of law only as long as the real law is not called in. Rule books, memos with enough initials, and minutes of the meetings between the production programming department and the shop superintendent serve as such legally unenforceable formal arrangements in hierarchies. In a contractual relation there is no other place to put the list of documents to be submitted with a request for reimbursement, or to specify who is in charge during a dispute over pricing a change order, or to arrange other matters for which one needs a hierarchy, except in the contract.

The normal expectation is that the client and the contractor should agree, formally and in writing, on such matters of joint administrative structure but that it would ordinarily not be worth anyone's while to go to court over it. We would not be surprised to find halfway through the contract performance a new rule from the client's accounting office demanding a new document before reimbursement (for example, a certification of the exchange rate at which currency was bought to pay the subcontractor), and one would not expect the contractor to sue for damages over such an increase in performances demanded. Putting these provisions in the contract has the virtue of explicitness more than the advantage of legal bindingness.

What usually has to be made binding under such circumstances is the overall control of the incentive system by one of the parties. The nearly hierarchical factual arrangements described by Macaulay (1966) for franchised car dealers were a reflection of the provision that cancellation was reserved to the manufacturer and that the manufacturer allowed a level of profit to the franchise holder that made it worthwhile for the car dealer to tolerate being pushed around.

That is, the function of the legally precarious flow of instructions generated by hierarchical structures built into contracts is to set up a formal organization—a hierarchy—that incorporates elements of the client organization and of the contractor organization into a new unity, under circumstances in which the traditional theory in this field would predict vertical integration.

When two powerful intellectual traditions have built powerful but idealized concepts, such as "market transaction" in economics or "contract" in law, into powerful intellectual systems, the concepts tend to shape perception. Everything appears as either the idealized version or something very different—"hierarchy." It is a great advance to conceive that dichotomy as a variable to be explained, as Coase and his successors have done. But things in the world are hardly ever dichotomies, and they are especially unlikely to be dichotomies when the economy sets a large number of intelligent men and women looking for the intermediate ground. Our argument has been that in many sectors of the economy, such intelligent search for contractual means of creating small hierarchies has been going on for generations.

From the point of view of this book, the central trouble with the economic model of a price-quantity transaction, and with the legal model of an enforceable contract, is that by excluding the uncertainty of the future, collecting news about what that future has brought in, and collecting information and making decisions to allow quick and rational response to that news, economists and lawyers have eliminated the organizational aspects of the networks of contracts. We have, however, agreed with the markets-and-hierarchies tradition that a hierarchy formed out of networks of labor contracts is a particularly easy way to set up information-collection and decision-making systems; that combination forms a constitutional mechanism by which many such information-collection subsystems can be created and integrated.

But other types of constitutions can organize and legitimate the creation of information-collection and decision-making structures. To figure out what they do, we first looked briefly (again) at what hierarchies in fact look like, how they are designed so that their structure can be changed without changing who is in charge. This short account is very much a compressed version of what we saw Du Pont doing internally when they introduced their multidivisional structure (see Chapter 4); it states the assumptions about what hierarchies are that are implicit in the processes that hierarchical Du Pont used to change how it responded to the news, to change its system of making decisions.

These constitutions generally specify how the labor contract is concretely used to create a system of authority; how people at the top can be trusted with other people's money; how an incentive system differentiated from the market can be set up to motivate employee performance, career development, or subcontractor performance; how routines and standard operating procedures can be created and, more important, improved; and how disputes can be resolved internally without the expense, delay, and uncertainty of the law. Such a constitutional system, in the markets-and-hierarchies tradition, is what enables hierarchies to outperform markets under conditions of uncertain specifications or costs, of small numbers in the market or first-mover advantages, or of other sources of "market failure."

But our assent to the core of the markets and hierarchies tradition, combined with the observation that networks of contracts between firms are the core organizing devices in many of the most uncertain parts of the economy, suggests that we have to look for how similar constitutional systems are set up with other types of contracts than those of the labor market. We find those constitutional devices written into the contracts between firms, where they are as legally precarious as they are in the law of the labor contract or the law of financial fiduciaries that are the legal basis of the constitutions of ordinary hierarchies within firms. Such organizational devices, such pseudohierarchies, do not need the certainties of contract law to make them run, any more than suits about the rights of employees versus employers are the normal way to make a corporate hierarchy run.

The uncertainties of research and development in the weapons business, or of contract construction, produce the problems of information processing that we have been analyzing throughout the book. When in Chapter 2, for example, we were predicting that the construction industry should have a high skill level because of its work-level uncertainty, we did not need to notice that those skills were tied together by contracts, rather than by a hierarchy, into a site organization.

Here we do not need to notice that, when contracts create a constitution in which a complex administrative task of coordinating many different tasks at a construction site can go on, the administrative task is substantially simplified by the skilled workers' being able to take up a lot of the uncertainty, which therefore does not have to be administered at the higher level.

The generalizations about the growth of information-processing structures toward sources of news about uncertainties that matter to the work do not depend on the work all being executed by a single legal entity, "an organization" as we would usually formulate it. Provided that in setting up the multiorganizational system that does the coordinated work the network of contracts forms a constitution that can create status systems, standard operating procedures, internal dispute-resolution systems, and the like, the network of organizations can, in the relevant respects, act like a hierarchy. Contracts as they actually exist in much of the economy are not to be explained by a branch of economic theory, nor by a branch of legal theory, but by a branch of organization theory.

Notes

1. Mansfield and others apparently do not predict this explicitly. They argue, following Arrow and others, that the private return to the innovating firm will generally be below the social return, because it is

difficult to appropriate all the returns from new information (Mansfield et al. 1977). Hiring as a subcontractor to develop new technology results in the subcontractor appropriating the value, as is documented by Scherer (1964, 381) for the relations between electronics manufacturers and airframe manufacturers; thus, subcontracting will rarely be used for R & D. Scherer (p. 372) quotes data which show that "only 4% of the four billion dollars in company-sponsored research and development performed during 1959 was contracted to outside organizations; the rest was performed in-house." It follows that R & D should be integrated to facilitate appropriation. The assumption that private firms never contract for R & D is implicit in the methods of Mansfield et al. (1977). See also Teece 1981, where amounts of in-house R & D in coal gassification and oil shale by oil companies are predicted on the basis of a theory of appropriability of returns.

2. Scherer (1964, 165, 178) compares civilian in-house R & D with weapons development contracts.

3. See Alchian and Demsetz 1972; and Newhouse 1982. On the general interpenetration of clients and suppliers, and the conditions that produce such interpenetration, see Reve and Johansen 1982.

4. Williamson's argument (1975) that more than authority—specifically the capacity to audit performances and incentive systems based on statuses and promotions—is required to make a hierarchy work is based on an analysis of Simon's paper (1957b).

5. See Scherer 1964, 145–146. Note that the theory that predicts the use of hierarchy rather than markets argues on the basis of competitive pressures on efficiency. These competitive arguments do not apply to governments, except perhaps in the long run in warlike periods. The explanation of why the American government does not develop its weapons in government arsenals, does not deliver Medicare and Medicaid through a national health service or through county, military, and veterans' hospitals, and does not build its own public buildings must be found in political history. Governments that do all these things with hierarchies show every evidence of being viable in the modern world, and in the medical case infant mortality statistics suggest they are more effective. Since we are here interested mainly in how hierarchies can be built with contracts, we will avoid trying to explain why the government uses contracts when the economic arguments suggest hierarchies would be more efficient. Perhaps government hierarchies are less efficient for special reasons, especially in the United States.

6. See Scherer 1964, 108–109; also Kidder 1981, 121–122. For a similar problem in software design, see Allman and Stonebreaker 1982, where it is estimated that "perhaps only a third of the total effort is required to get a large system to the stage where *we* can make it work."

7. Alchian and Demsetz (1972) define "manage" as "renegotiate with," which makes the same point.

8. See Scherer 1964, 308. Scherer (p. 159) gives returns on contracts by type of risk sharing for cost uncertainty, and documents (p. 226) the dependence of contractor willingness to share the risks of cost uncertainty on the amount of uncertainty present.

9. See also Moe et al. 1980, 324, 329, for the cost of having to recruit and train an unexpectedly large number of new workers on a project.

10. Three bids is a rough estimate based on miscellaneous sources on the construction industry in several countries.

11. Compare the reasoning behind the provision of Danish law that contractors assume the risks of cost uncertainties unknown to the clients: "the contractor will in many cases be in a better position than the client for limiting the impact of the [cost] uncertainties and can by virtue of his professional knowledge estimate the risk in advance to some degree"; my translation from Kriener 1976, 127.

12. See Klein, Crawford, and Alchian 1978; on opportunities to "renegotiate" the terms of construction contracts under way, see Kreiner 1976, 119. The ability to change the terms of a contract already in existence due to bargaining advantages developed during execution implies that "repeated-play" short-term contracts also would not solve the problems involved. This is why Klein and others predict vertical integration in such circumstances.

13. See Scherer 1964, 111. Western Electric insisted that components for missiles be shipped to them for measurement and testing before being sent to missile sites for assembly, even though the components were being made on contracts between the suppliers and the government; and some prime contractors accepted a zero-profit override to have component suppliers be subcontractors, rather than have them contract with the government, so the suppliers would report to and coordinate with them. Both facts indicate subcontracts with hierarchical elements.

14. Kreiner 1976, 91–119, has a good account of the variety of things that are hard for a client to observe in construction contracting.

15. "Second, while it is possible to conceive the fee as being directly functionally dependent on the act [of the agent, rather than being dependent on the outcome—as in fee-for-service agency relations rather than a typical sales agency relation] the theory loses much of its interest [because the agent by assumption will choose the act that is best paid], forcing a particular act" (Ross 1973). Physicians have less trouble conceiving of the interest of such fee-for-service arrangements than do economists.

16. Scherer (1964, 99) reports an r-square of .862. This figure is not in agreement with that given in Peck and Scherer (1962), reporting on the same study, where the reported r of .903 gives an r-square of .815. Either one is extremely high, and both show that contractor performance cannot be distinguished from client performance.

17. Granick suggests that this Soviet practice resulted in greater than proportional increases in average wages with increased productivity; periodic campaigns to revise the incentive pay scales reduced this creep (1954, 83–85, 245). For a comparison of Hungarian and American machine shop incentive systems, see Burawoy 1979. On incentive systems as characteristic of hierarchy, see Williamson 1975, 145; and Stinchcombe 1974, 123–150.

18. Williamson has gone some way toward restating his main hypothesis in continuous form in Williamson 1985.

7   Segmentation of the Labor Market and Information on the Skill of Workers

The Fundamental Uncertainty of the Labor Contract

No firm that hires a new person knows quite what it is getting, or in particular what it will get *on the average* over the eight or so years it can expect to employ the new person. Even while the person is employed the firm does not know exactly what it has got. Let us start with the measurement of performance after the worker gets the job, since if that is impossible to obtain, predictions of that performance at the time of hiring cannot help but be yet more inexact (March and March 1978).

We will analyze first performances of athletes in professional athletics, for statistical measurement of performance is surely better developed there than in practically any other area (Kahn and Sherer 1986). Measurement is done by outsiders rather than by management, so that managers need not decide on a cost basis how carefully to measure performance. Athletes on baseball, basketball, football, or soccer teams work under standard conditions, conditions very nearly identical to those of people who play the same positions on other teams. The objectives on all teams are identical: to score in a well defined set of ways in a standard number of games against a set of teams that are nearly identical in composition. The performance appropriate for different positions is also measured in standard ways, so that in baseball, for example, batting averages, earned run averages, or fielding averages span performances appropriate (in different mixtures) to outfielders, pitchers, and infielders.

The difficulties with even this highly developed measurement system for the work of athletes are well known. The first, most obvious difficulty is that the measurments are statistical, and (given that half of all the teams lose and the other half win, except in games like soccer where ties are common) they are statistical under conditions where certain kinds of uncertainty are maximized as far as the opposing teams and the overall managers of the competitive system can manage (for a description of the informal management of such a system of competition, Balinese cock-fighting, see Geertz 1973a). This means that every measurement is only as statistically reliable as the sample size permitted by a season of games (or the season so far) makes it. For example, scoring is a very unreliable measure in soccer, because the expected number of scores per person in a season is very low. Pitchers who pitch few games, or passing by backs other than the quarterback, present comparable problems. But these are only extreme forms of the common problem of random measurement error in all performance statistics.

In addition, different sports depend to different degrees on teamwork, and different positions or roles in any one sport matter more or less to the performance of others. Thus, individual performance statistics can-not adequately summarize performance, because the qualities reflected in one person's scoring (or other performance) include qualities of team-mates. This fact has shown up historically in American sports in the slower racial integration of the positions of pitcher and catcher in base-ball or of quarterback in football, where the importance of the position's contribution to teamwork makes measurement of performance difficult. Some measures of performance (e.g. the number of double plays in base-ball) are strongly affected by inseparability of teamwork performances.

Finally, some star performers are very popular with the fans, while some are a good deal less popular. Except for the factor of race (where it is fairly clear that in basketball a white star is more valuable to a team than a black star of equal performance, because there are more white fans than black fans, and whites prefer a star of their own race; see Kahn and Sherer 1986), the ability to get favorable notice in the news and bring fans to the stadium is not easily measurable.

So even in athletics, under the best of conditions, employers do not know quite what value they are buying for what they pay a worker.

Further, the very excellence of the measurement demonstrates a sec-ond point, that the performance of athletes over the course of their play-ing life and the length of that playing life are not well predicted by scouts or by recruitment contract rankings. Sports recruiters find out more surely than other personnel departments when they have made a mistake in judgment (in fact, the mistake rate of personnel departments may be the worst-measured performance characteristic of the business world, and surely is in the civil service). But of course, many sports have high injury rates as well. The long-run performance of an American football running back, even with a long series of knee operations, is not very well predicted by whether the knees held up through college.

This difficulty of predicting an athlete's performance at the time of recruitment occurs even though the situation in which the measurement of the talents and training of the recruit takes place—namely, college or amateur sports or farm clubs—simulates the actual work situation fairly well. This differs from the situation encountered by a recruiter of, say, engineers, who cannot examine many bridges built by a budding civil engineer, not even bridges built in a farm club that is not in the same league as a major civil engineering firm.

Consequently the contract of an athlete in any given year of his or her career depends intimately on current measurements of productivity, rather than on certificates consisting, perhaps, of batting averages from his or her college or farm club days. The bonuses for signing are of course a partial estimate of how much of the athlete's total value can be reliably predicted at recruitment time. In other parts of the economy, the labor contract has seniority provisions against layoffs and for moving up to better jobs by bumping less senior workers or for tenure after a six-year trial period, types of evidence of employer and employee unwillingness to make continuation and reward depend on current performance. These structures of tenure are wiped out in professional athletics by the possibility of good measurement of current productivity.

If seniority or tenure in the labor contract indicates poor measurement of current productivity, the employer—and even more, perhaps, the employee—must be uncertain about what the employer has in fact bought. This uncertainty is lower in athletics than in other sorts of work.

Part of the reason the possibility of measurement and prediction is so much worse in most jobs than in athletics is that the employer outside athletics will not be playing the same game as now in the future: the market will change, the technology will be improved, a different sort of teamwork will be needed because different groups will be working together, and so on. The artificial rigidity of the rules of sports makes it possible to predict what one will want in eight years in a third baseman. In eight years in the automobile industry, General Motors may be competing with the Japanese on quality rather than with Ford on style and price, and so may be wanting workers who will suggest how to avoid mistakes rather than workers who can keep the line going whether the carburetor gasket fits or not. An employer outside athletics wants to recruit now someone who will be good at doing whatever the firm decides to do in eight years, rather than someone who will still be good at what a third baseman has always done.

Part of the reason the labor market as a whole is less good than athletics at predicting productivity is that schools are not in general good simulations of work life; the measurements at career beginnings are of what makes potential recruits good at schoolwork, with an overemphasis on intelligence and an underemphasis on qualities of character. Insofar as school recommendations do comment on qualities of character, we would all be better off to ignore them, because ordinarily the teachers who write the letters have very little opportunity to observe those parts of life in which such qualities play a great role.

Part of the reason the labor market as a whole is worse than athletics at measuring productivity and rewarding it is that employees will not stand for rewards based on performance unless they get a lot out of it. One can hire professional athletes even though one is going to fire them at roughly thirty-five years old on the basis of declining performance statistics, to withhold seniority privileges, to make their future income uncertain depending on such things as the success or failure of knee operations, only because one is willing to pay a lot for the years they work.

Not knowing what one is buying, or even what one has bought, makes the labor contract a perennial information problem for management. It might be imagined that at least the worker knows what he or she produces, but this also is not true. What workers conceive as valuable to the firm is strongly determined by the jobs they occupy. Manual workers typically believe that what really holds a firm together is physical production; clerical workers believe that if the flow of paper does not go right, everything will come apart; managers believe that the bottleneck factor in company success is management; financial officials of the company believe that the proper structuring of debt and equities is the fundamental determinant of the mixture of risks and profits of stockholders and debt holders, and so determines whether or not the firm will continue to exist. Thus, at least some of them must overestimate their productivity for the firm. And employees very generally have virtually no idea what their talents would bring on the open labor market.

Institutional Substitutes for Measurement of Productivity

Mutiple personnel information systems in organizations and in the labor market are directed at filling in the gaps in this picture of poor measurement and poor prediction of the productivity of labor. These systems of information include certificates from the educational system and sometimes from the professional system as well (e.g., specialty boards in medicine); union membership in the crafts; promotion decisions in internal labor markets; informal respect in the work group; whatever experience firms have about whether men or women work out better under the salary, promotion, and incentive systems they typically set up for clerical workers; job evaluation schemes; recommendations by workers in the plant about new hires (a remarkable proportion of workers are recruited this way); footnote citations that distribute honor in the scientific community and so indirectly determine appointments, promotions, and salaries in universities; and so on.

The information that leads employers to prefer one kind of workers to another (e.g., that leads large manufacturing corporations to prefer people already employed there but that leads universities below the very first rank to prefer *not* to hire their own graduates as assistant professors) means that different *segments* of the labor force will have different opportunities: different incomes, different levels of employment security, different chances of promotion, and the like. Consequently, labor market segmentation is fundamentally a solution to a problem of the information structure about people and their performance that confronts organizations and employees. But since people's rewards depend on these flows of information, they have an interest in having the flows contain information that says they are better than others, whether that information is trustworthy or not (Edwards, Reich, and Gordon 1975).

The labor market part of the problem of organizations is shot through with agency problems, problems of the two parties to a contract having different amounts and kinds of information and wanting to use those information differentials to their own advantage. The example of an agency problem we gave in Chapter 1—whether a secondary school teacher's certificate of audiovisual competence was information about whether that teacher is likely to select good instructional films—demonstrates the deep problem of getting unbiased information about worker productivities. And it is this impossibility of gaining good information about employee performance that creates many opportunities for employees to monopolize opportunities, by monopolizing the chance to generate good information about their performance. We find relatively little monopolization in professional athletics (for instance, the residual racism in athletic teams' hiring and promotion is not at all comparable to the racism or sexism that still exists for jobs paying comparable salaries in corporations or universities), because in spite of the cautions we have outlined above, one can measure the productivity of athletes very well indeed. The purpose of this chapter is to examine the interplay of information on performance, agency problems biasing the information, and monopolization of opportunities by segments of the labor market.

Types of Information About Work Performance

An organization needs information about the immediate past work performance of a worker so as to allocate rewards fairly, and it needs information about future work performance in decisions about hiring, promotion, and retention. In order to be used as a basis for rewards, information needs to be, to some degree, "auditable," so that people do not simply get to choose their own reward levels. In order to be useful for predicting future performance, an employer needs information about response to a range of conditions that fairly represent the expected future of the work the person will do, and again the information needs to be auditable, so that workers do not unilaterally decide on their retention and promotion and potential recruits do not determine who should be hired by providing false information.

The general problem with information systems about employees is that the more accurate and wide-ranging a person's observation of the worker is, the more likely it is that the person will be a fellow worker (or a fellow student). This brings up two problems: the fellow worker may not be competent to render a judgment that would be accepted by a reward-giving or hiring executive; and the fellow worker may have his or her own fate intimately intertwined with the information given, and so be motivated to withhold or distort it. Informal pressures among fellow workers tend to discourage giving accurate information to management, especially if that information is negative (see, e.g., Halle 1984, 121–122, 138–144, 161–162). Information from a competitor for the same promotion might, however, be shaded in a negative direction for reasons of rational interest, while information from a fellow worker might be negatively shaded for vengeance if the worker had been too attentive to the evaluator's wife.

Information from hierarchical superiors tends to be based on less detailed observation but to have different, generally smaller, agency problems (but see the analysis below of why union firms are more productive, for contrary evidence). The information that a superior gives about the worker's performance gives the superior partial control over a reward for that worker. The superior, then, may trade the benefit of giving more favorable information to superiors for cooperation. While the organization generally benefits, in the short run, from the cooperation, the degraded information about the worker is a cost that must be paid in return. Of course, the cooperation required of a supervisor does not always contribute to organizational objectives, as sexual harassment cases demonstrate (cf. Charlton 1983).

Information is therefore often based on measures of performance that are easier to audit, such as units produced, hours recorded by a time clock, sales made, or (higher up the hierarchy) costs reduced, profits increased, delivery times reduced, scrap figures down, and the like. There are four broad types of difficulties with such measurements. The first is that they too can be manipulated by interested workers on the scene; for example, bargaining between workers and first-line supervisors about how much time should be allowed against a piece rate for down time of a machine is common in machine shops, because management cannot get accurate measurements of that down time from anyone but the workers and supervisors involved (Burawoy 1979).

The second difficulty with formal performance measurement is that the measures used may not be good estimates of true performance. In shoe factories in the Soviet Union where performance was measured by numbers of shoes produced under conditions of leather shortage, for example, factories produced only shoes of the smallest size (Granick 1954). When responsibility in dealing with extraordinary circumstances is a core function of a job, routine measurements of productivity tend to be worst exactly when the workers are doing the extraordinary parts of their jobs the best. For example, more soldiers under one's command are killed while one is successfully attacking or defending, and productivity of a chemical plant is lowest when the workers are putting out a fire.

The third difficulty is that such auditable measures tend to rigidify the measurement of performance, so that technical change or reorganization undermines the measurement system. With rigid performance measurement, the interests of workers embedded in the measurement system tend to lead to sabotage of technical and organizational change.

Fourth, such specialized measurement is generally expensive. One still needs the pyramid of supervision even if productivity is measured separately. One needs cooperation and the transmission of informal skills within the work group (and one has to pay the costs of cooperation) to deal with the ordinary contingencies of work, even if peer judgments are not used in the personnel process (cf. Blau, [1955] 1963). Because, for example, one cannot substitute the records of productivity, produced by an inspection department, for supervision by the foreman of a machine shop, measurement of performance by inspectors is an extra expense. Special performance measurement therefore tends to be narrowly focused on a few aspects of performance and to be done at a high level of abstraction, since it would be too expensive if it were not radically simplified.

For hiring and promotion decisions one needs to measure performances that will predict what kind of worker a person will be in the future. Even if one or the other of the performance measurement types outlined above has been carried out before the hiring or promotion, predictive information has four difficulties additional to those associated with the measurement of current and past performance.

First, the performances that the hirer or promoter tries to measure may not predict the sorts of performances that will be required in the future job. Ordinarily the person doing the hiring cannot predict exactly what the performance requirements will be for the job being filled, because of technical and organizational change or because personnel officers do not know much about the job themselves. A crucial factor in the prediction may be how well a person is accepted by the future fellow workers and supervisors who can teach him or her to do it well; personnel people can usually predict this only by using crude categories such as ethnicity and sex, and those are not very good predictors.

A second additional trouble is that the performances measured previously may be systematically different from those required in the job a person is being recruited for or promoted to. Often much of the information for recruitment is about schooling, and the performances measured there (typically tests in courses or general ability tests), while fairly well audited, are not good samples of the tasks required for success in jobs. Work done in a lower position is often not representative of what the worker will need to do in a higher position (particularly in terms of "responsibility," management of people, and management of information flows at a higher level of abstraction, all of which tend to be more important in higher positions), so that excellent performance lower down may not predict good performance higher up (this uncertainty can be partly controlled by letting people who might be promoted pinch hit for superiors when those are sick or on vacation).

A third broad additional difficulty with recuitment information is that people providing the information often have no commitment to the organization they are supplying information to, so that letters of recommendation all rank people as among the top 10 percent. This is one reason why the more auditable parts of people's previous experience (grades rather than recommendations, and grades in calculus rather than grades in sociology) tend to overemphasized.

A fourth broad difficulty with recruitment and promotion information is lack of comparability. It is well known that it is harder to get good grades at Swarthmore or Reed or some other leading places than at less distinguished colleges and universities, but there is no general formula to translate grades from one school into their equivalents at another. Similarly, within a company some supervisors will be well known to give generally very high ratings to their subordinates, others to be somewhat tougher, but no general translation to a standard degree of softness or toughness is likely to exist.

Even without such variations in the standards of the judges, there would be differences in what is being measured. An engineer who has been doing an excellent job selling airplanes produced by a particular company does not show the same virtues in his or her work as an engineer who has been doing an excellent job designing efficient heat transfer from the exhaust to the incoming air and fuel of the engines of those airplanes. Even if both workers have substituted successfully for their superiors, their superiors have different jobs as well. Thus, prediction of future performance is even more difficult than measurement of past and current performance.

A General Theory of Certification

By a "certificate" we will mean a summary of information about some performances of a worker or a candidate for a job that has been subjected to some sort of special procedures that are thought to make it more trustworthy (the general approach of this section is taken from Heimer 1984; see also Shapiro 1987). The first thing we have to do, then, is to distinguish different certificates according to the degree of formalization of both the sampling of performances and the protection of the trustworthiness of the judgments. At the extreme low end of formality is the "certificate" of seniority in a particular job. The universe sampled in the knowledge that a person has held a job for some time is the correct universe for assessing performance in that job (insofar as the job is not predicted to change much), but the sampling process tells us only that no negative information has come to light that was sufficiently serious to fire the worker. No particular efforts have ordinarily been made to check and protect the trustworthiness of the information, to make sure that everyone who should be fired has been fired.

At the high end of the variable of formality is the degree (with a transcript) from a particular college or other school, which ordinarily specifies in what courses performance was sampled and certifies that the judgments were made by people relatively uninterested in providing spurious information. One can be reasonably confident that much of the information was derived from pencil and paper tests or from writing assignments, and that the subjects of those tests would be recognizable by someone who had taken a similar course at another school.

Certificates can be produced as an offshoot of all the types of information systems described above, by fellow workers or bodies of peers, by superiors giving an overall judgment, by systematic performance measurement systems of a more or less numerical and auditable sort. Those providing the information may have sampled performances highly predictive or less predictive of job performance, may have more or less commitment to providing the hiring or promoting organization with accurate information, and may be providing information in a common metric (such as Graduate Record Examination scores) or in noncomparable form. The central *sociological* point of all this is that all information that is taken into account in recruitment, retention, or promotion tends to need legitimation. The main reasons for this are practical: performance measurement requires observation of a worker or recruit in performances that are relevant to the work he or she is to do; judgment of that information requires that the judge too be competent in the same performances; and transmission of the information requires honesty and discretion on the part of the transmitter.

Second, it is not only performances in school that become certificates. Seniority is almost always a part of the formal record, and is roughly of equal importance to education in determining job level, job security, and pay. Seniority is a crucial certificate of qualification, particularly for the job a worker now holds, because what it lacks in systematic measurement and trustworthiness of the judgments it makes up in relevance. The performances of which it is a sort of record are those that are crucial for doing the job. If labor market segmentation is due to differences in various populations' opportunities to give acceptable certificates of their competence in a job, then a big source of segmentation is the tendency of most jobs to be awarded next year to the person who holds them this year.

Seniority is also one of the components in promotion systems or "internal labor markets" that characterize large bureaucratic firms, the various levels of government (especially in educational, health, and military branches), and certain large nonprofit organizations such as private universities. Since in general not all workers get the same number and size of promotions, and since educational qualifications determine which promotion ladder different people are on within the same organization, seniority in this case is more complex than in the case of a job qualifying a worker for that same job. Most promotions go to whatever groups are now employed in large bureaucratic organizations, especially to those who entered from college. We have suggested in Chapter 2 some of what seniority in positions to which one is recruited from higher education may be certifying.

The other main source of certification in internal labor markets, again especially in those career ladders that start with recuitment from higher education, is the formal opinion of superiors. As one gets nearer to the top of the hierarchy, more of such opinions are formed in committee rather than by individual superiors, which means that to some degree the top ranks of the "internal labor markets" of large organizations must be treated as a subtype of craft and professional certification. At the top people are certified by a body of peers.

The third main type of certification is based on observation of work by people already certified as skilled in that work, and it is protected from the most extreme forms of interpersonal logrolling by a "committee of peers"–type structure. As Amitai Etzioni has pointed out (1975), committees of peers are actually made up of one's superiors, not one's peers. (The original notion presumably was that the peers are peers of one another, like the House of Lords, not peers of the candidate.) What the committee of peers structure means is that no one person is a particular hierarchical superior who has the certification within his or her own power. Instead, for example, the associate and full professors of a department meet as a committee to recommend to the dean whether a given assistant professor should be promoted, or the body of craftsmen meet to certify someone as a journeyman. Internal labor markets in corporations and large bureaucracies tend to be more craftlike toward the top than they are in the middle, because as one advances influence over promotion chances begins to pass away from a single hierarchical superior toward a group, the "management committee" or, in the extreme, the board of directors.

The basic idea of peer certification systems is that the true requirements of a role can be taught and judged only by those who can do the role themselves, who have teaching and supervisory responsibility for the candidate for the role, and who have multiple informal contacts with the candidate. Quite generally a strong seniority element is built into these certifications, as in the fixed term of apprenticeship in many traditional crafts or the fixed term of internship or residency of physician trainees. The expectation is often that anyone admitted to the peer tutelary period can learn to perform the roles involved, so years spent in the apprenticeship are in effect the only measures of competence in the certificate.

Quite often, however, there are additional examinations or performances (e.g., the traditional "masterwork" of some artistic crafts) or additional examination of the work (e.g., the assessment of published work by a committee on a promotion in a university). So while assistant professors rarely get promoted without a respectable five years' seniority in the job, they may not get promoted even with the seniority because their work is not judged to be up to the standard of the profession.

We will expect the features of the certification system for particular positions to vary with the character of the information problems involved in those positions. In general, the more the crucial uncertainties of the system in which a role is placed are dealt with in the role itself (as, for example, medical diagnosis in hospitals is dealt with by physicians, not managers), and the more the information to deal with those uncertainties tends to be concentrated at the lowest level, the more one has to rely on role holders (peers) for judgments. Thus in general, the higher the skill level of a role, and the more important the uncertainties dealt with by workers' skills in the organization as a whole, the more the organization must tap the information held by peers, that is, by the senior people who perform the role themselves and who work with the candidate.

When it is difficult for peers to explain what it is they do and to judge whether someone else is doing it well, and when bureaucratic superiors cannot measure output well because of poor observation or incommensurability of outcomes, as in secondary school teaching or police patrol work, then very general certificates of appropriate character and background for the work are combined with seniority (for a general description of police and teaching promotion and salary systems, see Spilerman 1986, 54–65), but usually with relatively small reward for seniority. Where the skill itself is obscure, but the output of interest to the organization is readily measurable and auditable, as among wholesale or real estate salespeople or athletic stars, certificates of competence and seniority usually play a very small role and rewards are based on measured performance. Where crucial uncertainties have to be dealt with by teamwork, making individual performance difficult to measure, as in continuous process manufacturing, seniority mixed with hierarchical superiors' judgment tends to dominate.

These general considerations are combined in different ways into five main kinds of institutional systems for certifying people for jobs in modern economies, which we will outline in the next five sections; these systems are based on (1) continuity or tenure in the present job; (2) promotions from within in large organizations; (3) craft and professional certification by peers; (4) recruitment of a person from within the family or of oneself as owner; and (5) the odd case of certification through work in a union shop. After examining these main institutional systems for certification of competence, we will look at how the opportunities to provide information and to have it disseminated to the people doing the hiring are distributed. If all people needed to get a job was to have the competences to do it, the labor market would be much more competitive than it now is, because competences can be learned in all sorts of ways. But one has to learn a competence in such a way that trustworthy information about that competence can reach a potential employer at a time when that employer is making a decision about whom to hire (for a fuller analysis, see Heimer 1984). Since one of the main forms of certification is being already in the job, and if someone satisfactory is in the job an employer does not make a decision, competition takes place mainly on the rare occasions of job vacancies.

But even in the case of job vacancies, only certain types of information are acceptable certificates to a potential employer for predicting a potential recruit's future performance. And since the information embedded in those certificates is generated in institutions that produce the opportunity for a person to perform, produce observations on that performance, and guarantee to some degree the integrity and comparability of the report of those observations, not everyone could conceivably provide certificates of competence because not all have access to those institutions. This situation produces a stratification of opportunities in the labor market. In general, those who cannot produce certificates of special competence occupy places in the "secondary" labor market, a market of open competition for bad jobs.

The Great Segmenting Factor Is Who Holds the Job Now

Around 1970 the status attainment literature, the literature about who got what jobs and how social origins influence what jobs they got, assumed that everyone got the highest occupational status they could, so it assumed uniformity of the values of workers choosing jobs (though these authors never discussed just what they were assuming). The "causes" in this literature, then, were amounts of people's resources, especially human capital resources, such as education, and ordinary capital or wealth, which facilitate or hinder that maximization (the clearest statement of this theory I have seen is Kelley 1972); in other words, the causes were not variations in subjective processes (e.g., in how much people value prestige versus money returns, or security versus higher average income), but rather variations in the situations that determine people's possibilities.

In the past decade, besides providing the main substantive material that has been used in the development of sociological methodology, the status attainment literature has provided an environment in which variations in labor market demands by firms have become principal variables for explaining the distribution of labor market outcomes. And the new variables are provided by institutional features *of the employers.*

Overall, the central institutional feature of employers is that, by and large, they will employ the same workers in the same jobs this year as they did last year. For example, the average job occupied around 1970 by a male worker under fifty-five falls vacant in Yokohama about once every eight years, owing to either promotion within the firm or movement between firms; in Detroit such a job would fall vacant about once every four years (Cole and Siegel 1979, 70–71). So in Japan, about seven-eights of the jobs occupied last year would still be occupied this year by the same man; in the United States, about three-quarters would be.

In 1970, the typical male worker between thirty-five and fifty-five in the Detroit study (Cole and Siegel 1979), left the firm he worked for on the average of every fourteen to twenty years; in Yokohama in 1971, the typical male worker left the firm on the average of every thirty-three years. If these men did not move among firms, then chances are they would change jobs within the firm only once in sixteen to twenty years in Detroit, once in twenty years in Yokohama. On average, then, if a job is occupied by someone over thirty-five, *nobody* is going to move into it any more often than about once every ten to fifteen years (roughly half the jobs being vacated by promotion, the other half by the worker leaving the job), in either Japan or the United States.

Jobs occupied by young workers are more likely than those occupied by older workers to fall vacant because of both kinds of mobility. Jobs occupied by workers in large organizations are more likely than those in small organizations to fall vacant due to *promotion*, while those in small organizations are more likely to fall vacant because of *mobility among firms.*

But the overwhelming institutional fact about the labor market is that the boundary around the worker-job pair is the most impermeable of labor market boundaries—among markets, perhaps only the housing market for owner-occupied housing has a lower rate of movement (the housing market as a whole, at least in the United States, has very roughly the same rate of movement of people as does the labor market). High-seniority workers in middle age move out of their jobs about as often as homeowners move out of single-family houses that they own.

This means that the overall structure of the labor market reflects the mobility patterns of people now working which took place up to forty years ago when they were young. The tendency of people to retain their jobs means that holding a job now does not represent an equilibrium created in the timeless instant of economic theory. About one-sixth of all lawyers in the United States are women, even though about one-third of all law school graduates in 1987 were women; past patterns of mobility into the legal profession will be cast in stone until the tight person-job ties between males and jobs as lawyers are dissolved by retirement or death (cf. Lieberson and Fuguitt 1967 on the comparable problem for the races; Caplette 1982). All sorts of firms have "internal labor markets" in the sense that the people who will occupy the jobs next year are mostly in the firm already.

What this comes down to is that the flexibility of the labor market in terms of *mobility* is mainly flexibility over what to do with the new cohort—people between twenty and thirty who are settling into the jobs that they will mostly then hold (except for promotions, if they are in the big firm–government sector). How this group settles in will heavily determine what the labor market looks like thirty to forty years from now. If 33 percent of law school graduates, but only 10 percent of engineering school graduates, are women, and if entry rates in those fields are about the same between 1986 and 1990, then in 2020–2025 the new recruits will be between sixty and sixty-five years old. A little over 33 percent of the lawyers and a little over 10 percent of the engineers aged sixty to sixty-five in 2020 (a few more of the men will have died than the women) will be women.

To put real numbers on this, in 1980 about 65,000 engineers out of 1,401,000, or 4.6 percent, and about 74,000 lawyers and judges out of 530,000, or 14.0 percent, were women (*Statistical Abstract of the United States, 1984*, 416). In 1981, about 7,700 out of 75,000 engineering graduates were women, or about 10.3 percent (*Digest of Education Statistics 1983–84*, 120); for law the figures are 11,768 out of 36,331, or about 32.4 percent (ibid., 126). By and large until 2020, the folks now in the profession will shape the sex composition of the legal and engineering elites. At around that time present law and engineering graduates will have moved into the elite to roughly double the respective percentages of women. So the fact that feminism has had a lot less effect on engineering training than on legal training recently will still be a fact set in stone in the elite of the engineering and the law elite labor force in 2020.

This means, however, that when the labor market aggregates *do* move because of some outside cause, such as a decrease in the number of elementary school–aged children, this movement has enormous implications for the only people who are mobile, namely the people just entering the labor market. For instance, the total number of teachers did not change much between 1975 and 1981, as a percentage of what it was in 1975 (see ibid., 49; *Digest of Education Statistics 1976*, 53). But because almost all the teachers already in service would hold onto their jobs, the adjustment of young people was tremendous. During that same period, the number of teachers *graduating* went down from 167,000 (*Digest 1976*, 118) to 108,000 (*Digest 1983–84*, 120), or by over a third. In the same years, the number of engineering graduates went up by over 50 percent, though surely the total number of engineers rose by only 3–5 percent or so; similarly, business administration graduates increased by over 75 percent, and computer science graduates more than tripled in just six years (*Digest 1976*, 119; *Digest 1983–84*, 120). These increases did not occur because things were really booming in this period, by factors of 1.5 to 6, in management, engineering, and computer work; rather *if* the dog of labor demand moves its hindquarters a little, the tail of demand for new graduates has to wag a lot.

The total size of the labor force has grown some lately: from about 95 million to about 114 million, or by about a fifth, in the eight years from 1975 to 1983 (*Statistical Abstract*, *1985*, 390). But jobs did not grow that much, so unemployment went from about 8 million to about 11 million (ibid., 390, 406). The unemployment *rate*, then, was about steady, at about 6 to 10 percent. But young people sixteen to nineteen had a rate of unemployment that varied from 16 percent to 23 percent, and for people twenty to twenty-four the rate varied from 10 percent to 16 percent (*Statistical Abstract*, *1987*, 390); that is, the total range of variation for teenagers was about twice that of the labor force as a whole. Roughly speaking, if unemployment overall goes up 1 percent, the unemployment rate for people out of school between sixteen and nineteen goes up 2 percent, and that for people out of school between twenty and twenty-four goes up 1.5 percent. In other words, the fluctuations of total employment hit the new cohort harder.

This tendency also shows up in wages. In the big firm sector, about a million unionized workers (miscellaneous journalistic sources, Spring 1985) have contracts that have separate scales for recently hired workers. Because the new cohort is so big, firms and other organizations can get good young workers more cheaply than good old workers. So companies not wanting to fight their unions agree with the older workers represented in unions that for the first ten or so years on the job new workers will get lower wages than the old workers in the same jobs, and they will progress up the seniority scale at a certain distance behind the older workers. So the adjustment in the wage rates responding to the increase in the total supply of workers is being disproportionately borne by young workers. (My advice to the reader is to be born in 1933, when the birth cohort was the smallest relative to the total labor force; one will have opportunities far beyond what one's merit would otherwise earn.)

In addition, the new cohorts take up the uncertainty disproportionately. New businesses are a lot more likely to fail than old ones, especially in new industries. For instance, the death rate of firms in the high-tech electronics industry is a lot higher than in the old-line industry of newspapers (Freeman, Carroll, and Hannan 1983). Newspapers by and large employ old people, electronics firms young people. So when firms fail, it is more often young people who have to scramble.

If employers looked only at comparative wage rates, they would in general prefer to lay off workers now holding the jobs they have and to hire instead teenagers at the minimum wage or, by moving the factory, to hire Koreans or Taiwanese. But clearly most employers prefer the people they have now to the people they might get by laying all the old workers off and starting anew in the cheapest possible labor market. Employers believe they know something valuable about the workers who now occupy jobs in their organizations that they do not know about other workers. Let us briefly speculate about what an employer might know about workers with seniority.

First, first-line supervisors would presumably complain about a worker's misbehavior if that behavior were critical to production. The silence of first-line supervisors that is indicated by seniority, perhaps supplemented by a vague investigation of whether the worker has "kept his or her nose clean," then, means that there is nothing wrong with a worker's performance in any crucial respect.

Second, those close to production, at least, know that a worker has to learn a lot informally from other workers about the quirks of the machines or procedures or clients and how to deal with them, and seniority in a particular job usually measures at least a minimal fit into the production work group. That informal learning also provides workers with clues to at least the minimal requirements of teamwork that make a particular operation go. Production lines or other "unskilled" systems run a good deal better than engineers alone can guarantee because workers usually cooperate to remedy defects in their machinery by babying it (Kusterer 1978), by helping one another deal with technical interdependencies, where trouble for one creates troubles for others, and so forth. The workers often know their local part of the production or service process better than their supervisors could teach them. Seniority in the job certifies that workers know the technical and social competences that are learned in the work group.

Third, some of the routines that workers are required to use on their jobs are used very often, and some of those may create troubles if done badly. For instance, tellers count money many times a day, and it is important that they should get this task right (Kusterer 1978, 79–80). Whatever those frequently used routines are, it is exactly those routines which workers presently in the job are highly practiced at. Thus, they may be more productive than workers with the same repertoire of skills but different amounts of practice in the skills most used in their jobs, because the others have practiced on other jobs. This is less true of course, the more rapidly the task composition of a particular job changes (for instance, it is less true of maintenance electricians whose tasks change very frequently than of construction electricians who may work for days on a single task). But in many organizations the task composition of particular roles is quite stable, and in such organizations the people in the job are certified to be better fitted for those jobs by practice than substitutes with the same repertoires of skills.

Fourth, workers who hold the job now and have held it for some time show, by continuing to hold it, that the incentive system for that job is adequate to keep them working at it. One of the best predictors of being willing to do a job is having been willing to do it for some time. Seniority in a job is thus a measure of character and motivation, which is uniquely a measure of how the workers will likely respond to the incentives that in fact they will be confronted with in the job. New hires have much higher turnover than old lags.

There are many rational reasons for an employer to prefer the workers it has, because their holding the jobs they do is information about what sorts of jobs they can hold. Many of the costs of turnover are of course the sheer bureaucratic trouble of hiring people or in the expense of training them. But many of the costs of turnover come from the fact that the information employers have about workers and their fit to the work system, to the routines and incentives of the work role, is worse in conditions of high turnover.

What makes these facts institutionally crucial is that people who could just as well have been hired in the first place but were not can never show that they hold the job, with all that that implies about whether they will have the job next year. The largest cause of labor market rigidity is the preference of employers to stick with the evils they know rather than fly to others they know not of.

Of course, the whole situation would be most unstable if it were not for the fact that workers also prefer employers they know they can satisfy, prefer informal systems on the shop floor to keep production going that they have learned to manage, prefer work that they have thoroughly mastered so they can, when they choose, perform it semiconsciously, and of course, prefer work where the incentives seem to them adequate to make it all worthwhile. The fact that workers have held jobs for a while shows them, too, that these are jobs they can hold.

Seniority on the job, then, is moderately reliable information about whether people can do the job, and perhaps the best available under conditions (which are normal) in which the management itself could not do the job very well. The stories of early union organizing days of managers stuffing tar paper into the furnaces to make smoke, to tell striking workers that they were managing fine, illustrates the difficulty of managers or staff workers learning the thousands of details involved in how the line really runs. Being an airplane engineer does not make one a fighter pilot, nor does managing a production line make one a semiskilled operative. Yet management is in a better situation to know how to do a semiskilled production job than a random worker picked from the street, so the workers with seniority will exceed such replacement workers even more than they exceed managers.

Thus, the central certificate in the labor market is the implicit certificate of already holding the job, a certificate that is especially valuable for certifying one for that particular job.

Segmentation by Internal Labor Markets: Promotions Go to Those Now Employed by Big Firms and Government

The second big institutional fact on certification is that big firms and government organizations have mobility within them among positions, presumably mostly promotions, while small firms in the classical small firm competitive sector have almost no promotions. Roughly three-eighths of all movements among jobs in both Japan (a low labor mobility society) and the United States (a high labor mobility society) are between positions within firms (Cole and Siegel 1979, 70–71), five-eighths between firms. These within-firm movements represent "internal labor markets" in the strong sense that even people who dissolve the person-job tie tend to move within the boundaries of the firm.

Such mobility structures are characteristic of bureaucratic organizations in the engineering-based industries (manufacturing of machines and generally metals fabrication, chemicals, oil, electricity generation and distribution, telephone and telegraph services), in finance, and in government (Stinchcombe 1979b, 231–233). The effect of the size of the

Table 3. Average Years Between Intrafirm Job Changes,
by Size of Firm, for Detroit and Yokohama

Size	Detroit (1970)	Yokohama (1971)
1–9	50	100
10–99	17	50
100–999	11	25
1000+	8	12

Source: Calculated from Cole and Siegel 1979, 80–81.

firm on the promotion rate is illustrated in Table 3, which shows that promotions are much more frequent in large firms than small ones. This is often called the creation by large firms of an "internal labor market," but it is crucial to recall that even people who do not change jobs are in the labor market: they sell their labor under conditions in which the employer could hire someone else, and it is just as much an internal labor market in the small firm sector when very few change either firms *or* jobs. The point here is *not* that a young woman who gets a nonclerical job in a big firm will be promoted more slowly than the men; rather very probably a forty-year-old woman does not now work for a large firm or the government in a job that leads to promotion, *and so* she is a lot less likely to get a promotion over the next twenty-five years than is a *man* of forty. Since there are very few promotions in the small firm sector employing a lot of women and blacks, and since promotions will go to people employed in firms where promotions take place, it is already a foregone conclusion that even with perfectly fair policies within firms on promotions, most promotions over the next couple of decades will go to white males. (It is important to note that the difference between large and small firms in promotion rates may be lower for women; in large firms women are disproportionately in dead-end jobs.)

But what is crucial from our point of view is that the information used to predict performance in the new job consists in large measure of observations of performances in the old job. In many jobs covered by a collective contract, that performance is certified by seniority alone. As we have argued above, this is not an information-free certification, and a person promoted to a higher-yielding machine in a machine shop because he or she has worked another machine for years is in fact a good bet.

Furthermore, jobs are ordinarily connected to other jobs in such a way that experience in one is thought to be relevant for experience in the other; there are "career ladders." This is clearest where the higher job is really the same as the lower job, as in the case of full professors and assistant professors. Where the higher job is as first-line supervisor of the work of people doing the same job, it is generally conceded that experience in the supervised job is relevant. Engineering supervisors are recruited from among engineers, software development supervisors from among programmers, floorwalkers from among salespeople, foremen in the crafts from craftsmen, and so on. This means that many promotions will be restricted not only to people within the larger firms and governments, but also to people on the first rungs of career ladders.

Where the information is judged by a committee of peers (again, this means a committee of superiors) in an internal labor market, the work of the candidate is to some degree observable by that committee. It is more observable in universities when the significant work is published writing; teaching work is not usually very observable in American universities. But in businesses, the higher one goes in the organization, the more everyday work is done in committee and by long telephone conversations among executives in different departments, which means that a variety of people who might promote a candidate for higher management have had dealings with the candidate. Thus, a candidate's work is more observable by the promotion committees toward the top of the managerial hierarchy than it is for first-line supervisors toward the bottom.

Promotion systems, or internal labor markets in the strong sense, make much use of the same seniority information that is used in retaining the same people in the same jobs. But in addition, if information about job performance is available to superiors by direct observation, and if the position being filled is of considerable importance to the productivity of the organization as a whole, performance evaluations are used as a supplement to seniority information (Rosenbaum 1981).

This in turn means that the certification of job performance for higher and more difficult jobs tends to be judged by a "committee of peers," though in most pyramidal organizations the hierarchical superiority of the peers is obvious. At any rate, the dynamics of recruitment to higher management and to supervisory positions in high-status staff departments tends toward the professional model, to be discussed in the next section. Generally in systems of promotion from within, promotions to lower positions are based primarily on seniority in the next lower job, promotions to middle positions are based primarily on evaluations by hierarchical superiors, and promotions to top positions are more similar to professional or craft recruitment based on evaluations by a committee of peers.

Worker-Controlled Recruitment in Professional and Craft Occupations

The third big institutional fact in job certification is that some employers hire certified skilled or professional workers from other employers in the same line of work, producing a pattern of mobility in which people get the same sorts of jobs they had before when they move to a new employer. In this case, the central boundaries in the labor market are around occupations as well as around firms (though sometimes *rather than* around firms, as in highly unstable industries such as building construction). Occupational associations such as craft trade unions or professional schools govern mobility into the occupation.

The fundamental generalization about entry into craft and professional jobs (and, as we have argued above, into higher management and top staff jobs in bureaucratic organizations) is *the more democratic control over recruitment into a set of jobs is*—that is, the more entry and training are controlled by workers in that set of jobs—*the fewer women, blacks, Mexican-Americans, or immigrant workers are employed in the group* (Heimer 1986b, 766; see also Cohn 1985; Glenn and Feldbert 1977).

There are three main places in the labor market where "co-optation" is a common method of recruitment—that is, where members of a body of workers help train, select, and find jobs for young potential members of the body. These are (1) the professions, especially the highest-status professions in a given area of work—for example, professors in prestige colleges and universities; lawyers, but not paralegals; dentists, but not dental hygienists; physicians, but not nurses or lab assistants in a hospital (but chemists who work for chemical or oil companies who do the same sort of laboratory work as lab assistants in hospitals *are* included here, because while lab assistants in hospitals are recruited and trained by pathologists, professional chemists do recruit their own followers [Schroeder and Finlay 1986]); (2) craftsmen (or craftspeople, if the generalization I am arguing for were not true), such as craftsmen in the construction trades; machinists of various kinds (e.g., tool and die makers, pattern makers); molders in foundries; pressmen and typographers in printing, at least before computer typesetting; cooks and chefs in fancy restaurants; long-haul truck drivers driving big rigs; and riverboat pilots in Mark Twain's day—such workers are usually recruited, trained, and certified by those who already occupy positions as craftsmen; and (3) top management, executives high enough that they are likely to be on the board of directors as well as to hold an executive position.

In each of these cases an older tradition of organizing recruitment applies, in which the training occurred only when someone who knew the trade allowed a novice to come into his office or shop and learn that trade (Jackson 1984, passim; Carr-Saunders and Wilson 1933; Lockwood 1958). Now recruitment in these crafts or professions is often by schools or by admission to practice in a hospital or some other organized and quasi-bureaucratic structure, but there is still "peer group" control over who gets in. A few other work settings are marked by recruitment with a peer group character, but these do not have the same labor-market-wide "occupational" form: in mining, new underground miners have classically been recruited by the working miners and so have had ethnic and sex continuity with the miners, while aboveground workers are hired by more bureaucratic methods and very often are of a different ethnicity than the underground miners. For example, in Arizona around the turn of the twentieth century the aboveground workers at a mine would be Mexicans, the belowground workers first Cornish tin miners, then later Anglos more generally (Boswell and Bush 1984, 141–142; see also Boswell 1986).

While professors in high-prestige places have a lot of control over recruitment, in junior colleges or in what are now called "state universities" the administration has generally more control over recruitment. The prediction, then, is that affirmative action with respect to race, gender, and ethnicity will have gone further in junior colleges and state universities than in prestige universities or tony liberal arts colleges.

How, then, does it come about that when workers control recruitment to their own ranks (when recruitment is "democratic"), the recruitment pattern is so discriminatory? It reminds one of the observation that to maintain the subjugation of a majority of another ethnicity stably in the long run, as is done in South Africa or Israel, there must be democracy within the ruling ethnic group. Only if, say, oriental Jews have a way to express their indignation over the treatment they get from the Ashkenazim, say, by supporting the Likud, can the more oppressed part of the Jews be prevented from joining their interests to those of the Arabs and undermining the solidarity of the ruling ethnicity. Similarly, the Boers in South Africa used an English-type parliamentary system to become the ruling ethnicity, then crowded out the English through the democratic system (democratic without blacks, needless to say) rather than allying with, say, the colored. Recruitment is one of the several cases in which democracy has undemocratic effects, and we would like to know why.

Let us consider professors aiming to hire another professor in their department. How often should one expect them to propose to the administration to hire the cheapest labor the university can get? The people who do the hiring are likely to be either only professors themselves (usually functioning in a recruitment committee) or (in the United States) a professor who is also a part-time administrator who gets practically no more money for being chair of a department and who will go back to his or her professorial role after a term as chair. The recruiters, then, have no interest in beating down the wages of the professorate, and quite often have the reverse interest. (Someone trying to hire me told me that he wanted to go to the administration proposing the highest salary we could support with arguments, because then we [it would only be "we" after I came, of course] could use that as a benchmark for what the others of comparable merit ought to be getting.)

Now contrast this situation with that of a dean of a junior college, say in Gary, Indiana. He or she is likely to be hiring quite a few teachers, and will soon learn that the college can hire University of Chicago graduate students to teach a course for a few thousand dollars; they will be pretty smart, quite likely female, but will accept low wages partly because they are willing to work part-time so they can work on their dissertation the rest of the time. For the vocational (and high school makeup) classes, the junior college needs to hire teachers full time, and if it is willing to hire women it can get exceptionally good people who thought they were going to be stuck all their lives teaching in a high school. The junior college can get women a lot cheaper than it can get men, for it would have to hire men away from a machine shop or an auto repair shop or an engineering job. And of course, if a junior college hires black people, since by and large they still cannot get really good jobs, it can probably get them cheaper, too. A dean's own salary will not go down in the future because he or she has recruited a lot of cheaper labor; the dean is not hiring his or her own replacement, just substitutes for more expensive full-time college teachers with advanced degress. And economizing on faculty salaries will surely increase the chances that a dean will be promoted or will increase his or her salary.

So the fundamental dynamic is set up. If an executive's future depends on minimizing the costs in a department or institution, then he or she will tend to hire less qualified workers, and will tend to prefer cheaper blacks, women, and immigrants, especially illegal immigrants, if the organization can use them. Pathologists, even though they are professionals, are not hiring their future replacement when they hire a lab assistant. Their future replacement will come out of a medical school (in 1981 that meant that three out of four of the replacements will be male, *Statistical Abstract, 1984,* 170), so a pathologist will not be beating down his or her own wages by hiring cheaper women lab technicians (with four years of training) instead of more expensive men chemists (with four years of training). On the other hand, in a chemical company if executives hire chemists to work in the lab they will very likely be hiring their own replacement, and the new hires' wages will shortly be competing with their own (Schroeder and Finlay 1986; Fitzgibbon 1988).

If the hirers are members of a group that co-opts and trains its own members, then if they beat down the wages of people coming in, they beat down their own wages as well. If hirers are executives who hire a lot of people who are *not* going to be promoted into their own positions, then if they beat down the wages of the people they hire, they themselves will get promoted faster. One of the easiest ways to beat down the wages of new hires is to hire disproportionately from among women and minorities. We thus predict that the more democratic recruitment is, the fewer women and minorities will be recruited; the more recruitment is in the hands of bureaucratic or entrepreneurial officials, the more women and blacks should be recruited. But for those minorities and women who do get hired by a body of fellow workers, the hirers have an interest in seeing that they get the same privileges and are not used by the organization to beat down the general level of wages. So those few women and minorities hired by a body of peers are less likely to be exploited (Heimer 1986b; Shack-Marquez and Berg 1982).

Gary Becker ([1957] 1971) argues that those who hire with the objective of minimizing costs will hire more blacks and women, on the assumption that it is entrepreneurs (who will never be replaced by the people they hire) who do the hiring; and in the competitive industries, where Becker finds most recruitment of women and blacks, entrepreneurs more often do in fact do the hiring.

The pressure for executives to hire women and minorities is intensified if there is a lot of competitive pressure on the organization. In a relatively labor intensive small firm sector such as apparel or contract construction, a firm may be in one of two basic situations. The first is where the cost of labor is standardized throughout a competitive market by craft unions, so that all employers are faced with the same wage rate for skilled workers (sometimes there is a nonunion sector that is less efficient, quite often with semiskilled workers that need a lot more supervision; that market situation will be analyzed below). In such conditions the employers do not mind too much turning over the recruitment of workers to craft trade unions, because then they get the same sort of workers as their competitors for the same wages. The second condition is that the competition over labor costs reigns unrestrained, and employers have to get the cheapest labor they can in order to stay competitive. In

Table 4. Competitive and Recruitment Conditions Determining the Sex, Race, and Citizenship Composition of the American Labor Force

	Union or Professional Recruitment	
	Yes	*No*
Competitive Pressure, Small Firm	White male, perhaps except for some segregated crafts (e.g., sleeping car porters): construction, machining	Black, female, Puerto Rican, Mexican-American, illegals, foreign born: textiles, apparel, food, many service industries
Lower Pressure, Oligopoly	White male: university faculties, physicians in hospital settings, top management of large firms	Fairly white male, often in industrial unions: auto, chemicals, oil, electrical equipment

competitive conditions with no shielding monopolies in the labor market, a rapid switch to women, blacks, immigrants, and illegals tends to take place (G. Becker [1957] 1971; Cohn 1985). So we get the four conditions described in Table 4.

Family Recruitment in Small Firm Sectors

A big institutional fact in some industries is that employers hire themselves and parts of their families to do some of the work of the firm. This is most characteristic of small-firm sectors of the economy, especially in farming and the service industries. People who have careers as owner of a firm are not governed by the same sort of relation between the supply of labor and the demand for labor that characterize other employment relationships, and these sectors tend to "oversupply" labor during downturns of the business cycle.

People do not seem to be very good predictors of their own work performance as entrepreneurs, as is evidenced by the large failure rate of small business enterprises. Roughly half of all new starts of small businesses in the urban economy go out of business in the first couple of years, indicating that the entrepreneur did not predict very well his or her own ability to make the enterprise go (or did not predict the other resources needed very well, which amounts to the same thing). In addition, the small businesses in the single-family residential and subcontracting parts of the construction industry tend to be destroyed on a large scale in business recessions and depressions, because construction activity is very sensitive to the business cycle. The same is true of architectural firms (Blau 1984, 115–132). Physicians, lawyers, dentists, and a few other kinds of professionals are ordinarily successful selling their own labor, but they have some government help in certifying their abilities in that work and in support of their monopoly.

For reasons that have nothing to do with entrepreneurial talent, about half of all small farming businesses disappear in each generation in modern countries whose urban economy is developing fast enough to absorb them. But all studies of, for example, adoption of innovations by farmers show large differences in productivity. Corporate farms and partnerships get roughly 50 percent more sales per acre than individual family farms (computed from *Statistical Abstract, 1987*, tables 1102–1103), which probably indicates poor judgment by many family farmers about whether they should be entrepreneurs in that business.

Thus, while overall the position of the owner of a business hiring himself or herself is a privileged one in the labor market, people do not show a great deal of ability in judging or predicting their own work performance. The certificate that a person gets from having owned a firm is to a considerable degree a certificate of foolhardiness.

Union Membership as a Certificate of Productivity

Union workers are about 10 to 30 percent more efficient than other workers (Freeman and Medoff 1984) and so do not run into hard resistance in bargaining up their wages until they exceed 30 percent above nonunion workers. In January 1979, the median male union member made about 28 percent more than the median male nonunion worker; unionized females made about 50 percent more, but there were very few of them (*Statistical Abstract, 1984*, 435).

Unionized workers are more often blue-collar workers in manufacturing or transportation (41.4 percent of male blue-collar workers were union members, 29.1 percent of female; figures in this paragraph are from *Statistical Abstract, 1984*, 435) as opposed to (a) service workers (males 24.7 percent, females 10.8 percent); (b) clerical and kindred workers (males 32.9 percent [many being post office letter carriers], females 12.2 percent); (c) professional, technical, and kindred workers (males 19.4 percent, females 26.5 percent [most of the unionized professional workers are teachers, and teaching is a heavily female profession, which is why more female professionals are organized than male ones]); (d) managers and administrators (males 8.4 percent, females 5.3 percent), and (e) salespeople (males 3.3 percent, females 5.1 percent).

In general, unionized workers work in industries where there is quite a bit of competition, though not as much perhaps as in a lot of small firm competitive manufacturing. Freeman and Medoff (1984) show that unionization of the work force only pushes down profits in the less competitive sector. That is, only when there are excess profits in an industry, because of oligopolistic advantages, do unions manage to get part of what would otherwise be profits. In competitive industries, union and nonunion firms have about the same profit rates. So the question is, how do union employers stay in business if they have to pay roughly 30 percent more for their workers?

The basic answer seems to be that unionized workers work harder or with more skill than nonunion workers. Apparently they get more work out per day than workers in nonunion shops or on nonunion crews. There are a number of different possible explanations for this.

In some craft trades like the printing industry, people evidently start in the nonunion firms (Jackson 1984, 263). After they get thoroughly trained, so that they can work faster and more accurately than somebody still in training or with only a few years' experience, they get themselves jobs in the unionized sector and join the union. When nonunion firms that pay about 30 percent less than union firms sell in basically the same market (though there are some kinds of printing that until recently were done only on a union basis), the only way the union firms can compete is to produce the same products using about 70 percent of the worker hours that the nonunion firms use.

A similar thing seems to happen in the construction industry, though there the market is perhaps more segregated. In metropolitan areas, most big jobs (most commercial and industrial construction, and almost all government construction) are run on a union basis; repair jobs on houses in most trades are run on a nonunion basis; and the building of houses is run both ways. In the competitive branches, especially housing construction, where union and nonunion overlap, the union construction firms have to get by while paying 30 percent more than other firms. Union firms usually do not get jobs for which the client pays by the hour, because it seems to a noncraft client so much more expensive to hire union labor, and they have no way of knowing this labor is more efficient. Perhaps they have also heard about union featherbedding, and so imagine that union work will be more expensive because of work rules. Almost all repair work is done by nonunion firms, because it is almost always done on an hourly basis.

But where firms bid for the jobs, the union firms can do all right. This means that the union firms must be about 30 percent more efficient than the nonunion firms in construction. Here again, I suppose the greater efficiency of union workers reflects the nonunion sector serving as an apprenticeship system for the union sector.

In factory work we find the same general picture, that union firms paying more than the nonunion firms are competitive, though they can't go too high above the nonunion wage and still make it. Here several different things seem to be going on. The first is merely that a union contract stimulates management to institute a speedup that they could have done with nonunion workers but somehow have not got around to. So part of the explanation is that union firms have more efficient managements, managements that drive the workers harder because they have to sell at the same price as their competition while paying higher wages. Incentive systems and industrial engineers are often part of the system introduced to speed up the work after the company goes union.

Second, because the system of industrial relations that is instituted under a union contract seems fairer to the workers, they may be willing to work harder and take orders more cheerfully. Grievances go into the grievance system rather than causing sullen workers to institute a secret slowdown because they think they are not being treated fairly.

Third, it may be that union firms can be more selective in hiring their workers than nonunion firms can. While most personnel recruitment processes cannot distinguish a good worker from a bad one, there may be some added fussiness in union firms about who is hired, and since the firm is paying more than other firms, it can get the better workers. For example, it seems that a lot of blue-collar jobs are filled through the recommendations of the firms' own workers (Granovetter 1973, 1974). It may be that in union firms managers that keep their ear to the ground and hear about good prospects among friends and relatives of their good workers can, because they are paying higher wages, generally get those friends and relatives. So union firms recruit from hard-working families and hard-working friendship circles, by following out the recommendations of their good workers and not listening to their shirkers.

The overall result, however, is that one way or another working for a union firm certifies that one can hold a job in a union firm, which in turn means that one can hold a job in which the whole system (whatever its origin) makes one considerably more efficient than workers in nonunion firms. Thus, the fact that union firms tend to offer their union jobs next year to their own workers, so that they too have the large majority of their jobs filled by the same person who had the job last year, results in the certificate of greater productivity being perpetuated in the same social groups who were more unionized last year. As the above data show, the more unionized groups are disproportionately the male working class.

Let us pick up the thread of the argument again. Certificates that give employers reason to pay above the going rate for unskilled labor are generated in five main ways: through holding the job now (seniority); through data collection within large firms and governments, leading to promotions; through certification of professionals and craftsmen by bodies of peers; through certification by owning a business that one is a manager; and through occupying a job in a union shop. Each of these conditions carries different amounts and kinds of information. Depending on what information is most problematic for particular roles in the organization, we would expect more than one certification system to be in place. For example, we have argued that in management the system for certifying competence for top roles is different from that for certifying competence for roles at the middle and bottom.

The central overall difficulty to which these various systems of certification respond is that the measurement, and more especially the prediction, of the quality of performance is problematic. About all we know about why union members are more productive is that they work in more productive organizations; but from a brute economic point of view, this means that the economy should (and does) pay union members more. While the preference for union workers is ordinarily imposed on firms from the outside and against their wills, that preference apparently allows them to pay their workers more. Similarly, much of the information that comes from the fact that a given worker now occupies a given job is inchoate, and has been hard to analyze systematically here. But since so many employers use that information to decide whom to employ next year, it serves as a certificate in the labor market. Seniority critieria are especially prominent when the qualities that constitute qualification for the job are also inchoate, as in teaching and police work. All such certificates, generated in different ways, and measuring different kinds of qualification for work, tend to preserve positions of privilege in the labor market.

The Secondary Labor Market

These big institutional facts (stability in jobs, internal promotions in large firms, occupational continuity in some occupations, family recruitment in some sectors, and the association of unionization with productivity) taken together distinguish, first of all, between people inside the boundary marking off the employed from those not employed. People now employed have a much better chance of being employed next year than those not now employed.

But a second distinction has preoccupied recent labor market sociology. This is the distinction between those inside any boundary that protects privilege *among those employed* (such as being employed by a large firm that gives promotions or higher pay, being qualified as a craftsman or professional, owning a firm that gives the owners employment, being employed in a unionized shop or crew), generally called the "primary labor market," and those employed but not protected by such a boundary, generally called the "secondary labor market." Roughly speaking, those outside the circles of privilege amount to about 25 percent of those employed. About one out of four jobs (and about one out of four jobholders) have high rates of interfirm mobility and high rate of mobility into the status of unemployment, and have low wages, low unionization, and other features showing lack of privilege.

The people who occupy these unprivileged jobs in most modern economies are disproportionately ethnic minorities, women reentering the labor market in middle age, teenagers, and people recently unemployed (Doeringer and Piôre 1971). In underdeveloped economies they are very often recent migrants from rural areas living in *favelas* or *bidonvilles* and working on the fringes of the urban service sector.

From the point of view of this chapter, what is distinctive about such populations is that they have very little opportunity to provide certification that will satisfy an employer with a good job on offer that they can be predicted to do well in that job. The main kind of certification that satisfies employers is that one already occupies such a job—and that is the hardest kind of certification for members of the secondary labor market to give. Those sorts of formalized information that justify promotion in internal labor markets are even more inaccessible to members of the secondary labor market, and the bodies of peers that govern self-recruited status groups have no reason to regard such people as potential peers, and much interest in keeping out low-wage labor.

Such lack of certificates no doubt reflects in part a true lack of competence, but this does not answer the sociological question of how such lack of certifiable competence (and perhaps of true competence) is systematically distributed. After all, people who end up with the good jobs were also born incompetent.

Conclusion

Almost all modern organizations must face a great deal of uncertainty in their predictions about worker productivity over the periods in which those workers will be employed. There is a great deal of uncertainty even when those workers are already employed, because all the forms of uncertainty analyzed elsewhere in the book make it uncertain exactly what one will be asking workers to do, exactly what incentives they will get if they do that, and exactly what the economic or other consequences for the organization will be if they do it. Organizations have even more uncertainty when they are recruiting new workers.

This uncertainty matters more for some organizations than for others. Generally speaking, if an organization is confronted with uncertainty that requires skilled variation of routines at the worker level (as, for an extreme example, is required in basic scientific research), then the problem of picking workers who can deal successfully with the uncertainty is crucial to organizational success. In those cases will expect organizations to develop personnel systems that make heavy use of information from fellow workers (peer review systems), with all the problems of motivated distortion of personnel information that this involves. Such peer systems are likely to apply only to the professional or craft subsection of the organization; thus, for example, the business office of a university will probably use little peer review.

Organizations that require a great deal of teamwork, and in which supervisors contribute strongly to teamwork, will be expected to use a good deal of hierarchical information from superiors and superiors of superiors in predicting workers' future performance. The ideal-typical "internal labor market," in which promotions are governed by hierarchical superiors, should be a normal outcome of uncertainties that revolve mainly about the amount of teamwork.

Most work that is neither too difficult nor too involved in teamwork but that is poorly measured by reliable managerial information, such as teaching or police work, should result in certification systems organized around seniority. The main certificate indicating that person can manage the job (whatever the job really involves) is that he or she has been managing it already. In particular, the higher apparent productivity of union firms, while likely as mysterious to union firm managers as it is to economists and sociologists, is apparently, whatever its cause, adequately preserved by keeping union workers on their jobs.

Work that can be easily assessed by auditable measures in an environment that is sufficiently stable that the work is repetitive and requires the same talents (and the same measures of talent) should be paid according to its marginal productivity, just as economists assuming perfect information predict. Traveling salespeople, athletes, and lettuce pickers seem to be the main examples.

The general result, then, is that information about worker performance is ordinarily very bad, and predictions of future worker performance even worse. People apparently cannot predict their own future performance as workers in businesses they start for themselves well enough to keep from going bust; and they can presumably be expected to do worse at predicting the performance of others. That is why the labor market institutions in most parts of the economy look so little like the institutions of commissions on sales, or superstar contracts in athletics, or subcontracting by piece of lettuce picked, which would be the ideal-typical outcome if employers actually measured marginal productivity in any direct way.

What one needs to know for analysis of institutions collecting and using information on workers is what information about the future performance of the work is contained in the main kinds of certificates employers use. We have tried to analyze what sort of information seniority, education, certified or formalized performance measurements from previous jobs, production outcome measurements, and the like contain, so as to give a functional analysis of labor market institutions.

This functional analysis gives something of a Panglossian view of labor market discrimination: the institutions that result in racial, ethnic, and gender discrimination are really all for the best in this best of all possible worlds. Of course, they are not best for all purposes, and especially not for the purposes of building a fair society. The political function of this analysis, then, is to try to suggest why discriminatory labor market institutions are so resistant to change, and to provide a basis for proposing ways to change them. The purposes these institutions best suit vary with the type of information system, and we have used this fact to explain where in the economy the different types of system are used. Knowing why institutions with a discriminatory effect are found where they are may be politically useful in undermining them.

The scientific function of this analysis is to explain why *some kinds* of labor market segmentation are found in *some parts* of the economy, different kinds in other parts. Given that explanatory purpose, it is not surprising that we do not succeed very well in explaining why in *all parts* of the economy, the general tendency is for *all* such institutions to discriminate against women, against racially oppressed groups, against teenagers, and against recent immigrants or guest workers.

The connection between information, judgment, and reward is central to the structure of status systems (Stinchcombe 1964, 25–40). Whenever information about work performance is central to the overall functioning of an organization, status systems will be shaped by the requirements of that information system. In colleges and secondary schools, the information requirements for the grading of students are easily satisfied, and the preservation of the reward value of the resulting certificates is of greater functional importance. For example, the proportion of students flunking first-year chemistry varies hardly at all with the average SAT scores of entering freshmen, because the reward value of a grade in chemistry is primarily the relative ranking it provides a student as compared with other premedical students, not the absolute grade level. Conversely, reliable performance of maintenance tasks in complex, and frequently modified, machinery will be hard to measure and predict, but crucial for a chemical plant. The status system of maintenance people in such plants will therefore be shaped by the problem of collecting meaningful information on craft workers' performance.

Thus, the requirements of grading chemistry students and qualifying maintenance workers are different, even though they both depend ultimately on chemical knowledge. Hence, we find grading by standardized tests by chemists who themselves were promoted by committees of peers in colleges, and no grading, but instead apprenticeship and craft control, for maintenance workers.

We therefore predict different kinds of stratification systems in organizations with different information requirements, and different status systems in different parts of the organization depending on the particular information required. We will expect promotion in universities to depend not on hierarchical information from the business offices, but on faculty committees of peers, with the accompanying difference in the motivation of high-status people in the business offices to hire women and minorities, those in the faculty to hire white males and other high-priced labor. But we will expect the very top ranks of both to have the same low proportions of women and minorities, because as one approaches the top of the business office hierarchy people are recruited more by committees of peers, rather than recommended for promotion by their own superiors—just as in the case of faculty. The variations between and within organizations in the stratification system are likely to be explained by variations in the information needed about people for different productive tasks.

8 Class Consciousness and Organizational Sociology

E. P. Thompson Applied to Contemporary Class Consciousness

Introduction

By class consciousness we mean the tendency of people to think of their position in the larger society in terms of their position in an employing organization. Workers are class conscious when they think of their grievances at work and their interests in politics as both derived from their employment relation to particular organizations. The central role of organizational position in class consciousness means that such consciousness is a legitimate subject of organizational sociology. But the fact that class consciousness is a conception of one's relation to the larger society means that it also falls within political sociology.

Chapter 7 was about how employers find out about workers and how that shapes the large structure of the labor market. Here the crucial point is that the whole object of an incentive system is to communicate to workers where their interests lie. Only if workers' interests can be connected to some sort of performance measurement will the incentive system motivate attentiveness, improvement of routines, physical effort, concern for profits, and the learning and teaching of skills. The information conveyed to workers about where their interest lies makes the system run, or makes it fail. Since performance measurement is problematic, as we showed in Chapter 7, what the incentive system communicates to the worker about his or her interest is subject to cultural interpretation. A particular kind of interpretation with large social and political consequences is class consciousness.

Our first task in this chapter is to define class consciousness. To do so we reanalyze E. P. Thompson's great work on the development of class consciousness in England, supplemented by some of David Lockwood's observations on the importance of employers' creation of categories of workers who have identical labor contracts. The result is a definition that takes into account the fact that class consciousness is a projection of organizational position on the interpretation of the larger economic and political order of society. Thus it involves both organizational and political consciousness.

The problem we immediately confront in deriving a theory from this definition is that people's relation to a larger society is determined by that society as well as by their organizational position. There are enormous variations in the relation of class consciousness to politics in various societies. Our second task in this chapter is therefore to describe that variation, and to isolate the main variables predicting variations in the type of class consciousness societies show. The two categories of forces we isolate are political and organizational, corresponding to the two components of the concept of class consciousness.

The political variation is the way working-class citizenship comes to be established, with the three main subvariants being definition of workers' citizenship by soviet-style revolutions (e.g., Russia, China), mobilization of disenfranchised workers in liberal societies (e.g., England, Scandinavia), and enfranchisement with little worker mobilization (e.g., the United States, Japan). Before the industrial revolution virtually no employed workers were citizens; after that revolution they were generally citizens as defined by one of these three subvariant definitions.

The organizational variation is the growth of employment of large numbers of workers with identical labor contracts, such as craftsmen all hired at an occupational wage rate, or semiskilled workers hired as assembly-line tenders at a wage determined by a category in a bureaucratic wage system. (The importance of categorical determination of the labor contract was argued in Lockwood 1958.) The proposition is that class consciousness is maximized when workers have had to be mobilized to achieve enfranchisement *and* when large groups of them are employed at uniform wage rates to do similar work. Before the industrial revolution few workers were employed as members of categories of workers having identical labor contracts; after the industrial revolution many were either artisans or factory semiskilled workers.

The organizational factor—that there are standard contracts for groups of workers so that the worker enters a predefined structural "slot" when taking a job—is the main way class consciousness is connected to industrialization. Factories and skilled trades in manufacturing cities produce groups of workers who fill slots in a previously organized production system on standard terms. Societies basically do not have working-class consciousness before industrialization.

But the problem of negotiating the position of groups of slot holders is defined differently in different political systems. Working-class consciousness is the result of the interplay of the organizational process of putting workers into slots on the one hand, and the political definition of what rights and liberties such groups of slot holders have on the other. These political definitions vary among the main types of political systems.

In the third section we take up E. P. Thompson's great analysis (1963) of the interplay between occupation and factory employment in England on the one hand and English political culture on the other. In nineteenth-century England, workers had to mobilize to gain the franchise. It was a liberal society in which workers had many political rights (perhaps the most important ones were "immunities" rather than rights, such as freedom from arbitrary search and seizure, a certain freedom of speech, etc.) and in which there was political competition in Parliament. Thus, England was the first country to produce a "modern" working-class consciousness in a liberal society.

Thompson's strategy is to show how the cultural themes of the English poor, especially the political themes, were used by English workers from about 1790 to about 1830 to interpret the meaning of occupational, industrial, and political oppression. This then forms the basis for understanding how working-class organizations such as trade unions came into existence, and why they formed political alliances on the left of the parliamentary system. We will then apply Thompson's cultural strategy (as we have extracted it), combined with Lockwood's analysis of the social and economic basis of groups of slot holders, to analyze variations in class consciousness in different parts of modern liberal economies.

Finally, we apply this general theory to explain why the service sector of modern economies is in general poorly unionized, and why so many workers in this sector do not vote for working-class parties. The two basic variables we identify are the tendency of service workers to have individualized labor contracts, and the tendency for the meaning of their work to be defined in terms of conservative symbols. Individualized labor contracts make their membership in categories with a common wage rate and common conditions of work problematic. The daily use of conservative symbols in work provides a framework for interpreting grievances and opportunities in non-class-conscious terms.

Unity in Diversity: Why Are Societies with Factories So Much Alike?

The fundamental causal forces associated with industrialization that bring about working-class consciousness are, then, the organizational one of *bureaucratization* of the wage relationship and the political one of *legalization* of the suffrage relationship. First I will say what these are, and why they are associated with the reorganization of production in the course of industrialization. This part of the analysis justifies treating class consciousness in a chapter in a book on organizational sociology.

BUREAUCRATIZATION OF THE WAGE CONTRACT

The fundamental innovation of industrialization, particularly in its factory form but also in its artisanal form, is that a large number of workers are hired by one employer to do essentially the same work in the same place, and are trained to do that work in essentially the same way (Lockwood 1958). This means that *within the firm* it seems unfair to make individual and different arrangements with each worker, and the social basis of the *individualization of contracts* between workers and employers disappears. The employer then makes the contracts of employment for categories of workers uniform and subjects the workers to uniform standards of work (e.g., uniform output criteria); the category of workers becomes a "collective worker." Consequently, the labor market wage rate becomes a social and psychological reality to the workers, because it is an explicit part of the incentive system.

This is in essence a collective contract before collective bargaining. Class consciousness as influence on the wage rate is collective worker participation *in the collective contract that already exists*. The organization of trade unions and other devices for worker representation is, in some sense, merely recognition in workplace politics of a condition that is created by the nature of factory production: namely, that there will be a collective contract for categories of workers.

In artisanal or craft-type production, the uniformity of workers is produced by a labor market–wide training and experience system, one in Western European and North American cities descended from medieval urban guild structures (see esp. Sewell 1986, 1980; Hobsbawm 1984, 214–251). Here ideas of the fairness of wage rates spread beyond specific employers to the local labor market as a whole; in the end there is a perception that all machinists in a particular place, for example Birmingham, ought to make the same wage. Generally the trade union structures to respond to this sort of market labor categorization form earlier, and are stronger, than those representing factory workers.

The crucial feature in the causation of trade unions is thus not really "bureaucratization" of the labor contract by a factory management. Instead it is that there is a socially established uniformity of workers, together with a uniformity of factual wage rates for that uniform class of workers *either* within the factory *or* in a local labor market. It is *universalism* of the labor market relation for a category of workers, rather than the *bureaucratization* emphasized by Lockwood (1958), that is crucial. Industrialization greatly increases the proportion both of urban craft workers in the society and of factory operatives; thus it lays the basis for class consciousness.

LEGALIZATION OF THE SUFFRAGE RELATIONSHIP

The workers' political situation described by E. P. Thompson for the England of 1790–1830 is one with different suffrage relations in different parliamentary districts (see, e.g., the analysis of active worker participation in Westminster: 451–471; all page numbers cited in the following with no further specification are to Thompson 1963). Such a system has many distinct types of local political arrangements, each with its own determination of who participates in politics and how influence is arranged. It is a much-reduced form of the nearly infinite political variety of local political relations under feudalism.

A feudal government in feudalism's heyday was a ramshackle central government built on an astounding variety of local political systems. As the central governments gained more power, there were all sorts of demands, both by the kings and by the populace, to make the system of local political organization more regular and uniform. For instance, there are demands by the *noble* house of the Estates General elected just before the French Revolution to award nobility only for merit, to make commercial taxes regular and uniform, to regularize the court system and make justice more legalized, and so on (Weitman 1968, 269–441; Markoff 1975).

Having such national uniformity imposed on local governments throughout the country, and a uniform set of criteria for who gets to vote and who can hold office and what each official can do and the like, means uniformity in local political influence will be nationally legalized. The introduction of such uniformity is of course full of conflict, because somebody loses every time the local political constitution is changed.

Legal uniformity of suffrage is an important political precondition for working-class consciousness, since it makes the political demands of different groups of workers in different parts of the country uniform. The legal uniformity of all the local political systems produced by a growing power of the national government usually divides the upper classes, as the reform movement in England that eventuated in the Reform of 1832 did—some parts of the upper class lost some political privileges (e.g., local aristocrats might lose their "rotten boroughs"), while other parts gained. The uniformity presents the opportunity for working-class mobilization to influence the national structure of suffrage, rather than only to influence the politics of particular parliamentary districts. The division within the upper classes during the reform movement may create opportunities to form alliances between the workers and the formerly disprivileged bourgeoisie.

When such an introduction of national uniformity takes place in an oligarchical or dictatorial context, one of the things that usually gets regularized and legalized is the underprivileged status of workers. Some workers who were previously enfranchised are likely to lose political influence, and at any rate the legal category of "workers who are disenfranchised" is created on a national scale. But that makes it obvious what a worker has to do if he or she wants to have more working-class influence on either national or local politics—to change the *national* conditions of suffrage so that the poor can vote, hold office, and so on. Oppressive legalized uniformity is a basis of working-class unity.

When democratic suffrage had already been introduced into many local systems before the working class grew, as in the United States, then there was very little pressure to form a nationwide working-class movement around the question of suffrage. When trade unions formed later, they tended to be less political than they were in England and most of Europe. Thus, it is nationwide mobilization for nationwide legalization of working-class suffrage that maximizes class consciousness.

URBANIZATION

Third in importance to bureaucratization of the labor relation and legalization of suffrage as causes tending to connect industrialization and industrialism to working-class consciousness is industrialism's urbanizing effect. In preindustrial Europe, even in countries like England where there was an agricultural proletariat, there was not class consciousness among workers in agriculture. A big reason for this was that agricultural workers lived in agricultural villages that were class heterogeneous. When industry came, especially factory industry, workers moved into small industrial towns and cities. The question of suffrage for the working class has thus always been a question of suffrage for the *urban* poor, and has been separate from the question of suffrage for small farmers or agricultural laborers.

E. P. Thompson's Conception of Working-Class Consciousness

The main thing that distinguishes the sociological approach to industrialism, and to the process by which societies became characterized by modern, efficient manufacturing and mass distribution, is its interest in class consciousness. Sociologists generally characterize *societies* as having more or less industrialism, and more or less class consciousness. That is, sociologists do not in the first instance ask the questions, how much does an individual person feel like he or she is a worker, object if his or her daughter marries someone other than a worker, feel that only workers' political and economic interests should be defended, and so on. These are questions about *individual identity* as workers, which the sociologist generally tries to answer *after* he or she has characterized the society in which the individual lives.

Thus, when we want to know whether, for example, a black worker in the United States thinks of himself or herself first and foremost as a worker or as a black person, a sociologist attacks this question by asking first, How far is the social, economic, and political life of black people in the United States organized around their status as workers, rather than around their status as black people? After having answered that question in sufficient detail so as to understand what is going on at the societal level, he or she tries to explore how this social state enters into a person's consciousness, into the self-definition and the definition of his or her individual social, political, and economic interests, *given* how the society is organized into classes and into ethnic groups.

E. P. Thompson asserts that the English working class had been "made" by the 1830s. What specifically did he mean by that? First, a broad characterization (see also Sabel 1982, 127–193): he meant that one can write sensibly about Chartism, a British movement favoring increased democracy in the British government that developed after the period Thompson covers, by asking how the working class responded to the movement. What one will be talking about is the working class as an organized political and social force with a sense of its own identity, a more or less reliable following, and a vision of itself and of its historical interests.

If, however, one writes about the reaction in Britain to the French Revolution at the beginning of the period Thompson treats (about 1790), one must write instead about this and that democratic tendency, with an occasional artisan, an occasional trade union–like group of workers, adhering to the movement. There would be no clear tendency for all sorts of workers to react alike to their common economic and political interests, which might have led them to favor the radical tendencies of the French Revolution. So one could *not* write a sensible history of the democratic tendencies in England (or Great Britain) related to the French Revolution from the 1790s to 1815, say, in terms of how the working class reacted to the Jacobin tendency.

We will say that a society is characterized by a high degree of class consciousness when the following two tendencies are strong. 1. Many members of the labor force define their main economic interests in terms of the wage rate of some group of workers, want that wage rate to be higher, and join and support some sort of trade union to raise that wage rate. The more they think of their own wage level as being set by the general wage level of all workers, the more this is "class consciousness" as opposed to "job rights" consciousness, but we want to include both broad (classwide) and narrow (job rights) definitions of class interest here. Class-conscious workers enter into conflict over the setting of general wage rates with the employers who pay those rates. Such working-class consciousness is in contrast to workers being interested primarily in the *prices* of commodities they produce (as small farmers or peasants are in many agricultural systems, and as some artisans were in preindustrial Europe) or in the size of government handouts (as most of the poor of Rome are reputed to have been) or pensions (as a good many Northern Civil War veterans were; see Skocpol and Orloff 1983) or social insurance benefit levels (as people over sixty-five are in the United States today; see Stinchcombe 1985d).

2. Political interests of the poor in society (often in many different concrete political organizations) are organized separately from the rich, creating a workers' movement that (a) favors the interests of workers in wages, and in trade union organizations that defend wages: that is, defends workers' "industrial" rights and interests; (b) favors the extension (or defense) of the franchise in politics to all workers, or at least all male workers, at least for the urban part of the economy: that is, identifies "democracy" with the political interests of urban workers and defends democracy so conceived; and (c) unifies a large part of the wage workers in the society in defense of the above two-pronged program (economic and political), as against one or more parties of the rich and powerful that oppose the power of trade unions, favor the reduction of wages, and favor restriction of the franchise to "the rich, the wise, and the well born."

Thompson is saying more specifically that only a small part of the working population in 1790, first, identified its main economic interests with the wage level of a group of workers, and with the corresponding trade unions that defended that wage level, and, second, identified its political interests with an increase in the political power of urban wage workers, especially by advocating extension to them of suffrage and the rights of political organization. There were "the laboring classes," but not "a working class," in 1790; by 1830 there was a substantial working class interested in wage levels, trade unions, and the extension of suffrage to urban male workers.

Such a definition of working-class interests provides "information" to workers in particular organizations about how to interpret the organizational incentive system. It tells them to look at it as a collective contract rather than as a reward for individual productivity. It tells them not only that those with opposed interests in the collective wage level also oppose the enfranchisement of workers and the political legitimacy of trade unions, but that their particular employer is a political opponent as well. It tells them that their individual troubles at work are grievances to be processed in the local collective bargaining system in the workplace, or in collective movements in the larger society. In short, it concretizes the uncertain future of the individual labor contract by placing it in the context of collective institutions of class.

Throughout his book Thompson is trying to show the immense variety of thought and experience of working people and their leaders (many of the leaders were, of course, workers, though many were not) in which these central characteristics of modern British history were formed. One of the hardest things to keep in mind when reading or writing history is that no one in 1790 knew how it was all going to come out by 1830. For one thing, in 1790 very few people worked for wages, and when they did it was mostly in the countryside where the social and political conditions were very different from those in the city of London or the later industrial districts of the north of England. For another, the whole idea of a "wage rate" had no legal existence, nor did it exist much in social practice or even as an intellectual construct. Ricardo, the first great theorist on the question of how wages in general came to have the level they do, was still a relatively unknown academic scribbler even by the end of Thompson's period (which ends about when Ricardo died). In 1790 nearly everybody thought that what a worker got paid was the result of a bargain that he or she as an individual came to with his or her employer. An individual worker who did not like this wage rate could go work for himself or herself (which did not seem so unrealistic in those days). Economic interests in 1790 did not naturally divide themselves into the interests of workers in higher wages and the interests of employers in lower wages. The idea of a collective bargain in which workers had some power over wages was an abomination. People did not know that they would be thinking in terms of collective wage rates by 1830.

Similarly, there was very little notion generally in 1790 of what anything that might be called "democracy" was all about, and certainly very little tendency to identify it with *political* interests of a body of working people. Working people did not vote, and the idea that they would know how to run things was as foreign as the notion that students might be able to run a university would be in the 1980s. Probably most workers in

1790 had very little notion that politics affected them, had no trusted representatives of their interest to formulate political objectives for them, and in other ways were psychologically and organizationally "noncitizens." Not conceiving that they were members of a political body, workers generally had no more political opinions about what ought to be done in England than we have about what ought to be done in, say, Japan, where we are noncitizens.

By low working-class consciousness at the societal level in 1790, we do not mean that folks did not have economic grievances about their situation or that they did not feel alienated from the political system because their grievances were not solved. We mean instead that there were few ties between economic grievances and collective action that raises wages in the economy, and also that there were few ties between workers' political grievances about their own powerlessness and any collective movement that favored democracy and defined it as the participation of working people in the shaping of political decisions. What Thompson is documenting is the hundreds of ways that ordinary people could come to think about their grievances and the experiences of their economic and political lives, and the ways that their leaders (some of them from other classes) could formulate their interests in the economic and political systems and get a following.

For example, ordinary people had no neat picture of a gradual development from a state of worker economic and political apathy to a state of collective interest in the wage bargain and of collective organization into a class party in favor of democracy (meaning universal urban male suffrage). Instead there was much working-class enthusiasm for a variety of movements, including Owenite socialism (formulated by an employer), which denied the class conflict by trying to organize work without wage relations; Methodism, which defined many characteristics of working-class culture as sins and interpreted the bad lot of workers as the result of their sinful lives; Jacobinism, whose adherents thought the democracy created by the French Revolution was a lot better than the parliamentarism of the rich that governed England; the Church and King mobs that went after Jacobins; craft trade unions whose leaders wanted to divorce craft questions from politics; and craft unionists who thought revolutionary political action and a sort of relatively innocent terrorism were necessary. The point is that history as it is lived is a lot more complicated than history as one might reconstruct it, if one knew in advance that in 1830 there would a working class organized to some degree into trade unions and ready to function together in a prodemocratic political movement.

What the last chapter of Thompson (711–896) is mainly about, then, is the great variety of thoughts that still had influence among workers after 1830. These ideas were the legacy of what we might, looking at it retrospectively, call "the struggle to define English workers as a class." Here Thompson defines the criteria he has used to sort through this enormous variety of political thought of the 1820s and early 1830s and to say that (balancing as one has to to respect the integrity of the thought of the people actually functioning on the scene) the English working class actually existed by 1830 in a historically significant sense.

The appropriate criteria for Thompson to use in identifying quotations from the documents as manifesting the existence of a class that is already made are (1a) that the interests of the workers are defined primarily in terms of wages; (1b) that the interests of workers are defined as being in opposition to those of employers; (1c) that workers are shown as being interested in building trade unions, in defending trade unions, in collective bargaining about wages and working conditions, and so on; (2a) that people connected to workers because they are leaders of trade unions, or elected officials appealing to a working-class constituency, or leaders of riots or other collective manifestations composed of workers, are in favor of democracy in the sense of extending the suffrage; (2b) that those same people defend politically the rights of trade unions and of other workers' organizations; and (2c) that those same people conceive of the opponents of democratization (i.e., their own political opponents) in class terms, as propertied and rich, as interested in lowering wages, as uninterested in the welfare of the working people. More concretely, we will be interested throughout the middle sections of this chapter in six features of ideological thought that we, following Thompson, have identified as being indicators of growing class consciousness. To supply catchwords, they are (1a) wage interest, (1b) economic conflict over wage levels, (1c) trade union organization, (2a) favor of democracy (universal suffrage) in politics, (2b) defense of class organizations (trade unions) in politics, and (2c) a class conflict definition of political conflict.

The fundamental observation we start off with is that there was very little class organization or class consciousness in the sense that Thompson defined it in eighteenth-century Europe, and that by the middle of the twentieth century it was practically universal in the advanced liberal societies (Western Europe, the United States, Canada, Australia, and New Zealand). So we start with the sociological observation that *in fact* class consciousness, *in the sense we* (following Thompson) *have defined it*, is a feature of industrialized societies; hence, it historically came about during the nineteenth century in all the societies then undergoing industrialization. The basic point of the Thompson book is little has in fact been said when that has been said, because we still have to explain *how* workers created the structures and consciousness that are the features of industrialized societies.

An additional reason for wanting to understand the connection of factory and craft organization to class consciousness is that at the present time, a lot of signs point to an erosion of class consciousness, in the sense defined above. This erosion seems somehow to be connected to the growth of the service sector and of bureaucratic management, involving the growth of middle-class employment.

Cross-national Variation in Class Consciousness

The argument above is that in many ways the central transformation of social structure that was introduced with industrialism is the political and economic organization of the working poor and their incorporation as citizens, as defined by the institutions built up with industrialism in the economic and political order of society as a whole. This was a basic transformation in how the poor of the society came to think of who they were, of what could be done about their economic situation, of what their political interests were, and of what they wanted the state to do about their condition. It is almost true to say that all societies that are industrialized have trade unions in one form or another, while very few underdeveloped countries do; it is also almost true to say that all industrialized societies mobilize the workers into politics under a system of universal suffrage and have parties that at least claim to represent the interests of the workers in opposition to other parties or political tendencies that oppose those interests. Most underdeveloped countries basically have neither trade unions nor worker political parties (Inkeles and Smith 1974).

But there are two major variations from the picture given by Thompson, that are represented by the Soviet Union on the one side and by Japan on the other. The core of this comparison comes out of Barrington Moore's great book *Social Origins of Dictatorship and Democracy* (1966) and, more specifically on the place of labor relations, from Reinhard Bendix's *Work and Authority in Industry* (1956; see also Walder 1986; Burawoy 1985, 156–208).

Class Consciousness in Soviet Societies

In the USSR, organizations that originated as working-class parties and trade unions became the political rulers, and wiped out the representatives of the upper classes. Then "reasons of state" became the responsibility of the ruling working-class party and of the trade union apparatus, and they devoted themselves at least as much to preserving rule, to building military might, and to increasing productivity as to representing the workers' interests which they had originally represented. A new middle class in the economy and a middle and upper class in the state grew up *within* the shell of organizations representing the ideology and political power of the working class.

One result of this evolution is that the upper class in the USSR does not live nearly as well as the upper class of most capitalist countries of the same level of development (e.g., Italy, Spain, Venezuela, Uruguay, Singapore, Hong Kong, and the oil states of the Arabian peninsula are perhaps at about at the same level of development as the USSR). Only a very upper-class person in Moscow has a three-bedroom apartment, for example, and the upper-class dachas outside Moscow that one hears about in anti-Soviet tirades are the sort of cabin that a third of the population of Norway have access to, a slightly crude version of a small one-family house. But the Soviet upper classes have *more* political power than the upper classes of these intermediate capitalist countries, because the tsarist noble and bourgeois classes and their political representatives have been destroyed.

From a *cultural* point of view, the powerful in the Eastern bloc are an unchallenged political ruling class with a very strong cultural "survival" of egalitarianism in economic privileges. But that ruling apparatus is also connected with the working class in a very different way than Western ruling apparatuses are (Walder 1986). In particular, the ruling group has deep penetration into the Communist party and the trade unions. The commitment of the trade unions and of the Communist party to productivity has meant, for example, that what we call "industrial engineering" (incentive systems and machine speedups) is more common, is defended by the trade unions against worker attacks, and results in at least "temporary" workers putting out more effort than American workers do.

Harasti (1978) gives an account of a machine shop that is a lot like the one studied by Burawoy (1979) in the United States. The findings indicate that there is cruder exploitation of these workers in Hungary, sponsored in many ways by the union, than in the core of monopoly capitalism in Chicago. Burawoy (1985, 156–208) argues that the core experienced and skilled workers in soviet factories help management respond to the great uncertainties of supply (cf. Granick 1954, 1967) and so are not treated as ruthlessly as the temporary workers described by Harasti (see also Walder 1986, 28–84).

The general picture in Eastern Europe and China includes working-class revolution, and then the incorporation of "reasons of state," including especially advances in economic productivity, into the agenda of the working-class movement. Thus the class consciousness of soviet societies is channeled and controlled by organizations with a strong interest in the success of factories, so that its consequences are much muted as compared to the class consciousness described by E. P. Thompson.

Class Consciousness in Corporatist Capitalism

When industrialization takes place under a strong right-wing "corporatist" regime that suppresses working-class organization as much as they can throughout the process, working-class political representation can be achieved either by revolution, leading generally to the creation of soviet societies, or by other means. Japan from about 1890 to 1945, Germany from 1933 to 1945, and to some degree Italy, Spain, and perhaps Brazil at various times are examples of conservative corporatism, with limited and sponsored working-class representation in conservative regimes.

The resulting institutional order after the corporatist regime in turn loses power (is overthrown) depends a lot on how democracy and the freedom to organize trade unions are subsequently introduced. The basic generalization is that if modern forms of class consciousness are introduced into such a system *without* being extracted from a reluctant right-wing government by a thoroughly mobilized working-class movement (workers were not mobilized to introduce suffrage and trade unions into Japan in 1945–1946, for example), then a country develops institutions of working-class consciousness like trade unions and left-oriented parties in a basically conservative environment. Worker organization for conflict with the upper classes is much less salient in Japan and similar countries than in countries like England and the United States, where a liberal regime presided over industrialization.

The United States is perhaps halfway between Britain and Japan in this regard, with the question of universal suffrage *not* having been solved in the United States through a mobilization for conflict with the upper class but mobilization nonetheless having been necessary to get the right to organize trade unions and to force collective bargaining on employers. There is therefore a Labour party with a socialist ideology in Great Britain, a Democratic party without much socialist history in the United States, and apparently permanent-minority left political parties in Japan. In Great Britain, trade unions have a fundamentally antimanagement attitude on productivity questions; in the United States, their attitude is suspicious but productivity deals are made in collective contracts; and in Japan, workers participate actively in increasing productivity.

Along the dimension of massiveness of working-class mobilization, ranging from Japan to Russia, France is probably further to the left than Great Britain; certainly it has more radical-left political parties representing the working class, and more cantankerous, if not more powerful, unions than Great Britain (Gallie 1983; Tilly 1986; Hobsbawm 1984). I would place most other European countries between France and Great Britain (cf., e.g., Esping-Andersen 1985 and Stephens 1986 on the Scandinavian countries; Kocka 1986 on Germany; and, for a general survey, Sturmthal 1953); all have more radical working-class movements than the United States. Especially in the political part of our definition of class consciousness, Europe is generally more left than the United States.

The Culture in Which
Class Consciousness Grew

The comparative picture sketched above suggests that, with some minor variation, the origins of trade unions and working-class parties in most liberal societies took a form similar to that described by Thompson for England. In this section we outline how Thompson analyzed the origins of class consciousness in England, to see how the static comparative sociology outlined above appears in a historical analysis.

The first few chapters of Thompson are meant to give the flavor of the cultural presuppositions of various sorts that *will become* relevant to the working-class definition of what is about to happen to workers with industrialization. The idea of culture that is manifested here is in some ways similar to that advocated by the French anthropologist Claude Lévi-Strauss, commonly called "structuralism." Lévi-Strauss argues that a culture consists not so much of a set of *beliefs* as of a *set of alternatives for interpreting things.*

"MEMBERS UNLIMITED"

The contrast in Thompson's chapter 1 (17–25) is between the corporate organization of political thought and working-class radicalism. The corporate idea is, for example, that our interests as artisans in the shoemaking trade are the interests of the corporation (the guild) of shoemaker masters and journeymen; this is in contrast with the notion that everyone (including shoemakers—on shoemaker radicalism, see Hobsbawm and Scott 1980) might be interested in, and better off, implementing radical ideas. The contrast here is between defining interests by the legal and economic interests of closed corporations rather than by universal and democratic legal and economic interests of "the people." Thus the contrast is between a closed artisan guild and the London Corresponding Society, a radical democratic group from around the beginning of the nineteenth century that started its rules with the words "That the Number of our Members be unlimited."

The point here is not that the notion of unlimited solidarities—what we would call "universalism" in sociological jargon—was common among the working class. Thompson knows that the London Corresponding Society was an elite group, with some two thousand members in 1793; he is therefore not describing the natural condition of the poor in the 1790s when he presents the London Corresponding Society's idea of a common interest in radical notions. He is just demonstrating that the cultural baggage of the London working class at the time included an alternative to the closed occupational corporation—namely, the London Corresponding Society, which had in common with the eventual shape of working-class consciousness that it extended solidarity beyond the craft. One alternative for interpreting workers' experience during industrialization, then, was in terms of the privileges of closed corporations, while another alternative was in terms of an unlimited number of members of the common people.

"CHRISTIANS AND SATAN"

The second and third chapters of Thompson's work (26–76) show that working-class culture was characterized not only by the heavy-handed protestant strains that would be manifested in Methodism, but by a hearty, fun-loving, drinking, brawling culture as well. This theme says that a harlot isn't really all bad, she partly represents good dirty fun; and that drinking and cock fighting may be objected to by stuffy parsons, but a real man likes a little amusement. Again, the point is not that there were not plenty of sober, God-fearing workers in the 1790s. Both sides of the contrast between bawdy ale drinkers and sober evangelicals defined themselves by contrast with each other, and so each "understood" the way of life of the contrasting group to some degree.

That contrast provided two ways of defining what it meant to be a worker in 1790s, and it would later turn up in a Methodist-versus-class-solidarity way of defining who the people were that a good worker would identify with. Again, part of the point is that the nascent working class could understand things either way: that, for instance, the poor could be bad because they were sinners or good because they were sober, and even a worker who had a good deal of the "bad" in him would understand the force of the argument from sin. The good Methodist likewise understood to some degree the defensive argument that a man wants a bit of fun after work, after all.

"THE FREE-BORN ENGLISHMAN"

Chapter 4 (77–101) shows that patriotism and respect for authority was contrasted with a positive affirmation of the value of *being let alone* and hearty objection to an official or other authority that oversteps what is rightfully due him (an official was of course sometimes a queen, but was usually a man, in England). Though of a later era, the line from Gilbert and Sullivan's *Pinafore* is indicative: "For a British tar [sailor] is a soaring soul/As free as a mountain bird." The song was convincing even in a society where in fact a Captain ran the ship with an iron hand: for he only did so in a context where working sailors had the right to have a bit of fun when in port *or* to be Methodists.

The basic contrast here is that of reverence for the crown and church as responsible for the nation and its soul versus an affirmation of

> freedom from absolutism (the constitutional monarchy), freedom from arbitrary arrest, trial by jury, equality before the law, the freedom of the home from arbitrary entrance and search, some limited liberty of thought, of speech, and of conscience, the vicarious participation in liberty (or in its semblance) afforded by the right of parliamentary opposition and by elections and election tumults (although the people had no vote they had the right to parade, huzza and jeer on the hustings), as well as freedom to travel, trade, and sell one's own labour. Nor were any of these freedoms insignificant; taken together, they both embody and reflect a moral consensus in which authority at times shared, and of which at all times it was bound to take account. (79)

The fundamental idea is "You can't push *me* around."

Again, the point is not that all poor men, in every situation, would think automatically about the proper limits of authority, about being free-born Englishmen (women were mostly not thought of as free born, though they were in fact often defended by the limits of authority involved in the legal version of the concept). In fact, there is a contrast between the notion that the upper classes know what they are doing and should be let do it, with coercion to back them up if necessary, and the idea "They can't push me around." As the relations of authority at work and in politics changed over the forty years between 1790 and 1830, workers could interpret those changes in terms of the contrast. Conservative workers would recognize what radicals were talking about when they used the phrase *free-born Englishmen*, and the radicals would recognize the notion that society would come apart if the rulers were not respected.

"PLANTING THE LIBERTY TREE"

The last chapter of Thompson's background portrait (102–185) is about late innovations in this general working-class tradition, elements of what we commonly call "the Enlightenment." Here the cultural contrast is between the clear light of reason and the obscurantism of tradition. The central figure in all this, according to Thompson, was Tom Paine, originally a corset maker but later a sort of professional revolutionary publicist in the American, French, and now English radical movements. The basic theme of the affirmation of reason is that anybody can read (or could if they were taught, and they ought to be taught), and anybody can reason. The Enlightenment analysis of social life is that when they do reason, people will conclude that the system is ridiculous when it tries by appeals to tradition to prevent the conclusions from being taken into account. Thompson is careful to point out that this radicalism is *not* class conscious by his definition; rather, it is what we would call "populist." In the Enlightenment position, it is not specifically class-conscious thought that is superior (that is, the Marxist position), but generally radical, "reasoning," thought of all kinds. The Enlightenment position defends what a Marxist nowadays would call "petty bourgeois radicalism."

The alternative view is that the institutions we live under have a remarkable wisdom of their own. If pressed, some people could give a rationalization of how that widsom came to be in institutions, ones often theological or aristocratic (wisdom is in the blood of the rulers). But the contrasting notion to the Enlightenment analysis is, roughly, that "the heart hath reasons that reason knows not of," without explicit theological reasoning. Tolstoy's short story ([1886] 1982) about the simple hermits on an island taught the Lord's Prayer by a passing bishop, who forget the words and so walk across the water to ask the bishop to teach them again, is a perfect expression of this attitude. It is not scripture that counts, but the good traditional hearts of the simple poor.

In Thompson's background chapters we have a description of the cultural materials out of which, so to speak, history—specifically workers and their leaders—would form an interpretation of working-class interests. The "left" poles of these contrasts—(1a) extensive solidarity,

(2a) hearty and sometimes rowdy male conviviality, (3a) a "you can't push me around" attitude, and (4a) secular reason—are subthemes of traditional English working-class culture; workers would view the events of 1790–1830 through these themes, eventually to arrive at the definition of their political and economic interests in class terms. Conversely, the "right" poles—(1b) narrow corporatism, (2b) puritanical rejection of the self (and of the worthwhileness of the self's body particularly), (3b) the view that the authorities have the interests of the whole society to look after and "know better than us," and (4b) the philosphy of "the heart hath reasons that reason knows not of," with its respect for tradition—form the cultural basis of interpretations within the working class that hinder the formation of class consciousness.

The distinctiveness of Thompson's approach to this question is seeing the whole process not as the inevitable unfolding of the "correct" interpretation of working-class interests, but as the intellectual struggles of a bunch of workers to figure out what was going on, in terms of the cultural heritage that they had. The cultural heritage is *not*, in Thompson, a "set of prejudices" that predetermine how that bunch of workers will see the English political repressions during the Napoleonic wars, the economic exploitation of the early industrial factories, and the reorganization of nonfactory work by the expansion of the market for skilled workers. Instead the culture is a set of intellectual tools and moral alternatives that can be used to define the meaning of events, and to define with respect to those events who is on our side, who is on the other side.

In Thompson, cultural causation operates like a person's vocabulary: vocabulary does not predetermine what that person is going to say, but provides a more or less limited set of alternatives in which to frame what he or she wants to say. One should think of Thompson in the background chapters as giving the cultural and moral equivalent of a dictionary rather than a sort of "proto-working-class doctrine."

The Cultural Perception of Exploitation, Oppression, and the Wage Bargain

This cultural background means that the facts of political oppression and of that special sort of exploitation characteristic of the introduction of industrialism are not sufficient to explain the shape of working-class solidarity that eventually developed in England. The reaction to those facts is, in Thompson's view, a creative response by the working class, using both the vocabulary of moral and social judgment that was part of their heritage and the further moral vocabulary that would develop during the period.

After an extensive quotation of a cotton spinner's analysis of what has been happening in Manchester, Thompson summarizes what was seen as "exploitation" in the *economic* relations in the new factories:

> the rise of a master-class without traditional authority
> or obligations: the growing distance between master
> and man: the transparency of the exploitation at the
> source of their new wealth and power: the loss of status
> and above all of independence for the worker, his re-
> duction to total dependence on the master's instruments
> of production: the partiality of the law: the disruption
> of the traditional family economy: the discipline, mo-
> notony, hours, and conditions of work: loss of leisure
> and amenities: the reduction of the man to the status of
> an "instrument." (202–203)

Thus, in Thompson's chapter on exploitation (189–212) there are two conclusions. The first is a statistical and material one, that probably between 1830 and 1845 or so workers' average real wages increased, but that that increase was not very substantial, and at any rate came after about forty years of war and other sorts of crisis in which real wages probably remained stable. What "stability" means in this context is not that everybody stayed the same, but that *an equal number got better off as got worse off*. So, to use an example of Thompson's, while the coal miner under forty who, working a lot harder with the new methods of extracting coal, was earning and consuming more, a coal miner over forty who was unable to work because of an injury, whose risk was increased by working too fast, or who missed being injured but was sicker than a worker of his age would have been in olden days because there was more dust in the mines, might have been worse off (211). What stability means for the first forty or so years of what we normally call the industrial revolution is that roughly an equal number of workers experienced "immiseration" as experienced "progress."

The second point is that a lot of what workers complained about did not have to do with exploitation, so much as with humiliation. The imposition of a factory discipline that kept workers from sending the "boy" out for a pot of ale in the middle of the morning is not so much a decrease in the standard of living as an interference with workers' lives in a way that is none of the bosses' business. The spinning mill owner did not consider himself really to be "in the same trade" as the spinner running the jenny. This meant it was not believable either for the employer or for the workers to present questions of economic welfare in a corporatist solidary fashion.

Thus, *even if* workers' lives turn out on average to involve about the same amount of tea and sugar after industrialization as before, if they think that they are entirely dependent for their way of life on someone who does not give a damn about their welfare, they feel they are at risk. They feel they have to use the methods of conflict and politics to protect themselves, rather than trusting to the good will of the upper classes. When people have to put their whole lives into the hands of a system, they want to assure themselves that that system is "trustworthy." Thompson's general point is that whatever the statistical flow of improvements and degradations, workers did not think they were dealing with a trustworthy system, a system in which the rulers cared about their fates, respected their action to defend those fates, and regarded them as persons with inherent value to be respected and protected.

Part of Thompson's point is about the creativity of the leaders, who had these materials to work with and used them to define the place of workers in the larger political order. But part of his point is that *since* these materials were part of the working-class culture, the leaders' creativity was not merely elite hermetic speculation; it was also a basis for *discourse* with the mass of the workers. Thompson, in his last chapter on class consciousness (711–832), pays a lot of attention to the discourse of several leaders of the trades unions of London, using their organizational connection to show that quite a lot of workers believed that these leaders were talking about the political and economic conditions of workers' lives.

But for most of the period that Thompson is talking about, such organizational connections were suppressed by the British government. How, then, is Thompson going to make a case that his spinner in Manchester is talking to the workers, is engaged in class discourse rather than in radical onanism (199–203)? He does this in part by showing the continuity in the themes between what the spinner says in 1818 in Manchester and what various contrasting views regarded as good and worthwhile working-class life a generation earlier, in the 1790s. It is because the 1818 spinner's discourse has themes from the culture of the 1790s poor that we can conclude it is part of a dialogue between the spinner and the rest of the working class. Both are concerned with what makes a respectable worker and what makes a trustworthy system to entrust a worker's fate to.

The main cultural themes in Thompson's work are those that apply to the working class as a whole (or even England as a whole); they are not distinctive to particular firms or trades. To explain variations in class consciousness within the working class of modern societies, we need to use the same strategy that we (and especially Thompson) have used to explain variations in class consciousness over time in England, but now to construct explanations at the firm and occupational levels. We want to turn variables that we have described across societies, and over historical time in England, into variables that can explain why hospitals have less class consciousness than chemical factories, but chemical factories less than automobile factories. That explanatory problem occupies the rest of this chapter.

Constitutionalism in Modern Organizations

Organizations that classify employees into categories and treat them alike produce class consciousness not only because they create collective bargains by their very structure, but also because they often do not live by those collective bargains. Once categories have been created that are supposed to be treated alike, workers get indignant when identically placed workers are not treated alike. Arbitrary authority threatens the legitimacy of structures that are supposed to be fair more than it does the legitimacy of structures that are supposed to be a network of individual bargains. But all such structures have been historically created in labor markets in which the normal structure was a matter of individual contracts, each different, and in which arbitrary authority was the ordinary course of events. Consequently, the growth of "constitutionalism" in organizations, with limitations imposed on management so that they are obliged to follow their own rules (the rules they are required to create by their productive process), reduces conflict between management and class-conscious workers (for a similar argument, see the contrast between British and American machine shops in Burawoy 1985). We can distinguish four broad types of constitutionalism in modern industrial organizations, which we call (1) due process, (2) job evaluation, (3) collective bargaining, and (4) good sportsmanship in the incentive games.

DUE PROCESS

Selznick, Nonet, and Vollmer (1969) argue that bureaucratic organizations in modern society (i.e., exactly those organizations having labor contracts that are standard for members of categories) tend to develop grievance procedures that limit the authority of supervisors and management. These grievance procedures provide an opportunity to accuse management of not following their own rules providing for equal treatment of people with similar jobs. The management as a whole has an interest in fair treatment, treatment according to universalistic personnel policy, whether or not they have agreed to those standards with unions.

Such structures of grievance processing tend to develop workers' rights to bring witnesses on their own behalf, to know the nature of the charges against them, to appeal, not to have the sanctions against them come into effect until the case is resolved, and so on. By equalizing the status and powers of workers and management before the grievance committee, the organization *increases* its capacity to use its authority in the way it has specified in the rules governing categories of workers (and of course *decreases* its capacity to use arbitrary authority). Such structures still create classes and class consciousness, but they are less likely to create class hostility and consciousness of class oppression.

JOB EVALUATION

A crucial part of the structure of uniform contracts for employees of a given category is the relation among the categories. Consequently, bureaucratic organizations are more likely than those with more individualized contracts to develop job evaluation schemes that specify the relations among the contracts that apply to various categories of workers. If these relations among categories are developed so as to seem fair to the workers, they tend to reduce the sort of job-conscious categorical hostility due to one category of workers not being treated properly as compared with some other category of workers. Many such schemes are introduced with extensive consultation of workers about what makes one job more worthwhile than another, and so worthy of higher pay (Soltan 1987, 158–171). If management agrees to limit itself so that it does not reward one category in the system without corresponding rewards for the others, thus keeping the relations among categories that seem fair to the workers, they again reduce the hostility in class consciousness. Of course, such a system tends to build into itself discrimination against women, when there is a consensus between management and the better-organized workers that categories of workers who are mostly women ought to get lower wages. In the long run this tendency may undermine the solidarity between male and female workers.

COLLECTIVE BARGAINING

Collective bargaining is rarely introduced by management in order to pacify and improve the productivity of its workers. However, a line of argument in economics has urged that collective bargaining provides the advantages of constitutionalism, and so improves work discipline. Schumpeter carried the argument furthest, stating that only a socialist government might be able to provide enough work discipline to save capitalism (1942, 211). The argument was prevalent enough in the group of labor economists at the University of California at Berkeley to cause them to start a series of studies in the late forties and fifties entitled "Industrial Peace Under Collective Bargaining." Recent demonstrations by Freeman and Medoff (1984) that union workers generally have higher productivity (10 to 30 percent higher) than nonunion workers in the same industry, making their wages higher even in very competitive markets, support this argument.

Even when management recognizes its interest in following the rules implicit in a modern firm structure that has identical labor contracts with large groups of employees, unions may still be necessary to discipline management to follow their own interest (R. Freeman 1976). Just as the English and American legal systems are legitimized by the fact that both the plaintiff (or prosecutor) and the defendant have lawyers, so the constitution of the modern bureaucratic enterprise is legitimized by categories of employees having their unions. Managements do not have enough good sense to keep their own structures in good constitutional working order, to legitimate their own authority; they need unions to give the workers voice, just as society needs opposing attorneys to give defendants voice.

GOOD SPORTSMANSHIP

Michael Burawoy (1979) observed that a large bureaucratic firm with incentive pay for machinists had changed its policy over the years so that it played the game more fairly now. In an earlier study of the same firm, the investigator found that when productivity went up so that many workers were earning incentive premiums, the base requirement before premiums were earned was boosted. But when Burawoy was there, people were permitted to keep their winnings without changing the base productivity.

Since Burawoy observed that the workers were treating the incentive system as a game, the appropriate image for describing this new behavior of management of not changing the rules every time the workers started to win is "good sportsmanship." Burawoy argues that this good sportsmanship by management tended to cause workers to focus attention on their personal performance and the size of their premiums, rather than on the basic terms of the game. But the basic exchange of money for effort was built into the terms of the game. Hence, management's practice of good sportsmanship tended to create ideological hegemony, a systematic lack of attention by workers to the inherently conflictual setting of the terms of the labor contract for the category of machinist. Thus it reduced class consciousness.

The overall prediction, then, is that the more constitutional the procedure of large bureaucratic organizations is (the more it is characterized by due process, consensual job evaluation, collective bargaining, and good sportsmanship by management in the incentive games it plays with workers), the less hostility there will be in the class consciousness that such structures inevitably tend to create.

Debureaucratization, or Individualizing the Labor Contract

The structures for reducing class consciousness all leave the basic categorical labor contract intact. An alternative strategy is to individualize the labor contract as far as possible. For example, a common practice in setting compensation levels in American university labor contracts is as follows. The university central administration computes the overall increase in labor cost it can afford the next year, then disaggregates this into percentage goals for different deans and heads of service divisions, usually reserving a contingency fund to deal with special cases. Deans and heads of divisions in turn give percentage goals to their department chairs, usually saving some allowance for special contingencies. Department chairs then divide this amount among the faculty, aiming to meet potential outside offers, to reward seniority, and to reward other special merits. Though the average increase is set by the central administration, that average is individualized in a set of complex and partly secret political processes that give everyone the impression that they have a special labor contract, one that recognizes their special merits or their most recent outside offers or the fact that they had bad luck with journal referees the last couple of years. Thus, the categorical judgment of compensation levels for faculty as a whole does not appear clearly in the process of negotiation between an individual faculty member and his or her department chair or dean.

There seem to be three main types of structures that work to individualize the labor contract (or to individualize the apparent labor contract, insofar as there is a concealed categorical labor contract behind the individual ones): promotions and careers as primary rewards, increasing the complexity of the category system, and individually negotiated salaries.

PROMOTIONS AND CAREERS

For promotion systems to undermine people's sense of having their economic fate determined by the fate of the category in which they fall, promotions have to be reasonably frequent. Two forces tend to increase promotion rates: a high rate of growth of the overall enterprise, creating vacancies at the top that can be filled from within (Stinchcombe 1974, 123–150), and a high proportion of total jobs above the level at which recruitment takes place (Blauner 1964, 131–132, 148–154). In complex status systems with many people several steps above the recruitment level, each retirement creates many promotions (White 1970). It has been alleged that part of the purpose of creating the complex stratification system with the manual work force of the steel industry was to create promotions that could undermine steelworker class solidarity (Stone 1975). More briefly, categories of jobs can be uniform while rates of promotion between categories are individualized, and this undermines the class consciousness–creating effect of categories of identical labor contracts.

COMPLEXITY OF THE CATEGORY SYSTEM

The complexity of the category system in which workers are classified has an effect in addition to that of creating possible promotions. The size of the group in which absolutely clear solidarity is created is in general inversely proportional to the number of categories. There may be, for example, laboratory technicians, nurses, occupational therapists, social workers, and bookkeeping supervisors with about the same level of pay and conditions of work in a hospital, and each job type may have several levels of seniority or specialization. But the heterogeneity of the category system may mean that a particular Laboratory Technician II does not know anyone else in precisely the same category as she or he is. The equivalent Social Worker (Psychiatric) IV, Occupational Therapist Supervisor, and Surgical Nurse may never recognize their implicit membership in a category with nearly identical labor contracts to Laboratory Technician II.

INDIVIDUALLY NEGOTIATED SALARIES

Sometimes category systems have some basis of merit, such as, for professors, the length of one's vita or the size of outside offers, that can justify separate treatment of category members for some part of their status prerogatives. All professors may have tenure, but only a few of them have salaries in the top 10 percent of professors' salaries. It is most often the salary that is detached from the rest of the category system and made part of a more individualized bargain, so we have named the strategy for its main manifestation. Bonuses, commissions, stock options, easy work loads, and other perks may also be individualized by applying legitimate measures of merit, hence reducing class consciousness in the relevant group of workers. In this case, while the labor contract is truly individualized, many subparts of it are treated in a categorical fashion.

Two other forces that can reduce class consciousness are to recruit workers from less conscious labor market segments, and to subcontract part of the work to firms that operate in distinct labor market segments.

LABOR MARKET SEGMENTATION AND CLASS CONSCIOUSNESS

When there are large categories of low-skilled workers without much chance of promotion in an enterprise, it may be possible to fill those categories with labor force segments who are, for other reasons, lower in class consciousness. In recent years this has meant especially women and teenagers (both have often been excluded from unions, a fact that tends to reduce their class consciousness). Even when large groups of clerical workers are employed under very standardized conditions, they are relatively unlikely to form unions (in the United States) if they are female. Similarly, the operatives in textile mills or cigarette factories are often Southerners or women or both, and have been less militant than one would expect given their work conditions and wages (Blauner 1964, 70–73). In many parts of the service sector, low-skill jobs have been filled by women or teenagers, which helps to explain the lower degree of class consciousness in fast-food restaurants or among grocery clerks.

Analysis of the size of this effect is very difficult, because part of the reason labor markets are segmented in the first place is so that women and teenagers can be recruited to positions in which the general conditions of the job (precarious tenure, low skill, few career prospects) discourage class consciousness. They are segmented in addition so that such low-wage labor can be kept out of jobs whose conditions are favorable because of strong trade union control. These processes do not uniformly work very well, as is evidenced by relatively high levels of organization among grocery clerks in some parts of the country and in some chains (Walsh 1988).

SUBCONTRACTING AND CLASS CONSCIOUSNESS

The fundamental context of bureaucratic uniformity outside the skilled trades is the firm. Workers doing identical work in different firms do not necessarily see themselves as being members of the same category, especially if they are in different local labor markets. Consequently, one consideration for an assembly firm in the "buy or make" decision (the decision on whether the firm should manufacture parts itself or subcontract to suppliers) is whether there are local labor markets in which the category of workers required to make the part get lower wages than that category does within the firm. For example, if machinists in rural Michigan are employed by General Motors, they will probably have to be paid wages comparable to Flint machinists. If, however, they are employed by a locally owned machine shop with good relations to the local vocational teachers, they can probably be paid wages comparable to auto mechanics in rural garages. And if (as is usually the case) auto mechanics in rural garages earn less than UAW machinists in Flint, a subcontractor can manufacture the part much more cheaply than General Motors can, if its efficiency is equal. Both groups of machinists may separately be quite class conscious, but that class consciousness is less likely to result in equal wages for the parts manufacturer and the assembly firm (Sabel 1982, 31–77). In fact, parts suppliers to the automobile industry do seem to have lower wages than automobile manufacturers.

Low Unionization of the Modern Service Sector: Theory

To deal with the general notion that the movement toward a service economy has caused some of the decline in class consciousness, we have a problem of defining the dependent variable. In E. P. Thompson there is no question what working-class consciousness is: the workers he quotes are all clearly workers, and the unions found in the industries he studies are clearly unions. But is, for instance, the American Medical Association, a "working class"–conscious organization, merely one made up of quite rich workers and consequently a lot more conservative in economic and political philosophy than, say, the United Auto Workers? The American Bar Association is very well organized, and often they take initiatives against reforms that would give legal services more cheaply, such as so-called no-fault divorce—that is, they defend the economic interests of legal artisans in much the same way stockingers and others in early-nineteenth-century England did. For these professional associations, the question is whether they are unions or not, and whether the group consciousness they show should be called a narrow form of class consciousness—class consciousness without alliances with other working-class organizations.

An excellent example of the problem can be seen in the fact that within the census occupational category of "Professional, Technical, and Related Workers," women are more likely to belong to trade unions than men are. This is because women are overrepresented in the teaching profession, one of the few professional occupations that are highly unionized. Fifteen or twenty years ago teachers were hardly unionized at all, because the National Educational Association included principals and superintendents (supervisors supposedly cannot be members of their workers' unions in the United States) and did not engage in collective bargaining. The law did not at that time provide for representation elections in public schools.

We will take as a rough indicator of a group's class consciousness whether or not its organizations apply for the legal right to be collective bargaining agents. This criterion can be defended by the theory of class consciousness above, and divides occupational organizations in a way that agrees with my intuitions.

Several sectors of the service industries, however, have considerable class consciousness even in the Thompson sense. Some of the most powerful early unions were formed by high-status railroad workers, who were quite well organized by the 1880s. The railroads were the first large-scale modern bureaucratic industry to be almost completely unionized in the United States. They were pretty well organized by the First World War (Licht 1983). Steel- (after the breaking of the Homestead strike in the 1890s) and autoworkers were not really organized until the mid thirties. Nevertheless, the overall picture is one of low class consciousness in the service sector.

Service-Sector Class Consciousness: Demography

THE DEMOGRAPHY OF CLASS CONTACT

A basic generalization from political sociology (Lipset, Lazarsfeld et al. 1954) is that the more one associates with workers, the more left one's opinions and voting will be and the more likely one is to be drawn into those activities that are connected to working-class milieux. If a person is a lowly wage worker but is working as a servant in an upper-class household in an upper-class section of town, he or she will be very unlikely to vote Democratic in the United States or Labour in England, very unlikely to learn to play darts in England or pool well in the United States, and very unlikely to join a union or to participate in a working-class demonstration. Conversely, a grocer with a store in a working-class district whose conversations with clients are all with workers, who lives over the store among all-working-class neighbors, and who shares the ethnicity and religion of the neighborhood and so meets working-class people in his or her voluntary associational life, is very likely to vote Democratic or Labour or to come out on demonstrations on behalf of working-class grievances or even to make contributions to the workers' strike funds when the community splits apart during a strike.

Many service jobs isolate the person from social contact with other workers and require intense contact with clients. Broadly speaking, clients are a cross-section of the class system, so contact with clients tends to move people in upper-class professions (e.g., the clergy) in a leftward direction in economic ideology (though in a more fundamentalist direction in theology), people in lower-class occupations in a rightward direction. The broad effect on the people who might otherwise join working-class organizations in the service sector is to decrease working-class consciousness (Hughes 1958).

This generalization depends a lot on the composition of the clientele. For example, U.S. senators are very upper-class folks with a clientele that is very nearly an exact cross-section of the population, on whom they depend and with whom they socialize a lot because they depend on them. It is also perhaps the upper-class group most evenly split between Democrats and Republicans, and it has more prounion members than practically any other upper-class profession. Some other specialized groups tend to be near half left, half right as well, such as labor lawyers, for obvious reasons. Those lawyers who specialize in creating new financial instruments or advising corporations on corporate reorganizations tend to be quite right-wing, while criminal and divorce lawyers or political lawyers (e.g., district attorneys) tend to be much farther left. In medicine, the physicians who talk to their clients (psychiatrists, pediatricians, general practitioners) tend to be farther left than those whose patients are mostly unconscious (surgeons, anesthesiologists) or not present (pathologists).

Generally speaking, the teamsters, railroad engineers, pilots, and so on in the service industries have little contact with clients and are quite class conscious, while male salespeople are very likely to talk to their client and very unlikely to be in unions. The more the demography of the workplace includes clients, and the more intense the interaction of service workers with clients is, the more those who might otherwise be disposed to join unions or to vote left will instead be nonunion and vote to the right.

GENDER DEMOGRAPHY IN SERVICE INDUSTRIES

Women are disproportionately recruited into the service sector, especially into its lower-status positions. Even when women are factory workers, they are harder to organize into unions than men (in 1980, 41.4 percent of male blue-collar workers were union members, 29.1 percent of females; in that same year, 24.7 percent of male service workers were union members, 10.8 percent of women [*Statistical Abstract of the United*

States, 1984, 441]). In many ways, the main kind of "peasant workers," in Sabel's terms (1982, 101–109), are women. He defines peasant workers as those whose main life is elsewhere than at their work, who are willing to work hard for poor pay in insecure jobs because they are making more than they could make where their life is. If more women than men are, like peasant workers, temporary jobholders entering the labor market from unorganized sectors (e.g., the household or the farm sectors), this should depress their class consciousness.

In general, women receive more intense and more moralistic socialization than men; and, in general, modern morality is conservative. In addition, women tend to bear the responsibility in the home for matters of taste, that is, for so managing the home that the social status displayed is as high as the family can afford (Bourdieu 1984). If anyone sits on the front porch in an undershirt and spits on the steps, it is probably the man; if in rural areas anyone is going to leave old machines out in the yard and give the impression of a junkyard office, it will probably be the man. So the generalization that we will come to below, that people more responsible for matters of taste tend to be more conservative, applies more often to women workers than to men.

Except when the right-wing candidate is belligerent and enthusiastic about state violence (e.g., conspicuously in favor of capital punishment), women in most countries vote more to the right. In most countries, women join unions less than men as well, and are less class conscious in opinion surveys. Women tend to work with other women, a fact that can reinforce them in their conservatism, since their co-workers are, statistically speaking, likely to be conservative too. Of course, when the co-workers are left-wing, organized, class-conscious women, the reverse holds.

Service-Sector Class Consciousness: Selling Status Symbols

Quite often the work of the service sector is producing or selling symbols, and quite often those symbols have a conservative tinge. People tend to come to believe and value anything they say, so if their work requires them to produce symbols with a conservative tinge, they tend to become conservative.

HIGH STATUS FRONTS TO SELL STATUS SYMBOLS

One kind of symbolization that people take up in many service roles conveys a sense of the kind of person they themselves are. Some of those symbols represent humiliation (more on this below), such as waitress uniforms. But quite a lot of the symbols falsely indicate that one is one-self upper class. For women, the symbols of being of a higher class than the job would indicate are (in 1987) skirts and dresses, medium makeup, and dyed hair. If a work setting tends to induce women to adopt such symbols of official public womanliness, it will tend to conservatize them as well. For example, one would expect beauticians to be more conservative than other craftswomen.

With men, the comparable grooming symbols today are frequent shaving (or frequent psuedoshaving, producing the sharp line around the beard to show that the man has not just let it grow), neckties with the associated dress shirts, polish on the shoes, and, at the extreme, "business" suits. The more a role requires people to dress like businessmen, regardless of the content and status of the role, the more likely it is that the workers will not have class consciousness.

CONSERVATIZING DEFERENCE

Some service-sector roles require symbolizing deference, especially toward clients. As Robert McKenzie and Allan Silver showed so effectively for England in *Angels in Marble* (1968), a deferential attitude is closely associated with voting Tory. Roles that have a lot of deference built into them, such as barbers or salesmen (or occasionally saleswomen) of expensive things such as haute couture and BMWs, should have less working-class consciousness than dime store clerks or checkout personnel in a supermarket; waiters should be less class conscious than servers in cafeterias; people who work in racing stables should be less disposed to join unions than other agricultural proletarians; and so on. A lot of the "emotion work" that Arlie Hochschild talks about in *The Managed Heart* (1983) comes down to showing deference to the client. Such emotion work in a role should in general decrease working class consciousness.

TASTE AS A CONSERVATIZING FORCE

Pierre Bourdieu (1984) gives a pretty complete outline for France of what sorts of things are *appreciated* by the relatively unschooled rich, and what sorts are appreciated by the rather well off but highly educated upper-middle classes. By and large, things more appreciated by the upper classes of either kind are the same sorts of things that women appreciate more than men. For example, well-to-do highly educated people are likely to appreciate classical music as well as modern popular music, to take their music sitting down in a concert rather than dancing at a night club, to prefer *The Art of Fugue* or *The Well-tempered Clavier* to "The Blue Danube" or the Hungarian Rhapsodies, to like Dali or Rousseau more than Raphael, to think of themselves as "artistic" rather than "conscientious," to think that even engineers ought to have a bit of humanities training in college, and so on. The same contrasts would be true of women as compared to men.

Quite a lot of the high-margin trade in the service sector comes from producing and selling goods that appeal to nouveaux riches, who have not yet had their tastes perfected by several generations of family with good humanities classes, or selling those goods that show more "old money" tastes. So we would expect people in the service sector selling such things as golf or tennis lessons, interior decoration, haute couture, slimming salons, and so on, to be relatively conservative. I suppose that in general French teachers in the United States would be more conservative than Spanish teachers for the same reason, even though there is probably more reputable left-wing symbolism in French culture than in Spanish; in the United States one by and large learns French in order to be fashionable, Spanish to be a social worker.

Conversely, the folks who make and sell beer (at least in countries where the working-class drink is beer) are likely to be leftists, and owners of pubs or beer halls are likely to be more left-wing than owners of wine shops or cocktail bars. Beer advertising symbolizes male working-class virtues, and beer halls appeal to male working-class clienteles rather than to middle-class couples (LaBonte 1987).

The argument would then be that the parts of the service sector displaying relatively little class consciousness are those that sell high-margin goods to the rich, perhaps especially those that sell mainly to the rich with smaller educational capital. But since those high margins in part reflect more service-worker labor, the high-margin trade should have a larger conservatizing effect than the thin-margin trade of goods aimed mainly at the working class and poor.

Service-Sector Class Consciousness: The Small Firm Effect

The third big force producing less class consciousness in the service sector is that supervision of service-sector workers is different from that of workers in the manufacturing sector.

SHORT HIERARCHIES

Most of the service sector, except transportation and utilities, is run on a small-firm basis, that is, the profit taker himself or herself, or the high executive who represents the profit taker, is only a few steps away from the worker in the hierarchy, and often works alongside the worker. This means several things. First, the superior is much more likely to supervise by pointing out the goals he or she is trying to achieve, rather than by "Bravermanizing" or routinizing the job. Second, someone with a commitment to profit making is nearby in terms of social distance: a worker can talk to the head of a restaurant or the owner of the McDonald's franchise in a way that is impossible with the chief executive officer of General Motors. Third, the mobility chances of a worker are not defined by seniority, but are of a capitalist character; thus, the same objective mobility rates operating in the service sector as in manufacturing would probably have a conservatizing effect in small firms, because there the mobility is more often into the capitalist role of owner rather than into the salaried role of foreman. Ambitious service-sector workers are probably more conservatized by their ambition than members of the manufacturing or other large-firm sectors.

FEWER CATEGORICAL LABOR CONTRACTS

Smaller firms are generally associated with not establishing categories of workers and attaching the same pay to all members of the same category and the same seniority. Pay is a bargain with individuals, not with a category of people, a fact that reduces class consciousness, as argued above (Lockwood 1958).

PIECEWORK COMPENSATION

Much of the supervision in the service sector is on a sort of "piecework" system, where *clients' decisions* make up the pieces that the workers are paid by. Commissions are common in sales work, tips common for waiters, hairdressers, and taxi drivers, and in addition getting part of the total take rather than a wage is common for taxi drivers. What is being elicited in these schemes is not "productivity" in some obvious sense, but the capacity to find and influence clients to take the service, buy the good, or give the tip. Such incentive systems are generally individualizing, making the workers think their wage depends on their own efforts rather than on a general wage rate (Burawoy 1979; Browne 1973).

But the kinds of piecework found in the service industries often make the worker dependent on figuring out what the client would like; this intensifies the effects of role requirements that press workers to associate with and be friendly to upper-class clients or to show deference. The more a role requires the worker to figure out the wishes of the client, the more the conservative character of the average client (as compared with the average worker) penetrates the worker's consciousness.

UNIONIZED ENVIRONMENTS AND CLASS CONSCIOUSNESS

In some parts of the service industry, however, the overall relation between a corporation and the employees is so shot through with union
elements that even people who would otherwise not be very class conscious end up in unions and sometimes talk like class-conscious workers.
A lovely case is airline stewardesses: they are female, wear the medium
amount of makeup that reflects their higher class of clientele, their job is
to be deferential and to figure out how to satisfy upper-class and upper-
middle-class clients, and until recently they were more or less explicitly
required to be "peasant workers," to leave the business when they got too
old. One would thus not expect them to very class conscious. But everybody else in the industry, even the executives in charge of the small work
group they are in (the pilots), are all unionized. Compared to anyone else
in waitress roles with an upper-class clientele, then, flight attendants are
pretty class conscious.

Conclusion

The organizational facts that create social classes, and so create the basis
of class consciousness, cannot be understood without understanding the
political culture in which class relations are understood by the workers.
We have tried to build a theory of what class relations look like in modern societies by combining organizational sociology with political history, taking inspiration from E. P. Thompson. We have perhaps made
E. P. Thompson into more of a theorist than he would be comfortable
with (he is supposed to believe that "theory is just laziness in the archives"), but the result is something that can be used to understand labor
relations of modern corporations, who create classes by creating job categories, and to understand why many modern service industries do not
create much working-class consciousness.

The fundamental argument of this chapter is that since class consciousness is the projection of organizational statuses onto a larger political and economic canvas, the cultural tools workers have to make these
projections go as far to explain class consciousness as does the organizational process that creates groups with identical labor contracts. Those
tools are part of general working-class culture, as our analysis of Thompson shows; but they are also shaped by the sorts of structures that exist
within the organization, such as grievance procedures, job evaluation
schemes, or individuation of the labor contract, to define the meaning of
the categories involved in labor contracts. They are also shaped by cul-

tural definitions erected by the work itself, especially in the service industries, where a good part of what a worker sells is a set of symbols of upper-class status.

But those cultural definitions cannot redefine everything. Or better, they can redefine everything, but not to be anything they please. The service sector is less class conscious in large measure because it does not in fact put as many workers into large groups with categorical labor contracts, as well as because within those categories workers have to present themselves as if they were upper class in order to sell diamond rings. Craftsmen and craftswomen, and the semiprofessionals who make up the craft trade-union structure of the airlines industry, serve an upper-class clientele just as jewelers do, but they do so in a structure that treats them as equivalent members of a category earning a standard wage rate. So while we will not expect, say, stewardesses or pilots to be as militant as mineworkers, we will expect them to be a good deal more class conscious than workers in retail jewelry. The projection of organizational status on the larger society depends in part on the symbols that accomplish this projection; but it depends also on the type of organizational status system in which it is embedded.

The argument of this chapter, then, has been that people get much of the information about their interests from the information in the incentive system of the organization they work for. In particular, they do not learn that they are part of a labor market, and thus that their wages will be competed down to the lowest level their employer can pay, from the obscure operations of that market itself. Instead they learn it from the categories in the incentive system of their employer. When uniform category systems of employer organizations are projected onto the larger canvas of the political system, they produce the raw material of class consciousness, of trade union organization, and of left egalitarian politics.

But the very fact that the way the incentive system of the firm or of the local skilled trade appears to people produces the basic view they have of their economic and political interests means that various features of that local scene can affect what they see to be their interests. Further, it means that the larger processes of worker enfranchisement and trade union organization can affect what workers see when they look at the local incentive system. For most of this book we have treated the uncertainties that organizational systems deal with as hard facts. Clearly they often must *be* hard facts, or objectively measured features of markets would not have observable effects on skill distribution or on divisionalization, and turning inventions into innovations would be just another job people do, instead of a major force for administrative changes. But equally clearly, it does not do to be dogmatic about how far facts are objective; some facts are more objective than others. How far an individual worker's interest is actually collective is not immediately given to workers in the labor market, as it is given that the customer will have the building built the way he, she, or it wants it rather than however is convenient for the construction contractor. So the degree to which a labor market looks to the worker in it as though it ought to be unionized is not as objective a fact about that labor market as is the degree to which the construction market looks like a set of contracts for unique buildings, designed to customer specifications.

Class consciousness thus illustrates a more general fact about modern society. Whatever the cultural apparatus that interprets facts in some sector of the economy, very generally the facts themselves were generated by the information-processing systems of organizations. The discovery process in the law is mostly applied to get access to organizational records to use as evidence in court, though the government may take a very different view from that of IBM about what those facts mean (Fishman 1981, 380–411). The facts used by the tax system are generated by accounting and payroll systems in organizations, though generally neither the organization nor the employee is favorably disposed to the uses made of those facts. The facts generated by the registrar of the university, a compilation of judgments of professors, are central to some of the certificates used in the labor market, though many professors are vaguely uncomfortable that their judgment of a student's understanding of Shakespeare is worth money in the labor market.

Thus, it is not unusual that left-wing parties and trade unions make use of the facts generated by the categories of the incentive systems of organizations. They make use of them partly because they can do no other. It takes a good deal of argument to get professors to see that the core determinant of their salary raise is what percentage everybody's increase has to add up to, as decided by the university administration, while it takes very little argument for an autoworker to see the same thing— and all that simply because the first percentage is individualized before the professor's note on next year's salary comes (and it comes after the school years ends, making comparison difficult), while the second is the percentage that appears in the autoworker's pay packet, identical to the percentage in other workers' packets.

No doubt the employers in automobile manufacturing would rather give the same impression of individuation that universities give, but they would have difficulty running an assembly line that way. Regardless of the source of the organizational difference in individuation, professors are hard to organize for collective bargaining, autoworkers are easy, and that hard fact for trade unions is created by the hard facts of the different incentive systems.

But trade unions make different use of such facts in the Soviet Union than in Great Britain or the United States, and different uses still in Japan. The same kinds of workers are disproportionately active in trade unions in all four societies, presumably owing to deep facts about the incentive systems appropriate for different sorts of production. But these similarities are overlaid by differences in the large structure for interpreting their meaning in the political culture as a whole. Such facts about variations in interpretation as those elaborated in this chapter are what give the limits to the "techno-Marxism" of the first seven chapters.

University Administration of
Research Space and
Teaching Loads
Managers Who Do Not Know
What Their Workers Are Doing

What Business Universities Are In

My purpose in this first section is to specify why the uncertainty of scientific advance is central to the work of universities, by trying to describe what business universities are in. This will then serve as a background for exploring why administration of university space and teaching loads is as it is and, in turn, for saying why what looks like a pretty haphazard system is actually more or less rational. Most research space is allocated as if to sovereign states—the departments and research centers. Teaching loads tend to be administered by departments, with relatively intense supervision by deans but little administration from higher up. I will argue that the very unpredictability of research, and hence of research space and faculty time needs, is the microscopic explanation of why the central space administration of a university is so rigid, and why the administration of teaching loads varies so much across departments.

The first problem is to explain why organizations that make most of their money from teaching should emphasize research so much. My argument compares what universities do to what banks do; that is, both banks and universities are *fiduciary* institutions. Fiduciary institutions are essential to create an exchange system that trades and pools different kinds of uncertainties. What a modern leading university in the United States or England buys is different from what it sells. It buys professors' achievement in a very uncertain world of advances in science and scholarship, and it sells prestige education. For the most part, the prestige education is in the well-established consensus part of the various disciplines; thus people in, say, chemistry, with many different approaches to what is an interesting research question, will be willing to use the same elementary chemistry book. Further, they will teach the standard use of the standard laboratory equipment in the teaching laboratories, although the equipment in their research laboratories is purpose-built and unique.

So a university buys in the high-risk market for scientific advance in chemistry, and sells mostly in the market for certifiably excellent and standard education in the profession of chemistry. (In the last four decades, the NSF and NIH have bought research services from the physical and biological sciences departments of leading universities on a scale never seen before 1945—so this argument applies in pure form only up to 1945.) The professor is hired to do research, which is a different sort of work from what the student (or the goverment) pays tuition for: teaching. The university buys research on the labor market on the general criterion that someone who knows chemistry well enough to advance it will, on average, be able to provide reliably up-to-date teaching of chemistry's consensus. The high-risk market for scientific advances, then, promises *less* risk that students will get out-of-date or wrong teaching.

The point is that students would be unable to hire in the high-risk market for scientific advances themselves because assessing the risks of being wrong about scientific advances requires evaluation by peers who understand the paradigms and their uncertainties and the details of laboratory procedure. A student is not in a position to judge whether a person has really advanced knowledge or is just some sort of crank. The correlation between students' evaluation of individual professors and the professors' research productivity is relatively low (I would guess it at around .2, based on the difference in teaching evaluations in the universities versus the state colleges in California many years ago). But the tuition that a university can get away with charging for a prestige education (whether it is charged to the state or to the individual student) is very highly correlated with the *average* scientific and scholarly productivity of the faculty.

In some sense the students (or their parents, or their state legislature), then, pay the university to hire in a market for scientific and scholarly competence that is so risky they cannot make good decisions in it for themselves. They pay the university to provide them with a pooled risk function that is a reliable certification of competence and up-to-dateness. Although parents could not choose the faculty at MIT themselves, they are confident that a certificate that one is a competent engineer (or scientist) given by MIT as an institution will be valuable in the labor market, because it will reflect real learning.

The Analogy of Universities to Banks

In the same general way, banks buy future income streams in businesses or home mortgages that have much larger fluctuations and risks than most savers are willing to bear. By pooling those risks and income streams, by keeping reserves, by maintaining FDIC insurance, and the like, the banks can sell savers a very different temporal pattern of income with a very different risk function than is found in the future income streams they buy from the businesses they are lending to. One's checking account or savings account is quite liquid, available on short notice at a high degree of certainty; the bank, however, is earning the interest on it with both higher risk and larger investments that are quite illiquid. The bank would lose a lot of money by insisting that a factory built with their loan had to be sold off to satisfy savers' demands.

In both banks and universities, we have to trust the institutions to run for us the risks we are not competent to run (or do not want to run) ourselves, so that we can buy a reliably liquid degree in engineering that can be cashed in for a job at Du Pont (even though MIT has bought in a very uncertain market of recent advances in quantum mechanics that we cannot understand), or so that we can reliably collect our savings account with interest when we want to make a down payment on a house (even though the interest was earned by an investment that comes to maturity at a different time and with more risk than we were willing to bear, maybe financing the R & D at Du Pont). And it is because we have to trust them to act for us in markets that we can't ourselves manage that I call them both "fiduciary" institutions.

Institutional Risk Management in the Anglo-Saxon versus the Latin World

Many Latin American universities, instead of buying the full time of a leading scientist as shown by recent discoveries and making him or her teach roughly half time, hire someone part time who earns a real living by part-time work elsewhere and who can be certified to know the consensual content of the course to be taught. That is, the labor that the university buys is almost exactly the same as the labor that the student buys: competent teaching of a course. The problem is the same as with a bank that lends out only to people or enterprises with very little risk and highly liquid resources: the client can get no increased returns owing to the bank's or university's intelligent participation in highly risky investments in capital equipment or new knowledge with a high average rate of return. Highly liquid and safe investments in savings accounts can have higher rates of return because banks pool risks for their savers. Likewise, highly competent and standard teaching can be obtained without much risk by letting the university invest in precarious research ventures on the basis of its specialized knowledge of where the various fields of research are probably going.

Because Latin universities hire as if they were students, over time the teaching in engineering schools and accounting schools does not change as rapidly with advances in knowledge in the average Latin American or Spanish university as it does in the average North American or British university. This means in turn that investments in human capital in Latin America and Spain give lower rates of return than in North America and England.

More or less the same thing is true in international comparisons of national capital markets. The kind of certainty that savers need is not produced by legal certainty. Instead it is produced by having a complex set of insurancelike institutions. Life insurance, for example, gives savers risks of being able to collect when they die that are different from what would be obtained if they had instead bought shares in the Prudential Building; the chances banks give of people being able to withdraw their savings to make a down payment on a house are likewise different from what those people would have had if they had owned a piece of a mortgage on Houston real estate.

With fiduciary institutions, investments can be made even if the investments do not provide the risks and the overtime pattern of savings and withdrawals that savers demand. Legal certainty will not do that, because even if a saver's piece of a Houston mortgage is legally certain, he or she cannot collect on it unless a buyer can be found in Houston, and nowadays (1989) a buyer cannot be found in Houston. My untutored impression is that banks in Latin America are not as good at pooling higher risks so as to give savers their required liquidity while investing in long-term economic development. Latin banks tend to want to lend on mortgages in real estate rather than on corporate bonds.

What Is the Uncertainty of
Scientific Research?
Betting Where New Knowledge
Is to Be Found

BETTING

The first point one has to get straight in order to address the sociology of science is that the strategy of actively pursuing new knowledge is a different process from that of examining purported new knowledge the extent to which it is knowledge. That is, doing science is not just following some rules of epistemology. What a scientist has to do is take the present state of knowledge, as he or she believes it to be, and make intelligent guesses about what else (or what different) is likely to be the case, and further guesses about the method by which the likelihood that the guess is right can be increased or decreased.

The second half of this guessing or betting process is the strategic part of epistemology. Epistemology is the study of various methods of increasing or decreasing the probability that various assertions about the world are true. There are lots of deep philosophical problems about how this can be done, what makes them work, and the like, which constitute the main body of what is usually called the philosophy of science. But a scientist is posed with the problem of how, as a practical matter, best to *affect* the subjective probabilities with which the body of scientists will hold a belief that he or she proposes to investigate. It is, in other words, a matter of empirical or theoretical *strategy*, a game in which the rules are in some sense epistemological standards, but the *conduct of investigation* is a matter of choosing the least-cost, highest-return method of beating that game.

So epistemology bears roughly the same relation to the problem of "establishing" new knowledge as the rules of football, soccer, or horse racing bear to winning in those games. Obviously, a person can be a very good judge of the rules for a horse race without being a very fast horse or even a championship jockey. Likewise, a person can be a good epistemologist without being much good at changing the probabilities of various beliefs that scientists hold. But conversely, an entity can be a very fast horse without being much of a judge of horse races, and being a successful scientist does not much predict intelligence in the business of epistemology or philosophy of science.

Behind the decision to seek new knowledge in a given place lies more than a strategy for affecting the probabilities with which scientists hold a belief. Even more important is deciding what set of beliefs it would be useful to try to affect, which involves all sorts of judgments of probabilities that there is something wrong with the whole apparatus—theoretical, observational, paradigmatic, etc.—on which our present judgments of the probabilities of various beliefs in the scientific system rest.

There are bets in theoretical work as well. For example, people who ought to know say that when Einstein's special theory of relativity was developed and published, there were results by a famous experimentalist which looked unchallengeable that showed that Einstein was wrong. Only many years later did someone determine that there had been a leak in the experimental apparatus. Einstein was engaged in looking for a way to integrate the theories of Lorenz and Maxwell and simply ignored the contradictory results, hoping, I presume, that there would turn out to be a "special" explanation of them. There did. The point here is that Einstein's bet was that a unified treatment of two theories, both of which had been empirically productive, was likely to be truer than either alone, and likely to generate predictions that would tell something about the world that we had not been in a situation to think of before.

Of course, there might not have been a leak in the apparatus, and Einstein might have been quite wrong. In such a situation, where one set of indications, such as the experiments, points one way, another set, such as more or less convincing theoretical arguments, the other way, a scientist must place bets as seems wise. He or she has to be willing to be wrong. A wonderful example is the fact that two different physicists have got the Nobel Prize for the discovery of transuranium elements (Zuckerman 1977, 212-213). In the Nobel address for the first discovery (in 1938; the other award was in 1951 for research carried out in 1940), Fermi (who practically all physicists would agree deserved the Nobel for *something*) pointed out that there seemed to be something wrong with the standard interpretation of the results of the experiments that "established" the existence of transuranium elements, because Hahn and Strassmann had found barium among the products of those experiments. Fermi's experiments involved bombarding uranium with neutrons, and the actual result was fission of uranium, not fusion of the neutrons with uranium atoms.

But regardless of the scientific facts, which of course I am not competent to comment on, Fermi had clearly been making bets (and getting them accepted in the scientific community, up to and including the Nobel committee) on the interpretation of his experimental results, and he had been wrong—and he knew it (another measure of his being a great physicist) at the time he accepted the prize for it. What had made the facts of the experiments interesting was their theoretical interpretation, and that, as it turned out, was wrong. Another interpretation, however, which perhaps unfortunately had a lot of practical applications, was also interesting, and it led to the famous experiments showing a nuclear chain reaction in a basement at the University of Chicago during World War II—also conducted by Fermi.

In some ways, what distinguishes great scientists is that they make a lot of bets in uncertain circumstances (their "originality") and a lot of those bets turn out well (their "competence"). But if even a great scientist makes a lot of bets in uncertain circumstances, he or she will lose a lot. Similarly, even if a bettor is so good at judging horseflesh (or judging jockeys) that he or she has a winning record at the racetrack, if the bettor bets a lot he or she will lose a lot as well as winning a lot. Fermi was not so humiliated at having been wrong that he avoided making the prize speech, or defensive enough to try to conceal that he was getting the prize for having "established" something that was apparently not true.

NEW KNOWLEDGE

It is, however, not only the change in the probability of a given bit of knowledge, immediately implicated in an experiment or other observation or immediately involved as a lemma of a new theoretical derivation, that determines whether scientists will regard what has been established as "new knowledge." The overall evaluation of scientists about how new, and how much, knowledge there is in a given bit of scientific work is how much that bit of scientific work *changes* the probabilities they themselves use in betting on where to find new knowledge. For instance, a new finding in parapsychology, even if believable (and this is itself a problem, regardless of how far the parapsychology work follows the rules of legitimate epistemology), will hardly affect the bets of practicing psychologists about where new knowledge is to be found, because the mechanisms, theories, experimental methods, and the like that are "useful" in parapsychology have nothing much to do with the mechanisms, theories, and experimental methods that are useful in psychology as a whole.

In contrast, the fact that one could build Tinkertoy-like models of DNA to explain features of the X-ray diffraction pattern, which are compatible with previous knowledge about the distances between atoms and other ions and which immediately suggest how gene reproduction in DNA and protein production in the cell might proceed, immediately and dramatically changed the bets virtually all molecular biologists made about where new knowledge was to be found (see Watson [1968] 1981). The biological mechanisms were those which genetic biologists and cell physiologists had been looking for, the atomic bonding theories used in building the models were solid theories about the structures of molecules, and the X-ray diffraction method was and is a reliable device for getting certain parameters of the structure of matter, and had won the Nobel Prize for people before. As a subjective estimate, about a third of the papers in the *Scientific American* nowadays are about research in molecular biology or cell physiology that depends heavily on the Watson-Crick *Double Helix* research; these papers represent, that is, research that has been following out bets about where new knowledge is to be found which would be very different if we did not know what we do about the structure of DNA.

Part of what determines how much a piece of scientific work affects the structure of probabilities in other people's minds, on the basis of which they place bets represented by their own scientific work, is of course its epistemological value. A solid experiment that could hardly have come out the way it did unless the theory it supports were true will affect the way people bet about related matters much more than would experimental results that could be due to almost anything, among other things the theory in question (see Stinchcombe 1968, 17–28).

But a lot will depend on how the results relate to the ongoing programs of work of the scientists who read them. For example, a result showing that sociology's sampling designs probably cause us grossly to misestimate the regression coefficients that relate sons' occupations to fathers' occupations would be much more valuable knowledge than a similar demonstration that we are grossly misestimating coefficients relating alienation from society to almost anything else. Many more sociologists work on the regression coefficients related to social mobility than on those related to alienation. This is because the social mobility coefficients play a central role in our theories of socialization for social roles, in our theories of rebellion in the political system or class consciousness, in our notions of what is distinctive about industrial society as compared with peasant or primitive societies. Regression coefficients relating to alienation are of interest only to a few social psychologists (e.g., in sociology, Melvin Seeman) and to a few political scientists who work with the Michigan election studies (e.g., Philip Converse). So when a sociologist demonstrates something about the bias of our sampling methods with respect to alienation (Stinchcombe 1979a; Stinchcombe, Jones, and Sheatsley 1981), the work of most sociologists will remain unaffected. The same is true of another big bias, that *households* of people who live alone are substantially undersampled, whereas *people* who live in big families are very substantially undersampled, in most noncensus studies— but when was the last time an average sociologist was fascinated by an article in which the central point had to do with living alone or with living in a large household?

The structure of theory is especially important for how wide the implications of a bit of scientific work will be. The absolute centrality of the DNA work is perhaps the best example of this point. Genetics depends on the study of how genes replicate. The central way genetic information is transferred to cell physiology is by protein synthesis, so the relation between DNA and protein synthesis, clarified by knowing how DNA is built, is central to cell physiology. Knowing how proteins themselves are built allows one to use various biological methods to investigate the structure of particular proteins, and suggests as well how one might synthesize proteins related to a particular protein (see Latour 1980, an analysis of work that depends on applications of these findings about DNA structure). Similarly, quantum mechanics was central to physics in the 1920s and 1930s because the relationships between energy and matter were theoretically involved in most branches of physics, not to mention in many branches of chemistry, and quantum mechanics suggested new directions of research on all those matters.

For our purposes, what this means is that the amount of uncertainty about what one is going to do next year in scientific work is very great. Only if many scientists would bet differently than a given scientist will it be worthwhile for that scientist to do work on a topic. Only if he or she has a different estimate from theirs about how the work will come out should he or she do the work. Consequently, it is the areas of maximum uncertainty that are most attractive to scientists, especially when they think they can bet more accurately than other people about how the experiment will come out. And as a result, university research consists of a shifting set of "projects," which are quite different this year from last, and will be quite different yet again next year.

This also means that the information about what would be strategic for a given scientist to do next year—what will get through a set of NSF referees, for example—will be concentrated among people in the small community of scientists who themselves know the probabilities attached to various beliefs related to the proposed research, in other words, who know what would be valuable knowledge if it were found. It is such "peers," usually a group of fewer than one hundred active researchers in a given field, who know whether a particular project is really directed at a problem whose solution will matter. Further, only they will know whether the procedure proposed in the research is sufficiently solid that other scientists will believe the results. And only they will know whether this is the sort of work that a particular scientist is likely to be competent to do properly, or whether it involves knowledge of a different field as well as the field in which the proposer has been trained.

It is this informational implication of the fact that it pays to do scientific research only on uncertain subjects that is central to the problem of the administration of scientific work in general, and to administration of space for research in particular.

The General Character of University Research Space Problems

University research using laboratories, then, is usually organized into projects. Projects have a finite life and then are not repeated, though the following project may have similar enough characteristics so as to have basically the same space requirements. Most research has to be done only once (or at most a finite number of times). This project character of research means that the activities that occupy a given piece of university space are always changing.

The values of square feet required for, say, chemical research that are entered in administrative documents are, in a sense, *actuarial* values: expected values of statistical processes that develop over time, with a good deal of variation over time due to chance. That is, they represent the number of faculty members and graduate students one expects to have in the chemistry department, the mix of sorts of research one can expect them to be interested in, the luck those people can expect to have in getting their research funded, and the amounts and kinds of space that all the resulting activities in projects can be expected to fit into. The problem of space planning (as represented, for example, in the figures of per person research space for different disciplines in Bereither and Schillinger 1968, 58–61) is therefore to estimate the expected value of the space requirements of a future flow of projects—the amount of space the university should be expected to provide as insurer that whatever the contingencies, all researchers will at the appropriate time get what space they need to house their research.

The assumptions built into that list of per person square foot requirements in Bereither and Schillinger's *University Space Planning* (1968) are that the department will continue to have the research distinction that on average it has had, and so will be able to get grants of about the same quantity as before; that it will have about the usual proportion of leaves, the usual ratio of graduate student projects to faculty projects, and the usual experience of other personnel contingencies; that the mix of research-space-intensiveness will not change drastically, so that there will not all of a sudden be large space users in departments that have not used much space in the past; and so on. Further, the way Bereither and Schillinger's book is written, it implies that the research space requirements estimated for the University of Illinois at Champaign-Urbana do not reflect happenstance differences from other universities in the relative distinction of different science departments, or differences in emphasis on space-using versus space-saving scientific topics or modes of investigation in particular departments at Champaign-Urbana. That is, attempts to give per person research space estimates in different disciplines make an insurance-type actuarial assumption that the universe sampled in the experience of space requirements in the past will continue to obtain in the future. Since one is predicting the requirements of a future mix of one-of-a-kind projects, this assumption is, of course, fairly shaky.

Space Is Not Easily Transferred

But the big difference between the administrative enterprise of university space allocation and that of an insurance company is that money to pay off insurance claims is fungible, easily transferred from the one who pays premiums to the one who has the accident. Space is not easily moved to where it is needed, nor are university people easily divided up so that one-third of their research is in one building, one-sixth in a second, and the other one-half in still a third. The animals have to be near the mazes they are to run, and the cadavers and their refrigeration near the dissecting tables.

Furthermore, each researcher is in some sense his or her own insurer, because he or she pays a lot of the cost of not having enough space to do the research. The university does not fail to get tenure because there was not enough space to do the research; the assistant professor does. That means that each person would like to have a reserve of space that can be used if needed; the department in turn wants to insure its faculty members; the school wants to have a reserve of space so that departments in need can get it; and so on. People do not feel they can trust people higher up to take care of them if they do not take care of themselves. So space temporarily empty but (if all goes well) to be filled when the grant is approved tends to be kept in a liquid reserve near the bottom of the hierarchy.

We have developed institutions in the insurance industry that most people can trust, though except in marine insurance these institutions are only a century or two old. People believe that when they have an accident the insurance company will pay them (out of other people's premiums), and in the meantime they will pay premiums (to pay for those who have accidents). The insurance company makes money by collecting interest on the reserves it keeps so that it can be trusted. Such institutions of trust exist only at the lowest levels in a university (and they are precarious even there). The result is that space resources are not as liquid as insurance institutions make money to be, because we trust insurance companies with our financial futures in ways we would not trust deans and provosts with our research futures.

Information Problems in Managing Space Risks

One of the basic reasons we have difficulty building research space fiduciary institutions more similar to insurance companies (which could take from one researcher who is not much of a space-user this year to supply someone who is an intensive space user this year, because we all know we will be taken care of when it comes our turn) is that there is a radical information assymetry between the lowest level, which does the research, and the higher levels, which would have to manage the transfer of space. An insurance company can be moderately confident that clients will not purposely run their cars into trees in order to collect the blue-book value because there are other disadvantages to being in accidents, such as being without a car, getting hurt, and so on. There are problems of moral hazard in insurance, but they are manageable.

But a professor misrepresenting his or her need for space *in case* he or she should need more (or because it would be nice to have more) can be checked only by someone who happens to know a lot about how many cadavers one has to keep refrigerated for a given kind of tissue sampling, or how big a machine has to be to crush little blocks of hardened cement to test the strength of materials with different curing conditions (see Hald 1952, 367), or whether an industrial engineer really needs a separate table for his or her PC or whether it can go on the desk instead.

The information needed to compare the space needs of different kinds of scientists is concentrated in the (separate) lowest units. This means that any possible confidence that, say, the vice president for research or the College of Arts and Sciences dean can take care of a professor's research space needs relies on that vice president or dean being able to compare the pleas of tissue samplers against those of materials scientists, and to distinguish the pleas of people who use a PC in place of a typewriter and can put it on their desks from those of people who use dedicated PCs with necessary peripherals that cannot fit on the desk.

So the "insurer" at a higher administrative level in a university cannot collect good enough information to redistribute space in a risky environment, because that insurer cannot tell at the times claims compete what the luck of the draw has in fact brought in in the way of space requirements for the different departments. The insurer cannot tell because the level of detail of space needs and the intelligence to bet realistically about space needs next year are located at the base of the organization, and the people with the information have no interest in spoiling their own chances to insure their research space needs by communicating exactly, in the vain hope that the administration will take care of them.

This deficiency of adequate information at higher levels also means that people at lower levels see higher-level attempts to manage space as an intervention by ignorant people into matters they do not understand. Scientists' experience is that their arguments, when they know them to be truly persuasive, never persuade at the next higher level, while sometimes specious arguments of other colleagues or other departments do persuade. Vice presidents for research see a lab empty and propose to reallocate that space, without knowing that this lab is merely between projects and is (virtually) certain to be filled two months from now. Deans who propose that new people will have to fit their research into the space vacated by the person who just retired do not realize that they have just cut out the three most distinguished candidates, who happen to be intensive space users, and have excluded us from the line of research that is where the discipline is going.

Space Is Not Sovereign Territory in All Organizations

The university pattern of departmental sovereignty contrasts with, say, the relative fungibility of shelf space in a supermarket. Space throughout the store is more or less similar in value for selling all the different varieties of goods; higher management levels can be trusted to give more space to a particular line of goods in a departmental supervisor's jurisdiction if the supervisor can show it will make more profits per foot of shelf space, with the information on which such estimates of profits are based having a common form and a common metric. Space in a supermarket is therefore much more reallocatable, much more adaptable to shifting buying habits and the chance variations of the clientele of this and that store, than is university space. As consumption of canned olives goes down and consumption of refrigerated delicatessen goods goes up, it is easy to replace all the scattered displays of fancy olives with a short shelf of severe cans, and to use the space saved for a delicatessen counter (for a general analysis of this change in supermarkets, see Walsh 1988, 185–220). The stable statistical character of supermarket sales make actuarial values good estimates of the value of a foot of space devoted to olives, as compared with a foot of refrigerated display of smoked salmon. Higher managers can collect accurate information on feet of shelf space without the cooperation of lower managers or clerks. All the determinants of fungibility of space are higher in supermarkets than in universities.

How Universities Administer Space

The result of these features of the inherent nature of university space administration is a sort of nested sovereignty, modified by rare invasions from higher levels with special justification. An individual has sovereignty over the research space allocated to him or her, except on occasion of retirement, leaving the university, or invasions under special circumstances by the department. But information on the underuse of space by an individual will not ordinarily be forwarded by a department chair to the dean's office, nor by the dean to the provost's office, because if anyone is going to get the advantage of invading a faculty member's historic space rights, it should be that department (or school), not other departments (or other schools).

On the occasion of new appointments or of retirements, or of major policy shifts such as an attempt to build up electrical engineering or to start a program in cognitive science, the question of departmental space may be reopened at a higher level. And of course, a school can open the question of space when it has free space to offer—if "it" (i.e., one of its donors) has just bought a building or renovated laboratory space or if it has abolished a department (or, less likely, abolished a higher administrative office). Then deans can make the negotiation with lower levels a situation in which everybody wins.

Similarly, a school is ordinarily immune from invasion of its turf by the vice president or provost level, unless there is a major redirection of the university or unless the higher level is responsible for getting a lot of money for a new building. Space becomes fungible at the next higher level only when it is worth the while, at that higher level, to go to a lot of "political" trouble to reallocate things, or when schools or departments are reasonably sure of winning by entering into relations with a higher level. What reallocation there is depends on the higher level having information (that it does not generally use for reallocation) about the actual uses to which space is being put, about space requirements of different sorts of activities, and the like.

Some of this information is the actuarial experience of the sort summarized above, that for example, chemistry will usually need four offices' worth of laboratory space for each employee sufficiently important to the department of chemistry as to occupy an office (calculated roughly from Bereither and Schillinger 1968, 82–83; chemistry departments of higher levels of distinction than that at the University of Illinois may need larger ratios). Some of the information on which higher-level invasions of prerogatives are based is obtained by keeping track of what one learned in past renovations—keeping the same person managing space renovation in the dean's office for years, so that one can consult him (or, in the rare case of a buildings expert who is female, her) when the time comes for reallocating space or for allocating new space. The assistant dean for space questions, unlike other assistant deans, should *not* be recruited from the faculty, because then vital space information will go back to the faculty at the end of a professor's administrative assignment.

The information needed to invade lower sovereignties cannot generally be collected by setting up a committee of faculty from various departments and telling it, say, to come up with ten thousand more feet for electrical engineering. Each committee member will systematically overestimate the probabilities of needing all the currently underutilized space in his or her department (for example, when all the grants applied for for next year all come in at once). The faculty representative from each department would be regarded as a traitor if he or she did not put the best face possible on that department's space needs, exactly because one cannot trust the higher levels to come up with space when it is really needed in the future.

The information source for invading the sovereignty of a lower level has to be kept autonomous from the lower level, firmly under the authority of the higher level. The assistant dean for space should have his or her career in the administration, not in the faculty. Space cannot in general be administered on a "federal" basis, because the federated units cannot ordinarily be persuaded to give accurate information to the authorities of the higher levels—because giving up space means taking a chance with the future research of the department.

Toward a Philosophy of University Space Administration

The argument above implies that the defense of territory by lower units against higher ones in university life is in part a rational response: it is the conservatism of an insurance company that resists spending all its reserves, because "time and chance happeneth to them all." This means that proposals for improving the space administrative system need to respond to the same needs that space sovereignty with occasional invasions does; that although space is very hard to make flexible, the nature of university research work requires that it be flexible; that flexibility is hard to arrange too far from the level where the flow of chance variations in research space needs is known well enough to respond rationally to it. The following elements of a possible philosophy of space management, then, are meant more to communicate the nature of a strategy than to be "recommendations." The purpose of this brief outline of a strategic response by higher administrations to the problem of space is to illustrate the implications of this analysis of the microfoundations of an institution that has not been very legitimate, because its ideology has not been explicitly formulated. First, one has to distinguish the sorts of information that are ordinarily now kept at different levels in the administration, and how that information relates to the microfoundations we have sketched above. The basic microfoundation advice would be that these information systems can be improved only if they respond to the information about uncertainties at the bottom of the system, at the level of the working scientist, in a way compatible with that scientists' interests, so that accurate information about the probabilities of space needs can become available to higher levels on the administration.

UNIVERSITY SPACE INFORMATION SYSTEMS

One problem of all accounting systems is the choice of levels of abstraction for different purposes (for the problem in manufacturing, see Chapter 3 above). A university space administrative system generally involves (1) a very highly abstracted ("accounting-type") system, which matches square feet of usable space ("net square feet") with budgetary units (schools and departments, institutes, centers, etc.); (2) an architectural system, which involves drawings and structural specifications; and (3) an informal network of experienced associate deans and building and grounds personnel, which stores away in administrators' minds a welter of specific facts about this and that bit of space and this and that department's needs. Much of this network's information is derived from remembering renovation planning for that space from the past. The following suggestions might improve the capacity of higher administrators to respond to the uncertainties.

The Square Feet per Budgetary Unit System. Comparison of tables in Northwestern University's general statistical report (Northwestern University Office of the Provost 1986, 111–119, 127–134) makes clear that grant dollars per full-time equivalent (FTE) faculty member is, other things being equal, a good predictor of the ratio of research space to office space. For example, of the various departments that do chemistry of one sort or another, those with more grants per faculty member also have more research space per office. Thus one would expect on a probabilistic basis that as departments change in relative luck at the sources of grant and contract money, they change in space needs as well.

The possibility of large fluctuations of a few grants suggests that the central file of space information should have a special file of the current space usage of all individual grants above a certain amount and, on big grant getters' grants, of changes in the grant dollars or the personnel employed. The totals of grants associated with these large grant getters (and large users of space) should be continuously updated, so that the university or school can respond more centrally and quickly to opportunities to reclaim space temporarily from a large user down on his or her luck, or to allocate space quickly to developing needs of someone whose research program has finally taken off.

The Architectural Drawings System. It is reasonably difficult for anyone without detailed institutional memory of the spaces involved to remember the crucial user-relevant dimensions of the space users occupy. Consequently, it is often not obvious what is possible when it comes to moving people around. What one perhaps needs is a set of user-relevant characteristics obtained from interviewing people about the space they use, telling what about the space is important to them. (I suppose the best sort of question to pose to working scientists would be those that ask: "What would be the difficulties of moving into X," where X is the name of a building or a different wing or floor of the same building.)

For some departments, floor strength for heavy equipment (or for heavy collections of books or materials) would be a relevant dimension, for others it would not. For most scholars, ceiling height would not be a relevant variable, but for archeologists with collections to store it would be. Similarly air circulation for animals, hoods to vent dangerous gasses (and air intakes that are not just below such vents), isolation from vibration, freedom from electromagnetic noise, ability to install multiple temporary telephone lines for telephone survey interviewing, refrigeration, humidity control, and the like are all characteristics of quality of space that are relevant to specific users.

The idea would be, then, to attach to the file of drawings a footnote for each room or other unit of space. The footnote would list important user characteristics of the space, elicited by interviewing the occupants or interviewing the people who planned the last renovation of that space.

Making Buildings and Grounds and Renovation Information Useful for Exchange. The central problem with the information in the "old boy network" of buildings and grounds, associate deans for administration, and associate provosts is that it can in general be easily used only at a higher level, one not involved in making the chancy flow of future projects match the space available. Most such responsive exchanges of space are made within departments or research centers, and if between departments, are easiest for deans to manage if the departments have come to an agreement beforehand. Part of the problem of bringing the space knowledge into contact with the knowledge of research demands is that central arenas of flexibility in research space assignments are the research centers rather than the departments. Providing channels between space officers in the deans' offices who deal with departments and research centers could improve those centers' capacities to negotiate space allocations. Such channels make the information of such deans' officials useful in the place where the microfoundations information on research needs for space is best—in facilitating exchanges among departments and centers.

INTERDEPARTMENTAL CONTRACTING

Part of the trouble in getting departments to let go of space temporarily underutilized is that losing space tends to be permanent, despite vague promises from the higher administration that if a couple of rooms are given now to, say, the interdisciplinary American culture program, when the department needs a couple of rooms for a new faculty down the road a piece, it will be taken care of. Since those administrators have neither a budget of space to allocate each year nor, in general, the power to take space away from someone else, the departments giving up space typically do not believe these promises. Arrangements could be made so that the department getting the space has it for a definite term (depending on the expected duration of the research program to which the space will be devoted) and will give back if (a) the department now giving it up needs it at that time and (b) the higher administration does not provide that department adequate alternative space. Then one would substitute for the weak guarantee by the dean alone a joint guarantee between someone who has space *and* someone who allocates space on behalf of the dean, making the promise more believable. The object here is to do for the miniature sovereign lords in the university what term leaseholds of agricultural land did for feudalism: creating a viable exchange system without giving precarious tenants permanent property rights.

DEPARTMENT AND CENTER ARCHITECTURE

Within departments or research institutes, the central problem is to reallocate space over the short run. One year a given faculty member's research employs five data entry clerks on souped-up PCs, and the next year only two research assistants doing runs at the computer center; in the meantime, another faculty member may go from taking samples from monkey cadavers to running experiments with live monkeys, expanding space needs greatly.

If there is some common research space that can be reapportioned, with movable partitions, power sources every few feet, several separable lighting controls, and telephone jacks everywhere, and if the departmental conference room can be chopped to different sizes, sometimes crowded, sometimes generous, depending on the overall strain on the research space resources, then this common space can serve as an insurance reserve. (Supplying movable drains, water sources, and exhaust hoods are problems that now seem technically impossible; the inventor who solves them will make physical science laboratory space administration a lot easier.) Such a reserve can pay this year's claims on space from space used by another faculty member or graduate student last year, in return for a guarantee to the second that if he or she gives up the space this year, it will be available again when NIH comes to its senses about support for that person's research. The general administrative principle here is that the higher the proportion of all departmental space that is in liquid reserve at the departmental level, the less individuals have to insure themselves against future expansion contingencies by keeping a hoard of space.

The Role of University-Level Research Policy

The description above means that space policy looked at from higher administrative centers is likely to take the form of rare episodes, each unique, each filled with the concreteness of particular buildings, particular space requirements, particular ties to strategic decisions about hiring new scientific personnel or starting new schools and departments. These are likely to involve two main forms of strategic policy: fund-raising priorities, and opportunistic interventions in lower-level space disputes.

Bereither and Schillinger's *University Space Planning* (1968) is directed mainly to the first of these questions: what kind of space, and how much, can we *bet* we will need for a strategic decision to expand, say, a chemistry department? Fund raising at the University of Illinois is of course mainly legislative, so one can imagine that a translation of chemistry needs into square feet will itself be enough to raise the money: the positivist use of actuarial numbers of square feet per FTE scientist makes straightforward sense to a legislature. In private universities, however, space needs, development priorities, and fundability by private donors and the federal government all have to be weighed in the determination of what sort of financing for building the administration should go after.

Opportunistic interventions tend to come when new space becomes available, when major expansions or contractions in departments are undertaken, when new, very distinguished people are hired, or when a distinguished person retires or dies. It is characteristic of these types of reallocations that only a few parts of the university are directly involved (and only a few pieces of space), that the interested parties are intensely concerned but hardly anyone else is, that detailed investigation of the space available and space needs is undertaken, and that therefore general policy considerations are swamped by the concreteness of the interests and information on a particular space problem. This means in turn that general policies at the university level are not much use. While the relative priorities of small parts of the university versus other small parts are of course policy issues, and ought rightly to involve the highest general policy authorities of the university, general university policies are hard to bring to bear on questions of such concreteness, where the constraints are many and powerful and the options therefore very restricted.

The basic thrust of the "recommendations" here for developing the institutions of space administration in universities might be phrased as: build institutions that facilitate exchange among the research entrepreneurs at the lowest levels. This will sound familiar to anyone who has dipped into economics after Adam Smith, for it says essentially that one has to build institutions that facilitate the market, rather than institutions that run things from the center. The argument against central economic planning is that since the information required to equate marginal costs to marginal revenue in thousands of lines of goods in thousands of factories and farms and shops is widely distributed, bureaucrats cannot do it efficiently. Similarly, in the allocation of university research space the knowledge required to bet on the productivity of that space in very diverse uses is not available to a space bureaucrat at the top of the system. Those to whom it is available, insofar as it is available at all, are the distinguished physicists or the distinguished anthropologists at the base of another university. That means that even within the organization, a more marketlike structure of administration is rational.

Even if a very bureaucratic registrar's office, counting credits toward graduation, is possible without substantially undermining the modernization of the curriculum, a very bureaucratic research space administration is not really feasible, because administering research space sensibly requires knowledge of the inherent uncertainty of betting on where new knowledge is to be found.

The Teaching Productivity of Scholarly Reputations

The distilled and concentrated form of the information from scientific and scholarly peers in other universities is the scientific or scholarly reputation. That reputation indicates that in general, as far as those peers can tell, a particular person is one who can bet well about where new knowledge is to be found, and so can make generally good judgments about such matters as what should go into the curriculum, whom the university should hire, what equipment should be installed in order to do reputable work, and the like. Students can be expected to know whether a teacher is communicating well what it is that he or she is supposed to be teaching; only that person's peers from elsewhere can be expected to know whether the teacher is likely to have good judgment about what to try to teach.

Thus the president, provost, or dean is not likely to be a competent judge of the decisions that go into deciding what the basic course in physical chemistry ought to consist of, how far the relative emphasis on different topics should be changed because of the new directions that are developing on the research frontiers. The way the president tells whether those decisions are *likely* to be well made is the same way that colleagues elsewhere tell: by looking at whether the faculty member who makes them (and his or her colleagues in the department) seems to be good at betting on where new knowledge is to be found.

The Rent of Reputations

Whether an American college or university can charge higher tuitions for its teaching does not depend much on what the *students* say about whether the faculty are effective at communicating what they are trying to teach. The tuition is heavily dependent instead on the general reputation the college or university has for "qualified" teachers. What qualification comes down to is the reputation the faculty has *among other scientists* for good judgment about scholarly matters and about research. Thus, we can use the tuition of colleges and universities (separately for private and state universities) in the United States as a measure of scholarly distinction of the faculty and not go far wrong.

But this means that the reputation of the faculty, especially among peers in other universities, multiplies what people are willing to pay for the teaching, much as a law firm being in a piece of real estate in the financial district multiplies what people are willing to pay for legal services. The payment of high salaries to distinguished professors, then, might be considered comparable to advertising expenses; yet just as advertising a law firm's address falsely as in the financial district will not serve the purpose, so in a university only outside certification of the advertisement that the faculty have good judgment makes it effective.

Thus, the extra salary of a distinguished professor is much more like the extra rent one pays for an office next to the big banks; the university, rather than hiring a particular scholar's labor, is renting his or her reputation. Of course, if there is positive evidence that the distinguished judgment of the scholar will not be applied to the curriculum, the effect·is lessened. Leading physicists at the Princeton Institute for Advanced Study do not have quite the same effect on Princeton's tuition as do leading physicists in the Princeton physics department, because it is known that the former do not concern themselves much with curricular matters and instruction. Still, the value of teaching young people in a department is increased by the department's or school's general reputation, and so one can charge enough for professors' services to support them doing half-time research. A school without distinguished physicists cannot charge enough (either to the state or to the students) to give their young physicists full salaries for doing half-time research, half-time teaching.

The opportunity for a young physicist to invest half time in his or her reputation by doing research, which he or she can later rent out at a higher price, is, from the point of view of the university, a rent paid in advance for the future value of the reputation. From the point of view of the young faculty member, it is a rent paid on his or her "promise." Peers, preferably from elsewhere as well as from the university itself, thus provide judgments of promise as well as reputation. They are the only ones who can supply reliable information to make the bet of future productivity that justifies the investment of "rent in advance"—payment for half-time research. Of course, without serfdom of faculty members for the advance rent, the returns from that investment may accrue to another university. But in fact, most distinguished scientists rent their achieved reputations to the same universities that invested in their early career, if the university retains them (see, e.g., Zuckerman 1977, 194–195).

Joseph Ben-David (1960, 1968–1969) argues that universities will make such investments in young people only when they are in strong competition for scientific distinction with other universities in the same country. But this means that maintaining the value of the teaching of a university or college depends more on maintaining the reputational capital it is renting than on the labor expended on teaching. This in turn means that the university ought perhaps to exploit the differential capacity of different faculty members to maintain their reputations, by giving the more talented (as measured by scholarly reputation) more time for research and those who bring in less reputational capital heavier teaching loads.

Getting the Work Done with Rented Reputations

This overall situation poses a dilemma for university administration: how to collect information on the value of the research of various individual faculty for the long-run reputational health of the university, and how to maintain that health with the money from high tuitions from students or higher budgets from state legislatures. That dilemma has at least two aspects: the determination of teaching loads for departments, and the determination of teaching loads for individuals within departments. Broadly speaking, the number of course enrollments per "regular" faculty member, and very often the number of courses taught per faculty member, is smaller in the laboratory science departments in liberal arts schools (and especially smaller in those departments whose members might teach in medical schools) than in the humanities and social sciences, and larger in liberal arts, law, and management schools than in medical, dental, and engineering schools.

Most university departments in the United States have formally equal teaching loads for all regular faculty members, with the load calculated in either courses or lecture courses (i.e., excluding graduate seminars) per year. Some departments in some universities, however, count the teaching of arts and sciences graduate students not as a teaching responsibility but as a research responsibility, and some do not count tutorial-like supervision of independent study or dissertations as formal teaching (*informally*, of course, such individual instruction is always considered real teaching). That is, unless there is outside pressure, as from a state legislature, for strict accounting rules, most universities are fairly lax about what is counted as a course and allow departments a wide latitude in making such definitions; under formal pressure, they may even invoke different informal rules to make the record look right in different departments. Different departments and different schools are also likely to have different formal standards of what is a normal teaching load.

Presumably, this might reflect the different amount of practical difficulty in teaching different subjects; the small student loads for elementary language instruction, for example, no doubt partly reflects the fact that the teacher has to hear the students recite in order to correct their pronunciation. But teachers of elementary language courses often have a very large number of courses, are not paid extra for their reputations, and have very little time left over for research; nor, often, are they on the tenure track, the central indication that the university does not want to invest in their reputations. Similarly, it is not usually feasible to have a very large medical school class gather on rounds to hear a discussion of the normal run of symptoms and diseases in a given specialty.

The main point here, though, is that the information systems that decide such questions are heavily decentralized to departments, and no doubt reflect the "normal investment in promising scientists" that leading universities make in the various disciplines. The reputation for research productivity that a chemist has to keep up with is, of course, that of faculty members at other leading schools, accomplished in the amount of research time those faculty have left over after doing their teaching. This may be different from what a molecular biologist has to keep up with, because many molecular biologists are in medical schools, where teaching loads are normally lower.

Within departments there are also variations in how teaching loads are adjusted to the potential payoff of investment in reputational capital. Some departments do this explicitly, by classifying people as "research active," with a lower number of courses or a larger credit for graduate teaching, and inactive, with a larger number of courses or a larger proportion of undergraduate lecture courses. Sometimes the way one qualifies as active in research is simply to say that one has research under weigh; I was once in such a department, and several of the faculty did not make that claim, though some others who had not published anything in a long time did. Sometimes, however, there is apparently departmental consensus on who are the active researchers, who are inactive (by which we mean that a strong chair's decisions about the distribution of differential teaching loads do not create intolerable strains), so a formal departmental decision allocates lower teaching to leading researchers, higher teaching to less active researchers. Probably this is more common in sciences with a strong paradigm, such as physics or economics, than in areas with a weak or multifaceted set of criteria for research value, as is characteristic of geography, sociology, or management science (cf. the classification of sciences in Whitley 1984, 158 and passim).

Sometimes in the physical and biological sciences qualification as an active researcher depends on whether one has a grant that supports graduate students and postdoctoral students. Very often faculty members do not do their own lab work, but instead get grants, provide and criticize ideas, and do much of the writing up of results. Sometimes research grants directly reduce teaching loads by buying part of the faculty member's time; a comparable arrangement is for faculty to have joint appointments with a research institute, which pays part of their salary, preferably by research grants. In both these cases some "outside" body in control of the money makes a judgment about the probable value of the research and selects some but not all of the faculty to get lower teaching loads by paying part of their salaries specifically for research. Such bodies use both the reputational information that university processes use and peer judgment of the specific project proposal submitted.

In some systems, particularly those outside the United States, teaching loads in universities are determined differently for different ranks, and the ranks that faculty members reach depend on how distinguished their research is. Professors (what Americans would call "full professors") in German-inspired or English-inspired systems are much rarer than in American universities, and not all scholars who get tenure as teachers become professors. Professors often have different teaching loads, and at any rate have a different mix of courses (in particular, more graduate instruction), than "lecturers," or whatever the lower ranks are called. Named or endowed professorships in American universities often carry reduced teaching, sometimes by having an endowed part of the salary in a research institute, and like European professorships are not expected to be available to all comers.

The overall implication of this rough outline is that a multiplicity of devices are used in an attempt to give faculty members a "fair" teaching load, so that they can build up their own reputations and thereby that of the university, thus also building up the tuition rate the university can sell its teaching services for. It is characteristic that teaching load devices are sometimes (a) excessively rigid, so that all faculty members have the same teaching load regardless of the return to investments in their reputations (especially the same within single departments or within universities); (b) corruptible, because they use information only from the interested parties or from local departmental colleagues; or (c) reliant on outside peer judgment (as in research grants, amounts of publication, differential promotions to professorships in European systems or to endowed professorships in the United States). Whatever the formal devices are for making the teaching labor contract varied, they are embedded in an informal system that furthers the same end—of protecting the reputational capital of the university through loose teaching loads for highly reputable researchers.

In forming a labor contract between a university and a particular scholar or scientist, there are a variety of sutble negotiations about how much emphasis on research there is to be in the contract, and so implicitly on how little teaching labor is to be supplied. When the intellectual preparation for one's teaching will be the same as the preparation for one's research (as indicated by whether the chair of the department asks what the candidate would like to teach, with few restraints about division between graduate, undergraduate, lecture, or seminar, versus a clear outline of which large undergraduate courses the professor must take on; and indicated as well by how few or many separate course preparations the candidate is expected to make), the proportion of the salary that is essentially rent for a reputation is implicitly set high, the proportion that is payment for teaching labor, low. Such "special privileges" of low teaching and high research have to be legitimate within the department, but they do not ordinarily have to be defended in any larger administrative setting.

There is generally pressure at the lowest administrative levels of the system—within departments—to set the general terms of the contract favorably (that is, to make more of the contract count as rent on an achieved reputation or an advance on a future reputation, as opposed to wages for teaching) for the department as a whole, and to create one or another formal device for differentiating that general mix of payment for teaching versus research reputation in the bargains with particular faculty members. The pressures for favorable (i.e., research-oriented) bargains are differentially effective across the disciplines, generally being more effective in the physical and biological sciences, particularly in those attached to the medical school, and less so (i.e., more oriented toward teaching) in disciplines at the humanities end.

It is hard to make the differentials among departments legitimate. Mostly they are made legitimate by not being public. Sociologists usually do not have much information on the general terms of the labor contract in chemistry—for example, how many courses chemists have to teach, how graduate instruction is counted, whether they can buy time off with grants, and the like. And of course conversely, chemists know very little about what the labor contract of a distinguished sociologist generally looks like.

Summary on the Academic Teaching Labor Contract

To explain why the contract for teaching labor in leading universities rarely shows evidence of any attempt by the employer to get more teaching for less money, why senior academics make much higher salaries than beginners for doing the same teaching labor for no more hours, why richer and more prestigious universities paying higher salaries require less teaching labor, we have to reconceive what the labor contract is for. If we conceive it to be a contract to rent a reputation, so that the labor supplied can be sold for higher prices to students and grant givers, many of these peculiarities are explained.

But the dependence of the value of teaching work on the teacher's scientific or scholarly reputation is itself determined by the overall problem of quality control in advanced teaching, given that the client who is going to pay a premium for quality cannot generally tell whether it is, or will be, high quality or not. Since one cannot, however, trust academics to correctly assess their own intellectual value, because then their salaries would depend only on what they tell their employer about how good they are. The evidence such academics might provide on their own value would not be likely to convince a parent that the bachelor's degree is worth as much as a small medium-quality house. So one has to use information coming from a body of informed judges who have no immediate interest in the faculty member's salary (or teaching work), but who will know (as best it can be known) whether what the candidate is likely to teach is likely to be true. One has to have departmental committees and deans to translate that scholarly reputation into promotion and tenure, but they cannot conveniently generate the original information that constitutes the true quality control.

Still, before that reputation can be sold in the form of higher tuition payments or larger subsidies per student from the state legislature, that reputation needs to build up over time, be generalized across time, and be generalized to the university as a whole. That is why American universities have to invest in the future research reputation of young faculty members, by paying them to do research whose value to the university will come mainly when they are senior scholars who are known to be first-rate by a wide community of scholars ouside the university.

Conclusion

The information about what is a worthwhile use of university research space and university faculty time is generated first of all at the lowest level of the university, as a scientist or scholar decides what will probably be of most use in the further scholarly work of his small research group scattered all over the world. The university has to pay high wages for him or her to produce knowledge that will, on average, be read by thirty to one hundred people in other universities, because only those people will be able to provide the information needed for quality control of the intellectual content of teaching. The university has also to provide the space for the research when the scholarship is space-using; the laboratories, when it is experimental; the libraries, when it is book-using; and the museums, when it is specimen-using. These two requirements derive from the basic fact about advanced teaching—that teaching the best we know inefficiently is much better than teaching what we knew a generation ago efficiently.

The requirements for research space and time confront the university with different sorts of agency problems. The kind of person who can teach an up-to-date version of some special field may be most reliably found by consulting the leading members of the small research community he or she is contributing to. Those people can be identified by consulting the larger research community (or subdiscipline) in which that small community is embedded. There are also multiple measures of the impact of a scientist that are more or less immune from gross agency problems, such as citations in other scientific work. By using scientific or scholarly reputation as an index of faculty intellectual quality, a university can, in the long run, make a case that their advanced instruction is worth more than the advanced instruction of less-research-oriented institutions. Thus, a labor contract that looks more like a contract for the rental of a faculty member's reputation does, to a considerable degree, solve the problem of whom to hire, retain, and promote, and of who should have authority over the teaching and research program of the university.

But the demands on university space generated by the series of research projects that constitutes the investment in that reputation is not so easily subject to peer review by outside sources. The outside sources who know pretty exactly whether an experiment provides evidence for or against a hypothesis do not know nearly as well how much equipment space, office space, and library space the line of research involved should take. They do not need an accurate assessment of the space needs of another scientist elsewhere for the work they wish to do; what they do need is an accurate assessment of the truth of that scientist's hypothesis for their work.

The agency problem here is that the people within the university who have the best answer on the quality of a person's research and on his or her space needs—namely, that very person—also have an interest in getting the lowest teaching loads and the lushest space allocation possible. One can use outside indicators of scientific and scholarly reputation to judge research productivity, and thus to provide a solid basis on which to rent the reputation and have that rental be a rational university investment; but one cannot use those same outside "peers" to solve the university space allocation problem, because they do not have, and have no reason to give, accurate information on the space needs. One may use general scholarly reputation to weigh an individual's pleas for more space, so that a person whose reputation makes him or her a six-hundred-pound gorilla gets space while a lighter-weight scholar does not; but the university needs too much knowledge of the substance of space needs to allocate space purely on the basis of reputation.

The basic hypothesis of this book is that administrations will grow information-processing and decision-making structures toward the sources of information about the crucial uncertainties of their work. We can reformulate our arguments here by saying that an information structure for the administration of space really has nowhere to grow. Those who have the best estimate of the actuarial value of their space needs over the next few projects are the scientists or scholars involved, and it is exactly they who can be expected to give only overestimates. The best compromise is to trust the informal assessment of colleagues within the department, in a system of departmental sovereignty over research space.

The baroque structures of the tenure and promotion review process in leading universities show that there are great problems in assessing who will have the most valuable reputation to offer to the university for rent. But the way those structures grow out, toward collecting information from the small research community in which a scientist or scholar is embedded, show that there is some solution to the agency problem in ascertaining what reputation a university should rent, at what price, and with what teaching obligations, to maintain that overall, institutional reputation. That overall reputation lets the university sell its teaching at much above what the cheapest teaching labor could be hired for.

10   Conclusion

Three Criteria for Theories of Organization

This book has been guided by three main criteria for theories of organization: (1) they should explain how organizations can be more rational than individuals (though of course they are not always); (2) they should be social structural and thus able to explain, for example, why 10 percent of an organization's parts can be absent on a given day and the organization still work the same way; and (3) they should explain variance deep inside organizations by variations in what the individual parts have to do—and by extension, they should explain variations among organizations as well as why some parts of a single organization are so different from others. After the general argument involving these three criteria together is discussed, each criterion will be presented in more detail with illustrations from the argument. Finally, the implications for research strategy in organizational sociology will conclude the book.

The first criterion is that the theory should provide the basis for explaining why societies that *can* organize large-scale complex organizations hardly ever leave anything important to individuals. Our explanation is that organizations ordinarily do all the things we have been analyzing in this book better than individuals do: they teach the advances in science better (Chapter 9); they produce both explosives and paints better (Chapter 4), drill for oil a couple of miles under the North Sea better (Chapter 3), and organize work better (better than we usually manage in our households) so that the people who do it have the appropriate skills (Chapter 7). The theory, then, has to explain why organizations are more rational than individuals.

If, as we will argue below, the variables we want to use in the theory are descriptions of uncertainties and of the social structures of those parts, and the units of analysis are the parts of the organization, the mechanism that connects them is a postulate of organizational rationality. In this book, the postulate of rationality is what connects conditions in the environment to the structure of parts of organizations.

But the concrete substance of rationality depends on what part of the total uncertainty a particular part of the organization has to deal with. Thus, rather than postulating one rationality for the whole organization (such as "maximize net present financial value") and assuming that the rest of the problems will be dealt with by an opaque "production function," we postulate many different rationalities depending on what uncertainty has to be dealt with to get a given subtask done. One of the many (and often the hierarchically dominant) rationalities of an organization is to maximize net present value. But that cannot be done, for example, without preventing blowouts and hence without dealing rationally with the risk of high-pressure gas coming into the drill hole.

Further, we do not connect the postulate of rationality to decisions (a mass of ethnography of decisions shows that they are not very rational), but to social structures that gather information and, more or less routinely, make decisions. The postulate of rationality, then, is much more a *guiding principle of growth of the structure* than it is a notion that a single utility is everywhere maximized in each decision. And this means that the tradeoffs "between rationalities" are ordinarily to be conceived of as competing principles of growth of different parts of the decision-making system.

For example, the structure for recruiting, retaining, and promoting faculty in a university is organized to deal with the uncertainty of whether people will do good research in the future, and grows into a baroque system of many levels of committees writing many letters to the outside "peers" to ask what decision the organization should make. The structure for assigning teaching is oriented to a structure of requirements for awarding degrees, for assigning course grades, for setting formal teaching loads and negotiating exceptions, often department by department, so as to get the teaching job done. They are interdependent structures because the tuition one can charge for the teaching is determined by university reputation for scholarship and because the research that builds the reputation takes time that might otherwise be used to teach. But the two structures do not grow at the same speeds and with the same authority in different colleges and universities, and the tradeoff between the values of teaching and research in a particular university is an outcome of the relative growth of two structures of rationality.

In some sense, this implicit choice is a long-run choice of utilities, and to some extent the tradeoff is determined by the hierarchically superior levels of the organization. But the rationalities built into the American semester-hours course-credit system that Thorstein Veblen so liked to make fun of are not the same as the rationalities built into the use of citation counts to measure reputation that old-fashioned faculty who think one ought to read a person's work to judge them (that includes me) like to make fun of. As this example shows, it matters a good deal whether the rationality is located theoretically in the organization as a whole or in its subparts—a point we deal with as the last of our three criteria. If it is located in the subparts, then relative rates of growth of the subparts are the dynamic component in the choice of utilities, and the utility function can be expected to change over time. But the rationality of decisions is also determined by the social structure in which those decisions are made, by how far that structure has grown to be able to bring good information about the kind of uncertainty that mainly matters and to organize the decision process so that that information can be used when it comes in.

The problem of whether one can trust the source of information is pervasive in organizations, because the timely information about subparts of the uncertainty tends to be concentrated among people whose special responsibility it is to deal with it—which means that they need not report the best information available if so doing is to their disadvantage. So the problem of the appropriateness of the social structure in which an uncertainty is dealt with has two main parts: whether the information collected is good, and whether the people who have the information have incentives to use it for the benefit of the organization or motives to misrepresent it so that they look better. Performance measurement systems in particular are shot through with problems of correctly measuring the environment confronted by the organization in a particular area of its functioning so that they can evaluate performance relative to that (see, e.g., Eccles and White 1988, on the difficulty of getting the appropriate "market price"—or "cost," which in economic theory is supposed to be the same—at which divisions of a multidivisional company sell each other their products).

The information system on a particular area of the environment, pervaded by a particular kind of uncertainty, "needs," then, to be constructed in such a way as to solve the main difficulties, substantive and motivational, for collecting information on that sort of uncertainty. The basic assumption of our theorizing to explain social structure variations within and among organizations is that we can explain much of the variation in different parts of different organizations by those needs. We hope that this approach can give us systematic answers about why we feel, when we come to the end of Olsen's analysis (in March and Olsen 1976) of how a nameless university chose a successor to a nameless dean, that we have not only a case study of a particular university but also a general case of an organization trying to hire on the basis of scholarly distinction (in spite of hiring also for an administrative job). We get that feeling of generality, we argue, because we know we are not studying a particular decision that just happened to come out the way it did; rather, we are studying a social structure shaped by the nature of the decision problem, which is shaped in turn by the kind of problem it is to get reliable information on scholarly distinction. And this brings us to our second criterion for theories of organization—that they explain variations in social structure rather than variations in the outcomes of particular decisions.

The big difficulty with approaching organizational life through decision making, as in the Simon and March tradition (Simon [1947] 1976; March and Simon 1958; Cohen, March, and Olsen 1972), is that the fundamental fact of the matter is defined, in the first instance, as what happens in a particular decision. The aura of generality about the best work in that tradition (e.g., March and Olsen 1976) comes from tracing what happened in a particular case back to something we recognize as general. For example, the ease with which a search committee for a new dean collects information about candidates who have written articles in books edited by the former dean would clearly be similar in the social structure of other universities, as all professors would recognize. The reason economists have trouble assimilating the results of such studies into their theories is exactly that their idea of generality is not of a social structure built into the organization's mode of proceeding, but of the human tendency to maximize self-interest narrowly conceived. Our basic argument here is that the things worth explaining about decisions in organizations are those that are due to continuing features of social structure. That is, we believe that one should follow one's intuition about what is explicable and general in Olsen's study of selecting a dean—which is not that people make mistakes about scholars' reputations because they do not have time and energy to get everything right, but that universities by their nature collect information by the method of scholars following out their own contacts to get good evaluations of the research that candidates are doing.

But of course, to be sources of variance in behavior between organizations and their parts, such features of the social structure have to be variables. Social structures of parts of organizations have enough constancy to be worth explaining, and enough variation between organizations and between their parts to give something to explain sociologically. Our purpose in this book has been to say what those social structural variables are, and why they are systematic in many different organizations. Our answer to the *why* question is that organizations grow social structures to handle decisions by creeping toward information about the main sources of uncertainty that matter of the organization. Of course, those sources of uncertainty are different for different parts of the organization.

The big trouble with some versions of the contingency theory of organizations (the classic source is J. Thompson 1967, but Thompson is also interested in internal variations) is that it tries to define one big uncertainty for the whole organization. But if an organization is drilling for oil in the North Sea, one part of the organization faces the uncertainty of whether high-pressure gas will blow a mile of pipe and other equipment out of the hole; another part faces the uncertainty of whether OPEC will fall apart (no longer uncertain, though economic theory taught that OPEC would come apart long before any practical people could assume it actually would), in which case only the rich fields would pay; another part faces the uncertainty of whether the marine insurance industry will be able to put together a coalition willing and able to insure the enormous investment in installations (Heimer 1958b, c); another part faces the uncertainty of whether the socialist government will let them keep the profits their contract with that government gives them; and so on. This is then not one big uncertainty, but lots of different uncertainties, and one collects the latest news about them in very different ways. Consequently, one has to build social structures to keep tabs on different parts of the environment, to respond on the very different time scales that these different uncertainties are uncertain on, to be competent to evaluate the risks as the news comes in, and so on.

The *and so on*s in the previous paragraphs are meant to suggest that an organization has to be built to respond better to each of the various contingencies it is faced with than the average individual could do, because it would be a very unusual individual who could monitor the information about exactly when high-pressure gas might come into a drill hole and what coalition of bureaucrats and politicians might convince the socialist government to be a reliable partner in its contracts with world capitalist enterprises. The standard operating procedure of the various parts of the organization, or the "program for decisions" in the Simon and March language (March and Simon 1958), is not only a system for taking discretion away from smart individuals who might have guessed better in a particular situation; it is also a system for collecting information so that the ordinary people who are likely to be at the point of decision at the crucial time are moderately likely to take the right decision both about blowout protection and about what tack to take to defend oil industry profits in Norwegian politics. The standard operating procedure that will do one of these things well is very unlikely to do the other well. A rubber stamp with *Bullshit!* on it (see Chapter 3) would destroy the delicate political balance, while it is likely to remind drillers to pay attention to what other drillers say, rather than to the papers sent out by people onshore, if they want to stay alive.

3) According to our third criterion—that the units of analysis should be parts of organizations—a theory that explains why, say, the labor contract for professors in a university is so different from the labor contract for engineers in a manufacturing firm (see Chapter 9; also Schroeder and Finlay 1986; Heimer 1984) should also explain why professors' contracts are so different from accountants' contracts within the same university. A casual inspection will show that less than half of the people in a university have jobs that depend on scholarly competence and reputation outside the university. The fact that most organizations have none, rather than less than half, has to be explained, to be sure; but so does the fact that the universities most devoted to scholarship have most of their people devoted to something else. A theory that is good for explaining the differences between organizations should be good for explaining differences between parts of a given organization.

This criterion means that the theory developed by Williamson (1975) to explain why some activities are organized hierarchically while others are organized in a market, for example, needs to be extended in two ways. In the first place, it should be able to predict when activities organized in the market itself will have more hierarchical elements in their contracts (as we tried to do in Chapter 6 and Williamson has attempted in his later work [1985]). But second, it should be able to predict which parts of an organization will be organized more hierarchically, and which more like a market (as we followed Chandler doing in Chapter 4, discussed for universities in Chapter 9, and is discussed in relation to the particular problem of internal pricing in Eccles and White 1988). The crucial points here are (1) that the transaction is too small a unit to shape a social structure, while a long series of transactions resolved with similar sources of news about similar uncertainties can shape durable parts of the social system, and (2) that the organization is too big a unit because the uncertainties it faces are too many and too various to have one dominant outcome.

At the opposite end of the variation in units of analysis (ranging from transactions to whole organizations) is the theory developed in organizational ecology analyses of failure rates of whole organizations (e.g., Aldrich 1979; Carroll 1987). The theory relates such rates to whole organizations' structural features and to features of their environments. Naturally, this misses a lot of failures that did not destroy the organizations because in other respects the organizations were successful (NASA still existed after the *Challenger* disaster). But more important from our point of view, it does not provide the opportunity to use nuanced measures of social structure—of whether, for example, the accounting department is so set up and so related to the rest of the organization as to give prior warning of failure of parts (see the discussion of Du Pont's use of accounting indicators to locate failing parts in Chapter 4), thus allowing structural changes to be made in the failing parts before the whole organization is brought down.

Everyone knows from experience with their own organization that there are enormous variations from place to place in the organization's social structure, in rights and incentives, in hours, in style of dress, in access to expense accounts, in autonomy, in responsibility for crisis management, in career prospects, and so on. If, as we have argued above, our central variables ought to be social structural, then we are required to be able to analyze these internal variations. They appear to the newcomer as part of the natural order of things; the newcomer to a university, for example, learns as a natural fact that professors are allowed to do pretty much as they please and be prima donnas, but that the rest of us are subject to the authority of our hierarchical superiors. But these differences persist and are part of the natural order of things for the next cohort of newcomers: they are part of the social structure.

Organizational Rationality

People who work for organizations are held to a higher level of responsibility to be rational than are people answering only to their individual desires needing to be maximized. Further, people who design information and decision systems in organizations are held responsible for both their own rationality and that of others who will be making decisions in the system. Consequently, the ideal of calculating all the tradeoffs among all the costs and benefits, the ideal of collecting all the information needed to make a rational decision (if only to cover one's ass), the ideal of considering benefits some distance in the future on roughly the same basis as benefits at the next moment—all are more nearly achieved in organizations than in individual lives. I take the "postulate" that organizations are more rational than individuals as an observation, and consequently as something we need to explain, as well as taking it as the basis for the reasoning in this book.

The empirical assertions of the arguments we have posed here can be turned on their heads to explain the connection between organization and rationalization. We can say of the argument about divisionalization in Chapter 4, for example, that the more we *observe* that organizations are divisionalized when they are in multiple markets (in the sense defined in Chapter 4), the more support there is for the proposition that organizations are sources of rationality. Similarly, when organizations use seniority as a certificate for selecting workers for moderately stable interdependent productive systems, but use more peer judgment of skill for certificates of workers' ability to deal with a variable flow of contingencies (as suggested in Chapter 6), we have further evidence for organizations as sources of rationality.

This book, however, has been written the other way around, with the rationality of organizations being postulated. Note that this is not a postulate that organizations do not make errors. Instead it is a postulate that one can explain variations in the social structure of different parts of organizations on the presumption that the structure of the information and decision system will grow toward those sources of uncertainty whose rational management will matter most to the organization. The evolutionary principle here is that the organs of an organization grow better adapted to their environment over time—in other words, that the rationality of an organization improves (see Carroll 1987 for evidence that new organizations fail more often than older ones).

At a particular time, for example, an organization may be trying to run the administration of a product innovation in the same way they run the production of housepaint. But this will create such tensions, such clear irrationalities, that if the organization keeps up its commitment to the innovation it will evolve a tighter integration of engineering, marketing, and production within the innovation's administration, will reward skill more strongly in the innovating subpart of the organization, will orient its marketing staff toward marketing add on innovations through regular contacts with former buyers rather than toward low price and steady supplies, and so on. Similarly, if cost reduction is a primary organizational imperative, we will expect the cost accounting system to grow more rapidly in the direction of a more detailed system of cost codes, of a more flexible system of anlaysis of costs, and of a system of financial categories that are more unique to the organization rather than dictated by the financial and tax institutions of the society. In short, the postulate is not that organizations are rational, but rather that as organizations become better organized, they will tend to improve their information and decision systems and so become more rational.

But our fundamental postulate here is that the core of organizational rationality is efficiency in news processing, not efficiency in maximization. The reason drillers are oriented mainly to other drillers is not that other drillers have maximization schemes that come to better answers over the long run, but that other drillers, especially those in the same fields, have news about where a drill crew is likely to get into trouble. What makes internal communication such a high priority is that only those other drillers will have news about what is two miles down the hole, *not* that only they will know what to do about a pocket of high-pressure gas or a stratum that tends to collapse. If they can find out where the high-pressure gas is likely to be, drillers' skills will allow them to minimize risks. And they get their skills from their colleagues only in the long run: in the short run they get news from them.

Likewise, the observation that universities wait for outside offers to find out how much their faculty members are worth (J. Thompson 1967) does not mean that the faculty and administration of other universities are so much smarter than our own. (For one thing, this could not be true for all universities.) Rather, it means that faculty and administrators at other universities have no reason to overvalue the reputations they are buying, whereas the best experts on those reputations within the first university—namely, the owners of the reputations—want to exaggerate them. News about reputations of one's own faculty has to be gathered outside the university partly because outside opinion is precisely what reputation consists of, but mainly because the news from inside is so easily and routinely corrupted.

Starting with the postulate that rationality for an organization consists mainly of reacting accurately to recent uncorrupted news, then, is a different theoretical orientation than imagining that the main source of rationality is the ability to maximize. For example, parts of one's own organization are systematically motivated to provide distorted news, as when one asks scholars how high their reputation is in order to determine their salary. The argument of this book is that one should react to this not only by asking what coalition in the organization will control what is actually maximized; one should also ask how the organization might grow its information and decision structures toward sources of uncorrupted news, so it can in the long run maximize what it set out to maximize.

One could, of course, use the same approach to explain the problem of individual rationality—that individuals grow competences and information-collection strategies which enable them to deal with those uncertainties that are most important for maximizing their utilities. But a whole life is too complicated to develop such personal competences throughout the range of all important uncertainties. In contrast, the problem of managing the uncertainties of a department within an organization is often sufficiently limited that specialized growth of social structural competence can pay off. Thus, within the department we will expect to find that individual competences for collecting and reacting to specialized uncertainties (i.e., skills) will grow (Chapter 2), and that specialized information and decision systems in that department will develop to detect, hire, improve, and retain those skills (Chapter 7). We will also expect specialized departmental information-collection systems to grow (Chapter 3) and authority to integrate information about a market with distinctive uncertainties collected by different departments to be integrated by divisional organization (Chapter 4).

All this complexity in the information and decision system, all the files, the specialized computer programs, the cultural elaboration of enclosed departmental systems, and the like, is much more than could be crammed into an individual. And it is all about a part of the environment—how to drill for oil at the bottom of the North Sea (Stinchcombe 1985e), how to produce and market passenger airplanes (Newhouse 1982)—that is much more specialized than the whole of an individual's life. If one imagines that what people and organizations are doing to be rational is solving a maximization problem with given data, there is no reason to believe that an organization should do this job better than an individual. If one imagines instead that rationality is efficient processing of news about uncertainties, it is obvious that organizations are likely to do it better than individuals, and that individuals are likely to do it better in their organizational roles than in their lives. Thus, the idea that organizations are more rational than individuals is intimately tied up with the conception of rationality as processing and reacting to news about uncertainties.

What Makes the Dependent Variables Social Structural?

The catch phrase we have used to denote the general class of phenomena we are trying to explain is "information and decision system." When we described the difference between cost accounting systems that collect data for use in improving a productive system and financial accounting systems, we were not trying to explain where all the numbers come from that enter into a particular estimate of how much a given machine will save, or how those are translated into an "expected time to payback" using assumptions of a stable future market. Instead we were interested in the fact that the cost accounting system will be used, among other things, for a series of ever-changing projects that involve buying many different machines and that need different sorts of data, often unique to the plant. Financial accounts have to answer the standard questions that tax authorities and capital markets routinely ask in a way that those markets can trust (e.g., in a way that is auditable). What is accidental and contingent about cost accounting numbers is what happens in distorting the numbers about a particular machine and resolving the residual uncertainties in a particular machine-buying decision; what is of the essence in accounting is the different characteristics of the systems responsive to the uncertainties of a series of cost-reducing "projects," as contrasted with systems oriented to satisfying the authorities and the capital market that they will get their share of responsibly and honestly calculated returns.

We have in general chosen to analyze social structural systems rather than cultural systems, the social relations across which information is transmitted and modified rather than the category systems with which it is analyzed. Gaye Tuchman (1978), for example, analyzes the social structure of information processing in the news business—the way story assignments create flexibility, say, or why the names of news sources are defined as individual newspeople's private property. But she also analyzes the culture that newspeople use to define the nature of a story: news stories may be spot news (a fire), soft news (the problem of battered children), continuing news (a bill's course through Congress), or "what a story" (the assassination of a president).

Tuchman shows that these categories do not exactly characterize what is going on in the world or what the final story will look like; instead they reflect the problems of scheduling the work that the flow of information about a story creates, and in that sense are an example of the kind of analysis the theory here would generate. The structural analysis shows why news organizations would need a quick system of classifying stories by what sorts of work-scheduling problems they will create. The agency problem of how to get newspeople to develop a network of news sources and the requirement that people be reassignable to stories outside their specialty, sometimes to become subordinate to lower-status people who were on the scene first, are things of the sort we have been building theories of. But the classification scheme developed in the informal culture of newspeople is not the sort of variable that enters much into our analysis here. The *content* of the culture used to define the uncertainties that, in our theory, create the structure, the content that sets the information and decision structure into appropriate motion, we have left to one side. Instead we want to know which different sorts of information for making which different decisions the structure has to be ready for, not which decisions it does in fact make when various uncertainties come in.

The reason for leaving the culture that is used to analyze uncertainties out of our theory is that that culture gets its stability only from the structure of stability of the social organization of which it is a part. For example, it is only because the decision about what goes into the newspaper has to be made in time to print it before it is delivered that the news collection problem is so pervaded by the problem of temporal organization of information collection. Consequently, the fact so ingeniously demonstrated by Tuchman, that the concepts used to classify news stories have to do with the temporal characteristics of the work that has to be done rather than anything about the resulting story or the nature of the event, is from our point of view to be explained by the social structure she also describes. There is of course no contradiction in adding a set of cultural variables to be explained by those social structural variables we have tried to explain here. Our only point is that this is a different job from the one we have tried to analyze here.

To put it another way, we do not analyze why the structures we have outlined here sometimes make mistakes, why with the best drilling crew in the world sometimes one stills gets a blowout, why a firm that stabilizes labor relations by playing the good-sportsmanship incentive game with its machinists goes bankrupt even when the system works fine, why no one was ready to cover John F. Kennedy's assassination (Tuchman 1978). These things must be dealt with in the classic studies of decisions, such as Allison's analysis of the Cuban missile crisis (1971), because when one studies a particular decision one has to explain why it came out the way it did. We have explained not the outcome of particular decisions but the structure because we did not have a theory of error, a theory of why even when the structure was well designed to deal with the relevant uncertainty the world still managed to fool it.

The advantage of such a strategy is that the social structure stays in place to be studied. When Olsen studies the biases of an academic search process, as part of a diagnosis of why universities are "organized anarchies" (March and Olsen 1976, 82–139), the interest is focused on the particular causes that made the process deviate from the ideal set forth in the university's decision-making procedure for faculty appointments. But it is very unusual for an organization to have the exact ideal from which this particular process deviates; most organizations do not collect reputational information from other organizations for hiring decisions. While it is true that faculty, for example, often do not show up for the meetings called to take crucial decisions, that is largely because universities do not put them on the relevant committees unless they have a good deal of other research work, graduate student supervision, and cosmopolitan responsibilities that clutter their schedules and take them out of town. Why should one have an ideal that causes it to be impossible to live up to it?

Our explanation of why universities are organized anarchies is given in Chapter 9; our argument would be only that organized anarchy is a diagnosis of the state of the dependent variable: what kind of information and decision system is appropriate for universities. Briefly organized anarchies are found in universities (but much less in teaching colleges or secondary schools) because only outsiders, "peers," can be trusted to give uncorrupted information on the crucial decisions of a research university and on the "reputation" of people it might hire or promote. Its information system, then, has to start with a person's peers inside the university, who will know how to collect information from the relevant peers outside.

Since a university can charge a good deal more for its services if it has a good reputation, it has to collect its information through the people who carry the main work load at the lowest level—its faculty. This inability to detach people from their other obligations to do crucial administrative tasks means in turn that universities must make their decisions in committees with only two-thirds of their members present, who are at best devoting only 5 percent of their working time to collecting the crucial information for an optimal decision, and who think the administrators responsible for the decision are an irritating and more or less useless excrescence on the body of scholars. Other organizations, the ones that can get full-time administrators to come to meetings for crucial decisions, do not have to get the information collected at the lowest level by people of the highest reputation as scholars. Thus, the shape of the errors made in organized anarchies, their general inability to invade the research space of departments and centers, and the complications of their personnel systems that bet on future research reputations in a wide variety of fields are determined by the nature of universities' uncertainties and by the difficulties of getting unbiased information within the organization on those uncertainties. These shape the kind of social structures needed to process decisions, which are more or less necessarily organized anarchies.

We have chosen here to theorize about the social structure rather than about the decisions because without the social structural context the errors appear merely as avoidable mistakes, weaknesses of the human beings rather than "by-products of the best we can do under the circumstances." We have provided the basis for analyzing the types of errors that may be distinctive of different sorts of structures. Just as we expect decisions to be made in universities with only two-thirds of the relevant people at the meetings, so we will expect drillers to pay too little attention to how to save money on spare parts, marketers of software innovations written for a given innovative computer to pay too little attention to clients who have bought a different computer than the computer they are trying to preserve the monopoly of, and the like.

Similarly, we have (Chapter 5) given grounds to expect, for example, that the ways in which the information and decision system for product innovations will differ from the larger organization in which it is embedded in similar ways in most organizations. Further, we have given grounds to expect that when this is not true, the innovations have even less likelihood of success than innovations generally do. Because the success of innovations is very uncertain in the best of circumstances, we will expect there to be a lot of errors in decisions even when the innovations are ideally administered. Our purpose, however, is to explain nearly universal differences between innovation management and other management, so we have concentrated on explaining the social structural requirements of innovation management.

We expect there to be similar tensions in all manufacturing firms between building an accounting department to support cost reduction planning and building one to certify profitability for the capital market, as analyzed in Chapter 3. These tensions, we argue, will tend to be a feature of the social structures of accounting departments in manufacturing firms, given that requirements for using the same data for different routine purposes are generally incompatible.

The variables to be explained, then, are social structural features of information and decision systems, because these can be detached from the particular decisions being made and because it is easier to generalize across organizations, and across subparts of organizations, when the value of the variable one is explaining is of the essence of the organization, rather than an accident of the decision.

Units of Analysis and Variations to Be Explained Within Organizations

Each substantive chapter of the book can be thought of as about a main type of social structure useful for dealing with particular kinds of uncertainty: skills in Chapter 2, manufacturing subsystems in Chapter 3, autonomous divisions in Chapter 4, specialized structures for introducing innovations in Chapter 5, interorganizational contracts in Chapter 6, personnel and labor market systems in Chapter 7, categories of workers subject to uniform incentives and output measurement systems in Chap ter 8, and specialized scholarly reputational systems in Chapter 9. That is, in each chapter a broad class of social structures is presented that responds to a distinctive amount and kind of uncertainty.

These different sorts of structures are partly autonomous, as they have to be to do significantly different jobs for the organization. But they can also operate simultaneously and together in determining the details of a given social system. Thus, for example, a drilling supervisor has a skilled job (as we analyzed in Chapter 2) because he must respond to many contingencies and must have a repertoire of responses ready for instant use. He is in turn embedded in a system that gets most of its information from within the drilling operation in that particular field, as discussed in Chapter 3. To explain the complete social structure of a drilling crew, we need to use the causes and structural adaptations to those causes that were outlined in the two chapters: why drillers are skilled in a way similar to machinists (Chapter 2) and why they are at the same time very different from machinists because the news about the uncertainties of their job does not come, as a machinist's does, from other parts of the organization than the drilling crew (Chapter 3).

The cost accountant who specializes in negotiations within the same firm about which costs should be allocated to the drillers, which to manufacturing operations, also needs to be skilled, as machinists and drillers are: to remember the precedents and the general policies on the matter, to understand the general purpose behind the policies so that discretion can be guided by those purposes, to know whom to consult, to make sure all the trails of paper about a given expense end up in the place corresponding to the cost allocation, with the correct signatures, and so on. But the general purposes behind the accountant's allocation are oriented to taxation law and to capital accounting practice and law, to the measurement of executive performance in a fair way for both drilling and operations, to trails of paper that lead from invoices from outside the organization through to the final cost allocation, and in general to information systems that have to be uniform both within the organization and, to some extent, across organizations (see Chapter 3). So the same basic types of features of jobs that make drillers, machinists, and accountants skilled are embedded in very different types of manufacturing information systems, because the uncertainties the skills respond to come from different places. One kind of skilled person listens mainly to other drillers; another listens to the requirements of the people using the machined part; the third listens to standards that spread throughout the organization, throughout the society, or, in the extreme, throughout world capitalism.

Some themes recur throughout many types of information systems.

For example, when some set of activities cannot easily be decoupled because the performance of one depends on the performance of another, because they cannot easily be separately measured, and because they have to be carried out under time pressure, the information for the activities needs to be processed by the same authority system and the activities need to be subject to common incentives, because they have common measures. I have called this, in one particular context, the "decoupling principle"—that activities should be subject to separate contracts only when they can be decoupled, in the sense of low interdependence, separate measurement of performance, or loose scheduling so that late and imperfect performance of one does not lead to late or inefficient performance of the other (Stinchcombe 1985e, 68–71). This decoupling principle applies not only to contracting practices for construction, but also to which activities should be administered in a centralized fashion by a division of a multidivisional company, which should be administered separately by the separate divisions of that company (see Chapter 4); to why innovations often have to be administered as minidivisions (Chapter 5); to why systems of subcontracts often include hierarchical elements (Chapter 6); to why the main decisions that depend on knowledge of the reputation of a given scholar in his or her research specialty have to be initiated in the scholar's own university department as supervised by the chair rather than elsewhere in the university (Chapter 9).

The form of the book suggests that such basic general principles are not sufficient for a substantive analysis. They will not tell us how integrated systems responsive to distinctive types of news about uncertainties are formed. The centralization of divisions analyzed in Chapter 4 is analyzed there in the light of the need to coordinate different parts of the organization to respond to a given market. The substantive generalization concerns the number of markets and their degree of uncertainty; the number of uncertain markets is used to predict the decentralization to divisions, because that is the way uncertainty affects divisionalization. In Chapter 5, in contrast, we are interested in a certain type of market—the market for an innovation—and how that market is connected to engineering, marketing, and manufacturing in a distinctive way in many different kinds of organizations. The argument of Chapter 5 concerns the common ways that different organizations are likely to respond to the problems of the uncertainty about how to develop an innovation and to manufacture it cheaply so that it will fit its developing market. Paint at Du Pont, while not an innovation, required a separate division that was internally centralized because its market was different from that of explosives, which were also not an innovation. Since the substance of the uncertainty of an innovation leads to a peculiar dependence of engineering on marketing and manufacturing on engineering, it generally requires centralization within the innovating subpart of the organization and differentiation from the rest of the organization.

The point here, then, is that centralization of authority in subparts of organizations often forms a part of the response to uncertainty when uncertainties are interdependent. But it plays quite a different role in determining the resulting structure when the uncertainty comes from, say, the difference between package goods and tonnage goods than when it comes from administering an innovation in a firm most of whose products are not innovations. So although the decoupling principle may be a fundamental one in explaining where we find centralization, exactly what its implications are for any concrete setting varies with the details of that setting. One has to be very careful in making the mapping from the components of the theory, such as the decoupling principle, to the organization of response to a particular type of uncertainty, such as differentiation of markets, innovation, or estimation of scholarly reputation.

Similarly, skill pervades our analysis. In Chapter 2 the basic description of what skill is ties it to uncertainties that have to be dealt with at the level of the workers and to the qualifications required of workers to produce that response. It appears again in Chapter 5 in the explanation of why innovating parts of an organization have higher skill levels. In Chapter 7, a large part of the analysis of why firms participate the way they do in the labor market has to do with their problem of finding, certifying, rewarding, and motivating skill use and skill acquisition. But the personnel system uncertainty in Chapter 7 about who is skilled is different from the uncertainty in Chapter 2 that requires skill; it has to be solved with a different structure of information processing and decision making, one that extends outside the organization and structures segments in the labor market (Pfeffer 1977).

Skill levels appear again as a basis for the similarity of labor contracts of artisans and other manufacturing and construction workers in Chapter 8, and consequently as a basis for class consciousness. The uncertainty that artisans and craft workers have about who is on their side, who on the other side, and how that analysis is influenced simultaneously by the information they get from the political system and the information they get from the incentive systems that are built into their craft labor contracts is neither the same uncertainty as creates the need for their skill nor the same as shapes the employer's problem of how to decide whom to hire. Of course, the incentive systems that employers design are influenced by both skill requirements and hiring uncertainties, so these can be regarded as ultimate determinants of artisans' class consciousness.

Thus, each chapter of the book can be thought of as specifying an interrelated set of variations in a complex of interrelated dependent variables, things to be explained about why some parts of an organization are different from other parts of the same organization, and also why some organizations are different from other organizations. We have picked out the dependent variable complexes according to our argument about what sort of uncertainty they are responsive to.

Restructuring Research on Organizations

The conception outlined above about what organizational analysis ought to be about has some implications for the practice of organizational research. Let me summarize them under three headings: (1) units of analysis, (2) types of variables, and (3) forms of theory.

UNITS OF ANALYSIS

By units of analysis I mean those units on which data are typically collected. That is, should one collect data on individuals, departments, transactions, organizations, systems of organizations, or what? The central criterion for determining appropriate units of analysis is that, with respect to the theory at stake, they should be strongly causally connected internally. The units of analysis have to be chosen so that they are the place where causes are connected to effects—functions to needs, decisions to situations, flows to stocks, structures to environments. The central argument of this book is that units of analysis should be subparts of organizations that deal with distinctive sorts of uncertainties, that are responsible for securing effective responses to different sorts of news. Whole organizations may sometimes be proxies for the right units of analysis when they are dominated by a single type of information-processing system, as when universities are dominated by departments in various branches of scholarship. But even in this case one gets stronger and cleaner results if one distinguishes faculties from building and grounds departments.

Ordinarily organizations themselves, because they have had to build different substructures to deal with different sorts of uncertainty, will themselves provide guides to the right units. Universities will tend to locate building and grounds far from the faculty in the administrative system, but will tend to locate sociology moderately near to physics, because estimating the reputation of a physicist is the same general sort of problem as estimating the reputation of a sociologist. One has to go to a much higher level to find a common superior for building and grounds and sociology than to find a common superior for sociology and physics.

Quite often, whatever is called a "department" in an organization will be the right unit of analysis; but if the uncertainty in question has to do with investments or other matters with a longer time horizon, divisions or subsidiaries may be the right units. But since we have been arguing that features of the social organization of news processing are to be the main variables, we do not want to have units that cannot have social organization with a high degree of continuity through time. We therefore do not want to have either individuals or decisions as the central units of analysis.

Since in the theory a social structure relates decisions to news about uncertainties, the units chosen have to be those that tie news to decisions. Consequently, we need to so choose the units that they have authority (with review, to be sure) over a class of decisions that is served by a common news-collecting structure. Since authority is very generally divided in much the same way specialized departments are distinguished from each other (we rarely find departments that do not make—or at least recommend—important decisions), this criterion usually coincides with the one that tells us to choose as units of analysis specialized sub-units. But it draws attention to the volume of the flow of information, short periods between transmissions of information, and the like, as a criterion for what is a unit of analysis. Thus, if it is true that some drug companies have a "vice president in charge of going to jail," who is responsible for everything affecting the quality of drugs but gets very little information about those things and makes very few decisions about them (John Braithewaite, personal communication), we would not want the different departments for which he or she is "responsible" to be a unit of analysis for our theory. His job is to go to jail when low quality is to be punished by the courts, not to unify quality control.

Units of analysis are fundamental aspects of the strategy of scientific inquiry and scientific theorizing. If people do not typically look at the units that connect a given kind of uncertainty to decisions, their theory is unlikely to be about such connections. Since our units do not have the natural skins that serve as boundaries around the units of analysis in much of psychology, and do not necessarily have legal existence as separate organizations as the units in ecological organizational theory have, we have to tell how to recognize those units in some detail. That makes the definition of units of analysis itself into a theoretical question. Our suggestion that one normally will not go too far wrong by using whatever is called a "department" as a unit of analysis is merely an empirical convenience. But that empirical convenience comes about because of an observation that connects it to the core of our theory—that usually departments connect news about a distinctive sort of uncertainty to the authority required to make decisions, just as a thing with a skin is a unit in psychology because it happens that things with skins are what connect motives to individual actions.

TYPES OF VARIABLES

The argument of this book implies that we need to look at two broad types of variables, one describing the variations in the kinds of uncertainty that affect the units of analysis, another describing variations in the information and decision structure of the parts of the organization that form the units. For example, the service provided by a university faculty member is more valuable and has a higher price if the university has a good reputation, a fact that describes one type of uncertainty, about how to estimate reputation, while customer satisfaction and the capacity to get the job done right are more important in a service like that of barbers or beauticians, a fact that describes a different sort of uncertainty, about adequacy of competence.

It is variations in this uncertainty that gets universities into the problem of estimating both the present and the future scholarly reputation in contracting for their faculty, while no such problems arise in contracting for barbers or beauticians. The complicated structure of peer evaluation, and the system of paying faculty members for research work that is monitored not inside the university but in the researcher's own field, reflect (or so we have argued) the fact that it is uncertainty of reputation that determines the price a university can charge for its teaching. We therefore expect peer review when such renting of reputations is rational, because news of reputations cannot reliably be collected by other means (of course, it is not all that reliable when collected by these means either). Similarly, hospitals that depend on referrals to their physicians by primary-care physicians or by other hospitals should be expected to use peer review and investment in future reputations of their staff in much the way universities do. Of course, such hospitals are often university teaching hospitals and so find it easy to adopt variations of usual university personnel procedures. But, to return to the point made above about units of analysis, we will not expect much peer review in the hiring of nurses in that hospital, or in the building and grounds department of the university, because neither service becomes much more valuable by increasing the reputation of the service givers.

We have given many examples of such variables: whether or not the structure of the program governing a worker's handling of uncertainty is analogous to a batch program or to an interactive program, and the corresponding skill level of the worker (higher for interactive, lower for batch; see Chapter 2); whether the accounts have to provide for comparisons among firms by outsiders and honesty of reporting to those outsiders rather than materials to analyze cost reduction projects, and the corresponding standard codes versus specialized detail and rigidity versus flexibility of the accounting structures (Chapter 3); whether a firm is in several markets or a single market (in a sense described in considerable detail in Chapter 4), and the corresponding divisionalization; whether the subpart of the organization is trying to maintain the monopoly position derived from having introduced a product innovation, and the corresponding network structure connecting users to the marketing department and the close intergration of engineering with marketing and manufacturing (Chapter 5). These examples suggest the generativity or fruitfulness of the theoretical approach. Many more examples are scattered throughout the book.

FORMS OF THEORY

The definition of the variables and units of analysis involve a simultaneous orientation of the theory to three main domains of fact: the sources of uncertainty outside the organization; the organizational objectives that make the uncertainty important to the organization; and the volume, error, and bias of the flow of information about the uncertainty. The theory connects the larger social structure and the available productive technology to the microstructure of organizations. But it does not connect every part of the larger structure to every micropart of the organizational structure.

The crucial indicator that some uncertainty outside the organization is shaping a part of an organization is that information or news about that uncertainty is flowing through that part and being reshaped by that part into such a form that it can serve as the basis of a decision. The citations to a faculty member's work in the scholarly literature are processed into an overall ranking of the impact that scholar has on his or her field, as required by the dean's office, that is, departments must demonstrate the distinction of a given faculty member, as compared with alternative candidates who might be hired instead. This indicates that the information in the scientific or scholarly community shapes the personnel process of the university. Similarly, the fact that the well plan for a given well is shaped in detail by the well reports for neighboring wells is what indicates that drillers care a lot about the information from neighboring drill crews and drilling engineers, and makes it less surprising that they stamp *Bullshit!* on information from purchasing on how they might save money buying spare parts.

The theory, then, is about a flow of interactions between the environment and the subpart of the organization. Further, the argument is that the *main thing* that is going on in those interactions, the part that matters, is what will shape the main outlines of the subpart's structure. Sometimes the theory will be about variations in what matters in the interaction. For example, the argument of Chapter 5 is that the things that matter when one is trying to preserve the monopoly advantage got from a product innovation are quite different from those that matter when one is selling competitive products in a straightforward way. Sometimes the theory will be about variations in the temporal aspects of the interaction flow, as when the information for the general office of a multidivisional firm is abstracted into longer-period measures of performance, because the temporal structure of investment and return is slower than the temporal structure of market variations and response (see Chapter 4). Sometimes the theory will be about variations in the degree to which one has unanalyzed information indicating that everything seems to be going all right, as when personnel systems make great use of seniority criteria (Chapter 7).

But the basic presumption of all the subvarieties of the theory is that it is massive flows of interaction between an organizational part and the uncertainties of the environment that shape organizational structure. All the theoretical structures, then, are not so much about critical events as they are about flows of interaction, flows of information about uncertainty, flows of impacts of uncertainty on important continuing objectives, flows of outcomes that show that things are (or are not) being handled by the system. The overall theory of this book, then, is about all the different sorts of things a flow of interaction between an organization and its environment brings in, and how that flow of interaction affects the structure of work flow in different subparts of the organization.

Bibliography

Abbott, Andrew. 1988. *The System of the Professions: An Essay on the Division of Expert Labor.* Chicago: University of Chicago Press.

Alchian, Armen, and Harold Demsetz. 1972. "Production, Information Costs, and Economic Organization." *American Economic Review* 62, no. 5 (December): 777–795.

Aldrich, Howard E. 1979. *Organizations and Environments.* Englewood Cliffs, N.J.: Prentice-Hall.

Allison, Graham T. 1971. *Essence of Decision: Explaining the Cuban Missile Crisis.* Boston: Little, Brown.

Allman, Eric, and Michael Stonebreaker. 1982. "Observations on the Evolution of a Software System." *Computer* 15, no. 6 (June): 27–32.

Alvarez, A. 1986a. "A Reporter at Large: Offshore—I." *New Yorker* (January 20): 34–70.

———. 1986b. "A Reporter at Large: Offshore—II." *New Yorker* (January 27): 39–83.

Apter, David Ernest. 1964. *Ideology and Discontent.* New York: Free Press.

Banfield, Edward. 1981. *Political Influence.* Glencoe, Ill.: Free Press.

Barber, Bernard, and Walter Hirsch. [1962] 1978. *The Sociology of Science.* New York: Free Press. Westport, Conn.: Greenwood Press.

Barnard, Chester I. 1946. "Functions and Pathology of Status Systems in Formal Organizations." *In* Whyte 1946, 46–83.

Becker, Gary S. [1957] 1971. *The Economics of Discrimination.* 2d ed. Chicago: University of Chicago Press.

———. [1964] 1975. *Human Capital.* New York: National Bureau of Economic Research. 2d ed. Chicago: University of Chicago Press.

Becker, Gary S., and George J. Stigler. 1974. "Law Enforcement, Malfeasance, and Compensation of Enforcers." *Journal of Legal Studies* 3, no. 1 (January): 1–18.

Becker, Howard S. 1960. "Notes on the Concept of Commitment" *American Journal of Sociology* 66 (July): 32–40.

Ben-David, Joseph. 1960. "Scientific Productivity and Academic Organization in Nineteenth-Century Medicine." *American Sociological Review* 25: 828–843. (Reprinted in Barber and Hirsch [1962] 1978.)

———. 1968–1969. "The Universities and the Growth of Science in Germany and the United States." *Minerva* 7, nos. 1–2: 1–35.

Bendix, Reinhard. 1956. *Work and Authority in Industry: Ideologies of Management in the Course of Industrialization.* New York: John Wiley; Berkeley and Los Angeles: University of California Press.

Bendor, Jonathan B. 1985. *Parallel Systems: Redundancy in Government.* Berkeley and Los Angeles: University of California Press.

Beniger, James. 1986. *The Control Revolution: Technological and Economic Origins of the Information Society.* Cambridge, Mass.: Harvard University Press.

Bereither, Harland D., and Jerry L. Schillinger. 1968. *University Space Planning: Translating the Educational Program of a University into Physical Facility Requirements.* Champaign-Urbana: University of Illinois Press.

Blau, Judith R. 1984. *Architects and Firms: A Sociological Perspective on Architectural Practice.* Cambridge, Mass.: MIT Press.

Blau, Peter M. [1955] 1963. *The Dynamics of Bureaucracy: A Study of Interpersonal Relations in Two Government Agencies.* Chicago: University of Chicago Press.

Blau, Peter M., and Marshall W. Meyer. [1956] 1987. *Bureaucracy in Modern Society.* 3d ed. New York: Random House.

Blauner, Robert. 1964. *Alienation and Freedom: The Factory Worker and His Industry.* Chicago: University of Chicago Press.

Boswell, Terry. 1986. "A Split Labor Market Analysis of Discrimination Against Chinese Immigrants, 1850–1882." *American Sociological Review* 51, no. 3: 352–371.

Boswell, Terry, and Diane Mitsch Bush. 1984. "Labor Force Composition and Union Organizing in the Arizona Copper Industry: A Comment on Jiménez." *Review, Journal of the Fernand Braudel Center* 8, no. 1 (Summer): 133–151.

Bourdieu, Pierre. 1984. *Distinction: A Social Critique of the Judgement of Taste.* Cambridge, Mass.: Harvard University Press.

Braverman, Harry. 1974. *Labor and Monopoly Capital: The Degradation of Work in the Twentieth Century.* New York: Monthly Review Press.

Brooks, Frederic P. 1975. *The Mythical Man-Month: Essays on Software Engineering.* Reading, Mass.: Addison-Wesley.

Browne, Joy. 1973. *The Used Car Game: A Sociology of the Bargain.* Lexington, Mass.: D. C. Heath.

Burawoy, Michael. 1979. *Manufacturing Consent: Changes in the Labor Process Under Monopoly Capitalism.* Chicago: University of Chicago Press.

————. 1985. *The Politics of Production: Factory Regimes Under Capitalism and Socialism.* London: Verso-New Left Books.

Caplette, Michele. 1982. "Women in Book Publishing: A Qualified Success Story." *In* Coser, Kadushin, and Powell 1982, 148–174.

Caplow, Theodore. 1964. *The Sociology of Work.* New York: McGraw-Hill.

Carr-Saunders, A. M., and P. A. Wilson. 1933. *The Professions.* Oxford: Clarendon Press.

Carroll, Glenn R. 1987. *Publish and Perish: The Organizational Ecology of Newspaper Industries.* Monographs in Organizational Behavior and Industrial Relations, vol. 8. Greenwich, Conn.: JAI Press.

Chandler, Alfred D., Jr. 1962. *Strategy and Structure: Chapters in the History of the American Industrial Enterprise.* Cambridge, Mass.: MIT Press.

————. 1977. *The Visible Hand: The Managerial Revolution in American Business.* Cambridge, Mass.: Harvard University Press.

Charlton, Joy C. 1983. *Secretaries and Bosses: The Social Organization of Office Work.* Ph.D. diss., Northwestern University.

Coase, R. H. 1937. "The Nature of the Firm." *Economica* 4, no. 16: 386–405.

————. 1988. "R. H. Coase Lectures [on 'The Nature of the Firm']." *Journal of Law, Economics, and Organization* 4, no. 1: 3–47.

Cohen, Linda. 1979. "Innovation and Atomic Energy: Nuclear Power Regulation, 1966 to the Present." *Law and Contemporary Problems* 43, no. 1: 67–97.

Cohen, Michael, James G. March, and Johan P. Olsen. 1972. "A Garbage Can Model of Organizational Choice." *Administrative Science Quarterly* 17, no. 1 (March): 1–25.

Cohn, Samuel. 1985. *The Process of Occupational Sex-Typing: The Feminization of Clerical Labor in Great Britain.* Philadelphia: Temple University Press.

Cole, Robert E., and Paul M. Siegel. 1979. *Work, Mobility, and Participation: A Comparative Study of American and Japanese Industry.* Berkeley and Los Angeles: University of California Press.

Coleman, James S. 1973. *The Mathematics of Collective Action.* Chicago: Aldine.

Coleman, James S., Elihu Katz, and Herbert Menzel. 1957. "The Diffusion of a New Drug Among Physicians." *Sociometry* 20: 253–270.

Commons, John R. 1924. *Legal Foundations of Capitalism.* New York: Macmillan.

Converse, Philip E. 1964. "The Nature of Belief Systems in Mass Publics." *In* Apter 1964, 206–261.

Cooper, Bryan, and T. F. Gaskell. 1976. *The Adventure of North Sea Oil.* London: Heinemann.

Coser, Lewis A., Charles Kadushin, and Walter W. Powell. 1982. *Books: The Culture and Commerce of Publishing.* New York: Basic Books.

Coulam, Robert. 1977. *Illusions of Choice: The F-111 and the Problems of Weapon Acquisition Reform.* Princeton, N.J.: Princeton University Press.

Crecine, John P. 1969. *Governmental Problem Solving.* Chicago: Rand McNally.

Cyert, Richard M., and James G. March. 1963. *A Behavioral Theory of the Firm.* Englewood Cliffs, N.J.: Prentice-Hall.

Dahl, Robert A., and Charles E. Lindblom. [1953] 1976. *Politics, Economics, and Welfare: Planning and Politico-economic Systems Resolved into Basic Social Processes.* New York: Harper and Row.

Doeringer, Peter, and Michael J. Piore. 1971. *Internal Labor Markets and Manpower Analysis.* Lexington, Mass.: D. C. Heath.

Drucker, Peter F. 1946. *Concept of the Corporation.* New York: John Day.

Eccles, Robert G., and Harrison C. White. 1988. "Price and Authority in Inter-Profit Center Transactions." *In* Winship and Rosen 1988, S17–S51.

Edwards, Richard C., Michael Reich, and David M. Gordon, eds. 1975. *Labor Market Segmentation: Conference on Labor Market Segmentation.* Lexington, Mass.: D. C. Heath.

Elster, Jon. 1983. *Explaining Technical Change: A Case Study in the Philosophy of Science.* Cambridge: Cambridge University Press.

Engels, Frederick. [1882] 1935. *Socialism, Utopian and Scientific.* Translated by Edward Aveling. New York: International Publishers.

Esping-Andersen, Gøsta. 1985. *Politics Against Markets: The Social Democratic Road to Power.* Princeton, N.J.: Princeton University Press.

Etzioni, Amitai. 1975. *A Comparative Analysis of Complex Organizations: On Power, Involvement, and Their Correlates.* New York: Free Press.

Farkas, George, and Paula England, eds. 1988. *Industries, Firms, and Jobs: Sociological and Economic Approaches.* New York: Plenum.

Faulkner, Robert R. 1983. *Music on Demand: Composers and Careers in the Hollywood Film Industry.* New Brunswick, N.J.: Transaction Books.

Ferber, Robert, ed. 1966. *The Measurement and Interpretation of Job Vacancies.* New York: Columbia University Press.

Finlay, William. 1987. "Workers on the Waterfront: Union, Labor, and Technology in the West Coast Longshore Industry." Iowa City, University of Iowa. Photocopy.

Fishman, Katharine D. 1981. *The Computer Establishment: The Inside Story of America's Most Dynamic Industry.* New York: McGraw-Hill.

Fitzgibbon, Heather. 1988. "The Business of Science: Emergent Careers in Industrial Chemical Research." Ph.D. diss., Northwestern University.

Flood, John A. 1982. *Barristers' Clerks: The Law's Middlemen.* Manchester: Manchester University Press.

Freeman, John, Glenn R. Carroll, and Michael T. Hannan. 1983. "The Liability of Newness: Age Dependence in Organizational Death Rates." *American Sociological Review* 48 (October): 692–710.

Freeman, Richard. 1976. "Individual Mobility and Union Voice in the Labor Market." *American Economic Review. Supplement (Papers and Proceedings)* 66, no. 2 (May): 361–368.

Freeman, Richard, and J. Medoff. 1984. *What Do Unions Do?* New York: Basic Books.

Gallie, Duncan. 1983. *Social Inequality and Class Radicalism in France and Britain.* Cambridge: Cambridge University Press.

Geertz, Clifford. 1960. *The Religion of Java.* New York: Free Press.

———. 1963a. *Agricultural Involution: The Process of Ecological Change in Indonesia.* Berkeley and Los Angeles: University of California Press.

———. 1963b. *Peddlers and Princes: Social Change and Economic Modernization in Two Indonesian Towns.* Chicago: University of Chicago Press.

———. 1973a. "Deep Play: Notes on the Balinese Cockfight." *In* Geertz 1973b, 412–453. (Originally in *Dedalus* 101 [1972]: 1–37.)

———. 1973b. *The Interpretation of Cultures: Selected Essays.* New York: Basic Books.

Glenn, Evelyn Nakano, and Roslyn L. Feldbert. 1977. "Degraded and Deskilled: The Proletarianization of Clerical Work." *Social Problems* 25 (October): 52–64.

Goldner, Fred H. 1965. "Demotion in Industrial Management." *American Sociological Review* 30, no. 5 (October): 714–724.

Gouldner, Alvin W. 1954. *Wildcat Strike: A Study in Worker-Management Relationships.* New York: Harper Torchbooks.

Granick, David. 1954. *Management of the Industrial Firm in the USSR: A Study in Soviet Economic Planning.* New York: Columbia University Press.

———. 1967. *Soviet Metal Fabricating and Economic Development.* Madison: University of Wisconsin Press.

Granovetter, Mark. 1973. "The Strength of Weak Ties." *American Journal of Sociology* 78, no. 6: 1360–1380.

———. 1974. *Getting a Job: A Study of Contacts and Careers.* Cambridge: Harvard University Press.

———. 1988. "The Sociological and Economic Approaches to Labor Market Analysis: A Social Structural View." *In* Farkas and England 1988, 187–216.

Green, Albert Edward, and A. J. Bourne. 1972. *Reliability Technology.* New York: Wiley Interscience.

Grilliches, Zvi. 1957. "Hybrid Corn: An Exploration in the Economics of Technological Change." *Econometrica* 25, no. 4: 501–522.

Hald, Anders. 1952. *Statistical Theory with Engineering Applications.* New York: Wiley.

Halle, David. 1984. *America's Working Man: Work, Home, and Politics*

Among Blue-Collar Property Owners. Chicago: University of Chicago Press.

Harasti, Miklos. 1978. *A Worker in a Worker's State.* New York: Universe Books.

Heimer, Carol A. 1984. "Organizational and Individual Control of Career Development in Engineering Project Work." *Acta Sociologica* 27, no. 4. (Reprinted in Stinchcombe and Heimer 1985, 257–295.)

———. 1985a. *Reactive Risk and Rational Action: Managing Moral Hazard in Insurance Contracts.* Berkeley and Los Angeles: University of California Press.

———. 1985b. "Allocating Information Costs in a Negotiated Information Order: Interorganizational Constraints on Decision Making in Norwegian Oil Insurance." *Administrative Science Quarterly* 30, no. 3 (September): 395–417.

———. 1985c. "Substitutes for Experience-Based Information: The Case of Offshore Oil Insurance in the North Sea." *In* Stinchcombe and Heimer 1985, 172–224.

———. 1986a. "Producing Responsible Behavior in Order to Produce Oil: Bringing Obligations, Rights, Incentives, and Resources Together in the Norwegian State Oil Company." Bergen, Nor.: Institute of Industrial Economics. Photocopy.

———. 1986b. Review of *The Process of Occupational Sex Typing* by Samuel Cohn. *American Journal of Sociology* 92, no. 3: 763–766.

Herskedal, Stig, and Frode Kristiansen. 1987. "Oljepriser og Mulig Produksjonsstans for Felt på Norsk Sokkel" (Oil prices and possible production halt for fields on the Norwegian continental shelf). Notat no. 100. Bergen, Nor.: Institute for Industrial Economics.

Hirschman, Albert O. 1963. *Journeys Toward Progress: Studies of Economic Policy-Making in Latin America.* New York: Twentieth Century Fund.

Hobsbawm, Eric. 1984. *Workers: Worlds of Labor.* New York: Pantheon Books.

Hobsbawm, Eric, and Joan W. Scott. 1980. "Political Shoemakers." *Past and Present: A Journal of Historical Studies* 89 (November). (Reprinted in Hobsbawm 1984, 103–130.)

Hochschild, Arlie. 1983. *The Managed Heart: Commercialization of Human Feeling.* Berkeley and Los Angeles: University of California Press.

Homans, George Caspar. 1950. *The Human Group.* New York: Harcourt Brace Jovanovich.

———. 1961. *Social Behavior: Its Elementary Forms.* New York: Harcourt Brace Jovanovich.

Homans, George Caspar, and David M. Schneider. 1955. *Marriage, Authority, and Final Causes.* New York: Free Press.

Huber, Richard. 1985. "Sears and the Multi-divisional Structure." Evanston, Ill.: Northwestern University. Photocopy.

Hughes, Everett C. 1958. *Men and Their Work.* New York: Free Press.
Inkeles, Alex, and David H. Smith. 1974. *Becoming Modern: Individual Change in Six Developing Countries.* Cambridge, Mass.: Harvard University Press.
Jackson, Robert Max. 1984. *The Formation of Craft Labor Markets.* Orlando, Fla.: Academic Press.
Jaques, Elliot. [1956] 1972. *The Measurement of Responsibility: A Study of Work, Payment, and Individual Capacity.* New York: Wiley.
Jones, Calvin, Paul B. Sheatsley, and Arthur L. Stinchcombe. 1979. *Dakota Farmers and Ranchers Evaluate Crop and Livestock Surveys.* Chicago: National Opinion Research Center.
Kahn, Lawrence M., and Peter D. Sherer. 1986. "Race Discrimination of Professional Basketball." Urbana: University of Illinois Industrial Relations. Photocopy.
Kanter, Rosabeth Moss. 1977. *Men and Women of the Corporation.* New York: Basic Books.
Katznelson, Ira, and Aristide R. Zolberg, eds. 1986. *Working-Class Formation: Nineteenth-Century Patterns in Western Europe and the United States.* Princeton, N.J.: Princeton University Press.
Kelley, Jonathan. 1972. "A Resource Theory of Social Mobility: Modernization and Mobility." Paper presented at the annual conference of the American Sociological Association, New Orleans.
Kidder, Tracy. 1981. *The Soul of a New Machine.* New York: Avon; Boston: Little, Brown.
Klein, Benjamin, Robert G. Crawford, and Armen A. Alchian. 1978. "Vertical Integration, Appropriable Rents, and the Competitive Contracting Process." *Journal of Law and Economics* 21, no. 2: 297–326.
Knorr, Karin, R. Krohn, and Richard Whitley, eds. 1980. *The Social Process of Scientific Investigation. Sociology of the Sciences*, vol. 14. Hingham, Mass.: Reidel.
Kocka, Jürgen. 1986. "Problems of Working-Class Formation in Germany: The Early Years, 1800–1875." *In* Katznelson and Zolberg 1986, 279–351.
Kreiner, Kristian. 1976. *The Site Organization: A Study of Social Relationships on Construction Sites.* Diss., Technological University of Denmark.
Kusterer, Ken C. 1978. *Know-how on the Job: The Important Working Knowledge of "Unskilled" Workers.* Boulder, Colo.: Westview Press.
LaBonte, Joanne. 1987. "Cultural Constraints on Advertising Content, or This Bud's for *Whom?*: A Case Study of American Beer Ads from Colonial Times to the Present." Evanston, Ill.: Northwestern University. Photocopy.
Latour, Bruno. 1980. "Is It Possible to Reconstruct the Research Process?: The Sociology of a Brain Peptide." *In* Knorr, Krohn, and Whitley 1980, 53–73.

Lawrence, Paul R., and Jay W. Lorsch. 1967. *Organization and Environment: Managing Differentiation and Integration.* Boston: Graduate School of Business Administration, Harvard University.

Leidner, Robin. 1988. "Home Work: A Study in the Interaction of Work and Family Organization." *In* Simpson and Simpson 1988, 69–94.

Licht, Walter. 1983. *Working for the Railroad: The Organization of Work in the 19th Century.* Princeton, N.J.: Princeton University Press.

Lieberson, Stanley, and Glenn V. Fuguitt. 1967. "Negro-White Occupational Differences in the Absence of Discrimination." *American Journal of Sociology* 73, no. 2: 188–200.

Lientz, Bennet P., and E. Burton Swanson. 1980. *Software Maintenance Management.* Reading, Mass.: Addison-Wesley.

Lindblom, Charles E. 1959. "The Science of 'Muddling Through.'" *Public Administration Review* 19 (Spring): 79–88.

————. 1977. *Politics and Markets: The World's Economic Systems.* New York: Basic Books.

Lindzey, Gardner, ed. 1954. *Handbook of Social Psychology.* Reading, Mass.: Addison-Wesley.

Lipset, Seymour Martin, Paul Lazarsfeld, et al. 1954. "The Psychology of Voting: An Analysis of Political Behavior." *In* Lindzey 1954, 2: 1124–1175.

Lockwood, David. 1958. *The Blackcoated Worker: A Study in Class Consciousness.* London: Allen and Unwin.

Macaulay, Stewart. 1963. "Non-contractual Relations in Business: A Preliminary Study." *American Sociological Review* 28 (February): 55–66.

————. 1966. *Law and the Balance of Power: The Automobile Manufacturers and Their Dealers.* New York: Russell Sage Foundation.

Mann, Michael. 1973. *Workers on the Move: The Sociology of Relocation.* Cambridge: Cambridge University Press.

Mannheim, Karl. 1929. *Ideology and Utopia: An Introduction to the Sociology of Knowledge.* New York: Harcourt, Brace.

Mansfield, Edwin, John Rapoport, Anthony Romeo, Samuel Wagner, and George Beardsley. 1977. "Social and Private Rates of Return from Industrial Innovations." *Quarterly Journal of Economics* 91, no. 2: 221–240.

March, James C., and James G. March. 1978. "Performance Sampling in Social Matches." *Administrative Science Quarterly* 23, no. 3: 434–453.

March, James G. 1978. "Bounded Rationality, Ambiguity, and the Engineering of Choice." *Bell Journal of Economics,* 9, 2 (Autumn): 587–608.

————. 1981. "Decisions in Organizations and Theories of Choice." *In* Van de Ven and Joyce 1981, 205–248.

March, James G., and Johan P. Olsen. 1976. *Ambiguity and Choice in Organizations.* Bergen, Nor.: Universitetsforlaget.

March, James G., and Guje Sevon. 1982. "Gossip, Information, and Decision Making." *In* Sproull and Larkey 1982, vol. 1.

March, James G., and Zur Shapira. 1982. "Behavioral Decision Theory and Organizational Decision Theory." *In* Ungson and Braunstein 1982, 92–115.

March, James G., and Herbert A. Simon. 1958. *Organizations.* New York: Wiley.

Markoff, John. 1975. "Governmental Bureaucratization: General Processes and an Anomalous Case." *Comparative Studies in Society and History* 17, no. 4: 479–503.

Marschak, Thomas, Thomas K. Blennan, Jr., and Robert Summers. 1967. *Strategies for R & D: Studies in the Microeconomics of Development.* Berlin: Springer Verlag.

McKenzie, Robert Trelford, and Allan Silver. 1968. *Angels in Marble: Working-Class Conservatives in Urban England.* Chicago: University of Chicago Press.

Merton, Robert K. 1973a. *The Sociology of Science: Theoretical and Empirical Investigations.* Chicago: University of Chicago Press.

———. [1942] 1973b. "The Normative Structure of Science." *In* Merton 1973a, 267–278. (Originally published as "Science and Technology in a Democratic Order." *Journal of Legal and Political Sociology.*)

Meyer, John W., and Brian Rowan. 1977. "Institutionalized Organizations: Formal Structure as Myth and Ceremony." *American Journal of Sociology* 83, no. 2: 340–363.

Mintzberg, Henry. 1973. *The Nature of Managerial Work.* New York: Harper and Row.

Moe, Johannes, et al. 1980. *Kostnads analysen: Norsk kontintalsokkel, del I og II* (Cost analysis: Norwegian continental shelf, parts I and II). Oslo: Royal Ministry of Oil and Energy, 29 April.

Moore, Barrington. 1966. *Social Origins of Dictatorship and Democracy: Lord and Peasant in the Making of the Modern World.* Boston: Beacon Press.

Nelson, Richard R., and Sidney G. Winter. 1982. *An Evolutionary Theory of Economic Change.* Cambridge, Mass.: Harvard University Press, Belknap Press.

Newhouse, John. 1982. *The Sporty Game.* New York: Knopf.

Noble, David F. *Forces of Production: A Social History of Industrial Automation.* New York: Knopf.

Northwestern University Office of the Provost. 1986. *Northwestern University Statistical and Faculty Summaries, 1985–86.* Evanston, Ill.: Northwestern University.

Okun, Arthur. 1981. *Prices and Quantities: A Macroeconomic Analysis.* Washington, D.C.: Brookings Institution.

Padgett, John. 1980. "Bounded Rationality in Budgetary Research." *American Political Science Review* 74, no. 2: 354–372.

———. 1981. "Hierarchy and Ecological Control in Federal Budgetary Decision Making." *American Journal of Sociology* 87, no. 1: 75–129.

Page, John S., and Jim G. Nation. 1976. *Estimator's Piping Man-Hour Manual.* 3d ed. N.p.: Gulf and Western Publishing.

Parsons, Talcott. 1939. "The Professions and Social Structure." *In* Parsons 1966, 34–49.

———. 1966. *Essays in Sociological Theory.* 2d ed. New York: Free Press.

Peck, Merton J., and Frederic M. Scherer. 1962. *The Weapons Acquisition Process: An Economic Analysis.* Boston: Division of Research, Graduate School of Business Administration, Harvard University.

Perrow, Charles. 1981. "Markets, Hierarchies, and Hegemony." *In* Van de Ven and Joyce 1981, 371–386; with rejoinders, 387–406.

———. 1984. *Normal Accidents: Living with High-Risk Technologies.* New York: Basic Books.

Pfeffer, Jeffrey. 1977. "Towards an Examination of Stratification in Organizations." *Administrative Science Quarterly* 22, no. 4: 553–567.

Piore, Michael J. 1975. "Notes for a Theory of Labor Market Stratification." *In* Edwards, Reich, and Gordon 1975, 125–150.

Powell, Walter W. 1978. "Publisher's Decision-making: What Criteria Do They Use in Deciding Which Books to Publish?" *Social Research* 45, no. 2: 227–252.

Reve, Torger, and Egil Johansen. 1982. "Organizational Buying in the Offshore Oil Industry." *Industrial Marketing Management* 11, no. 4: 275–282.

Rogers, Everett M., and Judith K. Larson. 1984. *Silicon Valley Fever: The Growth of a High Technology Culture.* New York: Basic Books.

Rosenbaum, James E. 1981. "Careers in a Corporate Hierarchy." *In* Treiman and Robinson 1981, 95–124.

Ross, Stephen A. 1973. "The Economic Theory of Agency: The Principal's Problem." *American Economic Review* 63 (May): 134–139.

Rossi, Ino, ed. 1982. *Structural Sociology.* New York: Columbia University Press.

Sabel, Charles F. 1982. *Work and Politics: The Division of Labor in Industry.* Cambridge: Cambridge University Press.

Schelling, Thomas C. 1960. *The Strategy of Conflict.* Cambridge, Mass.: Harvard University Press.

Scherer, Frederic M. 1964. *The Weapons Acquisition Process: Economic Incentives.* Boston: Division of Research, Graduate School of Business, Harvard University.

———. 1980. *Industrial Market Structure and Economic Performance.* 2d ed. Boston: Houghton Mifflin.

Schroeder, Sandra J., and William Finlay. 1986. "Internal Labor Markets, Professional Domination, and Gender: A Comparison of Laboratory Employees in Hospitals and Chemical-Oil Firms." *Social Science Quarterly* 67, no. 4: 827–840.

Schumpeter, Joseph A. 1942. *Capitalism, Socialism, and Democracy.* New York: Harper Torchbooks.

Schwartz, Barry. 1975. *Queueing and Waiting: Studies in the Social Organization of Access and Delay.* Chicago: University of Chicago Press.

———. 1978a. "Queues, Priorities, and Social Process." *Social Psychology* 41, no. 1: 3–12.

———. 1978b. "The Social Ecology of Time Barriers." *Social Forces* 56, no. 4: 1203–1220.

Selznick, Philip. 1949. *TVA and the Grass Roots: A Study in the Sociology of Formal Organizations.* Berkeley and Los Angeles: University of California Press.

———. 1957. *Leadership in Administration: A Sociological Interpretation.* Evanston, Ill.: Row Peterson; New York: Harper and Row. Reprint, 1984. Berkeley: University of California Press.

Selznick, Philip, Philippe Nonet, and Howard M. Vollmer. 1969. *Law and Society and Industrial Justice.* New York: Russell Sage Foundation.

Sewell, William, Jr. 1980. *Work and Revolution in France: The Language of Labor from the Old Regime to 1848.* Cambridge: Cambridge University Press.

———. 1986. "Artisans, Factory Workers, and the Formation of the French Working Class, 1789–1848." *In* Katznelson and Zolberg 1986, 45–70.

Shack-Marquez, Janice, and Ivar Berg. 1982. "Inside Information and Employer-Employee Matching Processes." Fels Discussion Paper, no. 159. Philadelphia: University of Pennsylvania, School of Public and Urban Policy.

Shapiro, Susan. 1984. *Wayward Capitalists: Target of the Securities and Exchange Commission.* New Haven, Conn.: Yale University Press.

———. 1987. "Social Control of Impersonal Trust." *American Journal of Sociology* 93, no. 3: 663–658.

Simon, Herbert A. 1957a. *Models of Man, Social and Rational: Mathematical Essays on Rational Human Behavior in a Social Setting.* New York: Wiley.

———. 1957b. "A Formal Theory of the Employment Relation." *In* Simon 1957a, 183–195.

———. [1947] 1976. *Administrative Behavior: A Study of Decision-making Processes in Administrative Organization.* 3d ed. New York: Free Press.

Simpson, Ida, and Richard Simpson. 1988. *Research on the Sociology of Work.* Vol. 4: *High Tech Work.* Greenwich, Conn.: JAI Press.

Skocpol, Theda, and Ann Orloff. 1983. "Why Not Equal Protection?: Explaining the Politics of Public Social Welfare in Britain and the United States, 1880s–1920s." Paper present at the annual conference of the American Sociological Association.

Slicher Van Bath, B. H. 1964. *The Agrarian History of Western Europe, A.D. 500–1850.* Translated by Olive Ordish. New York: St. Martin's Press.

Slichter, Sumner H., James J. Healy, and E. Robert Livernash. 1960. *The Impact of Collective Bargaining on Management.* Washington, D.C.: Brookings Institution.

Smelser, Neil J. 1959. *Social Change in the Industrial Revolution: An Application of Theory to the British Cotton Industry.* Chicago: University of Chicago Press.

Soltan, Karol. 1987. *A Causal Theory of Justice.* Berkeley and Los Angeles: University of California Press.

Somers, G., and M. Tsuda. 1966. "Job Vacancies and Structural Changes in Japanese Labor Markets." *In* Ferber 1966.

Spilerman, Seymour. 1986. "Organizational Rules and the Features of Work Careers." In *Research in Social Stratification and Mobility*, 5: 41–102. Greenwich, Conn.: JAI Press.

Sproull, Lee S., and Patrick D. Larkey, eds. 1982. *Advances in Information Processing in Organizations*, Greenwich, Conn.: JAI Press.

Stephens, John. 1986. *The Transition from Capitalism to Socialism.* Urbana: University of Illinois Press.

Stinchcombe, Arthur L. 1959. "Bureaucratic and Craft Administration of Production." *Administrative Science Quarterly* 4, no. 2: 168–187. (Reprinted in Stinchcombe 1986a, 177–195.)

———. 1964. *Rebellion in a High School.* Chicago: Quadrangle Books; New York: New York Times Books.

———. 1968. *Constructing Social Theories.* Chicago: University of Chicago Press.

———. 1973 [1967]. "Formal Organizations." In *Sociology: An Introduction*, edited by Neil J. Smeltzer, 23–65. 2d ed. New York: Wiley.

———. 1974. *Creating Efficient Industrial Administrations.* Orlando, Fla.: Academic Press.

———. 1979a. "Analysis of Errors." *In* Jones, Sheatsley, and Stinchcombe 1979, 164–198.

———. 1979b. "Social Mobility in Industrial Labor Markets." *Acta Sociologica* 22, no. 3: 217–245. (Reprinted in Stinchcombe 1986a, 86–121.)

———. 1982. "The Deep Structure of Moral Categories, Eighteenth-Century French Stratification, and the Revolution." *In* Rossi 1982, 62–95. (Reprinted in Stinchcombe 1986a, 145–173.)

———. 1983. *Economic Sociology.* Orlando, Fla.: Academic Press.

———. 1984. "Third Party Buying: The Trend and the Consequences." *Social Forces* 62, no. 4: 861–884.

———. 1985a. "Authority and the Management of Engineering on Large Projects." *In* Stinchcombe and Heimer 1985, 225–256.

———. 1985b. "Contracts as Hierarchical Documents." *In* Stinchcombe and Heimer 1985, 121–169.

———. 1985c. "Delays in Government Approvals in Norwegian Offshore Development." *In* Stinchcombe and Heimer 1985, 296–321.

————. 1985d. "The Functional Theory of Social Insurance." *Politics and Society* 14, no. 4: 411–430.

————. 1985e. "Project Administration in the North Sea." *In* Stinchcombe and Heimer 1985, 25–120.

————. 1986a. *Stratification and Organization: Selected Papers.* Cambridge: Cambridge University Press.

————. 1986b. "Norms of Exchange." *In* Stinchcombe 1986a, 231–267.

————. 1986c. "On Social Factors in Administrative Innovation." *In* Stinchcombe 1986a, 221–230.

————. 1986d. "Transforming Information Systems in Organizations: The Norwegian State Oil Company Begins Operations." Bergen, Nor.: Institute of Industrial Economics.

Stinchcombe, Arthur L., and T. Robert Harris. 1969. "Interdependence and Inequality: A Specification of the Davis-Moore Theory." *Sociometry* 32, no. 1: 13–23. (Reprinted in Stinchcombe 1986a, 58–69.)

Stinchcombe, Arthur L., and Carol A. Heimer. 1985. *Organizational Theory and Project Management: Administering Uncertainty in Norwegian Offshore Oil.* Bergen, Nor.: Norwegian University Press.

————. 1988. "Interorganizational Relations and Careers in Computer Software Firms." *In* Simpson and Simpson 1988, 179–204.

Stinchcombe, Arthur L., Calvin Jones, and Paul Sheatsley. 1981. "Non-Response Bias for Attitude Questions." *Public Opinion Quarterly* 45: 359–375.

Stockfisch, Jacob A. 1973. *Plowshares into Swords: Managing the American Defense Establishment.* New York: Mason and Lipscomb.

Stone, Katherine. 1975. "The Origins of Job Structures in the Steel Industry." *In* Edwards, Reich, and Gordon 1975, 27–84.

Sturmthal, Adolph. 1953. *Unity and Diversity in European Labor.* New York: Free Press.

Teece, David J. 1976. "Vertical Integration and Divestiture in the U.S. Oil Industry. Stanford: Stanford Institute for Energy Research.

————. 1981. "Asset Revaluations and the Appropriability of Returns from Inventive Activity." Stanford Business Research Paper no. 425. Stanford.

Thompson, E. P. 1963. *The Making of the English Working Class.* New York: Vintage Books.

Thompson, James D. 1967. *Organizations in Action: Social Science Bases of Administration.* New York: McGraw-Hill.

Tilly, Charles. 1986. *The Contentious French: Four Centuries of Popular Struggle.* Cambridge, Mass.: Harvard University Press, Belknap Press.

Tolstoy, Leo. [1886] 1982. "The Three Hermits." In *The Raid and Other Stories,* translated by Louise Maude and Aylmer Maude. Oxford: Oxford University Press.

Toong, Hoo-Min, and Amar Gupta. 1982. "Personal Computers." *Scientific American* 247, no. 6: 86–107.

Tosi, Henry, Ramon Aldag, and Ronald Storey. 1973. "On the Measurement of the Environment: An Assessment of the Lawrence and Lorsch Environmental Uncertainty Subscale." *Administrative Science Quarterly* 18, no. 1: 27–36.

Treiman, Donald J., and Robert V. Robinson, eds. 1981. *Research in Social Stratification and Mobility*. Vol. 1. Greenwich, Conn.: JAI Press.

Tuchman, Gaye. 1978. *Making News: A Study in the Construction of Reality*. New York: Free Press; London: Collier Macmillan.

Ungson, Gerardo, and Daniel Braunstein, eds. 1982. *New Directions in Decision Making: An Interdisciplinary Approach to the Study of Organizations*. Boston: Kent.

Van de Ven, Andrew, and William Joyce, eds. 1981. *Perspectives on Organization Design and Performance*. New York: Wiley.

Veblen, Thorstein. [1919] 1954. *The Engineers and the Price System*. New York: Viking Press.

Vernon, Raymond. 1960. *Metropolis 1985: An Interpretation of the Findings of the New York Metropolitan Region Study*. Cambridge, Mass.: Harvard University Press.

———. 1966. "International Investment and International Trade in the Product Cycle." *Quarterly Journal of Economics* 80, no. 2: 190–207.

Walder, Andrew G. 1986. *Communist Neo-traditionalism: Work and Authority in Chinese Industry*. Berkeley and Los Angeles: University of California Press.

Walker, Charles R., and Robert H. Guest. [1952] 1979. *The Man on the Assembly Line*. Cambridge, Mass.: Harvard. Reprint New York: Arno.

Wallace, Anthony F. C. 1972. *Rockdale: The Growth of an American Village in the Early Industrial Revolution*. New York: Norton.

Wallerstein, Immanuel. 1974. *The Modern World-System: Capitalist Agriculture and the Origins of the European World-Economy in the Sixteenth Century*.New York: Academic Press.

———. 1980. *The Modern World-System II: Mercantilism and the Consolidation of the European World-Economy, 1600–1750*. New York: Academic Press.

Walsh, John. 1988. "Technological Change and the Division of Labor in Retail Trade: The Supermarket Industry from WWII to Present." Ph.D. diss., Northwestern University.

Watson, James D. [1968] 1981. *The Double Helix: A Personal Account of the Discovery of the Structure of DNA*. Norton Critical Edition, edited by Gunther S. Stent. New York: Norton.

Weintraub, E. Roy. 1979. *Microfoundations: The Compatibility of Microeconomics and Macroeconomics*. Cambridge: Cambridge University Press.

Weitman, Sasha. 1968. *Bureaucracy, Democracy, and the French Revolution*. Ph.D. diss., Washington University.

White, Harrison. 1970. *Chains of Opportunity: Systems Models of Mobility in Organizations.* Cambridge, Mass.: Harvard University Press.

———. 1981. "Where Do Markets Come From?" *American Journal of Sociology* 87, no. 3: 517–547.

Whitley, Richard. 1984. *The Intellectual and Social Organization of the Sciences.* Oxford: Clarendon Press.

Whyte, William Foote. 1948. *Human Relations in the Restaurant Industry.* New York: McGraw-Hill.

———. 1961. *Men at Work.* Homewood, Ill.: Dorsey Press.

———, ed. 1946. *Industry and Society.* New York: McGraw-Hill.

Williamson, Oliver. 1975. *Markets and Hierarchies.* New York: Free Press; London: Collier Macmillan.

———. 1979. "Transaction Cost Economics: The Governance of Contractual Relations." *Journal of Law and Economics* 22, no. 2: 233–261.

———. 1985. *The Economic Institutions of Capitalism: Firms, Markets, Relational Contracting.* New York: Free Press; London: Collier Macmillan.

Winship, Christopher, and Sherwin Rosen, eds. 1988. *Organizations and Institutions: Sociological and Economic Approaches to the Analysis of Social Structure. American Journal of Sociology,* Supplement, vol. 94. Chicago: University of Chicago Press.

Wolfe, Tom. 1979. *The Right Stuff.* New York: Bantam. [As cited by Perrow 1984, 359.]

Zetka, James. 1988. "The Hegemonic Foundations of U.S. Automobile Industry Development: Market Structures, Workplace Authority Structure, and Labor Militancy." Ph.D. diss., Northwestern University.

Zuckerman, Harriet. 1977. *Scientific Elite: Nobel Laureates in the United States.* New York: Free Press.

Author Index

Subject Index

Accounting, 12, 15, 348; auditing, 94, 202, 228; capital, 77–78, 86–87; cost, 62, 109–110, 218–219; cost comparisons, 84–85, 94; cost reduction, 85–86, 94; financial, 86–87, 94
Actuarial values, 321
Administered pricing, 197, 226–228, 230–231
Adverse selection, 16
Agency, 15–16, 201–203, 322–324
Air force, 52–53, 212–213
Airplanes, 66–67
Apparel industry, 68, 146
Apple Computer, 174, 211
Appliances, 67
Arbitration. *See* Conflict resolution
Architectural drawings, 328
Architecture, 329–330
Arizona, 128
Artisans, 33, 40–44; in manufacturing, 53–57. *See also* Craftsmen; Skilled workers
Assembly lines, 39–40. *See also* Fordism
Athletics, 240–243

Auditable performance measurement, 245
Auditing. *See* Accounting
Authority: arbitrary, 295; authorizations and, 89–93; conflict over, 61–62; in contracts, 197, 222–226; in investment in innovations, 176–179; in labor contract, 200–201
Automobiles, 67, 295, 301

Banks, 313–315
Barker, James M., 133
Batch computer routine, 34–38, 62
Beer production, 64
Bell Telephone, 164, 182
Benefits, division of, 185–189
Betting, on new knowledge, 315–320
Big firms, 258–265
Bilateral monopoly, 204
Bills of quantities. *See* Administered pricing
Birmingham, 40
Bottleneck factors, 6
Bragg, Lawrence, 4
Budgeting, 89

Compositor: G & S Typesetters
Text: 10/13 Janson Text
Display: Janson Text
Printer: BookCrafters
Binder: BookCrafters